STUDENT REVOLT IN 1968

Student Revolt in 1968 examines the origins, course and dissolution of student protest at three universities in the 1960s – the Free University of Berlin in West Germany, the campus of Nanterre in France, and the Faculty of Sociology at Trento in Italy. It traces how student revolts over space, speech, sociology and cultural democratisation catalysed a dynamic protest movement within universities in the mid-1960s that expanded dramatically beyond the university in 1968. Differing visions of democratisation – mass access to education, the dissolution of high culture, the democratic control of the university – clashed and competed in a radical re-evaluation of the meaning of university education and democratic culture. The study also evaluates the most ambitious experiments in higher education in the 1960s – the 'Critical Universities' of West Berlin and Trento, which sought to establish democratic control of higher education before dissolving in the politics of social revolution – and offers a new and clear-sighted perspective on the 1960s.

BEN MERCER is Lecturer in the School of History at the Australian National University. He is the author of numerous journal articles, including in *French Politics, Culture & Society*, *Journal of the History of Ideas* and *Journal of Modern History*, and a contributor to *The Oxford Handbook of European History 1914–1945* (2016).

NEW STUDIES IN EUROPEAN HISTORY

Edited by
PETER BALDWIN, University of California, Los Angeles
CHRISTOPHER CLARK, University of Cambridge
JAMES B. COLLINS, Georgetown University
MIA RODRÍGUEZ-SALGADO, London School of Economics
and Political Science
LYNDAL ROPER, University of Oxford
TIMOTHY SNYDER, Yale University

The aim of this series in early modern and modern European history is to publish outstanding works of research, addressed to important themes across a wide geographical range, from southern and central Europe, to Scandinavia and Russia, from the time of the Renaissance to the present. As it develops the series will comprise focused works of wide contextual range and intellectual ambition.

A full list of titles published in the series can be found at:
www.cambridge.org/newstudiesineuropeanhistory

STUDENT REVOLT IN 1968

France, Italy and West Germany

BEN MERCER

Australian National University

CAMBRIDGE
UNIVERSITY PRESS

University Printing House, Cambridge CB2 8BS, United Kingdom

One Liberty Plaza, 20th Floor, New York, NY 10006, USA

477 Williamstown Road, Port Melbourne, VIC 3207, Australia

314-321, 3rd Floor, Plot 3, Splendor Forum, Jasola District Centre, New Delhi - 110025, India

103 Penang Road, #05-06/07, Visioncrest Commercial, Singapore 238467

Cambridge University Press is part of the University of Cambridge.

It furthers the University's mission by disseminating knowledge in the pursuit of education, learning and research at the highest international levels of excellence.

www.cambridge.org
Information on this title: www.cambridge.org/9781108735957
DOI: 10.1017/9781108696111

© Ben Mercer 2020

This publication is in copyright. Subject to statutory exception and to the provisions of relevant collective licensing agreements, no reproduction of any part may take place without the written permission of Cambridge University Press.

First published 2020
First paperback edition 2021

A catalogue record for this publication is available from the British Library

Library of Congress Cataloging in Publication data
NAMES: Mercer, Ben, 1977– author.
TITLE: Student revolt in 1968 : France, Italy and West Germany / Ben Mercer.
DESCRIPTION: Cambridge, United Kingdom ; New York, NY : Cambridge University Press, 2020. | Series: New studies in European history | Includes bibliographical references and index.
IDENTIFIERS: LCCN 2019037027 (print) | LCCN 2019037028 (ebook) | ISBN 9781108484480 (hardback) | ISBN 9781108735957 (paperback) | ISBN 9781108696111 (epub)
SUBJECTS: LCSH: Student movements–France–History–20th century. | Student movements–Italy–History–20th century. | Student movements–Germany (West)–History–20th century. | College students–Political activity–France–History–20th century. | College students–Political activity–Italy–History–20th century. | College students–Political activity–Germany (West)–History–20th century. | Université de Paris X: Nanterre–History–20th century. | Università degli studi di Trento–History–20th century. | Freie Universität Berlin–History–20th century.
CLASSIFICATION: LCC LA707 .M47 2020 (print) | LCC LA707 (ebook) | DDC 378.1/98109409046–dc23
LC record available at https://lccn.loc.gov/2019037027
LC ebook record available at https://lccn.loc.gov/2019037028

ISBN 978-1-108-48448-0 Hardback
ISBN 978-1-108-73595-7 Paperback

Cambridge University Press has no responsibility for the persistence or accuracy of URLs for external or third-party internet websites referred to in this publication, and does not guarantee that any content on such websites is, or will remain, accurate or appropriate.

Contents

Acknowledgements   *page* vii
List of Abbreviations   ix

Introduction: History, Myth and Memory of 1968   1

PART I   EDUCATION AND CULTURE   23

1. The 'Devouring Monster': The University in the 1960s   25
2. 'New Managerial Class' or 'Social Doctor'? The Ambiguities of Sociology   47
3. 'Books for All': The Democratisation of High Culture   67
4. 'Knowledge Is Over': The Intellectual Politics of 1968   88

PART II   THE POLITICS OF REVOLT   105

5. 'The Space of Autonomy Must Be Created': The Politics of Democracy   107
6. 'We Represent Nothing': The Crisis of Representation   130
7. 'We Began to Talk': The Seizure of Speech   155

PART III   CRISIS OF THE UNIVERSITY   175

8. 'Question, Doubt and Criticise': Free Speech at the Free University   177
9. 'Student Power': Vietnam at Trento   206

10 'An Asylum for Delinquents': The Space of Revolt at Nanterre 230

11 'A Golden Ghetto': The Critical University 254

Conclusion 285

Select Bibliography 290
Index 296

Acknowledgements

This book is the product of over a decade of research and writing. In that time I have accumulated an enormous number of intellectual and personal debts that require acknowledgement. Jonathan Steinberg first suggested this project and I hope it reflects some of his inimitable breadth and limitless intellectual curiosity. At the University of Pennsylvania, I benefited from the sharp intelligence and friendly dispositions of Warren Breckman, Benjamin Nathans and Roger Chartier. Richard Bosworth has been an ever-encouraging and critical reader for more than two decades.

I wish to acknowledge financial support for research and writing from the University of Pennsylvania, the Deutscher Akademischer Austauschdienst, the City University of New York and the Australian National University. I would also like to thank the staff of the Museo Storico del Trentino, the Bibliothèque de documentation internationale contemporaine at Nanterre, the *Archives départementales* Hauts-de-Seine and the APO-Archiv in Berlin. In my research stays in Europe, I owe thanks to Lilian Catéro, Vincenzo Calì, Gustavo Corni, Mark Gilbert, Eric Lancelloti and Lucia Pinasco, among others.

I have benefited from a number of friends and colleagues who read various chapters or whose conversations have aided this book. In Australia and then elsewhere, I've enjoyed the challenge of conversations with Vaarunika Dharmapala, Reto Hofmann, Jeska Rees and Yavor Siderov. At Penn I drew on the intellectual friendship of Francesca Bregoli, Nick Di Liberto, Susan Epting, Andrew Heath, Tehyun Ma, Anne Oravetz Albert, James Saporito and Sarah van Beurden. At the College of Staten Island, Zara Anishanslin, Melissa Borja, John Dixon, Mark Lewis and John Wing were wonderful colleagues. The book chapter reading group in the School of History at the Australian National University provided numerous insightful suggestions for revision and I would like to thank Gemma Betros, Frank Bongiorno, Nicholas Brown, Tania Colwell and Carolyn

Strange. Alex Cook in particular provided extra and invariably generous criticism.

I completed the manuscript during a fellowship at the Humanities Research Centre at the Australian National University, and I would like to thank the Centre and in particular Will Christie for his support. An earlier version of Chapters 3 and 4 appeared in the *Journal of the History of Ideas*, Volume 72, Number 4 (October 2011). My thanks also to Liz Friend-Smith at Cambridge University Press and to the anonymous readers for their thoughtful feedback. All errors are, of course, mine.

Finally, I owe a great deal to my family. This book would never have been possible without the support of my parents, Jan and Iain. I owe endless thanks to my wife, Consuelo Martínez Reyes, for more than a decade of intellectual conversations, companionship and encouragement that made writing this book such an enjoyable experience. Lastly, thanks to my daughter Isabela, who teaches me more every day.

Any work of history that attempts a comparative analysis of this range runs the risk of intriguing everyone but pleasing no one, inviting the interest of three historiographical fields but disappointing specialists of each. It can only be hoped that the benefits of comparison outweigh the inevitable deficiencies of the presentation.

Abbreviations

AStA	Allgemeiner Studentenausschuß
CGT	Confédération générale du travail
CLER	Comité de liaison des étudiants révolutionnaires
FDP	Freie Demokratische Partei
FNEF	Fédération nationale des étudiants de France
Intesa	Intesa Universitaria Cattolica
JCR	Jeunesse communiste révolutionnaire
JEC	Jeunesse Étudiante Chrétienne
JUC	Jeunesse Universitaire Chrétienne
MSI	Movimento Sociale Italiano
NPD	Nationaldemokratische Partei Deutschlands
PCF	Parti communiste française
PCI	Partito Comunista Italiano
PSI	Partito Socialista Italiano
PSIUP	Partito Socialista Italiano di Unità Proletaria
PSU	Parti Socialiste Unifié
SDS	Sozialistische Deutsche Studentenbund
SFIO	Section française de l'Internationale ouvrière
SHB	Sozialdemokratische Hochschulbund
SPD	Sozialdemokratische Partei Deutschlands
UEC	Union des étudiants communistes
UGI	Unione goliardica italiana
UJC(ml)	Union des jeunesses communistes marxistes-léninistes
UNEF	Union nationale des étudiants de France
UNURI	Unione nazionale universitaria rappresentativa
VDSt	Verein Deutscher Studenten Berlin-Leipzig

Introduction: History, Myth and Memory of 1968

A revolution, a mass revolt, the turning point of post-war European history (or a point of no return), the culmination of decades of social change: the events of 1968 are evoked in the most grandiose of terms. To interpret them historically is to enter a debate on the meaning of the entire post-war period and the origins of contemporary society. Yet however momentous the events, the beginnings were small. In 1965, debate erupted at the Free University of Berlin over a five-year-old ban from university grounds imposed on a journalist who had criticised the institution. The following year (in 1966), around 150 students at the Faculty of Sociology in Trento occupied their institute to protest the Italian parliament's decision to grant them degrees not in sociology but political science. Then, in 1967 students at the new campus of Nanterre on the outskirts of Paris unilaterally declared the right of female students to welcome male students into university dormitories. In 1968 these disparate protests each burst forth from the university, triggering enormous demonstrations in West Berlin, the largest strike in French history and a decade of social turmoil in Italy. How did such humdrum issues engender crises of the state? How did debates about freedom of speech, the minutiae of curricula and the regulation of dormitories generate mass movements that threatened to sweep aside the politics and societies of post-war Europe?

Interpretations of 1968 have struggled to reconcile the quotidian origins of the revolts with the explosive charge they unleashed, the revolutionary appearance of events with the seemingly meagre results. Direct consequences of the protest movements of 1968 are difficult to identify. What was achieved other than a few curricular changes and modified university regulations? Were the revolutions of 1968 merely sound and fury which, once they subsided, signified nothing? Interpretations range from the portentous to the diminutive, from the beginning of the end of capitalism, and 'the only "general" insurrection the overdeveloped world has known since World War II', to an imaginary revolution played out in the shadow of triumphant consumerism.¹ The image of revolution has confined much interpretation of 1968 to the task of either defending or demythologising the events. The mythos of political revolution is privileged over, or punctured by, an emphasis on transformations in youth culture. Yet the search for identifiable legislative or political consequences only obscures the nature of the conflict of the 1960s in western Europe. The struggle of the Sixties was never over narrowly political ends, but the politics of social and cultural relations in their broadest sense. The 1960s in western Europe witnessed an extended and escalating conflict over the meaning of postwar prosperity and democracy. This conflict emerged in the most mundane matters – relations between teachers and students, parents and children, forms of teaching and the limits of free speech – and in 1968 was expressed in its most politicised and confrontational form.

This book analyses the 1960s as an experimental laboratory of different visions of political, social and cultural democratisation. This approach helps to contextualise the events of 1968 in the wider social transformations of the decade and to foreground the relation between cultural and political change rather than opposing them. The sustained prosperity of postwar western Europe created a new, utopian horizon of expectations of a newly democratised society. However, democratisation held many different meanings. For some, it meant the triumph of an egalitarian and meritocratic social mobility on the back of the economic boom, for others a less praiseworthy process of social and cultural levelling – what contemporaries labelled 'mass society.' Democratisation could mean the liberation of personal autonomy from authoritarian political and social structures, or the transformation of those institutions through direct democracy. The democratisation of culture promised new realms of freedom, but also subjection to the tyranny of commodification in consumer culture. The protest movements held no single position on this spectrum. 'What do I care about Vietnam, when I have orgasm difficulties', infamously declared the West German radical Dieter Kunzelmann, emphatically prioritising personal freedoms over international politics.² Yet thousands

---

¹ Kristen Ross, *May '68 and Its Afterlives* (Chicago: University of Chicago Press, 2002), 4. For the beginning of the end of capitalism, see Angelo Quattrocchi and Tom Nairn, *The Beginning of the End: France, May 1968* (London: Verso, 1998). Surely it was too soon to tell, as Zhou Enlai supposedly said in 1971 in reference to the 1968 revolts in France. See Rowan Callick, *The Party Forever: Inside China's Modern Communist Elite* (New York: St. Martin's Press, 2013), 232.

² As quoted in Dirk Moses and Elliot Neaman, 'West German generations and the *Gewaltfrage*: The conflict of the Sixty-Eighters and the Forty-Fivers', in Warren Breckman, Peter E. Gordon, A. Dirk Moses, Samuel Moyn and Elliot Neaman (eds.), *The Modernist Imagination: Intellectual History and Critical Theory* (New York: Berghahn Books, 2009), 268–295, 272. For the broad anti-authoritarian

of others perceived an innate connection between sexual and post-imperial repression. The details of democratisation proved fertile ground for social conflict. Competing ideas of democratisation undermined themselves and each other. Minimum and maximum definitions collided and reality confounded expectations as Europeans fought to secure the meaning of technological and cultural change.

This study explores these dilemmas of democratisation in the 1960s through an analysis of three university revolts in France, Italy and West Germany, based on case studies of the campus of Nanterre, the university of Trento and the Free University of Berlin (FU). While higher education was not the sole site of social conflict in the late 1960s, the university cultivated the protest movements of the 1960s. Higher education serves as an ideal locus to examine the contradictions of the protest movements, as it embodied the postwar promise of social mobility, mass education and the 'democratisation' of high culture. Each of these universities was of relatively recent vintage, incarnating a promise of democratic education. All three were centres of sociology, a newly legitimised social science heralded as the adjunct to a democratised political culture. All three incubated a student movement well before the protests expanded to other universities and broader society. Each drew on a distinct, peripheral, locale: Berlin, a divided city on the frontline of the Cold War deep inside the Communist German Democratic Republic; Nanterre, an isolated institution on the fringes of Paris – the cultural, intellectual and political capital of Western Europe; and Trento, a small, conservative Catholic town not far from the Brenner Pass. Despite the differences, in each case a student movement with a strong family resemblance emerged early and almost simultaneously. In West Berlin and Trento, two versions of a 'critical university' – the *Kritische Universität* and the *Università Critica* – rose, then fell, as the most coherent and developed application of radical democratic ideas to the institutions of higher education. These universities epitomised the tensions, triumphs and failures of democratisation in the 1960s. They reveal the revolts as an intense political and social struggle over the meaning of the democratisation thought implicit in postwar economic progress.

---

impulse of the 1960s, see Timothy Scott Brown, *West Germany and the Global Sixties* (Cambridge: Cambridge University Press, 2013). On Kunzelmann, see Aribert Reimann, *Dieter Kunzelmann. Avantgardist, Protestler, Radikaler* (Göttingen: Vandenhoeck & Ruprecht, 2009).

Nanterre – Trento – West Berlin

The three case studies demonstrate the unity beneath the diverse origins of student revolt. While these campuses, especially Nanterre and the Free University of Berlin, have been studied before, they have never been examined together. The Free University of Berlin was founded in 1949 by dint of student pressure in opposition to Humboldt University in the Soviet Sector. With this heritage of student activism and its famous 'Berlin Model' of student representation at all levels of the university hierarchy, the FU stood as the most 'advanced' and 'modern' institution of higher education in the Federal Republic. The 'political mandate' of the Berlin students was singular in the Federal Republic, held to be democratic, 'progressive and exercised a great power of attraction'.[3] Residents of West Berlin were exempt from the requirement for military service and the city also offered the prospect of contact with students at Humboldt as well as books from the German Democratic Republic. While the university counted as a symbol of progress, West Berlin had 'an atmosphere of front city, a mix of fear, threats, stagnation, cronyism, narrow-minded arrogance and uptight individuals'.[4] One student recalled that 'the city still looked really destroyed. Many façades had bullet holes, the plaster peeled away, and whole wings of buildings were destroyed from bombs and had left large holes. Somehow the Nazi period hung in the walls, and I often had a very oppressive feeling'.[5] The Free University, in a peculiar, isolated outpost of the Federal Republic, appeared a beacon for radical democratic student politics.

The Faculty of Sociology at Trento – or the Istituto Superiore di Scienze Sociali (Higher Institute of Social Sciences) – was, like West Berlin, an experimental outpost of higher education. Opened in 1962, the Institute was the first faculty of sociology in Italy and began to operate without the degree recognised by the Italian state. The institute was founded by progressive members of the Christian Democratic Party, conceived as a motor of modernisation for both the backwater of the Trentino and Italy as a whole. The institute at Trento was the purest expression of dreams of

---

[3] Jürgen Horlemann, 'Zwischen Soziologie und Politik: Rekonstruktion eines Werdegangs', in Heinz Bude and Martin Kohli (eds.), *Radikalisierte Aufklärung: Studentenbewegung und Soziologie in Berlin 1965 bis 1970* (Weinheim: Juventa Verlag, 1989), 215–238, 221.
[4] Tilman Fichter and Siegward Lönnendonker, *Kleine Geschichte des SDS: Der Sozialistische Deutsche Studentenbund von 1946 bis zur Selbstauflösung* (Berlin: Rotbuch Verlag, 1977), 86.
[5] Ute Kätzel, *Die 68erinnen: Porträt einer rebellischen Frauengeneration* (Berlin: Rowohlt, 2002), 242.

Introduction: History, Myth and Memory of 1968

modernisation through a democratic science: entirely dedicated to sociology, open to students from technical secondary schools (to whom most university doors remained barred) and with a degree not yet recognised by the Italian government at its opening. Students set out for Trento from all over Italy, despite not always knowing where they were bound: 'those from the Trentino were few, three quarters came from outside. It was the first truly national university. Like everyone else, I thought Trento was near Trieste'.[6] Some found the distance a liberation from family and social origin, but once again students were struck by the contrast between the university and its hinterland. The student leader Mauro Rostagno described Trento as this 'crazy, stagnant, closed city ... city of the valleys, narrow-minded, mountain dwellers, the city of the Council, of prince bishops, the alpini. The faculty of sociology was a delirium. Its lure drew everyone on the loose in Italy, a faculty in and of itself self-selecting. Thus at Trento suddenly nested this colony of crazy birds'.[7]

The campus at Nanterre, the banlieue just outside the western edge of Paris, opened in 1964 as a Faculty of Letters and Human Sciences in order to relieve an overcrowded Sorbonne. Nanterre, like the FU and Trento, boasted an image of modernity. The new Faculty had a liberal dean in Pierre Grappin, an emphasis on the new disciplines of the social sciences and, although students did not sit on its Faculty council, assistant professors did. The location did not appear propitious: 35 hectares of land transferred from the military and bordered by a shantytown of North African immigrants.[8] A wall topped with barbed wire recalled its military origins and 'gave the university domain the forbidding appearance of a penitentiary camp.'[9] The French historian of Britain François Crouzet described the campus as

> [a] desolate no-man's land, on which stood a number of corrugated iron sheds. With a number of buildings under construction, it became in winter

---

[6] A. Manzoni (ed.), *Facoltà Occupata. Certo eravamo arroganti, certo eravamo giovani ... ma avevamo ragione. Sociologia, 1962–2002* (supplemento al quotidiano *Trentino*, 2002), 41–43. This is true particularly after the first two years. The percentage of students from the Trentino and Alto Adige dropped from 69.6 per cent in its first year (1962–1963) to 29.9 per cent in 1966–1967.
[7] Mauro Rostagno and Claudio Castellacci, *Macondo: La storia del 'luogo magico' di Milano, nel racconto del suo principale protagonista* (Milan: SugarCo, 1978), 62.
[8] On Nanterre, see Daniel A. Gordon, *Immigrants & Intellectuals: May '68 and the Rise of Anti-Racism in France* (Pontypool: Merlin Press, 2012).
[9] René Rémond, *La règle et le consentement: gouverner une société* (Paris: Fayard, 1979), 63.

an ocean of mud. Surrounded by railroad tracks, factories, and large grey blocks of cheap apartment houses, and with the infamous shanty towns of Nanterre not far away, this grim and depressing neighbourhood had none of the amenities – the cafes, cinemas, and shops – which students frequented in the Latin Quarter.[10]

Pierre Grappin lamented the absence of windows in the lecture halls: 'the builders told me ... darkness was chosen because it aided concentration'.[11] Students founds themselves relatively isolated at a site where 'there was no environment, no café nor drink machine, a couscous joint a bit far away, a shantytown which fascinated and to which some went, especially an activist elite and left-wing Catholics in particular, and the cemetery in the background'.[12]

In their novelty and openness, these three institutions offered a greater space for the development of student movements and conflict over the structure of the university than elsewhere. The establishment of new faculties and degrees, particularly in the social sciences and especially in sociology, acted as the calling of an Estates General about education and society. Students arrived at the new institutions with their *cahiers de doléance*, with further reforms promised but unelaborated. While outbreaks could occur elsewhere – the Sorbonne exploded (or imploded) in mid-1968 without any indication of a similar development to the struggle at Nanterre – the lengthy development of the struggles at West Berlin, Nanterre and Trento illuminate the origins of the conflict that crystallised in 1968. Each campus had unique features, but all shared a rhetoric of anti-imperialism, anti-authoritarianism, autonomy and democracy. Local concerns were expressed alongside, and in an international lexicon that evoked, Berkeley and Vietnam. In all instances, a broad revolt against academic authority fed the protest movement and radicalised most quickly under the impact of police intervention. All embarked on a politics of 'free speech', challenged the content and function of higher education and rejected the administration of university space by academic authorities. Yet these common concerns expressed themselves in diverse configurations according to context.

---

[10] François Crouzet, 'A university besieged: Nanterre, 1967–69', *Political Science Quarterly* 84 (1969), 328–350, 329.
[11] Pierre Grappin, *L'Île aux peupliers: de la Résistance à Mai 68: Souvenirs du Doyen de Nanterre* (Nancy: Presses Universitaires de Nancy, 1993), 237.
[12] Nelcya Delanoë, *Nanterre la Folie* (Saint-Amand-Montrond: Seuil, 1998), 61.

History and Myth

Any attempt to historicise the events of 1968 must be cautious. Even as the protagonists of the era fade from the scene, discussion of '68 still evokes an engagement and identification characteristic of participants. This is as true of those who seek to historicise events as those who romanticise them. Each new history of the period aims finally to consign it to the past and academics routinely call for the 'historicisation' of the period. Yet that clarion call has been made for quite some time, often sounded by the participants of the Sixties themselves. Nor is the period so easily tamed. Controversies about the meaning of the 1960s and 1968 erupt regularly. An optimistically entitled 1998 volume *1968: Vom Ereignis zum Gegenstand der Geschichtswissenschaft* (1968: from Event to Object of History) was reissued (unchanged) a decade later as *1968: vom Ereignis zum Mythos* (1968: from Event to Myth). So much for historical scholarship! The assumption that a certain distance from the events of the 1960s would naturally facilitate a dispassionate and less partisan approach to the past appears naïve. Any attempt to write the history of 1968 must grapple with the persistence of its mythical and symbolic dimension.

The events of 1968 did not become myth; they were born as myth. From their inception, critical observers sought to disassociate the events from their grandiose interpretations. As early as July 1968, Raymond Aron wrote with the objective 'to demystify, desacralise them'.[13] To do so, he measured the May events in France against the yardstick of a seizure of power by the working class: 'Since the Communist Party retained control of the working masses and had no aim of insurrection', Aron asserted, 'it consisted of psychodrama'.[14] While Aron evoked the limits of the protest movement, sympathisers and protesters emphasised that the events merely marked a beginning: *ce n'est qu'un début* – 'it's only a beginning' or *la lutte continue, la lotta continua* – 'the struggle continues'.[15] Some proclaimed the beginning of the end of capitalism, others the beginning of post-material politics or the emergence of a new revolutionary actor, interpretations which awaited their validation in a distant or not-so-distant future. All assumed that the events portended much more than was demonstrable

---

[13] Raymond Aron, *La révolution introuvable: réflexions sur la révolution de mai* (Paris: Fayard, 1968), 13.

[14] Aron, *La révolution introuvable*, 35.

[15] For 1968 as a beginning from a historiographical perspective, see Odd Arne Westad, 'Was there a "global 1968"', in Chen Jian et al. (eds.), *The Routledge Handbook of the Global Sixties* (London: Routledge, 2018).

in the immediate reality. The power of the events lay in this protean capacity. 1968 began, as Sunil Khilnani put it, as 'an interpretation in search of an event'.[16]

Beginnings are more easily perceived retrospectively than prospectively. The one now most associated with 1968 is the beginning of the end of the Soviet Bloc. Yet few in the early 1970s had the prescience of the political scientist François Fetjö who thought that 'the Czechoslovak leaders and intellectuals ... might have helped in accelerating the slow awakening of conscience in the Soviet Union. One may hope ... that the next Dubček will appear in the nerve centre of the system: Moscow'.[17] While there is no direct line between the events of 1968 and 1989 in Eastern Europe, Western Europe's 68 lacks even an imagined terminus.[18] Subsequent history proved unkind to proclamations of capitalism's demise. The inflated claims for the revolts of 1968 have suffered from the condescension of posterity more than demystification. Thus, three decades later, Arthur Marwick wrote in his landmark work *The Sixties* that 'the great events of 1967/1969 really had remarkably little in the way of long term consequences'.[19] Michael Seidman unfavourably compared the historical significance of May '68 to the D-Day landings of 1944.[20] Yet these are debates as much about what constitutes an event of historical importance, and how that is measured, as they are thoughtful contributions to the interpretation of history.

A historicisation of 1968 cannot simply puncture contemporaries' grandiose assessments of events. Contesting the protagonists' point of view can only with difficulty extricate itself from contemporary criticism of the protest movements. Rather, it is important to understand why such grand

---

[16] Sunil Khilnani, *Arguing Revolution: The Intellectual Left in Postwar France* (New Haven: Yale University Press, 1993), 122. On the memory of 1968, see Ingo Cornils and Sarah Waters (eds.), *Memories of 1968: International Perspectives* (Oxford: Peter Lang, 2010); Ross, *May '68 and Its Afterlives*; Michelle Zancarini-Fournel, *Le Moment 68: une histoire contestée* (Paris: Seuil, 2008).
[17] François Fetjö, *A History of the People's Democracies: Eastern Europe since Stalin* (New York: Prager, 1971), 317. On 1968 and 1989, see Kevin McDermott and Matthew Stibbe (eds.), *Eastern Europe in 1968: Responses to the Prague Spring and Warsaw Pact Invasion* (Cham: Palgrave Macmillan, 2018), 2–3.
[18] With some exception for German historiography, which has at times embraced a mythology of the 'normalisation' of Germany.
[19] Arthur Marwick, 'Youth culture and the cultural revolution of the long 1960s', in Axel Schildt and Detlef Siegried (eds.), *Between Marx and Coca-Cola: Youth Cultures in Changing European Societies, 1960–1980* (New York: Berghahn, 2006), 43. See further Arthur Marwick, *The Sixties: Cultural Revolution in Britain, France, Italy, and the United States, c.1958–c.1974* (Oxford: Oxford University Press, 1998).
[20] Michael Seidman, *The Imaginary Revolution: Parisian Students and Workers in 1968* (New York: Berghahn, 2004), 282.

narratives of a watershed moment proved so appealing. One reason for the insistence on 1968 as a beginning was its experience as refutation of the widely promoted idea of an 'end of ideology'. The proclamation of a beginning resonated in an environment of declared endings and created the experience of caesura for participants. The gulf between the events and their extravagant interpretation grew from the failure of the reigning intellectual schema to understand them. The revolts of the 1960s appeared as harbingers of the new, and while critical voices could perceive the overstatement in the most inflated interpretations, they often judged by standards that failed to capture the new reality, registered as much irritation as insight, and sought to dismiss instead of understand.

Attempts to historicise 1968 thus need to wrestle critically with the problem that demythologisation formed part of the cultural struggle over 1968 from the beginning. A new history of the era cannot adopt the terms of this debate without question. The events of the late 1960s do not need to signify the end of capitalism or prefigure an imminent revolution to be important. Likewise, there was indeed much psychodrama in 1968, but politics is sometimes little else. Rather than seeking to identify the enduring consequences of a complex set of occurrences to confirm or deny their importance, this study views those events as a particular manifestation of long-term trends, shot through with contingency. The revolts explored here matter for the concrete ways the practical possibilities of radical democratic culture both did and did not play out in the specific circumstances of 1968.

The '68 Years and the Long 1960s

I seek to frame the events of 1968 (1967 or 1969, depending on the location) in relation to the era of the Sixties more broadly. The attempt to historicise 1968 in a wider time frame, and a consequent tension between event and process, marks much of the historiography.[21] In the shadow of mythologisation of 1968 (and especially May '68 in France), a great deal of valuable historiographical work has shown how what was imagined to have begun in '1968' can be discerned much earlier. Various French historians have elaborated the concept of the '68 years (*les années 68*).[22] Outside of

---

[21] Timothy Scott Brown, '1968. Transnational and global perspectives', *Docupedia-Zeitgeschichte*, 11.06.2012: DOI: http://dx.doi.org/10.14765/zzf.dok.2.272.v1

[22] Philippe Artières and Michelle Zancarini Fournel, *68: Une histoire collective 1962–1981* (Paris: La Découverte, 2008); Dominique Damamme et al. (eds.), *Mai–Juin 68* (Paris: Editions de l'Atelier,

France, historians have usually opted for the 'long 1960s' or, increasingly, the 'global Sixties'. Yet these thoughtful attempts to reconceptualise 1968 are not without their own pitfalls.[23] The chronological reconfigurations furnish yet another way to aggrandise or diminish the most troublesome moment. The expanded geographical range provincialises national narratives in a cornucopia of Sixties and 68s that defy generalisation.

'*Les années 68*' (the '68 years) has the virtue of expanding the field of analysis beyond the year (or, for France, beyond the mere month of May). Defined as the ongoing construction of a veritable 'public sphere' of contestation',[24] the term identifies an important element of the 1960s: the ability of small minorities to achieve a political and cultural effect far beyond their size: 'the leftist "groupuscules" … formed only limited political spaces, but these "microcosms" held the power during these "68 years" … to find a social reception larger than their strict political influence would allow one to suppose'.[25] Such a definition wisely refrains from measuring the movements by their political influence and places at the heart of the analysis the gap between strict political and wider public influence. Yet the '1968 years' defines much of the rest of decade by its relation to '68 and the retention of the magical number belies the argument that the year 'is only a moment' of a longer process.[26] This is, rather, one moment that is allowed to stand for the whole. The most elegant solution to this problem is the one suggested by Julian Jackson, who points to '68 as a pivot which 'made "the 1968 years" that followed possible … [and] also gave new meaning to experiences that had preceded May.'[27] While 1968 is clearly the most emphatic expression of the power of social movements to create a public sphere of contestation, understanding the events of that year requires conceptualising their relation to the rest of the decade in a manner that does not see 1968 as the decade's culmination.

While '*les années 68*' magnifies the year, drawing the decade into its orbit, the 'long 1960s' (first proposed by Arthur Marwick) dissolves it into the decade. The notion of the 'long 1960s' (roughly 1958 to 1974) rightly

---

2008). In English, Julian Jackson et al. (eds.), *May 68: Rethinking France's Last Revolution* (Basingstoke: Palgrave Macmillan, 2011).

[23] See also Richard Vinen, *The Long '68: Radical Protest and Its Enemies* (Allen Lane, 2018), where the definition remains vague.

[24] Robert Frank, 'Introduction', in Geneviève Dreyfus-Armand et al. (eds.), *Les années 68. Le temps de la contestation* (Bruxelles: Editions Complexe, 2000), 18.

[25] Ibid.   [26] Ibid.

[27] Julian Jackson, 'Rethinking May 68', in Jackson et al. (eds.), *May 68*, 6. There is much to be said for this formulation. However, 'the 1968 years' is a conceptual frame limited to French historiography – something that attests to the ongoing power of May–June 1968 in France.

Introduction: History, Myth and Memory of 1968

recognises the dates of 1960 and 1970 as arbitrary signifiers. Problems arise, however, in justifying an alternative set of dates. An exasperated reader might wish for a 'long 1950s' and 'long 1970s' to dispense with the difficulty of defining the Sixties altogether. Attempts to elaborate the specific content of the long 1960s rapidly descend into lengthy, descriptive lists.[28] Similarly, the work of French historians to move beyond a narrow image summed up as 'May, Paris, student' has produced an enormous wealth of knowledge, described charitably as 'polyphony' or critically as 'cacophony'.[29] Tasked with defining a long decade, Marwick relies on a set of very broad generalisations. He numbers some sixteen characteristics of the 'long 1960s',[30] which together form a cultural revolution, understood in a minimalist sense as 'social and cultural transformation'.[31] The Sixties, he affirms, 'were characterised by the vast number of innovative activities taking place *simultaneously*, by unprecedented *interaction* and *acceleration*'.[32] While this definition captures some of the effervescence of the era, it remains descriptive and superficial.

The idea of a 'long' century has worked best where, as in Eric Hobsbawm's 'long nineteenth century', it stood for the long-term working out of the twin industrial and political (British and French) revolutions, or in the 'short twentieth century' for the long-term effects of the double cataclysm of the First World War and the Russian Revolution.[33] No similar long-term narrative serves the Sixties. The events that might offer a narrative arc for the postwar era, the long-term impact of the Second World War, the rise of a post-imperial world and the postwar economic boom, are much bigger than any single decade. For this reason, 'long' and 'short' designations may work better for centuries. Indeed, all decades can be long or short, depending on one's point of view. They can even be decade-length. The important task is not to identify a chronological container that has a superficial plausibility. Any number of alternative dates could be proposed. Instead, historians must specify the precise relationship between the short- and long-term historical phenomena.

---

[28] For a useful breakdown, see Brown, '1968. Transnational and global perspectives'.
[29] Isabelle Sommier, 'Mai 68: Sous les paves d'une page officielle', *Sociétés Contemporaines* 20 (1994), 63–82, 65. For polyphony, see e.g. Philippe Artières, 'Ouverture', in Artières and Zancarini-Fournel, *68: Une histoire collective*, 11. On cacophony, see Julian Jackson 'The mystery of May 1968', *French Historical Studies* 33.4 (2010), 625–653, 633.
[30] Marwick, *The Sixties*, 17–20. [31] Ibid., 801. [32] Ibid., 7.
[33] E.J. Hobsbawm, *The Age of Revolutions, 1789–1848* (London: Weidenfeld and Nicholson, 1962) and *The Age of Extremes: A History of the World, 1914–1991* (New York: Pantheon, 1994).

The Global Sixties

In the 'global Sixties' the decade is as geographically wide as it is chronologically long, especially once events around the world are released from a presumed normative standard set by Berkeley or Paris. The choice of the most capacious spatial and temporal boundaries affirms the multitude of beginnings and endings to the story of the Sixties. The 'global Sixties' can start in 1954 (Dien Bien Phu), 1955 (the Bandung Conference), 1956 (the Hungarian Revolution), 1959 (the Cuban Revolution), 1964 (Berkeley Free Speech Movement) or 1966 (Chinese Cultural Revolution), among others. The end can be discerned in 1973 (at the fall of Allende or the OPEC oil crisis), the death of Mao (1976), the German Autumn (1977) or the elections of Mitterrand, Thatcher and Reagan (1979–1981). This diversity needs to be embraced. At a minimum, the 'global Sixties' began and ended in different places at different times. Even for individuals in the same location the 'Sixties' could begin and end at different moments.[34]

There is thus no single origin to the Sixties. Any model of diffusion, in which the 'Sixties' began in a particular location and then spread, can only betray the diversity of events and prove deeply reductive.[35] The international origin of radicalism was a favoured theme of the protest movements' critics who sought to designate their opponents' ideas as foreign imports, whether from China, Cuba or the United States. Protesters, by contrast, proclaimed the international nature of their rebellion, affirming its universality and importance against charges of triviality in content and consequences.[36] This claim has echoed in the presentation of 1968 as 'the first global rebellion'.[37] Yet, as Timothy Scott Brown has noted, the global character of the 'Sixties' is more often asserted rather than analysed.[38] A common approach simply affirms the manifold nature of events. While globalisation is invoked to demonstrate the importance of 1968, it is unclear what significance 1968 has for the history of globalisation.

---

[34] For a useful brief overview of the global Sixties, see Tamara Chaplin and Jadwiga E. Pieper Mooney, 'Introduction', *The Global Sixties: Convention, Contest and Counterculture* (Abingdon: Routledge, 2018), 1–12.

[35] Wolfgang Kraushaar, 'Die erste globale Rebellion,' in *1968 als Mythos, Chiffre und Zäsur* (Hamburg: Hamburger Edition, 2000), 37.

[36] For a good exploration of the international, see Robert Gildea, James Mark and Annette Warring (eds.), *Europe's 1968: Voices of Revolt* (Oxford: Oxford University Press, 2013).

[37] Kraushaar, 'Die erste globale Rebellion'. See also Daniel Sherman et al. (eds.), *The Long 1968: Revisions and New Perspectives* (Bloomington: Indiana University Press, 2013).

[38] Brown, '1968. Transnational and global perspectives'.

Introduction: History, Myth and Memory of 1968

Recent research on the global 1960s has demonstrated the variety of events across the world, producing a 'kaleidoscope' effect.[39] That result can be disorienting for analytical purposes. Attempts to discern a common theme either slip towards greater geographical precision or invite contradiction. Thus '1968 in the global imagination' can be interpreted as 'the end of class-based politics, at least in Europe and North America'[40] for one historian, but mark 'the reappearance of working class action as a major radical force in contemporary societies' for another.[41] Not without reason did the editors of the journal *The Sixties* argue that the 'sheer diversity of the era's social activism … and the complexity of its dynamics … militate against theorizing *in general* about the Sixties.'[42] Nonetheless, several features of the global space in which revolt flourished can be delineated: the rise of the 'third world' in an era of decolonisation, compounding a challenge to Cold War ideologies evident (for global Communism) at least since the mid-1950s and symbolised (for the United States) by the Vietnam War. These ideological realignments proved especially provocative amid the aspirations generated by sustained economic growth and expectations of global economic development. Protest emerged in a globally minded world. Small wonder that students in West Berlin invoked Vietnam when US Secretary of Defense Robert McNamara had already insisted that the 'defense of Berlin starts at the Mekong'.[43]

Historians have been on firmer empirical ground when pointing to actual connections between activists across national borders, as opposed to generalising about the global content of the 1960s, although the novelty of international linkages can be overstated.[44] Radical students in particular

---

[39] See 'Introduction' to 'AHR Reflections: 1968' in *American Historical Review* 123.3 (June 2018), 707. See further the remainder of that issue, and the 'International 1968' forums in the *American Historical Review* 114.1 (Feb 2009) and 114.2 (April 2009).
[40] Westad, 'Was there a "global 1968"?', xxii.
[41] Gerd-Rainer Horn, '1968: A social movement *sui generis*', in Stefan Berger and Holger Nehring (eds.), *The History of Social Movements in Global Perspective: A Survey* (London: Palgrave Macmillan, 2017), 530.
[42] Jeremy Varon, Michael S. Foley and John McMillian, 'Time is an ocean: The past and future of the Sixties', *The Sixties: A Journal of History, Politics and Culture* 1.1 (June 2008), 3. Italics in the original.
[43] See Quinn Slobodian, *Foreign Front: Third World Politics in Sixties West Germany* (Durham: Duke University Press: 2012), 92, and Alexander Troche, *"Berlin wird am Mekong verteidigt." Die Ostasienpolitik der Bundesrepublik in China, Taiwan und Süd-Vietnam, 1954–1966* (Düsseldorf: Droste, 2000). For an early and important, if somewhat limited, attempt at a global framework, see Carole Fink, Philipp Gassert and Detlef Junker (eds.), *1968: The World Transformed* (New York: Cambridge University Press, 1998).
[44] See Christopher Leigh Connery, 'The World Sixties', in Rob Wilson and Christopher Leigh Connery (eds.), *The Worlding Project: Doing Cultural Studies in an Era of Globalization* (Berkeley: North Atlantic Books, 2007), 77–78.

saw themselves as part of an international movement, explicitly rejected the language of nationalism and formed a relatively small, transnationally mobile elite that facilitated a multidirectional, if uneven, flow of information, ideas and practices.[45] Quinn Slobodian has argued for the importance of Iranian exiles in West Berlin.[46] Martin Klimke has demonstrated the multiple connections between students from the United States and West Germany.[47] A variety of links connected protest movements in France and its former empire.[48] Daniel Gordon has put immigrants back into '68, and '68 into the history of immigration.[49] Connections traversed the iron curtain.[50] The reality of these connections (and the presence of international students as well as immigrant workers) is another reason for the strength of the global imagination in 1968.

The three student movements considered here all framed their rebellions within an international imaginary. All invoked the war in Vietnam, Che Guevara, the Chinese Cultural Revolution, and the United States (the Berkeley Free Speech Movement in particular, but increasingly also Black Power). Beyond that shared framework, most striking is the diversity of references. A global connection tangibly present in one location is largely absent in another. Student movements divided internally in their inspirations. The impetus for revolt that some found in international Marxisms came to others via the Catholic Church. High theory spurred some to activism. Popular culture could do the same. This book thus suggests the contingency of intellectual sources and connections in the development of '1968', a contingency that simultaneously explains their diversity, and points to the breadth and depth of the underlying crisis of authority that protest movements exploited.

---

[45] See Gildea et al. (eds.), *Europe's 1968.*; Belinda Davis, 'A whole world opening up: Transcultural contact, difference and the politicization of new left activists', in Belinda Davis et al. (eds.), *Changing the World, Changing Oneself: Political Protest and Collective Identities in West Germany and the U.S. in the 1960s and 1970s* (New York: Berghahn, 2010), 255–273.

[46] Slobodian, *Foreign Front.*

[47] Martin Klimke, *The Other Alliance: Student Protest in West Germany and the United States in the Global Sixties* (Princeton: Princeton University Press, 2010).

[48] See Françoise Blum, 'Années 68 postcoloniales? "Mai" de France et d'Afrique', *French Historical Studies* 41.2 (2018), 193–218; Burleigh Hendrickson, 'From the archives to the streets: Listening to the Global 1960s in the former French empire', *French Historical Studies* 41.2 (2018), 319–342; Burleigh Hendrickson, 'March 1968: Practicing transnational activism from Tunis to Paris', *International Journal of Middle East Studies* 44.4 (2012), 755–774.

[49] Gordon, *Immigrants & Intellectuals.*

[50] See James Mark and Anna von der Goltz, 'Encounters', in Gildea et al. (eds.), *Voices of Revolt*, 131–163. See also Richard Ivan Jobs, 'Youth movements: Travel, protest, and Europe in 1968', *American Historical Review* 114.2 (2009), 376–404, who argues that in important ways, 1968 in Europe remained Eurocentric.

Interpreting '68

Making sense of the Sixties and 1968 thus confronts a number of problems: the inflated claims and derisory dismissals of contemporaries, the sheer variety of phenomena and the difficulty disentangling events and long-term processes. Expanding the time frame and spatial scope of analysis is a useful corrective to the contemporary myopic obsession with events, but it can also lead to interpretative bewilderment. It is a truism that 'the events of 1968–69 ... were only possible because of deeper changes taking place in ... society throughout the sixties'.[51] Philipp Gassert has identified this relationship between long-term change and social protest when he noted, 'the rebels of 1968 stormed barricades that had been abandoned by their former defenders'.[52] Placed in the context of long-term social and cultural changes, the protesters and their pretensions to historical importance can look small indeed, the inheritors of sociocultural change posing as their creator. At best, the events of 1968 are conceded to have sped up a process that was already underway.[53] Yet such a view is as much an illusion as the claim to earth-shattering transformation of society, substituting the heroic self-importance of the contemporary with the Olympian disdain of retrospection. Those who stormed the barricades in 1968 did not know they were abandoned, nor how many ramparts would fall. Their desertion was clear only in retrospect. Other bastions remained unbreached. To be sure, the victories of protest movements were most secure when grounded in social and cultural change already in process, but neither the underlying socio-cultural change nor the events themselves were unidirectional or uniform. The protest movements

---

[51] Marwick, *The Sixties*, 8.
[52] Philipp Gassert, 'Narratives of democratization: 1968 in postwar Europe', in Martin Klimke and Joachim Scharloth (eds.), *1968 in Europe: A History of Protest and Activism, 1956–1977* (New York: Palgrave Macmillan, 2008), 315. Broadly on democratisation see Martin Conway, 'Democracy in postwar western Europe: The triumph of a political model', *European History Quarterly* 32.1 (2002), 59–84; Martin Conway and Volker Depkat, 'Towards a European history of the discourse of democracy: Discussing democracy in western Europe, 1945–60', in Martin Conway and Kira Klaus Patel (eds.), *Europeanization in the Twentieth Century: Historical Approaches* (Basingstoke: Palgrave Macmillan, 2010), 132–156; Martin Conway, 'The rise and fall of Europe's democratic age', *Contemporary European History* 13.1 (2004), 67–88; Jan-Werner Müller, *Contesting Democracy: Political Ideas in Twentieth-Century Europe* (New Haven: Yale University Press, 2011); Geoff Eley, *Forging Democracy: The History of the Left in Europe* (Oxford: Oxford University Press, 2002).
[53] Gerd Langguth, 'Die "68er"-Bewegung und gesellschaftlicher Wandel in der Bundesrepublik – Motor, Katalysator oder Profiteur', in Gerrit Dwork and Christoph Weissmann (eds.), *1968 und die 68er: Ereignisse, Wirkungen und Kontroversen in der Bundesrepublik* (Vienna: Böhlau Verlag, 2013), 191.

did not seek only what was achieved. They held numerous and conflicting goals, short- and long-term. These varied from minor, such as greater discussion in the classroom, to major, such as educational reforms, or the rejection of Emergency Laws in West Germany. Beyond these specific aims, they adopted guiding ideological principles – whether democratisation, the end of 'professorial power', or socialism. Many aspirations remained just that. Others were realised, but without the expected dividend; they did not always prompt the greater transformation of society desired. Indeed, the at-times utopian demands of protesters could only end in disillusion.

This account aims to restore this sense of open-endedness and multiplicity to the transformations of 1968. The struggles of the late 1960s owe much to the broader changes of the decade but are all too often flattened in the wider frame.[54] Reduction of the events of the late 1960s to longer-term socio-cultural change fosters an evaluation of individuals and social movements by how well they understood their historical trajectory. Political struggle appears as irrational (or, in polite terms, naïve and idealistic). Protesters are largely consigned to the dustbin of history, as if they should have stayed at home to wait for historical forces to accomplish their goals for them.[55] If the 'folly' of student radicals appears most obvious, their most dedicated opponents are rendered irrational. Thus Michael Seidman remarks how 'the constant victories of forbearance during the 1960s make some of the authorities' disciplinary actions at Antony and Nanterre unfathomable in retrospect'.[56] Something which now appears unfathomable or irrational registers a failure of historical understanding, or at best, an indication of how successfully events redefined the rational. For this reason – the immediate, almost unchallenged characterisation of attitudes or mentalities as archaic – the decade of the Sixties is one peculiarly susceptible to relatively simplistic narratives of progress. The Sixties have ceded their revolutionary power to become a placid origin myth of a tolerant, democratic, progressive society. If only because those gains frequently appear tenuous, it is necessary to rethink this story in all its contradictions.

The view of the late 1960s as split between naïve, idealistic radicals and authoritarian reactionaries (with common-sense liberals caught in the middle) serves a narrative of progress in which the former missed the truly

---

[54] For a re-evaluation of the event of 1968 in the French case, see Boris Gobille, 'L'événement mai 68: Pour une sociohistoire du temps court,' *Annales. Histoire, Sciences Sociales* 63.2 (2008), 321–348.
[55] Marwick, *The Sixties*, 675.   [56] Seidman, *The Imaginary Revolution*, 280.

important historical changes and the latter stood on the wrong side of History. The result is at best inaccurate. Plenty of students began with the assumption that the revolution was not possible in the foreseeable future (although they often changed their minds). Some university administrators who called the police counted themselves as men of the Left and cannot be simply dismissed as archaic reactionaries. The narrative of liberal progress, or 'modernisation', or most simplistically the debate over whether the 1960s is the decade in which the Federal Republic of Germany finally became part of 'the West', is simply inadequate in representing these complexities.[57] More importantly, this interpretation jettisons the contemporary perception of 1968 as a watershed, only to adopt the viewpoint that the 1960s fostered of its predecessor decade.[58] Perhaps the Sixties' most successful and enduring accomplishment is the invention of the 1950s as the decade of 'stuffy conservatism', the epitome of a 'rigid, conformist, deferential and authoritarian environment'.[59] A significant number of influential individuals rapidly came to view the social, family and school arrangements of the earlier era as stale, conservative and authoritarian, an image that soon attained the status of common sense. The invention of the 1950s is not the primary focus here, and the point is not to deny the substantial cultural changes across the postwar decades. Rather, this book aims to capture not just a struggle between authoritarianism and progress, but between different visions of liberalisation, egalitarianism and democracy.

This conflict is most evident in the short-to-medium term within the Sixties, and the focus here is on the period from around 1964 to 1968. Viewed from a distance, the balance sheet inevitably appears insipid. Arthur Marwick contrasts 'a "revolution", or "transformation" in material conditions, lifestyles, family relationships, and personal freedoms for the vast majority of ordinary people' with an apparently self-evident

---

[57] See Axel Schildt, *Ankunft im Westen. Ein Essay zur Erfolgsgeschichte der Bundesrepublik* (Frankfurt am Main: Fischer, 1999), and Axel Schildt, Detlef Siegfried and Karl Christian Lammers (eds.), *Dynamische Zeiten: Die 60er Jahre in den beiden deutschen Gesellschaften* (Hamburg: Hans Christians Verlag, 2000). For a designation of 1968 as 'decidedly anti-liberal, anti-democratic (at any rate anti-parliamentary) and anti-Western', see Gerd Koenen, *Das rote Jahrzehnt: Unsere kleine deutsche Kulturrevolution 1967–1977* (Cologne: Fischer Taschenbuch Verlag, 2001), 24. On Italy, see Stuart J. Hilwig, *Italy and 1968: Youthful Unrest and Democratic Culture* (London: Palgrave Macmillan, 2009); Robert Lumley, *States of Emergency: Cultures of Revolt in Italy from 1968 to 1978* (London: Verso, 1990); and Peppino Ortoleva, *I movimenti del '68 in Europa e in America*, 2nd ed. (Rome: Editori Riuniti, 1998).

[58] Including, of course, critics of the 'Sixties' who idealise a well-ordered 1950s as its counterpoint.

[59] Nick Thomas, *Protest Movements in 1960s West Germany: A Social History of Dissent and Democracy* (Oxford: Berg, 2003), 248.

observation that 'certainly there was no political or economic revolution, no fundamental redistribution of political and economic power'.[60] Many activists of the era also assess the revolts as a failed political revolution alongside a successful cultural one.[61] But an important question in the latter part of the decade itself was precisely the social and political consequences of the cultural revolution. Despite his occasionally critical observations on the student movements, Jürgen Habermas hoped they would contribute to a 'democratisation of decision-making processes in all sectors of society'.[62] This optimistic view has proved tempting. Thus Philipp Gassert argued in 2008 that 'the protest movements were prime movers and shakers in the transformation and modernisation of European societies. Thanks to 1968, the West had become more democratic'.[63] This is, however, a long-term affair: 'Although the movements of 1968 did not immediately democratise existing institutions, by calling for cultural self-determination, by criticising authoritarian structures, and by strengthening counter-hegemonic values, in the long run they contributed to strengthening the democratic impulse all over Europe'.[64]

There is no doubt that the protests of 1968 served as legitimation and inspiration for subsequent democratic politics. However, the notion of a 'democratic impulse' is too vague, and lumps together in one category an enormous variety of phenomena: the widespread acceptance of electoral politics, anti-authoritarianism, cultural and political autonomy, direct democracy, levelling tendencies, consumerisation and secularisation. The emphasis on democratisation, as its Habermasian origins suggest, appeals most in the Federal Republic of Germany. With Nazi authoritarianism casting a long shadow, the failure of the diverse attempts at direct democracy and cultural autonomy in the 1960s can be recompensed by the tardy embrace of electoral democracy by European conservatives. Yet to set the acceptance of electoral democracy as the bar for democratisation in no way corresponds to the goals of most protesters in the 1960s. This long view is not so much wrong as incomplete.

---

[60] Marwick, *The Sixties*, 15.
[61] See Peter Wagner, 'The project of emancipation and the possibility of politics, or what's wrong with post-1968 individualism?', *Thesis Eleven* 68 (February 2002), 31–45.
[62] Jürgen Habermas, *Toward a Rational Society: Student Protest, Science and Politics*, trans. Jeremy J. Shapiro (Cambridge: Polity Press, 1987), 49. On liberalisation and Habermas, see Arndt Neumann, 'Time is on your side. Ein Kommentar zu Detlef Siegfried's *"1968" – eine Kulturrevolution? Sozial. Geschichte Online* 3 (2010), 117–132.
[63] Gassert, 'Narratives of Democratization', 309.   [64] Ibid., 320.

The long-term perspective obscures as much as it reveals, either by rendering the conflicts of the 1960s incomprehensible, or by eliding the distance and the difference between 1968 and the present day it is held to have created. The meaning of a set of events such as 1968 should probably not be sought primarily in a set of identifiable achievements. As the editors of *The Sixties* have observed, the gap between aspirations and accomplishments constitutes a distinctive feature of the period.[65] Indeed, the long term is rarely kind to utopianism. The disparity between hope and reality was to be expected for protest movements that rarely prioritised parliamentary political or legislative change and embodied no consensus on the details of the society they sought. Faced with a lack of achievements, Gerd-Rainer Horn has proposed that 'the most truly radical potential of 1968 lay precisely in its highlighting of the *possibilities* of a different organization of social life.'[66] After five decades, 1968 is no longer a beginning, it is only its possibility. Without doubt, the late 1960s revealed great vistas of social transformation, even if many of them were short-lived. But it may be in the experience of the short term, rather than any set of achievements, that the long-term significance is to be found.

Democratisation and Its Discontents

Rather than the strengthening of a generalised 'democratic impulse', the 1960s was an extended struggle over different visions of political, social and cultural democracy, which often contradicted and undermined both each other and themselves. Part I of this book elaborates this dynamic in culture and education, tracing its evolution from the early 1960s to the crisis of 1968. Higher education embodied these tensions from the very beginning of the decade. As Chapter 1 demonstrates, many intellectuals and even politicians in the early 1960s came to view the university as an instrument of technocratic modernisation and social mobility capable of almost limitless growth. The largely unplanned expansion of the student body undermined these expectations. Instead, the university emerged as a site of struggle. Students opposed technocratic goals in favour of democratic ones. Egalitarian visions of open access to higher education fell apart as overcrowded institutions contemplated ways to restrict access. The changed physiognomy of the 'mass university' led to another axis of conflict, not over access but rather the content and purpose of education.

[65] Varon, Foley and McMillian, 'Time is an ocean', 3.
[66] Horn, '1968: A social movement *sui generis*', 516.

Nowhere was this more evident than in the field of sociology, as Chapter 2 shows. Sociology was a recent invention (as a degree, not as a discipline): a German *Diplom* in sociology was possible first at Frankfurt in 1955, the *license* in France in 1958; the *laurea* in Italy only in 1966. On the blank slate of sociology, academics and students imagined a discipline that would either train cadres in the technocratic administration of modern society or educate critics of the existing social order. In the absence of a traditional curriculum and defined careers for sociologists, every aspect of the discipline invited contestation. This conflict expressed itself in paradigmatic form at Trento, where the struggle over the ambiguities of sociology forged a student movement increasingly dedicated not just to a particular view of the discipline but to the radical-democratic restructuring of the university.

The vision of a 'mass' university drew on a wider cultural phenomenon of the 'democratisation of high culture', itself exemplified in western Europe in the mass market for paperback books. As Chapter 3 shows, advocates of 'democratic culture' proved as uncertain of its meaning as the champions of 'democratic' education. Did democratisation mean easier access to high culture or its redefinition? Where some saw the desacralisation of high culture as democratic, others perceived a process of commodification, laced with contempt for culture. The revolts of the late 1960s saw these stark alternatives in action. Transposed to the university, the dynamic of democratisation via cultural desacralisation proved both invigorating and self-defeating. Chapter 4 traces how the demands for democracy in the cultural sphere shifted between visions of democratisation as increased access to knowledge, as the rejection of distinctions between high and low culture, and as anti-intellectualism, creating a dynamic that ultimately rejected the university altogether for the field of politics.

The university mattered not only as a site of cultural democratisation, but also as a political space amid widespread dissatisfaction with the parliamentary democratic politics of the postwar era. Part II of this book examines this construction of the politics of revolt, from the national level to the local, before investigating the nature of politics in 1968 itself. The mid-1960s were marked by the growth of neo-fascist parties in Italy and West Germany, the French embrace of Gaullist authoritarianism, and the electoral isolation of the Left. Postwar aspirations for a new democratic culture to put the era of fascism, Nazism and imperialism firmly in the past appeared to have been defeated by the realities of electoral politics. The youth groups of political parties atrophied as their parent organisations smothered demands for greater autonomy. Chapter 5 demonstrates how this dual democratic deficit – in the workings of electoral democracy and in internal party politics – combined with the lack of representation for students within the university structure itself to forge a new political space in the university. Chapter 6 explores how new movements occupied this space by adopting the tactics of provocation and direct democracy to demand autonomy and self-government. The protests proved successful at creating a mass movement and paralysing the university, but soon faced internal criticisms of male charismatic authority and pressure to shift from the disorder of general assemblies to a more organised and hierarchical form of politics.

The student assemblies and the protest movements more broadly were characterised by an outpouring of speech. This 'seizure of speech', from provocative interruptions of professors and the demand for debate to the interminable verbal marathons of general assemblies, defined for many the experience of 1968. Chapter 7 analyses this phenomenon. At times, the revolts took on the features of participatory democracy. A space to speak and to be heard was created by provocation and the silencing of professors. At other times the forms of student speech – variously informal, irreverent, aggressive, vulgar, and opaque – established new, unspoken hierarchies.

Part III of this book delineates the crisis of the university in each of the three campuses. While the case studies can be found in each chapter, here the events at each location are examined in turn. The Free University of Berlin, the focus of Chapter 8, exemplifies how the politics of speech could generate institutional crisis in the university. At Trento (Chapter 9), the content and purpose of sociology served this function in the most successful expression of the demand for self-government within an institution of higher education. At Nanterre (Chapter 10), the dean's oversight of student dormitories coalesced with issues of speech and education to generate conflict over academic control of university space.

After incubating at these campuses for years, the revolts burst out of the university in response to a set of specific incidents. The death of the student Benno Ohnesorg in June 1967, shot in the back of the head by a policeman while observing a protest against the Shah of Iran in West Berlin, transformed the situation in the Federal Republic of Germany. In France, with the campus of Nanterre closed by May 1968, its students gravitated to the Sorbonne, where further police intervention escalated the protest to immense proportions and led to the building of barricades in Parisian streets. At Trento, in the absence of brutal police intervention, the extension of protest to the Catholic Church led to a siege of the institute by the local population. From 1968, the revolts were no longer solely or even primarily located in the university.

Despite the radicalisation of revolt leading students away from higher education to a more straightforward political contest, students at West Berlin and Trento created 'Critical Universities' that sought to reshape higher education in the protest movement's image. The final chapter explores the West German and Italian Critical Universities, briefly considered but aborted at Nanterre, where politicisation proceeded most intensely after the general strike of May 1968. The student-run *Kritische Universität* at West Berlin, which operated from mid-1967 through mid-1968, developed counter-courses to those offered by the Free University until it collapsed amid the contradictions of the project and overwhelmed by the political struggle. At Trento, the *Università Critica* operated from mid-1968 into 1969 as a unique experiment in joint control of the institute between students and professors before it too crumbled in the midst of intense pressure to embrace full-time political struggle and not a project derided as a 'golden ghetto in a society of shit'.

The history of 1968 is, of course, not exhausted by these case studies. The story of the Sixties is much broader than the sphere of higher education and the actions of students, academics and intellectuals. Yet there are wider implications to be drawn from this experience. The ephemerality of the 'critical universities' that marked the high tide of student revolution within the university cautions against their romanticisation. Nonetheless, the breadth and depth of aspirations to remake education and society cast the subsequent decades in the shadow of their utopianism. The disproportion between the size of these movements or the events they provoked and their impact on the political and historical imagination stems in part from this expression of political desires in their most radical form. Aspirations for democratisation did not disappear in the wake of 1968, but continued in a variety of other, if less spectacular, forms. Yet while it is possible to draw a long-term legacy of democratisation, it is equally viable to interpret the late 1960s as marking many of the limits of democratisation. Those limits are most evident in the failures of the protest movements to achieve their goals. But equally important are the self-limitations revealed in the events: the way in which democratic impulses coexisted with or gave rise to forms of intolerance, authoritarianism and populism. There is no cause for complacency in the events of 1968. They offer as much to challenge as to celebrate.

PART I

Education and Culture

CHAPTER I

The 'Devouring Monster'
The University in the 1960s

The university of the early 1960s embodied the promise of a new society. The path to economic growth, social mobility, cultural democratisation and personal fulfilment all appeared to lie through the institutions of higher education. The modern economy, industrial vigour and new scientific knowledge are all 'based upon the creative capacity of man and upon his education', proclaimed the OEEC's director of the Office for Scientific and Technical Personnel.[1] That ethos enthused numerous proponents of university expansion in the early years of the Sixties. By the latter half of the decade, however, the vision was much more pessimistic. Raymond Aron compared French students to 'rats ... [that] from an excessive density in a given space, manifest all the signs of disorder which in the human world we associate with neurosis'.[2] One such student put the matter more bluntly. Asked how the university is viewed, he wrote 'A devouring monster, in which the elect are few'.[3] The euphoria of the early 1960s had collapsed into an image of rats and monsters, or worse.[4]

The 'mass university', as it was called, provided one of the most visible features of the student revolt of the late 1960s, and observers drew a causal connection between the two. Whether overpopulation (rats) or underproduction (the devouring monster), the problem was one of number: too many students in too small a space, too many graduates for too few jobs, too few survivors in a Darwinian university. The short time in which some universities exploded intensified the disorientation. Less malicious than

---

[1] Alexander King, 'A Foreword by the Director', in Office for Scientific and Technical Personnel, Organisation for European Economic Co-Operation, *Forecasting Manpower Needs for the Age of Science* (Paris: OEEC Publications, 1960), 7.
[2] Raymond Aron, *La révolution introuvable: réflexions sur la révolution de mai* (Paris: Fayard, 1968), 54.
[3] Bibliothèque de documentation internationale contemporaine [BDIC] F delta 1961(1) – II(1), 'Enquête sur les étudiants du 1er cycle de Tours' (1).
[4] For the worse, see Roger Masters' exploration of the 'biological roots' of the student revolts, which lay in the aggressivity of adolescent apes seeking a role in the social structure. Roger Masters, 'Les racines biologiques d'une révolte', *Preuves* 215–216 (1969), 74–81, 74–75.

Aron, dean of Nanterre Pierre Grappin's elegiac depiction of the university crowd placed the transformation in less than a year:

> One evening of November 1966, I violently experienced the coming change ... In the hall of the Faculty, exiting a large lecture theatre came towards me a tight crowd of students, advancing in rows of six or seven. At five meters of their advancing front, I froze. They passed to my right and left. Not one reaction from anyone. I stood rooted to spot. It was a revelation for me: in that mass of two hundred students, no-one recognised the dean any longer, or wanted to ignore him. The previous year, in 1965, we still knew each other ... There was no hostility, to tell the truth, in that crowd of students. No curiosity either. They simply went on their way. It was their indifference that struck me. On my return home, I depicted the scene to my wife, adding in the form of conclusion – that anonymous crowd frightened me.[5]

Yet the teeming Sorbonne preceded Nanterre's swarm. Before becoming dean of Nanterre, Pierre Grappin ranked as one of the few Sorbonne faculty members actively engaged with the issues provoked by the expanding student body. Far from being frightened by the oncoming crowd, he took the stairs to the student association's office to discuss the matter, 'the only professor of the house, they told me, to have ever taken that path'.[6] The sudden rise of student anonymity fails adequately to explain Grappin's newfound fear.

University overcrowding was not new, in France or elsewhere. One member of the Naples law faculty resorted to a loudspeaker to connect two lecture halls – in 1960.[7] Long before 1968, the numbers at the Sorbonne passed the 2,000 students for which it was built. More than 30,000 registered in the Faculty of Letters at Paris in the early 1960s.[8] Student numbers peaked not in 1968 but after. A brief burst of new construction between 1970 and 1975 barely stemmed the tide.[9] In France, expenditure per student in the mid-1960s surpassed that of the 1970s.[10] The era of

---

[5] Pierre Grappin, *L'Île aux peupliers. De la Résistance à Mai 68: Souvenirs du Doyen de Nanterre* (Nancy: Presses Universitaires de Nancy, 1993), 241.
[6] Ibid., 227.
[7] See Antonio Santoni Rugiu, *Chiarissimi e Magnifici: Il professore nell'università italiana (dal 1700 al 2000)* (Florence: La Nuova Italia, 1991), 256.
[8] See Raymond Aron, 'Some aspects of the crisis in French universities', *Minerva* 3.2 (1964) 279–285, 280.
[9] Guy Neave, 'Patterns', in Walter Rüegg (ed.), *The History of the University in Europe. Volume IV: Universities since 1945* (Cambridge: Cambridge University Press, 2011), 31–69, 44–45.
[10] See Louis Lévy Garboua, 'Les demandes de l'étudiant ou les contradictions de l'université de masse', *Revue française de sociologie* 17.1 (1976), 53–80, 60. See also Raymond Boudon, 'The French university since 1968', *Comparative Politics* 10.1 (October 1977), 89–118, 91.

overcrowding thus neither began nor reached its nadir in the late 1960s. While Aron's 'rodents' and Grappin's 'anonymous crowd' memorably capture the speed of university growth in the 1960s, they cannot suffice as an explanation for the student revolts. There is scant empirical evidence that the student masses encountered a crisis of jobs.[11] Students proved equally politicised outside of Paris, and outside of France, with greater space and fewer competitors. Contestation at the Faculty of Sociology at Trento began with a little more than 600 enrolled. Overcrowding could become a cause of revolt, but was in no way its precondition or primary impetus.

Numbers mattered, not for their size but their meaning. The burgeoning mass of students marked for some the democratisation of higher education and the triumph of social mobility, for others the motor of a modern economy. The advent of mass higher education transformed the university into the preferred instrument of social change.[12] Higher education increasingly assumed the role once reserved to primary, then secondary schooling. Indeed, its prominence stemmed from the universalisation of the latter. Yet proposals for university reforms greatly outnumbered actual pieces of legislation in the 1960s. The Federal Republic of Germany, in which education was a state responsibility, lacked a federal Minister of Education until 1969. In Italy, various legislative proposals were put forward, but none enacted until two decrees in 1968 (themselves thought to be temporary measures pending a substantial reform which never happened). Only France began a reform of higher education, which divided the four-year degree into two cycles, creating a *diplôme* at the end of two years and the *license* after four, and attempted to shift the teaching from magisterial lectures to small seminars. The growth of the university sector occurred in the context of great expectations, but a decidedly meagre legislative output.[13]

---

[11] See Louis Gruel, *La rébellion de 68: Une relecture sociologique* (Rennes: Presses Universitaires de Rennes, 2004), in which he effectively dismantles assumptions about a lack of jobs and perceptions of downgraded degrees.

[12] On the era more generally, see James Bowen, *A History of Western Education. Volume III: The Modern West Europe and the World* (New York: St Martin's Press, 1981), 530. See also Walter Rüegg and Jan Sadlak, 'Relations with Authority', in Rüegg (ed.), *History of the University in Europe, IV*, 73–123, 105, who suggest that the student movements' motivations and goals were largely extrinsic to the university. This obscures the centrality of the university to issues of social reform in the 1960s.

[13] For an account of the relation between the student protests and university reform in West Germany, see Anne Rohstock, *Von der 'Ordinarienuniversität' zur 'Revolutionszentrale'? Hochschulreform und Hochschulrevolte in Bayern und Hessen 1957–1976* (Munich: R. Oldenbourg Verlag, 2010). For an account of the reaction to democratisation in the 1970s, see Nikolai Wehrs,

University expansion did not rely upon reforms of higher education. In all three nations, higher education admitted any student with a final certificate from the upper secondary school system: the *baccalauréat* in France, the *Abitur* in West Germany or a diploma from a *liceo classico* in Italy.[14] The French parliament had declared higher education to be free in 1875. In West Germany, the Basic Law conferred the constitutional right of every German to freely choose their profession (thereby limiting any restriction on entry to university, save that of the ability to accommodate students). In Italy, the constitution promised the right of the highest levels of education to the capable and deserving, regardless of financial resources. The most significant pieces of legislation for the university in the 1960s were not proposals for higher education reform, but those which modified the secondary school system. In France, the reform of January 1959 extended compulsory education to 16 years. In Italy, the 1962 creation of the unified middle school did the same to age 14.[15] In West Germany, with some variation by state, compulsory education already extended to 14 or 15 years. Thus one historian of Italy has argued that 'the student revolt arose not because of lack of reform, but as a consequence of an attempted reform, namely the raising of the compulsory school-leaving age to fourteen years'.[16] As secondary replaced primary education as the lowest common denominator, the tertiary sector displaced secondary schooling as the high road to social mobility. Two further factors drove university growth: the arrival in higher education of the baby-boom generation and the increase in the number of women attending university. Both of these groups sought something different. The soaring numbers of students mattered less for their sheer quantity than for the implicit promise of a new society, built on the principle of democratised education.

The Educational Catastrophe

The expectations that accompanied university expansion explain why, just a few years before 1968, a brief consensus emerged that there existed not

---

Protest der Professoren: Der "Bund Freiheit der Wissenschaft" in den 1970er Jahren (Göttingen: Wallstein Verlag, 2014).

[14] An important exception is the Grandes Écoles in France.
[15] On the Italian education system, see Luigi Ambrosoli, *La Scuola in Italia dal dopoguerra ad oggi* (Bologna: Il Mulino, 1982).
[16] Percy Allum, 'Italian society transformed', in Patrick McCarthy (ed.), *Italy Since 1945* (Oxford: Oxford University Press, 2000), 27.

too many students, but too few. In a series of articles in *Christ und Welt*, the philosopher and theologian Georg Picht dramatically directed public debate in the Federal Republic of Germany to the theme of educational planning, or, more precisely, the lack thereof. Rapidly transferred into book form, *Die deutsche Bildungskatastrophe* (The German Educational Catastrophe) sketched an image of imminent disaster in West German education, a drought of educated individuals. The book won the inaugural Theodor Heuß Preis, which recognises democratic initiatives, in 1965. The PEN-Club elected him a member. The book's impact, Picht joked in 1973, incriminated him as 'the chief culprit for the overproduction of *Abiturienten*'.[17] Yet Picht's warning was not new even in 1963. No novice to the field of education (his father Werner was one of the earliest proponents of adult education), Picht had participated for a decade (1953 to 1963) in the German Committee for the Education System and the Advisory Board for Educational Planning of Baden-Württemberg. *Die deutsche Bildungskatastrophe* followed this long engagement and testified to its failure.[18] Unlike his committee work, the articles in *Christ und Welt* addressed the public before politicians, and aimed at provocation rather than policy: 'The public must finally take note of the truth, and politicians must set themselves to make those hard decisions demanded by a national emergency of the first order.'[19] Picht's book addressed education not as a policy issue, but as a public and national crisis.[20]

Die deutsche Bildungskatastrophe was not new either in its message or rationales for university expansion, but rather in its framing and resonance. A mere year before Picht's articles of February 1964, the economist Friedrich Edding advanced a similar agenda in his volume *Ökonomie des Bildungswesens*, with no equivalent response. Edding's book collected a

---

[17] Georg Picht, 'Vom Bildungsnotstand zum Notstand der Bildungspolitik', *Zeitschrift für Pädagogik* 19.5 (1973), 665–678, 665.
[18] Picht identified the lack of funds for the educational programmes put forth by the education ministers. See Georg Picht, *Die deutsche Bildungskatastrophe* (Olten: Walter-Verlag, 1964), 42; Sören Messinger, 'Katastrophe und Reform: Georg Pichts bildungspolitische Interventionen', in Robert Lorenz and Franz Walter (eds.), *1964: Das Jahr, mit dem "68" Begann* (Bielefeld: Transcript Verlag, 2014), 247–258. For a brief comparison of Picht to the demands of scientific development in the German Democratic Republic, see Wolfgang Lambrecht, 'Deutsch-deutsche Reformdebatten vor "Bologna". Die "Bildungskatastrophe der 1960er-Jahre', *Zeithistorische Forschungen/Studies in Contemporary History* 4 (2007), 472–477.
[19] Picht, *Bildungskatastrophe*, 17–18.
[20] On Picht's media strategy see Nicolai Hannig, 'Georg Picht: Strategien eines Medienintellektuellen in der westdeutschen Öffentlichkeit', *Vierteljahrheft für Zeitgeschichte* 66 (2018), 617–644.

series of interventions between 1953 and 1962, and closed with an appeal for a 'New Deal through educational policy'.[21] Despite the programme of social justice implied by the Rooseveltian reference, a purely economic rationale was central to Edding's case: the assumption, articulated as early as 1958, that 'the *demand for staff on the upper levels* of responsibility appears to be *increasing particularly fast*. It is mainly this general development of expert staffs where only recently one highly educated personality could master the task, which makes the expansion of education on the higher levels inevitable.'[22] If the argument of economic inevitability proved insufficient, Edding added the incentive of international competition: 'all the nations around us are moving towards a rapid increase of the quota of the academically educated ... Why is it assumed here ... that we can remain stagnating in educational endeavours?'[23] After economic necessity and national survival, the expansion of higher education also answered the demand for social equality.[24] Edding offered economic, patriotic and moral justifications for educational planning. Picht's 1964 tocsin combined all three but drew deeply on the language of national catastrophe: 'The governments and parliaments must now act. Should they not do so, it is today certain who is responsible for the third great collapse of German history in this century.'[25]

While both tasteless and trivial, comparing a potential crisis of the education system to the 'catastrophes' of 1918 and 1945 certainly helped to obscure the quite different politics of educational expansion. The prospect 'that in 1970 France will be the centre of Europe'[26] no doubt aimed to win to the cause of educational planning those for whom the word 'plan' reeked of Communism.[27] *Christ und Welt* was not a journal

---

[21] Friedrich Edding, *Ökonomie des Bildungswesens. Lehren und Lernen als Haushalt und als Investition* (Freiburg im Breisgau: Rombach, 1963), 412. See also Ursula Kirkpatrick Springer, 'West Germany's turn to *Bildungspolitik* in educational planning', *Comparative Education Review* 9.1 (February 1965), 11–17.

[22] Friedrich Edding, *Internationale Tendenzen in der Entwicklung der Ausgaben für Schulen und Hochschulen* (Kiel: Institut für Weltwirtschaft, 1958), 163. Italics in the original.

[23] Friedrich Edding, 'Bildungsforschung als Grundlage der Bildungsplanung', in Deutscher Hochschulverband (ed.), *Bildungsplanung und Bildungsökonomie* (Göttingen: Otto Schwartz & Co., 1964), 57.

[24] Edding, 'Bildungsforschung als Grundlage der Bildungsplanung', 60. Cf. Edding, *Ökonomie des Bildungswesens*, 404.

[25] Picht, *Bildungskatastrophe*, 87. The echoes of Friedrich Meinecke's *Die deutsche Katastrophe* hardly seem accidental.

[26] Picht, *Bildungskatastrophe*, 26.

[27] See the parliamentary debate in March 1964 reported in Picht, *Bildungskatastrophe*, 103.

noted for its radicalism. The editor, Giselher Wirsing, a one-time SS Hauptsturmführer,[28] presented the imminent German 'catastrophe' as the result of 'a falsely understood conservatism, which can only be perceived as *restaurativ*'.[29] He had invited Picht to write a series of articles, 'to present the German educational catastrophe as it would appear to an observer who represented no interest in this field and was bound to no party'.[30] Picht himself wrote in the context of his religious engagement, declaring in 1963 that 'the educational question is ... the field on which it will be decided if the Church recognises its responsibility'.[31] But for the purposes of an 'apolitical' presentation, Picht chose the spectre of economic disaster: 'we must at least double the number of *Abiturienten* and the number of academics must also rise significantly if West Germany is not to go to the dogs in the course of the development of scientific civilisation'.[32]

National and economic catastrophe played to the centre-right and the ostensibly 'apolitical'. But the discourse of democracy lay just beneath the surface, and in some instances took centre stage. The sociologist Ralf Dahrendorf, Picht's companion on the Beirat für Bildungsplanung Baden-Württemberg and future parliamentary representative for the FDP, deployed the language of rights. Where Picht's alarm had begun with 'educational catastrophe means economic emergency',[33] Dahrendorf asserted that 'educational policy is infinitely more than the maidservant of economic policy ... it can ... only be effected in connection to the idea of a civil right to education'.[34] Nonetheless, Dahrendorf insisted that framing education in terms of rights rather than economics did not imply a goal of social equality, that 'a free society is always a society that gives inequality large space....'.[35] Despite such qualifications, the spectre of social equality and planning lurked in the debate on higher education.

A broad consensus began to emerge on the expansion of higher education that encompassed divergent political positions and rationales. For

---

[28] On Wirsing, see Norbert Frei and Johannes Schmitz, *Journalismus im Dritten Reich* (Munich: C. H. Beck, 1989), 173–180.
[29] Giselher Wirsing, 'Einführende Leitartikel aus "Christ und Welt"', in Picht, *Bildungskatastrophe*, 12.
[30] Picht, *Bildungskatastrophe*, 6.
[31] Georg Picht, 'Die Krise der Kulturpolitik und die Aufgabe der Kirche', *Lutherische Monatshefte* 2.9 (1963), 468.
[32] Picht, *Bildungskatastrophe*, 28.   [33] Ibid., 17.
[34] Ralf Dahrendorf, *Bildung ist Bürgerrecht: Plädoyer für eine aktive Bildungspolitik* (Hamburg: Christian Wegner Verlag, 1968), 22–23. See also Dahrendorf's letter in *Hochschulgesamtplan Baden-Württemberg* (Villingen: Neckar Verlag, 1967), 19–21.
[35] Dahrendorf, *Bildung ist Bürgerrecht*, 26.

Picht, education was the privileged field for the engagement of the Protestant Churches; for Wirsing, an opportunity for a true conservatism; for Dahrendorf, the fulfilment of a civil right and for Edding, a crucial component of a modern economy and a qualified gesture towards creating social equality.[36] Despite the different rationales, each demanded a politics of educational planning and expansion and placed the university at the centre of social change. The discourse of national catastrophe helped to hide the divisions. But a latent tension existed between the nationalist, technocratic, liberal and egalitarian visions. When the German universities did expand, the languages of catastrophe and of rights returned, but not in the meaning given to them by Dahrendorf and Picht.[37]

The Technocratic Age

In the national stakes of educational reform, France appeared to have taken an almost insurmountable lead over its European competitors. France threatened to dominate the continent within a decade, Picht warned, unless urgent measures were introduced to prevent such misfortune. French politicians evinced little of the squeamishness West Germans exhibited at the idea of planning. Paris also hosted the offices of the Organisation for Economic Co-Operation and Development, which, since the formation in 1958 of its Committee for Scientific and Technical Personnel (of the then Organisation for European Economic Cooperation), had played an important role in promoting research and policy development on the nexus of education and economics. The OECD researchers argued, unsurprisingly, that the coming world required more people like themselves. The Committee for Scientific and Technical Personnel defined its task in 1960 as 'to promote ... the formulation of policies for increasing the supply of scientific, technical and other qualified manpower'.[38] West German policy experts were not alone in envisioning higher education's expansion.

---

[36] The FDP politician Hildegard Hamm-Brücher, whose *Auf Kosten unserer Kinder? Wer tut was für unsere Schulen – Reise durch die pädagogischen Provinzen der Bundesrepublik und Berlin* (Bramsche/Osnabrück: Nannen Verlag, 1965) painted a dismal picture of the West German education system, and the Basel-based Gottfried Bombach should also be mentioned.
[37] Picht, for one, remained defiant. See Picht, 'Vom Bildungsnotstand zum Notstand der Bildungspolitik', 666.
[38] Henning Friis, 'Preface', in Seymour E. Harris (ed.), *Economic Aspects of Higher Education* (Paris: OECD Publications, 1964), 7.

Two assumptions underpinned the OECD programme. First, a growing technical ability to predict educational requirements, and second, the capacity and need of the modern economy to produce and employ ever greater numbers of educated personnel. The 1960s offered a brave new world. Philip H. Coombs, then the US Assistant Secretary of State for Educational and Cultural Affairs, stated to an OECD conference in 1961 that 'mankind is entering a new and bolder environment where poverty need no longer exist and where education is the vital prerequisite of clear thinking by democratically governed peoples'.[39] Education contained the promise of a new, democratised society free from the burden of poverty. Yet a pessimistic underside lurked within this optimistic, utopian vision. Coombs declared 'the combination of greatly increased demand for education and restrictions upon supply has produced in Western nations a serious educational deficit. If allowed to persist, this could eventually spell disaster for free societies'.[40] The Cold War – especially in the wake of the Sputnik shock of 1957 – provided an important global dimension to the existential stakes of expanded education systems and ensured that at the international level, the prospect of potential disaster tinged the optimism associated with economic planning and higher education.[41] The OECD funded conferences, research and predictions of educational needs in the late 1950s and early 1960s. An international cohort of enlightened bureaucrats eagerly took up the technocratic triumphalist narrative of the 1960s. Yet the educational euphoria always contained the creeping fear of defeat in a Darwinist struggle for survival of the most educated, even in France. While West Germans anticipated with discomfort French economic dominance of Europe, their French equivalents warned inaction in education threatened to reduce the nation to the rank of 'an intellectually underdeveloped country'.[42]

Raymond Poignant, counsel (Maître des requêtes) to the Conseil d'Etat, and rapporteur général to the Commission on Scholarly, University and

---

[39] Philip H. Coombs, 'Preface', in Organisation for Economic Co-Operation and Development (ed.), *Policy Conference on Economic Growth and Investment in Education, Washington 16th–20th October 1961* (Paris: Organisation for Economic Co-Operation and Development, 1962), 5.

[40] Philip H. Coombs, 'Educational planning in the light of economic requirements', in Office for Scientific and Technical Personnel, Organisation for European Economic Co-Operation, *Forecasting Manpower Needs for the Age of Science* (Paris: OEEC Publications, 1960), 30.

[41] Coombs, 'Preface', 6.

[42] Louis Cros, *'L'explosion' scolaire* (Paris: Publication du Comité Universitaire d'Information Pédagogique, 1961), 44.

Sporting facilities of the Commissariat général au Plan, articulated the most sophisticated argument for further expansion of the French higher education system. Poignant advanced a multi-causal rationale for expansion that identified demographic factors, social demand and state policy in addition to the axiomatic OECD insistence on economics. Nevertheless, the technocratic imperative remained central, as Poignant outlined at an OECD training course for human resource strategists in Italy in 1962: '[France] is now experiencing a shortage of semi-skilled and skilled manpower. As the supervisory personnel needed ... are either non-existent or in short supply, the concept of "economic needs" is now posed in absolute terms in France, and is likely to remain so until 1975.'[43] A few years before Raymond Aron's 'rats' populated French universities, Poignant conceived almost no limits to growth: 'an unlimited proportion of people with a secondary or higher education can be employed by the economy'.[44] To an even greater degree than West Germany, French bureaucrats evinced a boundless faith in the limitless potential of higher education.

The French debate did not lack for warnings similar to Picht's evocation of national catastrophe. The economist Jean Fourastié, Poignant's colleague in the Commissariat du Plan, the man who later coined the phrase *'les trentes glorieuses'* to describe France's postwar economic boom, expressed better than Poignant the appropriate sense of urgency:

> We will surely not have what is needed so that the French economy fully utilises the most recent production techniques and French enterprises are all ultra-modern. What is needed are engineers, physical sciences, but also social sciences, human sciences, psychologists, accountants ... in much larger numbers than we have and than we will have. *The strangulating bottleneck of human progress, even in a country like ours, is the lack of qualified citizens.* In other terms, we are a relatively backward country in relation to what we could be, because our citizens are not sufficiently educated.[45]

---

[43] Raymond Poignant, 'Establishing educational targets in France', in OECD The Mediterranean Regional Project, *Planning Education for Economic and Social Development* (Paris: OECD Publications, 1962), 216. See also Raymond Poignant, 'Les Problèmes posés par la planification dans l'enseignement', in Institut Pédagogique National, *Planification et enseignement* (Paris: SEVPEN, 1963), 7–17.

[44] Poignant, 'Establishing educational targets in France,' 209.

[45] Jean Fourastié, 'Les données économiques du problème de la planification', in Institut Pédagogique National, *Planification et enseignement*, 46. The italics are from the original. See also Jean Fourastié, 'Les exigences nouvelles du progrès économique et technique', in Francis-Louis Closon (ed.), *L'Éducation nationale* (Paris: Presses Universitaires de France, 1965), 43–53.

Fourastié merely recited the technocratic consensus.⁴⁶ The necessity of unlimited university expansion rapidly attained the status of self-evident truth.

Bureaucrats and administrators consistently stressed the apparently apolitical, technical rationale for the growth of higher education. But democratic and egalitarian implications were never entirely absent, although often merely treated as an added bonus rather than the principle. Thus Louis Cros, creator of the Institut Pédagogique National, explained that technological progress had dissolved any tension between the economy and social reformer's goal of extending all education to the greatest number: 'for the first time in history, *idealist aspirations and practical necessities in matters of education have ceased to contradict each other*'. At long last, 'the most advanced education for the greatest possible number of children' was not only desirable but necessary.⁴⁷ A new era had begun. With the understatement characteristic of the prophets of education, Cros declared 'The problem is immense. It has to do with the creation of the school of a new civilisation.'⁴⁸ Much has been written about the utopianism of students in 1968, but they were hardly unique. Even the sceptical Raymond Aron admitted the need for 'giving to an increasingly large number of persons a secondary or higher education'.⁴⁹ As Marzio Barbagli described, 'a new priesthood of sociologists and economists, supported and financed by governments and foundations, preached the virtues of education ... that all that was required for man's ills to be ended, tyrannies crushed, poverty, unemployment, and underdevelopment extinguished, was for education to be planted, take root, and grow healthy and robust'.⁵⁰ The promised reconciliation of democratic, egalitarian aspirations and technocratic, economic 'necessity' reflected the educational reformers faith

---

⁴⁶ Coombs, 'Preface', 6.
⁴⁷ Cros, *'L'explosion' scolaire*, 43–44. Italics in the original. See Bernard Pudal, 'Ordre symbolique et système scolaire dans les années 1960', in Dominique Damamme et al. (eds.)., *Mai–Juin 68* (Paris: Editions de l'Atelier, 2008), 62–74, 66. See also Christelle Dormoy-Rajramanan, 'Mai–Juin 1968: acme d'un context de crise universitaire', in Charles Soulié (ed.), *Un mythe à détruire? Origines et destin du Centre universitaire experimental de Vincennes* (Paris: Presses universitaires de Vincennes, 2012), 61–81.
⁴⁸ Cros, *'L'explosion' scolaire*, 41.
⁴⁹ Raymond Aron, 'The Education of the citizen in industrial society', *Daedalus* 91.2 (1962), 249–263, 252. Just two years later Aron wondered whether 'is it desirable that the state should devote considerable sums of money and, what is more, the precious talents of its teachers to the vain attempt to give a traditional academic training to boys and girls who are not capable of benefiting from it?' Aron, 'Some aspects of the crisis', 282.
⁵⁰ Marzio Barbagli, *Educating for Unemployment: Politics, Labor Markets and the School System. Italy 1859–1973*, trans. Robert H. Ross (New York: Columbia University Press, 1982), 1.

in economic progress, not the reality of the Sixties. Cros' 'school of the atomic age' would indeed be explosive, but not in the way he expected.

Faith in technological progress long predated the 1960s. Yet that decade witnessed a renewed certainty in the ability to empirically document the precise requirements of the economy (and as a consequence to develop policy 'scientifically'). As long ago as 1956, at the International Symposium on the Problems of Automation held at Milan, Jean Fourastié vaunted the power of 'techniques of prediction' which 'allow full employment to be realised within a nation'.[51] At the same conference, the Italian Gino Martinoli precociously drew a direct link between technological change and its educational preconditions: economic progress 'is subordinated to the availability of technicians'.[52] The former manager of Olivetti, Martinoli's short paper prompted his appointment as head of a commission instituted between the Minister of Education and the Associazione per lo sviluppo dell'industria nel Mezzogiorno (Association for the development of industry in the South or SVIMEZ).[53] The result, *Mutamenti della struttura professionale e ruolo della scuola: previsioni per il prossimo quindicennio* (Changes in Professional Structures and the Role of Education: Predictions for the Next Fifteen Years), in Martinoli's own words 'obtained consensus and provoked notable interest'.[54] Translated immediately into English, the report served as a model for other predictions, as Raymond Poignant noted.[55]

Thus in Italy, too, a nation where, in 1958, 39.4 per cent of university graduates expected to remain unemployed,[56] and where, as Martinoli himself had noted 'we are still talking of the battle against illiteracy',[57] an audience suddenly appeared for the thesis of university expansion. The contours of the argument conformed to the international model.

---

[51] Jean Fourastié, 'Les répercussions économiques de l'automation et le problème de l'emploi', in Consiglio nazionale delle ricerche, *Convegno Internazionale sui Problemi dell'Automatismo*, vol. 3 (London: Pergamon Press, 1959), 2054. See also his intervention 'Conditions et conséquences sociales du progrès technique', 2278–2281.

[52] See Gino Martinoli, 'L'automazione e la necessità di una adeguata preparazione culturale in Italia', in Consiglio nazionale delle ricerche, *Convegno Internazionale sui Problemi dell'Automatismo*, vol. 3 (London: Pergamon Press, 1959), 2308–2321.

[53] See Carlo D'Amicis and Mirella Fulvi (eds.), *Conversando con Gino Martinoli* (Città di Castello: Fondazione Adriano Olivetti, 1991), 98.

[54] Ibid.

[55] Martinoli was no stranger to the OECD conferences on this issue. He was present at the November 1959 Hague conference that became *Forecasting Manpower Needs for the Age of Science*.

[56] See Barbagli, *Educating for Unemployment*, 224.

[57] 'Statement by Mr. Gino Martinoli (Italy)', in *Annals of Collective Economy* 34.2–3 (1963), 291.

Technological progress demanded more educated personnel,[58] higher education required expansion to fulfil this need, and such expansion felicitously served the goal of social equality ('In modern societies social mobility realises itself above all through scholastic institutions').[59] Last but not least, Italy appeared to the Italians, no less than the Federal Republic to the West Germans and France to the French, as precipitously poised in the education stakes. The current institutions, Martinoli warned in 1965, 'can provide at most for 50–60% of the needs for qualified, technical personnel, of higher personnel, middle management, scientific researchers, managers, of teachers'[60] needed within the decade. The title of one report put the thesis in its greatest simplicity: *L'economia italiana ha bisogno di laureati* (The Italian economy needs graduates).[61] Yet for all the resonance of these appeals, Martinoli himself retrospectively conceded that 'very little has changed in the institutions and the situation of the Italian educational system in the last thirty years'.[62] His own contributions culminated in his 1967 manifesto *L'università come impresa* (The University as a Business).[63] Destined for a short life-span, the book nonetheless was one, as Norberto Bobbio would testify, 'in which many of us saw ourselves reflected'.[64] Indeed, the greatest success of the flurry of reformist manifestos of the late 1950s and early 1960s was not their research, nor any actual policy achievements, but their expression of the political desires for social reform of enlightened intellectuals.

The Democratisation of Higher Education and Its Discontents

Despite being unplanned, ever greater numbers of students entered higher education in the mid-1960s. Regardless of their policy impact, the prophets of university education had nonetheless effectively set the agenda for understanding that expansion, and the extent to which it fulfilled national, technocratic and democratic aspirations. The idea that sheer quantitative increase equated to democratisation proved the first

---

[58] Associazione per lo sviluppo dell'industria nel Mezzogiorno (SVIMEZ), *Mutamenti della struttura professionale e ruolo della scuola: previsioni per il prossimo quindicennio* (Rome: Giuffrè, 1961), 47–49.
[59] Ibid., 59.
[60] Gino Martinoli, 'Evoluzione tecnologica e aspirazioni umane in Italia nell'ultimo ventennio', *Economia e storia* 12 (1965), 384.
[61] Comitato Nazionale per la Produttività, *L'economia italiana ha bisogno di laureati* (Rome: Edizioni Scientifiche S. P. E. I., 1961).
[62] D'Amicis and Fulvi, *Conversando con Gino Martinoli*, 104.
[63] Gino Martinoli, *L'Università come impresa* (Florence: La Nuova Italia, 1967).
[64] Centro di documentazione Mauro Rostagno [CMR] B.14 f.1 (Fondo Calì).

assumption to fall. To begin, the advent of mass higher education was decidedly uneven. Advocates of almost unlimited university expansion invariably stressed the economic requirements for education and the demand for technically skilled, scientific personnel. Raymond Aron noted that the university conferred degrees which gave access to professions, and that thus 'the division of students among faculties must correspond to social needs'.[65] As evidence of this relation he cited the growth in science students from 1949 to 1960. In Italy, Gino Martinoli forecast that the scientific and technical and economic faculties would outstrip those of law and letters.[66] In France, Raymond Poignant predicted the relative increase in the students of science and engineering. He thought they would account for some 43 per cent of all students by 1970, in contrast to 18 per cent in 1949.[67] They were all wrong. Numbers of science students stagnated in relative terms. The relative weight of the science and engineering faculties in France declined in the 1960s, never reaching the commanding heights predicted, a mere 19 per cent still in 1970 and declining further that decade.[68] To be sure, the university produced a greater number of engineers and technicians, but the most visible growth occurred in the bastion of traditional high culture, the arts faculties.

The prediction of the ongoing expansion of higher education proved correct, although West Germany's take-off lagged slightly behind those of France and Italy. However, the expansion of the universities did not occur evenly across the faculties. Humanities and arts experienced exponential growth, not the sciences or technical fields. In Italy, between the mid-1950s and 1970 the number of students in arts faculties multiplied sixfold. In France, the number of arts students increased fivefold during the same period. In West Germany, by 1970 the number of students in the arts and social sciences was more than six times that of the mid-1950s. While the university no longer resembled the privileged preserve of a miniscule minority, nor did it mean the seamless recalibration of faculties to the exigencies of an ever-more technically oriented job market capable of absorbing limitless numbers of graduates. Expansion did not reflect the supposed 'social needs' for technical personnel.

Not the demands of the job market but the pressure of supply from below explained the growth of the university. What policy experts usually

---

[65] Raymond Aron, 'Quelques problèmes des universités françaises', *Preuves* 159 (1964), 10–22, 20.
[66] See Gino Martinoli, *L'università nello sviluppo economico italiano* (Rome: Giuffrè, 1962), 30.
[67] Poignant, 'Establishing educational targets in France', 218.
[68] On Italy, see Ambrosoli, *La Scuola in Italia*, 180.

presented as a fortunate by-product of economic growth – social mobility and aspirations for equality – appear more important as drivers of university expansion than the demands of the market. Yet the social transformation via the university remained ambiguous. Optimists pointed to a gradual growth in the numbers of students from working-class backgrounds, but empirical studies demonstrated persistent inequality in access to higher education.[69] One major source of growth was rarely mentioned: women. Once again, the arts faculties incarnated the changing physiognomy of the university. Between the mid-1950s and the end of the 1960s, the percentage of female students at Italian universities increased from around 27 per cent to 38 per cent; in French universities the percentage of female students increased from 36 per cent to 44 per cent; and in West German universities the percentage increased from 19 per cent to 30 per cent (with parity achieved Europe-wide around 1990).[70] The increase in female students was overwhelmingly achieved via the arts faculties. If those disciplines are excluded, the actual percentage increase of female students plummets from 12 per cent to 2 per cent.[71] Indeed, by 1970–1971, 63 per cent of all women in Italian higher education were arts students; in France 52 per cent of all women studied in the Faculté des Lettres et Sciences Humaines, while in West Germany, some 70 per cent of female students turned to the humanities and social sciences. For the student body as a whole the respective figures were 32, 35 and 30 per cent. A mere 12 per cent of West German law students were women. Thus the university population explosion of the 1960s occurred predominantly in faculties (arts and letters) that, apart from teaching, did not lead directly to a profession, and in a population (women) previously excluded from higher education (and who remained excluded from more prestigious degrees such as Law, Medicine and Engineering).

University expansion thus opened up a set of contradictions. Expected to serve economic growth via providing technical and scientific personnel, the greatest increase occurred in fields that did not lead directly to employment. Advocates of higher education planning did not have hordes

---

[69] See Yossi Shavit and Hans-Peter Blossfeld, *Persistent Inequality: Changing Educational Attainment in Thirteen Countries* (Boulder: Westview Press, 1993).

[70] These figures are derived from the *Annuaire statistique de la France*, *Annuario statistico italiano* and the *Statistisches Jahrbuch für die Bundesrepublik Deutschland*. French figure is for 1966–1967 only. See Ulrich Teichler, 'Graduation and careers' in Rüegg (ed.), *The History of the University in Europe*, 319–368, 353.

[71] If the arts faculties are excluded, the percentage of women at Italian universities rises only from 18 per cent to 20 per cent, at French universities from only 28 per cent to 32 per cent, and in West Germany from a little more than 13 per cent to 15 per cent.

of arts graduates in mind when they extolled the limitless capacity of the market to absorb degrees. To be sure, arts students were not terrorised by the prospect of unemployment in the 1960s.[72] But the enormous size of the arts faculties, their detachment from vocational outcomes and the feminisation of the student body suggests university expansion served a very different function to that imagined by educational planners, one marked less by technocratic planning than the appropriation of high culture. Yet access to higher education in no way equated to its completion.

The numbers of students registered at university were highly deceptive. Many never completed a degree. Attrition marked each university system, although the exact scale is difficult to calculate. To give just one example, 105,480 Italian students entered the university in 1965; only 60,651 were awarded a degree in 1970. Estimates of attrition in France were higher than 60 per cent.[73] One study of almost 7,000 arts students saw just 46 per cent successfully complete the first year.[74] Another study recorded 25 per cent of an incoming student body eventually attaining an arts degree.[75] Gino Martinoli estimated the 'scholastic output' in Italian universities at 44 per cent, and just over 20 per cent for some faculties.[76] Attrition was not a new phenomenon, but the idea that it reflected the failure of the education system rather than the abilities of individual students was.[77] Abandonment of university took on a different meaning in the context of widespread notions of democratised access to higher education. As student numbers expanded, so did the number of 'rejects' from the mass university. Open access at entry to the university appeared merely to postpone the process of selection to the first years of university. That process of selection, furthermore, favoured the most privileged sectors of society. One study reported the need to work condemned poorer students to failure,[78]

---

[72] See Gruel, *La rébellion de 68*.   [73] See for example Aron, 'Some aspects of the crisis', 280.

[74] Only 43 per cent registered for the second year, while 21 per cent began the first year again. Nonetheless, the number who eventually passed the first year rose only to 48 per cent; Noëlle Bisseret, *Les inégaux ou la sélection universitaire* (Paris: Presses Universitaires de France, 1974).

[75] Mattei Dogan, 'Causes of the French student revolt in May 1968', in Stephen D. Kertesz (ed.), *The Task of Universities in a Changing World* (Notre Dame: University of Notre Dame Press, 1971), 306–322, 310.

[76] Martinoli, *L'Università come impresa*, 8–9. These figures did not change much over the succeeding decades. See Sheldon Rothblatt, 'Curriculum, students, education', in Rüegg (ed.), *The History of the University in Europe*, 238–275, 258–259.

[77] See Antoine Prost, 'La démocratisation de l'enseignement: histoire d'une notion', in Claude-Isabelle Brelot and Jean-Luc Mayaud (eds.), *Voyages en histoire: mélanges offerts à Paul Gerbod* (Paris: les Belles Lettres, 1995), 119–129, 126.

[78] Bisseret, *Les inégaux*, 99.

while Pierre Bourdieu and Jean-Claude Passeron popularised the image of the university as a consecrator of inherited cultural capital.[79] The mass university, despite its size, appeared little more democratic than its elite predecessor in equalising access from all social classes and genders.

The Social Boundaries of the University

The arts faculties – to which the greatest number of new students flocked in the 1960s – formed the base of the student movements of the late 1960s. So was Raymond Aron correct in diagnosing a rat-like student psychosis, the effect of too great a population in too small a space? If there is any truth to Aron's argument, it lies not in the problem of physical space but the social and symbolic boundaries of the university. Student movements invariably sprang into action not to protest overcrowded universities as such, but to combat the administrative response to expansion, which typically took the form of restrictions on entry to the university and the length of time students could remain registered. Inevitably, one of the most charged issues of a 'democratised' university revolved around the problems of access and selection. Almost any process of selection contradicted the ideal of democratisation.

As early as 1963 at the Freie Universität Berlin, the Law Faculty notified students who had been enrolled for longer than nine semesters that further study would no longer be possible beyond the winter semester of 1963–1964. By July of 1964, that deadline was rescinded in favour of immediate deregistration.[80] The Allgemeine Studentenausschuß (AStA), the student executive, protested the one-off measure, but as the Law Faculty pointed out, in the three weeks following the decision only seven students applied to extend their period of study.[81] In February 1966, however, the admissions committee of the Law Faculty voted to impose henceforth a limit of nine semesters. In May the same year, the Medicine Faculty also limited the length of time a student could remain registered. In June, the *Wissenschaftsrat* in its 'recommendations for a new organisation of study at the universities' advocated for the shortening and rationalisation of all courses of study. That same month, in defence of the

---

[79] In English, Pierre Bourdieu and Jean-Claude Passeron, *The Inheritors: French Students and Their Relation to Culture* (Chicago: University of Chicago Press, 1979). See Pudal, 'Ordre symbolique et système scolaire', 72.
[80] See Pressestelle der FU Berlin (ed.), *Hochschule im Umbruch: Teil III: Auf dem Weg in den Dissens (1957–1964)* (Berlin: Pressestelle der FU Berlin, 1974), 160 and 172–173.
[81] Pressestelle der FU Berlin (ed.), *Hochschule III*, 174.

'*Zwangsexmatrikulation*' (forced de-registration), the law professor Karl August Bettermann declared that 'He who is not finished after nine semesters provokes the suspicion that something is not quite right with his study, and indeed in his individual domain, and not in the institutional domain of the university.'[82] In this, Bettermann merely restated the traditional explanation for student attrition. But in the new context of a mass university, the explanation appeared as merely another form of social exclusion.

Students in the mass university no longer subscribed to the notion of individual responsibility for a phenomenon so widespread. As the student association of the Freie Universität pointed out, 'according to the statistics of the Law Examination Office law students in Berlin study for an average of 9.5 semesters; therefore the maximum length of study will fall short of the actual average number of semesters. We must conclude from this, that in Berlin only an elite will complete their exam'.[83] What to the administrators and often to the faculty of the university appeared a move of rationalisation, was to the students a form of social selection. They understood overcrowding as a cause, not the effect, of the length it took to complete their studies. Indeed, length of study grew in West Germany across the post-war decades. The percentage of students studying in their ninth semester or later reached 12 per cent in 1950, 18.8 per cent in 1955–1956 and almost 27 per cent in 1967–1968. To the students, the problem of university space had to be understood as the choice between two alternative approaches, 'disciplinary measures at the end of study (*Zwangsexmatrikulation*)' or 'effective reform'.[84] Yet the vision of rats proved compelling. By 1968, the 'recommendation' of the *Wissenschaftsrat* for limitations on length of study had become an 'emergency measure': 'The introduction of the *numerus clausus* is an emergency measure. It cannot solve the problem of overcrowding, but tightens its expression.'[85]

---

[82] Pressestelle der FU Berlin (ed.), *Hochschule im Umbruch: Teil IV: Die Krise (1964–1967)* (Berlin: Pressestelle der FU Berlin, 1975), 101. See also Wilhelm Hennis, 'Germany: Legislators and the universities', in Hans Daalder and Edward Shils, *Universities, Politicians and Bureaucrats: Europe and the United States* (Cambridge: Cambridge University Press, 1982), 1–30. Hennis blames the increasing amount of time needed to attain a degree on new professors too specialised to teach well.
[83] Archiv APO und soziale Bewegungen [APO] Berlin FU Allgemein Konvent 1966 18. Konvent 'Anhang zum Tagesordnungspunkt 8e) der 4. (o.) Sitzung des 18. Konvents. Erklärung des Konvents zur Rücktritt der Studentenvertretung der Juristischen Fakultät'.
[84] Ibid.
[85] Klaus Schroeder (ed.), *Hochschule im Umbruch: Teil V: Gewalt und Gegengewalt (1967–1969)* (Berlin: Pressestelle der FU Berlin, 1983), 291.

A fundamental divide opened over how to understand and respond to 'overcrowding'.

The same politics of access emerged in France, where the population problem of the universities moved to centre stage at the *rentrée* of 1967. The opinion of Raymond Aron was well known ('I ask myself if, truly, the eternal principles of democracy require that all those who wish to learn English do a degree at the Sorbonne?').[86] The dean of Nanterre, Pierre Grappin, had already announced his support for selection before entry to university, suggesting it would be better 'to orient the "average" bacheliers elsewhere than the university'.[87] The best response to the 'poor output' of French faculties, he argued, was 'to be more demanding at entry', and 'to those who would try to say it is undemocratic to harshly select future students, one would respond that selection according to intellectual capacity and work is an assuredly democratic measure'.[88] Two visions of democratisation contradicted each other. The mirage of open access confronted the illusion that selection was democratic.

Meeting in June 1967, the Conseil de la Faculté at Nanterre discussed Grappin's proposal to establish 'a sorting at entry',[89] whether by automatically accepting only students with a *mention* at the baccalauréat or by eliminating those who had failed an exam. The sheer increase in numbers had been aggravated by the Fouchet Reforms, which had shifted the emphasis from the *cours magistraux* (large lectures) to *travaux dirigés* or *travaux pratiques* (seminars), without providing a complementary increase in teaching staff. As Grappin pointed out 'the main problem is in effect that of the *travaux pratiques*, which are obligatory, but which can only be so within the limits of the capacity of the Faculty'.[90] To faculty and administrators the problem appeared as a simple matter of resources. Paul Ricoeur merely thought that in the context of the 'traditional attachment to the policy of the open door', 'the reason why control at entry has become necessary must be made completely clear'.[91] However, open access was not simply a traditional attachment, but a fundamental component of the supposed democratisation of higher education. The university

---

[86] Raymond Aron, 'Point de vue d'un sociologue sur le colloque de Caen', *Revue de l'enseignement supérieur* 4 (1966), 209–214, 211–212. See also BDIC GF delta 85, 'Révolution dans l'université? Le colloque de Caen ... (GEH info janvier 1967)'.
[87] Pierre Grappin, 'Au-dela de la réforme', *Revue de l'enseignement supérieur* 4 (1966), 9–14, 11.
[88] Ibid., 11.
[89] ADHS 1208W/2 'Université de Paris. Faculté des lettres & sciences humaines de Nanterre. Conseil de la Faculté année universitaire 1966–67. 8ème Séance. Nanterre, le 10 juin 1967'.
[90] Ibid.   [91] Ibid.

reforms – introducing obligatory attendance at the *travaux pratiques*, limiting the possibility of taking a year again (when in some subjects up to 80 per cent failed their exam), creating a new, shortened degree which could be achieved after two years and demanding an early and definitive choice of study while at the same time failing to increase the material resources necessary to accommodate the increased numbers of students – functioned as 'barrier after barrier which attempts to cut back our right to study'.[92] The response to overcrowding proved that greater numbers would not mean greater equality: 'the Fouchet reform favours the children of the dominant classes who, by their social origin, possess the economic means and the cultural inheritance necessary to overcome the barriers created. The selection by failure put in place by the reform is a selection by class.'[93] The turn to selection and deregistration anchored the image of a conservative, undemocratic and inegalitarian university.

The democratisation of the university was supposed to have removed the economic and social constraints that once restricted higher education, leaving only the ability of the individual as a limit to tertiary education. Instead, the numbers who qualified for university outstripped the capacity of the institutions of higher education to accommodate them. The crisis of overcrowding posed a choice for the mass university on how selection for higher education would occur. Some administrators and faculty preferred to view attrition as the student's fault and grumbled that the growth of numbers clearly marked a decline in quality. Others argued for a selection by exam at entry instead of by attrition over the course of the degree, emphasising the meritocratic value of an early barrier instead of the survival of the fittest (or wealthiest) in the context of open access. Students opposed any formal selection, doubtful of the meritocratic credentials of an exam and demanding the expansion of funds to the university sector to match the greater numbers. In the absence of such funding, however, a socially regressive selection by attrition existed by default. The problem of selection called into question the depth of democratisation of higher education.[94]

Only a few years separated the optimistic pronouncements of enlightened technocrats like Louis Cros (*'idealistic aspirations and practical*

---

[92] BDIC F delta 813(1), Bulletin des Comités de Lutte Contre le Plan Fouchet. n.2.
[93] BDIC F d. 813(3), Programme d'orientation et plan de travail. Présenté au conseil d'administration de l'Association fédérative des groupes d'étudiants de Nanterre le mardi 19 décembre 1967.
[94] On selection, see Dominique Damamme, 'La "question étudiante"' in Damamme et al., *Mai–Juin 68*, 114–129, 118.

necessities in education have ceased to contradict each other')⁹⁵ and the emergence of an overt struggle between university students and administrators in which the latter stressed practical necessity of curtailing access to higher education. In the case of West Germany, some of the first attempts to jettison the surplus population occurred even before Georg Picht's warning of a *Bildungskatastrophe*. Alain Peyreffitte, the new Minister of Education in France in 1967, expressed the contradictory visions of the university perfectly when he stated that 'There are not enough students in France, but there are too many at university.'⁹⁶ The reformist modernisers uniformly insisted on a massive increase in funding to accompany the expansion of the universities. They were disappointed. But they also tended to posit the scientific needs of the economy as the prime mover of the mass university and scientific and technical personnel as its product. Here, too, they were mistaken. Government reforms, where they existed, most readily adopted the idea of the need for specialisation of degrees and rationalisation of the traditional university without endorsing unlimited access to and growth of higher education.

Yet the size of the universities increased, whether wished for, planned, or not. Attempts to narrow the point of entry to the universities gave the impression that the extension of compulsory schooling to the age of 16 in France in 1959 and the introduction of a unified middle school in Italy in 1962 (extending compulsory education to 14) had simply shifted some of the work of social stratification from the secondary schools to the tertiary system. The reformist utopias of the late 1950s and early 1960s were one attempt to understand, control and link the growth of higher education to a broader political vision of social progress, pitted against the small, anachronistic hierarchical and elitist university of tradition. As the 1960s (and the size of the universities) progressed, the spectrum of reformers polarised towards its progressive, democratic and its technocratic ends. As much as overcrowding, or the perceived archaicisms of the university, the student movements came into being in response to the narrowing of the idea of university reform.

The protests of the late 1960s were never narrowly about educational reform. Indeed, the most radical activists were often uninterested in the university, instrumentally embracing discontent within higher education

---

⁹⁵ Cros, *'L'explosion' scolaire*, 43–44. Italics in the original.
⁹⁶ As quoted by Jean-Pierre Duteuil, *Nanterre, 1965–66–67–68: vers le mouvement du 22 mars* (Paris: Acratie, 1988), 94.

to generate support.[97] The incidents that created mass mobilisation tended to be confrontations with police or other clashes with authority.[98] Nonetheless, the university came to embody the use of administrative authority in contrast to vague, diffuse aspirations for anti-authoritarian and democratic values and epitomised the hypocrisy that many protesters felt widespread in contemporary society.[99] The ideals of the modernisers foundered on the capacity of institutions to accommodate students, but access to higher education was only one definition of democratisation. Methods of teaching, the content of curriculum, relations of authority, the governance of the university, the very definition of culture itself, all emerged as sites of conflict over competing visions of democratisation.[100] Advocates of the university's expansion offered an image of the content of education starkly at odds with that of protesters. In 1968, the student Daniel Cohn-Bendit scorned how 'a bureaucratic society and economy demands a growing number of engineers, technicians, scientists, teachers, administrators, sociologists, organisers to develop production, to manage it "rationally", to administer the tentacular machinery of the state, to adjust the 'psychology' of individuals and groups'.[101] Having sought to study educational planning, Cohn-Bendit lasted fifteen days.[102] He switched to sociology.

[97] Rohstock, *Von der 'Ordinarienuniversität' zur 'Revolutionszentrale'?*, 409–410.
[98] Gruel, *La rébellion de 68*, 35.
[99] On the importance of hypocrisy to 1968, see Rebecca Clifford, Robert Gildea and James Mark, 'Awakenings', in Robert Gildea et al. (eds.), *Europe's 1968: Voices of Revolt* (Oxford: Oxford University Press, 2013), 45.
[100] For the way in which the university was condemned as 'bourgeois' not just for the social origins of its students, but for its pedagogy, see Dominique Damamme, 'Laboratoires de la réforme pédagogique' in Damamme et al. (eds.), *Mai–Juin 68*, 247.
[101] Daniel Cohn-Bendit and Gabriel Cohn-Bendit, *Le gauchisme: remède à la maladie sénile du communisme* (Paris: Seuil, 1968), 40.
[102] Daniel Cohn-Bendit, *Une envie de politique: entretiens avec Lucas Delattre et Guy Herzlich* (Paris: La Découverte, 1998), 18.

CHAPTER 2

'New Managerial Class' or 'Social Doctor'?
The Ambiguities of Sociology

The stereotypical protester of the 1960s was the sociology student. Sociology embodied the promise of a newly democratised system of higher education more than any other discipline. Instead of a supposedly old, archaic, elitist university dedicated to the consecration and transmission of high culture, sociology was conceived as either a practical education for a highly educated populace in a modern economy dedicated to the scientific administration of society, or a radical critique of the inequalities of power and wealth in the contemporary world. Both visions assumed the university must play an increasingly important role in society. Both demanded that the imagined boundary between broader society and the university be renegotiated. Whether subordinating higher education to vocational goals or alternatively subordinating politics, society and the economy to the critique of sociology, higher education could no longer constitute an ivory tower of unhurried reflection. Sociology incited the fantasies of both technocrats and radical democrats, the two constituencies that wholeheartedly endorsed university expansion. The 'mass university', before its advent, appeared to be everything to everyone. So too sociology, as a new degree, was a field whose vocational, intellectual and moral value remained to be determined. It was particularly susceptible to the discontents generated by the gap between the ideals of democratisation and the reality of mass higher education. Nowhere was this more evident than at Trento, in the first faculty of sociology in Italy.

New Frontiers

If the technocratic faith in university expansion, modernisation and even democratisation through education achieved only polite interest at the level of national policy, adherents emerged more easily within the university or at the local level. Thus, in his program of office in 1961, the Trentino Christian Democrat politician Bruno Kessler envisioned the construction of a Trentino Institute of Culture alongside a plan of urban development.[1] Economic and cultural development were indissolubly tied. In 1962, deploring that 'in Italy public and private entities that intervene to encourage or favour the processes of growth on the basis of sociological knowledge are scarce, if not inexistent',[2] he proposed a university institute of social sciences, (an *Istituto Universitario di Scienze Sociali*) which would confer a degree in sociology. The institute would 'form teachers and researchers in social sciences and prepare staff for private enterprise (in sectors important for social growth), and for public offices, particularly in local firms who can deal with social questions'.[3] The origins of what would become the Faculty of Sociology lay in the demand for trained, technical personnel. The institute would be a 'little factory of white collar employees', as one letter to the local newspaper described it.[4] Convinced that the creation of what would later become the first Faculty of Sociology in Italy was to 'have made an act of social reform',[5] Kessler embodied the optimism of the early Kennedy era: the university was Trento's 'new frontier'.

The *Istituto Universitario di Scienze Sociali* was conceived as an instrument of cultural and social modernisation. The 'new frontier' was invoked 'against cultural barriers' to economic growth. The very idea of social sciences, when previous suggestions for a university in Trento centred around a possible offshoot of the Università Cattolica at Milan specialising in forest sciences, already implied a broader horizon than hitherto thought possible.[6] Other, less noble, considerations also played a role. As Kessler confessed two decades later, 'the University project also had the function of counterbalancing the diminished importance which Trento would have had with the full autonomy given to the Province of Bolzano'.[7] Yet if local rivalries played their part in founding the institution, the national and international context determined its nature. The most important influence in the creation of an Institute of Social Sciences was Beniamino Andreatta,

---

[1] Vincenzo Calì, 'Università e ricerca tra movimenti e istituzioni: il caso trentino', in Giuliana Gemelli, Girolamo Ramunni and Vito Gallotta (eds.), *Isole Senza Arcipelago: Imprenditori scientifici, reti e istituzioni tra Otto e Novecento* (Bari: Palomar, 2003), 152.
[2] 'Kessler, contro "le barriere culturali" annuncia la "nuova frontiera"', in special issue of *Didascalie: rivista della scuola trentina*, 'La lunga marcia del Trentino per la sua Università' 9.1 (2000), 34.
[3] Ibid. [4] Giancarlo Tomazzoni, 'L'università a Trento', *Il Cristallo* 9.1 (1967), 9–27, 9.
[5] CMR B.14 f.2 (Fondo Calì), Norberto Bobbio, Untitled document.
[6] See Bruno Kessler, 'Alle origini dell'Università', in Redattori di Vita Trentina (eds.), *60 anni di Vita Trentina: 1926–1986* (Trento: Vita Trentina Editrice, 1986), 39.
[7] Ibid. See also Alberto Franceschini, 'La nuova frontiera: la nascità dell'Università di Trento', *Didascalie* 9.1 (2000), 33.

'the cultural soul of Kessler'[8] as Paolo Prodi labelled him. Andreatta, a native of Trento based in Bologna, where he founded the Institute of Economic Sciences and later the Faculty of Political Science, formed part of the group of intellectuals based around the journal *Il Mulino* and was economic advisor to Aldo Moro in the 1960s. Influenced on the one hand by Anglo-American scholarship (he both studied at Cambridge and returned as visiting professor in the 1950s) and on the other by the Catholic social reformers based around Giuseppe Dossetti and the journal *Cronache sociali*, Andreatta himself authored development plans for the Emilia-Romagna.[9] For Andreatta, the Istituto Universitario at Trento served the processes of social modernisation, 'the insertion of Italian culture and institutions (and with them those of Trento) in the most advanced areas of the Western world; a reformist welfare state, on Keynesian bases, which would translate into social, cultural and existential growth'.[10] A precocious precursor to the entry of the socialists into coalition with the Christian Democrats under the guidance of Aldo Moro in December 1963, the university institute at Trento embodied the optimistic hopes for reform associated with the opening to the centre-left. While the legislative balance at the national level proved negligible, the university at Trento exceeded expectations.

The opportunity to create an institution from nothing was rare. Existing institutions nonetheless sought to position themselves on the intellectual frontiers of the 1960s, making best use of their peripheral status. The Freie Universität Berlin stood on a very different frontier to the University Institute of Social Sciences and already counted more than a decade of existence by the 1960s. Yet not unlike Trento, the FU was in the process of repositioning itself in relation to a newly autonomous near neighbour. The erection of the Berlin Wall in August 1961 transformed the Free University, which in the 1950s drew up to a third of its students from the German Democratic Republic (and minimal numbers from the Federal Republic outside West Berlin).[11] The Wall dried up an important source of skilled labour in the Federal Republic and partly accounted for the

---

[8] A. Manzoni et al. (eds.), *Facoltà Occupata. Certo eravamo arroganti, certo eravamo giovani ... ma avevamo ragione. Sociologia, 1962–2002*, supplemento al quotidiano *Trentino* (2002), 10.

[9] See in particular Comitato Regionale Emilia Romagna di Democrazia Cristiana, *Sviluppo economico e pianificazione territoriale* 2 (Rome: Edizione Cinque Lune, 1968). See also Comitato Regionale Emilia Romagna della Democrazia Cristiana, *Piano di sviluppo dell'Emilia-Romagna* 1 (Rome: Edizione Cinque Lune, 1968), 24.

[10] Paolo Prodi, as quoted in Manzoni et al. (eds.), *Facoltà Occupata*, 10.

[11] James F. Tent, *The Free University of Berlin: A Political History* (Bloomington: Indiana University Press, 1988), 258.

plausibility of Picht's alarmist warnings of a *Bildungskatastrophe*. Less than a year later, the West Berlin Senate outlined the preconditions for the 'further development of Berlin as a central site for education, science and art'.[12] On the understanding that 'the economy requires a training site for middle management',[13] the Senate insisted that the universities of Berlin must 'be built up, preferably in the shortest time span'.[14] In particular, the 'expansion above the previous development goal requires a new, significant increase of the grant to the Freie Universität'.[15] Much like Trento, West Berlin aimed to compensate for its geographical marginalisation by placing itself at the frontier of education.

The university submitted to the social demand for a managerial elite. In return, society was expected to accept the academic veneration of knowledge. The politics of education for a new technical elite corresponded to a '*Verwissenschaftlichung der Politik*', a scientification of politics. At the Karlsruhe Party Conference in 1964, the SPD announced the names of thirty-six Professors with whom it would henceforth consult.[16] By 1967, the office of the Chancellor expanded to include a small staff for 'planning', which in the Social-Liberal Coalition became an entire department. The faith in expertise and modernity, anchored in an exuberant optimism about economic and social progress, elevated the political and social sciences to new heights of importance.[17] In the burgeoning politics of cultural and economic modernisation, the Freie Universität of Berlin could claim a special place. West Berlin boasted Willy Brandt as mayor and the Freie Universität a reputation as progressive due to the 'Berlin Model' in which students were represented at all levels of university government.

The politics of educational expansion, justified through an apolitical technocratic vision of rational planning that foresaw the necessity for large numbers of experts in an ever more technical and specialised modern economy, in turn envisaged the domestication of politics via the application of knowledge. Perhaps the simplest exponent of scientific politics was the Frenchman Michel Crozier, who perceived in the early 1960s a cultural

---

[12] *Der Tagesspiegel*, 25 May 1962, 11.   [13] Ibid.   [14] Ibid., 12.   [15] Ibid.
[16] Not all of whom agreed. See Wilfried Rudloff, 'Verwissenschaftlichung der Politik? Wissenschaftliche Politikberatung in den sechziger Jahren', in Peter Collin and Thomas Horstmann (eds.), *Das Wissen des Staates: Geschichte, Theorie und Praxis* (Baden-Baden: Nomos Verlagsgesellschaft, 2004), 216.
[17] Hans Günter Hockerts, 'Planung als Reformprinzip: Einführung', in Matthias Frese, Julia Pauls and Karl Treppe (eds.), *Demokratisierung und gesellschaftlicher Aufbruch: Die sechziger Jahre als Wendezeit der Bundesrepublik* (Paderborn: Ferdinand Schöningh, 2003), 249.

revolution in which 'knowledge eliminates the necessity of force'.[18] Greatly overestimating the progress of reason, Crozier declared that 'men no longer depend on myths like that of the invisible hand which will harmoniously regulate conflicts of interests' and heralded a new form of rationality in which 'the resistance of human means is no longer unforeseen. It can be taken into account in advance and one can make predictions without having recourse to coercion to assure the accuracy of the predictions.'[19] The social sciences would serve the 'constantly increasing appropriation of action by the scientific intelligence'. To be sure, not everyone was as naïve. Raymond Aron warned that 'politics is not reducible to a science because the selection of a group of persons who will be called upon to decide for everyone does not involve a method which is fully amenable to reason'.[20] Having previously worked at the Centre Nationale de la Recherche Scientifique, Crozier took up his first university position in 1967 at the University of Nanterre.

Created to release pressure on the already overcrowded Sorbonne, Nanterre embraced a more modern liberal image under its dean, Pierre Grappin. Decidedly peripheral by Parisian standards (especially before the construction of the RER), Nanterre, like Trento and West Berlin, offered the opportunity for experimentation. The campus boasted a particular strength in 'the specialists of human and social sciences (philosophy, psychology, sociology, ethnology, demography, linguistics) [who] represented ... a third of the professors and lecturers – a proportion never before reached in a Faculty of Letters'.[21] In contrast to the norm, the Conseil de la Faculté did not restrict its membership to professors. A department of sociology 'the creation of which was debated, even advised against' was nonetheless established.[22] At Nanterre, announced the dean, 'the human sciences, from linguistics to the different sociologies to human geography, are today our field of discovery'.[23] The periphery of

---

[18] Michel Crozier, 'The cultural revolution: Notes on the changes in the intellectual climate of France', *Daedalus* 93.1 (Winter 1964), 520.

[19] Crozier, 'The cultural revolution', 520. Cf. Pierre Bourdieu and Jean-Claude Passeron, 'Sociology and philosophy in France since 1945: Death and resurrection of a philosophy without a subject', *Social Research* 34.1 (Spring 1967), 163–164. See also Claude Gruson, 'Planification économique et recherches sociologiques', *Revue française de sociologie* 5.4 (1964), 435.

[20] Raymond Aron, 'Education of the citizen in industrial society', *Daedalus* 91.2 (1962), 255.

[21] Epistémon, *Ces idées qui ont ébranlé la France. Nanterre, novembre 1967–juin 1968* (Paris: Fayard, 1968), 22.

[22] Pierre Grappin, *L'Île aux peupliers: de la Résistance à Mai 68: Souvenirs du Doyen de Nanterre* (Nancy: Presses Universitaires de Nancy, 1993), 239.

[23] Pierre Grappin, 'La Faculté des Lettres et Sciences Humaines de l'Université de Paris à Nanterre', *Annales de l'Université de Paris* 36.1 (1966), 5–9, 7.

Paris, the borderlands of the Trentino and the isolated enclave of West Berlin proved fertile ground for new institutions, the politics of educational expansion, and a progressive vision of social sciences as the indispensable tool of a new society. All three were centres of sociology.

Two Cultures of Sociology

The advance of sociology accompanied the expansion of the universities, two symbols of a scientific society. In France, the reform of January 1959 that extended compulsory education to the age of 16 came less than a year after the creation of the *license* in sociology. In another decree of July 1958, the Facultés des Lettres became the Facultés de Lettres et Sciences Humaines. Those who proposed the ever-greater expansion of the university understood that transformation as one away from a humanist culture towards the social sciences. Jean Fourastié, emphasising that the economy required not merely technical personnel, insisted a humanist education be tempered by science:

> the need is and will be great for persons competent in economics, sociology, psychology, human relations, administrative sciences, in arts ... But on condition that these humanists do not faint in front of a fraction, a logarithm, exponential or statistical calculus. The Republic, Renault, Citroën, Saint-Gobain and Péchiney need philosophers – and will need even more in 1975 than today – but philosophers who listened as seriously to their mathematics, physics, chemistry and natural science professors as to their professor of philosophy.[24]

At Trento, Bruno Kessler viewed the establishment of the Institute of Social Sciences as the vanguard of a new scientific culture: 'We contradicted Italian academic culture ... we said: "it is useless that we create graduates capable of talking and talking and talking and incapable of measuring phenomena"'[25] C. P. Snow's 1959 lecture *The Two Cultures* articulated the thesis in emphatic terms.[26] In a common claim to exceptionalism, Gino Martinoli argued that the division of 'two cultures'

---

[24] Jean Fourastié, 'Les exigences nouvelles du progrès économique et technique', in Francis-Louis Closon (ed.), *L'Éducation Nationale* (Paris: Presses Universitaires de France, 1965), 48–49.
[25] Kessler, 'Alle origini dell'Università', 39.
[26] C. P. Snow, *The Two Cultures* (Cambridge: Cambridge University Press, 1998). (This is a reprint of Snow's *The Two Cultures and the Scientific Revolution* (Cambridge: Cambridge University Press, 1959) that features an introduction by Stefan Collini.) Snow was a great proponent of expansion of the universities in Britain and a supporter of the Robbins Report.

applied to Italy even more than England.[27] Raymond Aron added France.[28] The discipline of sociology appeared perfectly placed to inoculate humanists with scientific rigour.

Sociology not only incarnated a new relation of science to society, of practical intellectual initiative, and appeared the logical locus for the greater numbers who flocked to the university in the scientific society, but the discipline also distinguished itself for its academic staff. As Alain Touraine noted, because sociology was not taught in the *lycée* system and because of the novelty of the degree, of the teachers of sociology at Nanterre 'only a single one of them had ever taught first as an assistant then as professor in the Faculty of Letters'.[29] Sociology was new and its teachers youthful. Poised between the philosophical tradition from which it had slowly won autonomy (sociologists such as Pierre Bourdieu were all trained in philosophy departments) and the promise of applied enlightenment in administration and economy, sociology and sociologists were particularly susceptible to the tensions inherent to the university's transformation in the 1960s.

The intellectual, institutional and political pressures that exerted themselves on sociology found expression within the discipline itself. The discipline split towards the poles of critical theory and empirical research. In France, the advocates of empirical 'American' sociology clustered in the CNRS, the Weberians around Raymond Aron at the Sorbonne.[30] In the Federal Republic of Germany, sociology appeared divided between the Kölner Schule's empirically oriented, Parsons-influenced structural functionalism and the critical theory of the Frankfurt School. As one student noted, 'whoever wanted to be politically progressive had to opt heavily for the latter und and brand the first as positivist, politically conformist and *restaurativ* ... The peculiarity of the Berlin situation was that both schools were represented here, together with a third ... [that of] Otto Stammer,

---

[27] Gino Martinoli, *L'Università come impresa* (Florence: La Nuova Italia, 1967), 22.
[28] Aron, 'Education of the citizen', 256.
[29] Alain Touraine, *Le mouvement de mai ou le communisme utopique* (Paris: Seuil, 1968), 106–107.
[30] For a concise introduction to sociology in France and 1968, see Jean-Louis Fabiani, 'Sociologie et sociologies, entre isolement et contestation', in Philippe Artières and Michelle Zancarini-Fournel, *68: Une histoire collective 1962–1981* (Paris: La Découverte, 2008), 191–198, 192. For the diverse orientations of French sociology, see also Henri Lefebvre, *L'irruption de Nanterre au sommet* (Paris: Éditions Syllepse, 1998); Edgar Morin, '1968: Sociologie critique et sociologie critiquée', in Edgar Morin, *Sociologie* (Paris: Fayard, 1984), 281–291; Michel Trebitsch, 'Voyages autour de la révolution. Les circulations de la pensée critique de 1956 à 1968', in Geneviève Dreyfus-Armand et al. (eds.), *Les Années 68. Le temps de la contestation* (Bruxelles: Editions Complexe, 2000), 69–87, 81–82; Christelle Dormoy-Rajramanan, 'La sociologie nanterrienne "autour de 68". Entre expertise et contestation', *Revue d'anthropologie des connaissances* 12.3 (2018), 481–511.

who imparted to us the classics such as Weber, Michels, Mannheim, Marx and Pareto and whose political sociology did not fit into this schema.'[31] The creation of the *Diplom* in sociology – first in Frankfurt in 1955, then in Berlin in 1956 – necessarily focused attention on the field's definition and purpose. No consensus prevailed over what the study of sociology entailed.

No agreement existed on the professions for sociologists either. The introduction of Sozialkunde in German high schools created one domain. From 1956, positions for sociologists were available in the Pädagogischen Hochschulen. But teaching was not the vocation most commonly identified as the destination of sociologists by those who created its curriculum. In the Studienführer of the FU Berlin, Otto Stammer outlined the possibilities as follows: 'public authorities, state and municipal administration', 'the great industrial firms' and 'personnel management'.[32] These sectors required the statistical and sociological thought, empirical social research, economic training or expertise in human relations. The presupposition of a panorama of jobs available in social administration drew its power from the faith in planning so characteristic of the early 1960s. Helmut Schelsky, one of the most prominent West German sociologists, proclaimed the melding of politics and science, a 'fusion of state and modern technology' in 1961: 'in place of the people's political will steps the law of things'.[33] In a 'scientific civilisation', politics itself evaporated: 'The better the technology and science, the less leeway for political decision.'[34] The fantasy of the scientific and apolitical administration of society contained a kernel of social reform: Schelsky had famously declared the

---

[31] Peter Weingart, 'Wider Dogmen und Legende – Soziologie als Wissenschaftskritik: Anfangsbedingungen der Frauen-forschung in der Berliner Soziologie', in Heinz Bude and Martin Kohli (eds.), *Radikalisierte Aufklärung: Studentenbewegung und Soziologie in Berlin 1965 bis 1970* (Weinheim and Munich: Juventa Verlag, 1989), 113. For an overview of postwar German sociology, see M. Rainer Lepsius, 'Die Entwicklung der Soziologie nach dem Zweiten Weltkrieg, 1945–1967', in Günther Lüschen (ed.), *Deutsche Soziologie seit 1945* (Opladen: Westdeutscher Verlag, 1979), 25–70. See also Erhard Stölting, 'Der kurze Frühling. Die deutsche Soziologie um und nach 1968', in Richard Faber and Erhard Stölting (eds.), *Die Phantasie an die Macht? 1968 – Versuch einer Bilanz* (Berlin: Philo Verlagsgesellschaft, 2002), 194–213.

[32] Otto Stammer, *Studienführer der Freien Universität Berlin* (1962) as quoted by Hans-Joachim Lieber, 'Autobiographische Reflexionen zum Thema: Soziologie im Beruf', in Karl Martin Bolte and Friedhelm Neidhardt (eds.), *Soziologie als Beruf. Erinnerungen westdeutscher Hochschulprofessoren der Nachkriegsgeneration* (Baden-Baden: NOMOS Verlagsgesellschaft, 1998), 54.

[33] Helmut Schelsky, 'Der Mensch in der wissenschaftliche Zivilisation', in Helmut Schelsky, *Auf der Suche nach Wirklichkeit* (Düsseldorf-Köln: Eugen Diederichs Verlag, 1965), 453.

[34] Ibid., 458.

advent of a levelled middle-class society. The advocates of the scientific society assumed a democratisation of economic prosperity and social opportunity even when they foresaw the progressive attenuation of the political sphere. To some, sociology seemed the epitome of the scientific supervision of society. However, the novelty of the discipline, the variety of its intellectual poles, and the vagueness of the degree's professional outcomes encouraged a second sociological culture, more self-consciously political and critical of contemporary society.

If faculty members frequently envisioned the creation of a class of qualified social managers in an era after the end of politics, many West German students 'saw sociology as the science of emancipation, that is as the science that could *also* help one feel out or to understand one's own societal standpoint'.[35] As the 1960s began, the discipline of sociology, like the university, appeared the privileged path to social emancipation and reform. These hopes could be indulged easily enough at the beginning of the decade, briefly free from refutation. But as the 1960s progressed, the discipline of sociology became more defined and the nature of the new university clearer, there would also be a reckoning of expectations.

Trento: The Crisis of Sociology

The tension between the two cultures of sociology emerged early at the University Institute of Social Sciences at Trento. As elsewhere, sociology functioned as a polyvalent symbol, open in meaning and alluring in its infinite implications. Great aspirations attended the promise of sociology: 'many arrived at Trento for the fascinating and suggestive thing that called itself sociology'.[36] Students were drawn to the emancipatory, critical function of the new social science. One student survey suggested that the majority of those who enrolled in the Istituto Universitario di Scienze Sociali did so 'on the basis of the idea of a social doctor ... there was a perception that society was sick'.[37] By contrast, the first director of the institute, the mathematician Mario Volpato, envisioned the formation for society not of a medical but a managerial class:

> a sociological approach to bring together the abstract and specialised language typical of the university with the more pragmatic language born of the concrete problems of the business world ... the idea of sociology was

---

[35] Jürgen Horlemann, 'Soziologie und Politik: Rekonstruktion eines Werdegangs', in Bude and Kohli (eds.), *Radikalisierte Aufklärung*, 215.
[36] Aldo Ricci, *I giovani non sono piante* (Milan: SugarCo, 1978), 47.   [37] Ibid., 48.

born as a course of study for the formation of a managerial class capable of being a bridge between university research and the needs of civil society.[38]

Despite the ostensibly apolitical rationale, for the Christian Democratic politicians and intellectuals who established the university, the goal was to 'guarantee an adequate presence of Catholics also in this sector of the cultural world ... a very delicate sector, for its relations with the world of political culture'.[39]

The creation of a *laurea* in sociology was designed to furnish a cohort of Catholic intellectuals who could shape Italian political culture. The first obstacle to that goal came from the political world itself. The Istituto Universitario di Scienze Sociali, speedily founded in 1962, enrolled 226 students in its first academic year, rising to 622 in 1965–1956. Those students arrived with the legal recognition of a *laurea* in sociology merely promised and when in May 1965 the Italian Senate approved a draft recognising the Istituto Universitario at Trento, the title of the *laurea* was no longer sociology.[40] The political immobilism of Italian government appeared to have triumphed over expectations both for the scientific management of society and the project of critical emancipation.

Scienze politiche e sociali ad indirizzo sociologico (political science with sociological direction) ran the new title of the Trento *laurea*. A number of factors determined the modified title: firstly, the resistance of faculties of political science to a rival degree;[41] secondly, the tendency of the Socialist Party, partners in coalition with Christian Democracy, to barter recognition of the *laurea* in sociology with a recognition of a Faculty of Economics and Commerce in Siena,[42] and thirdly, the problem of how a new degree would be integrated into a planned (but never implemented) wide-ranging reform of the university. The university administration at the Istituto responded with resignation, rationalised as realism, tinged with the fear of losing any distinction to the degree offered at Trento: 'obviously in

---

[38] Lino Scalco, *Mario Volpato: Maestro e pioniere tra ricerca, politica ed innovazione* (Padova: Cooperativa Libraria Editrice Università di Padova, 2002), 580.

[39] Museo storico del Trentino [MST] Fondo Libera Università di Trento, b.1, fascicolo 'Avvio Università, 1962–63: Promemoria colloqui riunioni'. 'Appunti Riservati' 15 November 1965.

[40] The first draft of the law was presented in December 1962 but lapsed due to the dissolution of parliament. The vote of 18 May 1965 was supported by the DC, PSI, PLI and PSDI and opposed by the PCI and PSIUP.

[41] See MST Fondo Libera Università di Trento, b.1, fascicolo 'Avvio Università, 1962–63: Promemoria colloqui riunioni'. Letter from Prof. Miglio to Giulio Bianchi di Lavagna Commissario del Governo per la Regione Trentino Alto Adige. 4 May 1965.

[42] See MST Fondo Libera Università di Trento, b.1, fascicolo 'Avvio Università, 1962–63: Promemoria colloqui riunioni'. 'Appunti Riservati'.

conducting this battle, we must be realists. There is no need to go chasing butterflies.'[43] Yet while the majority of the faculty and administrators of the Istituto Universitario adjusted readily, if not always enthusiastically, to the *fait accompli*, the student response was inverse: 'At 16.00 [4:00 p.m.] the student assembly met. It was a particularly tense assembly, for the state of mind of the participants who felt themselves ignored, defrauded and deceived, and for the clear division which immediately manifested itself'.[44] While the majority favoured a flat refusal of the new degree, a group led by the Catholic Marco Boato 'although bitter and frustrated, held that the compromise had to be accepted given that in the circumstances there was no alternative and a refusal of the degree would seriously endanger a future recognition with serious consequences for the students who would not have any recognition of the studies they had completed'.[45] Typically, the first division at Trento emerged between the political tactics of refusal and compromise.

If the founders of the Istituto Universitario di Scienze Sociali assumed the modified *laurea* would nonetheless still create expert administrators and carve out a space for a Catholic sociology, for most students the change in name signified a complete contradiction with how sociology had been understood hitherto, professionally, politically and intellectually. Those students nonetheless most inclined to accept the modified *laurea* phrased their dissatisfaction in terms of the job market: 'Tomorrow, when an expert in sociology is requested, you will find yourself *on the same market* as hundreds of other graduates in Law and Political Science, *more or less with the same chances.*'[46] Why bother having made the trip to Trento if the degree held the same value as every local faculty of political science? For many the faculty of political science embodied reaction: 'founded by the Fascist regime to form its own bureaucrats and ideologists',[47] its 'curriculum ... one of the most rickety in the Italian university system'.[48] Pointedly, the students expressed their revulsion for the *laurea* in political science in the language of modernity and progress so frequently invoked at the beginning of the decade. The 'University of Trento takes its place as an element of rupture and overcoming of an academic culture that has

---

[43] MST Fondo Libera Università di Trento, b.1, fascicolo 'Avvio Università, 1962–63: Promemoria colloqui riunioni'.
[44] Bruno Tellia, 'L'avventura del '62', *Didascalie* 9.1 (2000), 66.   [45] Ibid.
[46] CMR B.4 f.3 (Fondo Movimento Studentesco Riccardo Scartezzini), 'Caro collega, – [signed] U. G. I. (Unione Goliardica Italiana), C. D. U. (Comunità Democratica Universitaria)' Dated 21 December 1965. Italics underlined in original.
[47] Ricci, *I giovani*, 44.   [48] Rossana Rossanda, *L'anno degli studenti* (Bari: De Donato, 1968), 47.

dominated and continues to dominate Italy, that has seriously mortgaged the social sciences'.[49] The institute stood at the 'vanguard of the process of renovation of the Italian University' for the 'modernity and novelty of the studies'.[50] The students conceived sociology as an instrument of the democratisation of a sclerotic, elitist culture. The fact that 'students from all high schools can enter the Faculty of Social Sciences of Trento ... gives proof of the overcoming of an elitist vision of culture as essentially erudite'.[51] The students at Trento now mobilised the ideological matrix of educational expansion, social sciences, social progress and technocracy in political form. Contestation began not in protest at overcrowding, but the failure to fulfil the promises of a modern, democratic education. At the beginning of 1966, six months after the Senate's approval of a draft for the *laurea* in *Scienze politiche ad indirizzo sociologico*, the students at Trento occupied the university.

The occupation of the Istituto Universitario began on 24 January 1966, voted by all four student associations. Henceforth the students referred to themselves as the Movimento Studentesco di Trento, marking a break with past political formations. 'A type of union action, outside of the political crystallisations', the occupation aimed at public opinion, 'in order that the democratic denunciation of their misrecognition stimulates the centres of power, until now "neutral", to take an active, positive, role in this problem'.[52] The demands of the students – 'an institutionalisation of the Social Sciences in Italy, a break with the old schemes which permeate national culture, of a scientific adjustment of the country to the broader European context' – resembled the rhetoric once put forward by the founders of the faculty. But the administration's response was decidedly ambivalent. After all, their conceptualisation of the institutionalisation of the social sciences never embraced such outright political activity. The Collegio Commissariale, the governing body of the Istituto Universitario, declaring itself largely satisfied with a *laurea* in *Scienze politiche ad indirizzo sociologico*, stated that it 'had no objections to those who wish to make last steps towards the government and parliament, in order to carry off the title

---

[49] CMR B.4 f.3 (Fondo Movimento Studentesco Riccardo Scartezzini), 'Società attuale e conoscenza sociologica'.
[50] Ibid.
[51] CMR B.4 f.6 (Fondo Movimento Studentesco Riccardo Scartezzini), 'Un terremoto all'Università', *Alto Adige*, 27 gennaio 1966, 3.
[52] CMR B.4 f.1 (Fondo Movimento Studentesco Riccardo Scartezzini), 'Perché facciamo l'occupazione'.

of the laurea originally proposed by the promoters'.[53] This less than enthusiastic endorsement was followed by an 'exhortation to the students, in their own interests, to return to order and assume the task of adjusting to the solution which the parliament will adopt',[54] and a mandate to the president, should the demonstrations 'reveal themselves damaging to the prestige of the Institute, to take the necessary steps'.[55] In public statements to the press, the faculty and administrators of the university, while insisting that they agreed substantively with the students, stressed the danger of a 'political instrumentalisation',[56] the need for 'a realistic vision of things',[57] and appeared most concerned to hold exams on schedule.

Yet by early February all the political parties at the local level had agreed to back the *laurea* in sociology and the proposed law was blocked in the Chamber of Deputies. The occupation of the faculty was suspended on February 10. The teaching staff of the Istituto, readjusting to the new reality, released their first unequivocal statement in favour of the *laurea* in sociology at the end of March. The sociology degree was finally recognised in June 1966 and Trento produced the first graduates in sociology in Italy. The students celebrated victory. With some degree of exaggeration they proclaimed that the 'institutionalisation of the *laurea* in sociology in our nation signifies without doubt one of the most important cultural conquests of the post-war era'.[58] In terms that still echoed the founders of the institute, the students of sociology declared that 'a society such as ours can no longer permit itself the luxury of resolving complex problems which pose themselves urgently in the manner of a dilettante. There is the need instead of a whole new class of prepared and qualified intellectuals. This new figure of the professional sociologist must come from the Faculty of Trento...'[59] However, a gulf separated the founders' project of creating a 'managerial class capable of being a bridge between university research and the needs of civil society'[60] and the student vision of a 'new class of prepared and qualified intellectuals'.[61] The achievement of a *laurea* in

---

[53] CMR Archivio Marco Boato, Busta Trento Sociologia Anno 1963–1968. f. 'TN 1966. Sociologia 1966.' 'Comunicato Stampa' of Colleggio Commissariale presided over by Prof. Marcello Boldrini. 20 January 1966.
[54] Ibid.   [55] Ibid.
[56] CMR B.5 f.5 (Fondo Movimento Studentesco Gabriella Ferri), *Alto Adige*, 1966, 'Un'occupazione "attiva"', 4.
[57] Ibid.
[58] CMR B.5 f.5 (Fondo Movimento Studentesco Gabriella Ferri), *Alto Adige*, 1966, 'Una conquista culturale per la società moderna', 4.
[59] Ibid.   [60] Scalco, *Mario Volpato*, 580.
[61] CMR B.5 f.5 (Fondo Movimento Studentesco Gabriella Ferri), 'Una conquista culturale per la società moderna', 4.

sociology would make this chasm only more obvious, for while the title of the degree was now known, its content remained vague. The law recognising the *laurea* in sociology demanded the Istituto Universitario submit to the Minister of Education a statute and curriculum within six months. Furthermore, while students conceived the occupation initially in instrumental terms, by its end, they saw it rather as 'the base of a culturally advanced discourse'.[62] The struggle over the *laurea* had produced the *movimento studentesco di Trento*, armed with a political instrument, the occupation, a critical conceptualisation of sociology, and an awareness of the resistance of the administrators of its own university.

From Sociology to Society

The degree in sociology achieved, the question of its meaning remained undecided. The recognition of the *laurea* had left the constitution (*statuto*) of the university and its curriculum open, requiring their submission to the Minister of Education for his approval within six months. The students, flush from the successful struggle to denominate the degree as sociology, demanded a special commission composed equally of students, professors and the *assistenti* (assistant lecturers), for the elaboration of both. The tripartite conceptualisation of reform demonstrates just how quickly the student movement at Trento had abandoned the traditional structures of the university. The students sought to extend the democratic ethos to the constitution of the university itself and to ensure that the social sciences not be slighted in the curriculum as they had been in the degree title. Rejected in their proposal for a specially constituted commission to study the matter, the students learned in October 1966 of a draft curriculum that equally disregarded their desires. The second occupation of the Istituto Universitario di Trento began on 21 October 1966.

Beneath a superficial consensus on the importance and modernity of sociology lay two very different understandings of that modernity. All agreed on the methodological contribution of empirical sociology. Gino Martinoli, in his manifesto *L'università come impresa*, lamented how at 'all levels of the Italian school system, the Aristotelian tendency, essentially deductive, prevails over rational and objective research, and the exercise of inductive arguments, of going from the observable facts to theories and

---

[62] B.4 f.1 (Fondo Movimento Studentesco Riccardo Scartezzini). Untitled document. Signed 'Gli studenti occupanti'.

laws, has only minor importance'.[63] Likewise, the first director of the Istituto Universitario, Mario Volpato, evoked the division between 'philosophical' and 'scientific' cultures of sociology, the first undertaking 'general and theoretical formation' while in the second, 'the sociologist is entrusted with a technical formation, similar to that of the engineering disciplines'.[64] On one side lay abstraction, on the other practical, empirical methodology. Students employed a similar distinction, but dispensed with the apolitical and technocratic aura to emphasise the political weight of sociological research. In 1965, Intesa, the Catholic student association at Trento, defined its task as ensuring that *'the most important discourses ... do not remain at the level of abstract deductive formulations, and instead are adequately "historicised" and filled inductively with all of the political import that they have*'.[65] Such a project could hardly satisfy the mathematician and head of the Institute, Mario Volpato, for whom 'the mathematician *par excellence* is the man free ... of every prejudice',[66] and, as one professor later recalled,

> in the crescendo of contestation, having entered the lecture hall for the daily lesson, went to the board with chalk and for a quarter of an hour filled the black space with white symbols, formulae, algebraic expressions, and whatever else was meant to represent, or rather be, the demonstration of technical neutrality and of the objectivity of science. Turning to the students: 'Demonstrate to me – he asked – how this blackboard of technical-scientific language can be right or left, cannot but be neutral and impartial to every social, political and ethical action.'[67]

For the students, by contrast, sociology could not be neutral.

Within the consensus over sociology's modernity lay fundamental divergences over its political purpose. The students understood modernity to mean democracy as much as empirical methodology: 'A modern university must be able to develop systematically 'science' and 'democracy', complementarily, posing itself thus as a dynamic centre of civil society, a

---

[63] Martinoli, *L'Università come impresa*, 27.
[64] Mario Volpato, *Alcune scelte per un corso di laurea in sociologia* (Trento: Istituto Universitario di Scienze Sociali Trento, 1964), 11.
[65] CMR B.4 f.1 (Fondo Movimento Studentesco Riccardo Scartezzini), 'Gruppo Democratico Intesa Trentina. Un rinnovato Movimento Universitario per lo sviluppo dell'Università e della società italiana. (Contributo per il Congresso Nazionale di Trieste, elaborato dal Segretario ed approvato dall'Assemblea del GDIUT) Trento, 1965'. Italics underlined in original. The author is Marco Boato.
[66] Volpato, *Alcune scelte*, 18.
[67] Filippo Barbano, 'La sociologia di Trento. Il mio coinvolgimento', in Fabrizio Cambi, Diego Quaglioni and Enzo Rutigliano (eds.), *L'Università a Trento, 1962–2002* (Trento: Università degli studi di Trento, 2004), 147.

real and authentic organ of public intelligence in the nation'.[68] While Martinoli's critique of the abstract culture of Italian academia formed part of a social vision of expanded and liberalised university access, Volpato's served a much narrower project of producing a new technocratic class, and the draft curriculum he produced for Trento showed it. Volpato and two colleagues – Marcello Boldrini, Professor of Statistics at the University of Rome, President of the International Institute of Statistics, and President of ENI (Ente Nazionale Idrocarburi) and the Jesuit Padre Rosa – created a sociology degree with a prominent space for mathematics and statistics.

Students were not the only critics of the draft. Franco Ferrarotti warned of the danger of the 'cult of measuring, quantitatively precise, but substantially incapable of capturing the historical significance of social phenomena'.[69] For the students, the proposed curriculum 'permits the formation of professional sociologists in a merely technical-bureaucratic sense'.[70] Just as the expansion of higher education demanded 'an adequate qualitative adjustment, in the sense of the gradual passage from an elitist conception to a more democratic conception of the university', so too the teaching of quantitative techniques needed to be accompanied by qualitative methods: ('Methods and Techniques of Social Research', 'History of Sociological Thought', 'History of Social Research').[71] Furthermore, democracy within the university meant more choices and autonomy for students to plan their own study: 'the student themselves can exercise the principle of academic liberty, constructing the curriculum from a vast range of choices, according to their own (and not someone else's) professional-scientific interests'.[72] A variety of demands began to characterise student political discourse: the affirmation of liberalised access to education, understood as the overthrow of a restricted, privileged and elitist culture; complemented by the liberalisation of curriculum, not conceived out of any superficial notion of the student as 'consumer', but rather as a facet of autonomy from entrenched political and social interests.

The liberty to plan one's program of study was one element of the autonomy that for the students was a crucial characteristic of the sociologist. Rather than political or economic demands controlling academia and the definition of sociology, the independence of the degree would be

---

[68] CMR B.2 f.1 (Fondo Movimento Studentesco G. Palma), 'Documento del movimento studentesco della Facoltà di Sociologia di Trento. Osservazioni circa lo Statuto e il Piano di Studi nella diversa elaborazione della Direzione e della Commissione studentesca'.
[69] MST Fondo Libera Università di Trento, b.2. Letter from Franco Ferrarotti to Mario Volpato, 3.
[70] CMR B.2 f.1 (Fondo Movimento Studentesco G. Palma), 'Osservazioni circa lo Statuto'.
[71] Ibid.   [72] Ibid.

guaranteed, and that autonomy brought to bear on society. Only with the liberty and breadth of the students' conceptualisation of the degree in sociology could be 'avoided serious phenomena (such as for example the preconditioning of careers) which today invalidate the autonomy of the university from the establishment, and in the long term will damage the professionalism itself of the sociologists'.[73] By contrast, the administrators of the university promoted the instrumental function of the Istituto. In the debates between students and faculty over the constitution and curriculum, Beniamino Andreatta proposed a school of administration in addition to sociology: 'The Italian market cannot support an annual absorption of 300 sociological specialists. Therefore: a proposal to structure the teaching for the preparation of business or public personnel fusing with a school of administration'.[74] For the students, such an idea placed far too much emphasis on the 'demand side and strictly subordinates the supply side to it'.[75] A degree conceived as subordinate to professional outcomes threatened to undermine the autonomy and independence that students hoped they would take from the university into society.

The occupation came to an end when Trento was flooded in November 1966. But the struggle over the nature of sociology forged an informal alliance between a progressive fraction of the faculty and a majority of the students – 67.8 per cent of the students voted for the occupation and 28.4 per cent against, with 3.8 percent abstaining (and voting against the occupation did not signify outright opposition to its objectives). The mathematical and statistical emphasis of the first draft of the curriculum disappeared. For the first time in the history of an Italian university a student would sit (with an advisory vote) on the Consiglio di Amministrazione. Whereas the first occupation at Trento had primarily academic goals, albeit framed within a broad political understanding of the import of the social sciences for the modernisation of Italy, the second emerged from and sought concessions in both academic study and political representation. Furthermore, the academic goals were understood as inherently political – the attainment of autonomous study that would facilitate a critical approach to society. Both study and the governance structure of the university would be democratised. The students emerged with a fully formulated conception of the role of sociology as a 'critical science' (not

---

[73] Ibid.
[74] CMR Archivio Marco Boato, Busta Trento Sociologia Anno 1963–1968. f. 'Trento 1966–67 2ª occupazione. Statuto e piano di studi. Boato Documentazione'. 'Riunione del pomeriggio'.
[75] Ibid.

a 'technical operation'), and 'a vision of the university as an autonomous factor of democratic, cultural and civil growth in the social context, a community governing itself through the full and equal participation of all of its components'.[76] Not only sociology and the social sciences, but the university as a whole, had a particular role to play in the modernisation and democratisation of society. Sociology was understood not as a tool of the administration of society, but as a means to radically call it into question: 'Sociological research in its proper sense always poses a "political" problem and is thus always and necessarily in direct relationship with a determined social reality. As soon as research ceases to be an academic exercise with an end in itself, and poses a "true" problem, it calls into question the whole of a society, with its values, its ordering, its customs and institutions'.[77] From the debate over the meaning of sociology, emerged a debate on society as a whole. The political struggle at Trento was just beginning.

Why Sociologists?

The precocious emergence of the student movement at Trento stemmed in part from the political opportunities afforded by the institution's creation. Elsewhere, debates over sociology, democratisation and the social sciences swirled and eddied, but these often lacked a straightforwardly political struggle to sharpen their expression. Nonetheless, a similar evolution of the sociological degree, without the same level of conflict, occurred at the Freie Universität. To receive the *Diplom* in sociology required both successfully participating in an empirical sociological piece of work across the course of two semesters and passing an exam on the foundations of statistical methodology.[78] As a consequence, Hans-Joachim Lieber (rector of the Free University in 1967) noted, 'a good portion of the students who strived for the sociological degree had to try three or four times to receive the big statistical examination certificate, because as a rule they had either no or an insufficient mathematical knowledge'.[79] In 1970, the requirement for both an empirical piece of work and the statistical competence was dropped in favour of successful fulfilment of one or the other. As Lieber noted, 'that the majority of the sociologists did not go into social practice in the narrow sense, but rather stayed as assistants or tutors at the

---

[76] V. Capecchi et al., 'Dall'avarizia alla politica', *Bozze 1978* 1.3 (1978), 41–66.   [77] Ibid., 44–45.
[78] Hans-Joachim Lieber, 'Der Diplomsoziologe und das Berufsbild des deutschen Soziologen: Erwartungen und Wirklichkeit am Beispiel der Freien Universität Berlin', in Lüschen (ed.), *Deutsche Soziologie seit 1945*, 260.
[79] Ibid.

universities and high schools', an 'aberration', given the intended professions for the *Diplom*.[80]

As in Trento, so at the Freie Universität; the evolution of sociology did not conform to the intentions of its planners. One study noted that over 40 percent of graduates of sociology in West Germany since the Second World War remained employed in the universities.[81] When surveyed, students in sociology at the Freie Universität saw their professional goals most frequently 'in the field of the press or mass communications, of education and welfare systems or in scientific research and teaching'.[82] Conceived to be the intellectual adjuncts to social planning and administration, sociologists instead emerged as teachers, journalists, writers and critics. Yet if the professional outlook of sociologists altered, the ambition to be the agents of social and political change endured.

The novelty of the sociology degree and the speculative nature of the career paths that awaited sociologists created a space for intellectual and political conflict, although some critics preferred to believe reductively that 'sociology in France as elsewhere seems to attract young people who dislike the society in which they live'.[83] Those who embarked on a sociology degree did so with much greater capacity for self-illusion than that which normally accompanied a choice of degree, for there were no pre-established curricula or careers. The same potential for misrecognition characterised the creators of sociology degrees. The swelling of the student body, especially in the social sciences, brought these contradictions to the fore. Thus in France, in March 1968 four students at Nanterre authored a tract, 'Why sociologists?' comparing the 'uncertainty of students regarding their future profession' to the 'theoretical uncertainty ... where the invocation of science ... only highlights ... the confusion of the diverse doctrines taught us'.[84] A decade on from the institution of a degree in sociology and the advent of de Gaulle to the presidency, the two events appeared intertwined: 'sociology's take-off is ever more linked to the social demand for rational practice in the service of bourgeois ends: money, profit, the

---

[80] Hans-Joachim Lieber, 'Autobiographische Reflexionen zum Thema: Soziologie im Beruf', in Bolte and Neidhardt (eds.), *Soziologie als Beruf*, 55.

[81] Renate Mayntz (ed.), *Soziologen im Studium: Eine Untersuchung zur Entwicklung fachspezifischer Einstellungen bei Studenten* (Stuttgart: Ferdinand Enke Verlag, 1970), 78.

[82] Ibid., 111.

[83] François Crouzet, 'A university besieged: Nanterre, 1967–69', *Political Science Quarterly* 84.2 (June 1969), 328–350, 335.

[84] The full document is reproduced in Jean-Pierre Duteuil, *Nanterre, 1965–66–67–68. Vers le movement du 22 mars, Préface de Daniel Cohn-Bendit* (Paris: Acratie, 1988), 187–190, 187.

maintenance of order'.[85] For French sociology 'the cult of statistics (finally a scientific terrain!) are the key to all problems. The study of society has succeeded in this *tour de force* to depoliticise all teaching . . . to legalise the existing politics. And all this joined in a fruitful collaboration with ministers and technocrats seeking to create their executives, etc. . . .'[86] The project to create a class of administrators and technocrats had been understood only too well. Amid the malaise over careers for sociologists, the radical students sought to 'clarify the generally repressive meaning of the occupation of sociologist', one dedicated to the 'organisation, rationalisation, production of human merchandise according to the economic needs of organised capitalism'.[87] The tension between different visions of sociology, conceived as an ideology of modernisation, became increasingly difficult to obscure, and emerged most clearly at a moment when the expansion of higher education revealed the fault lines inherent not merely in sociology but the university itself, in its role as the chosen institution of social modernisation.

More than any other discipline, sociology embodied the hopes and disappointments of the mass university, cast adrift between technocratic and democratic ideals. Sociology was predisposed to express these tensions, but the phenomenon proved much broader than that discipline. The discontent at the democratisation of the university exploded in a myriad of ways, from control over access to higher education to the governance of the university, the content of curriculum, styles of teaching and the authority and prestige of the professor.

---

[85] Ibid., 187.   [86] Ibid., 189.   [87] Ibid.

CHAPTER 3

'Books for All'
The Democratisation of High Culture

The advent of the 'mass university' (as contemporaries liked to call it, even though it never served a majority of the post-secondary school-age population) marked a significant shift in the meaning of higher education, now no longer the preserve of a tiny elite. That transformation elicited both laments of a decline in quality and paeans to the prospect of democratisation. Both visions exaggerated. The most evident decline occurred not in the quality of students but, rather, the social status of the professor. Democratisation of access was much more restricted than its proponents proclaimed. Overcrowding and attrition, not degrees for all, characterised the mass university. Yet while access to higher education was far from democratised, the high culture it conferred was nonetheless drastically recast for the new, 'democratic', dispensation. Just as the growth of the mass university merely revealed the tension between the promise and reality of access to elite education, turning the project of disseminating higher learning into a conflict over its content and form, so too the confrontation of high culture and the mass student body only served to sharpen a debate over the social meaning of culture itself. If the overcrowded lecture hall epitomised the social transformations that created the mass university in 1968, its graffiti-spattered walls proclaimed the desacralisation of high culture.

The collapse of cultural authority was embodied most clearly in the explosion of speech that accompanied the student revolts. The hierarchical lecture hall in which the professor expounded the fruits of science and high culture to a passive and deferential audience was substituted by the raucous debates of the student assembly. A 'marathon of endless arguments' was how Raymond Aron described it. 'The Parisian, French students talked, talked, talked during nearly five weeks ... and they found the utmost joy in talking'.[1] He explained rampant speech as an emotional release, the joy

---

[1] Raymond Aron, *La révolution introuvable: réflexions sur la révolution de mai* (Paris: Fayard, 1968), 31.

of escape from the solitary crowd: 'This sort of juvenile fraternity in a semi-delinquent community is the overcompensation for the solitude in which French students ordinarily live'.[2] By contrast, Aron felt his own freedom of speech sharply circumscribed. With *Le Figaro* threatened by strikes and its own printer, it had become difficult 'to write clearly and distinctly what one thought of the revolution in progress'.[3] The revolution of May, briefly, left both students and Raymond Aron equally unable to express themselves unreservedly in one of France's largest national daily newspapers.

The holders of cultural authority felt silenced, the culturally dispossessed instantly empowered. When one striking Parisian worker replied to a journalist 'I don't know what to say, me, I don't have any culture', another interrupted to tell him 'Don't say that ... Knowledge is over (*Le savoir, c'est fini*). Culture today consists in talking'.[4] A multitude of meanings hid in these few words: that knowledge from books no longer counted; that the right to talk came from experience, not learning; that no deference was due to high culture; indeed, that everyone had 'culture', no one's better than anyone else's; or that power came from the control of who speaks, and thus revolution from talking. And talk the student movements did. They seized speech, as Michel de Certeau put it, 'the way, in 1789, the Bastille was taken',[5] even if to critics (and in retrospect) there appeared much talking about nothing. 'I have nothing to say, but I want to say it', read one inscription on the walls of the Sorbonne.[6] Opponents and critics of the student movements sought to reaffirm the hierarchy of knowledge over talking, and savaged the lack of content in so much speech, characterising the protests as culturally bereft, an assault of the laziest or least willing to learn, who employed in graffiti or tendentious tracts the most vulgar and unsophisticated of intellectual tools. The acid observation of the Italian journalist Carlo Casalegno could stand for many critics of the talking culture: 'Now one can graduate without opening a book'.[7] High culture had been overrun by the illiterate but loquacious hordes.

---

[2] Ibid. [3] Ibid., 22.
[4] Evelyne Sullerot, 'Transistors et barricades', in Philippe Labro et al. (eds.), *Ce n'est qu'un début* (Paris: Éditions et publications Premières, 1968), 158.
[5] Michel de Certeau, *The Capture of Speech and Other Political Writings*, trans. Tom Conley (Minneapolis: University of Minnesota Press, 1997), 11.
[6] Edgar Morin, 'La commune étudiante', in Edgar Morin, Claude Lefort, and Cornelius Castoriadis, *Mai 68: La brèche, suivi de vingt ans après* (Paris: Editions Complexe, 1988), 29.
[7] Carlo Casalegno, 'Architettura e rivoluzione', *La Stampa*, 29 September 1970, 9.

High culture, as a relationship between a set of canonical texts, the institutions which consecrated them, the practices and attitudes it legitimated, and the authority it conferred to the social groups that saw in their mastery the mark of their distinction, came under attack in each of its components in 1968. This cultural confrontation was much broader than that played out in the university. However, the burgeoning population in the institutions of higher education made those bastions of high culture particularly vulnerable. As had occurred with the mass university, the apparently innocuous goal of expanded access (whether the consequence of greater numbers at university, the mass production of cheap books, or the possibility of diffusing high culture through television) instead created a crisis. Cultural democratisation could be conceived not only as an increase in access to the undisputed good of 'high culture', but its redefinition, or as a refutation of both the existence and value of 'high culture' itself. Access, alter and abolish: the protest movements pursued each of these conflicting approaches to high culture in the revolts of 1968, leaving its opponents either speechless or confusedly denouncing the collapse of culture. However, the origins of this challenge to high culture were much deeper than the disparaging diagnoses of juvenile delinquency or assault of the unlettered.

Ma-Ma-Ma?

One response to the student movements reaffirmed that culture did not mean talking, but rather the mastery of knowledge sanctioned by tradition and the university. Another engaged the students as the product of Marx and Marcuse, a heretical high culture but one nonetheless with pretensions to scientific knowledge and the reading of great books. The Italian radical monthly *Espresso* drew a map of the intellectual origins of the student revolts which managed to omit the most important text in Italy (Don Lorenzo Milani's *Lettera a una professoressa*) but named Marx and Freud the godfathers of the movements. The German journalist Rudolf Walter Leonhardt deployed the term 'Ma-Ma-Ma' to describe the 'curious mixture of Marx, Mao and Marcuse that dictates not only the vocabulary but the frame of reference of the students'.[8] The nomination of intellectual patrons facilitated a particular sort of engagement with the students. Most critics of the movements felt much more at ease elaborating their differences with Herbert Marcuse than dealing with disruption in the classroom.

[8] Rudolf Walter Leonhardt, 'Ma-Ma-Ma', *Die Zeit*, 2 February 1968, 9.

Identification of the 'idols' and 'Gods' of the protesters infantilised them, rendering them errant children of master thinkers and the wrong ones at that: 'At least once upon a time they read Lukács', the Italian philosopher Francesco Barone complained.[9] Marcuse symbolised a perverted high culture, but one that could comfortably be treated with some condescension. The throngs of Marx and Marcuse's disciples threatened less than the spectre of barbarian hordes at the university's gate.

For the most part, students reacted defensively to the attempt to identify their ideological origins, recognising the implicit trivialisation. A journalist interviewing the sociologists at Trento asked about their ideological inspiration: 'One speaks of Mao, Marx, Marcuse, Debray, Guevara, of Black Power, of reviews like *Quaderni rossi, Quindici, Quaderni piacentini, Nuovo impegno, Lavoro politico*'. 'We reject all labels', came the curt reply.[10] 'Marcuse, who's that?' quipped Daniel Cohn-Bendit to the *Nouvel Observateur*, even though he himself knew well, having read Marcuse in English.[11] But student leaders did not always use the reticence employed when seeking to evade the shadow of Marcuse. When Daniel Cohn-Bendit and his brother published their book *Le gauchisme* in 1968, they affirmed it could be substituted by 'an anthology of the best texts that appeared in *Socialisme ou Barbarie, L'Internationale situationniste, Informations et correspondence ouvrière, Noir et Rouge, Recherches libertaires*, and to a lesser degree, in the Trotskyist reviews'.[12] Indeed, the leaders of the student movements perhaps had more in common with professors' understanding of high culture than the majority of the protest movement. Their intellectual canon might have been different, but it existed nonetheless; like the priests of high culture, they mastered a dense and difficult language abstruse to outsiders, and they liked to contrast their own critical capacities to the passive conformity of the student masses. The tendency of academics to engage the student revolts on the grounds of high theory, Marx and Marcuse, acknowledged this affinity. However, the identification of specific ideological origins, whether by opponents or protagonists of the

---

[9] 'Giuste proteste e rivolta anarchica degli studenti alla Normale di Pisa' *La Stampa*, 25 February 1968, 3.
[10] *Alto Adige*, 5 March 1968, 3.
[11] See Michel Trebitsch, 'Voyages autour de la révolution. Les circulations de la pensée critique de 1956 à 1968', in Geneviève Dreyfus-Armand et al. (eds.), *Les années 68. Le temps de la contestation* (Brussels: Editions Complexe, 2000), 71.
[12] Daniel Cohn-Bendit and Gabriel Cohn-Bendit, *Le gauchisme: remède à la maladie senile du communisme* (Paris: Seuil, 1968), 18. Cf. Cornelius Castoriadis, 'The Movements of the Sixties', *Thesis Eleven* 18/19 (1987), 26–27.

student movements, only obscures the depth of the challenge to high culture in 1968.

The origins of the protest movements did not lie in a discrete set of intellectual texts. The small reviews of the New Left, their influence much greater than their print runs, undoubtedly influenced some of the at times even smaller groups that found themselves at the heart of the revolts of 1968.[13] Yet the large numbers who made 1968 a mass movement rarely read these authors before the events turned them into best-sellers. Cohn-Bendit noted that 'in the movement, there is not ten persons who have read Marcuse'.[14] More to the point, they could not have even had they wanted to, as most of Marcuse's works went untranslated into French until 1968 itself.[15] The leaders of the protest movements, already politically active before 1968 and who placed great value in their theoretical sophistication and knowledge of heterodox Marxism, were not representative of the mass of students – politicised by rather than before 1968 – who sought out a radical political culture once the revolts began. Indeed, the politicised minority frequently disdained the reading habits of the majority. In 1967 the Situationist International scorned how the 'student, like everyone else, is proud to buy paperback re-editions of a series of important and difficult texts which "mass culture" pours out at an accelerated rhythm. Only he does not know how to read. He contents himself by consuming them visually.'[16] A typical intellectual itinerary might perhaps be the Italian student Marianella Sclavi, who described her reading prior to the student revolts as Jack London, John Steinbeck, Luigi Pirandello, Voltaire, Raïssa Maritain, Albert Schweitzer, Camus and Sartre, among others.[17] As the 68er and historian Peppino Ortoleva resignedly noted 'an attentive reading of the documents demonstrates that, if sought, it is possible to find "traces" of almost all pre-existing cultural production'.[18] Not Mao, Marx,

---

[13] On the relation of the New Left to 1968, see Ingrid Gilcher-Holtey, *Die Phantasie an die Macht: Mai 68 in Frankreich* (Frankfurt am Main: Suhrkamp, 1995), 104.
[14] Labro et al. (eds.), *Ce n'est qu'un début*, 29.
[15] See Trebitsch, 'Voyages autour de la révolution', 71–73. In Italy, many of Marcuse's works were published in 1967, while the West German publication preceded both. See also Henri Lefebvre, *L'irruption de Nanterre au sommet* (Paris: Éditions Syllepse, 1998), 20–27.
[16] Membres de l'Internationale Situationniste et des étudiants de Strasbourg, *De la misère en milieu étudiant, considérée sous ses aspects économique, politique, psychologique, sexuel et notamment intellectuel et de quelques moyens pour y remédier*, 2nd ed. (Paris: Ch. Bernard, 1967), 10.
[17] See Marianella Sclavi, 'Le origine del '68 a Trento: come si creano e come si distruggono una, due tre, tante fantasie', *I Giorni Cantati* 1.1 (1981), 75–77.
[18] Peppino Ortoleva, *I movimenti del '68 in Europa e in America*, 2nd ed. (Rome: Editori Riuniti, 1998), 107.

and Marcuse, nor the New Left, but the mass distribution of the entirety of high culture could be indicted for the revolts.

The protest movements sprouted not from a particular set of ideas, but rather emerged from and reinforced a transformed relation to high culture, one which threatened to upend entirely the traditional relations of cultural authority in- and outside the university. For the Situationist International, the convergence of high and mass cultures, in which others discerned a cultural democratisation, produced instead a visually voracious but intellectually supine student. The idea of 'high culture' acted as a soporific, while the practice of high culture – the ability to read critically – remained the property of an elite. Yet it was precisely this diffusion of high culture through mass circulation books that began the reconfiguration of the relation between the idea, the practice, and the authority of high culture. The primary concern of the protest movements was talking, not knowledge: whatever the ideas consumed and the words produced, they deliberately sought to seize control of, or alter the circulation and distribution of, discourse. That goal underlay a variety of actions from interrupting a professorial lecture, to the reproduction and distribution of particular texts, to the grandest of schemes in the 'critical university'. In contrast to the effort to control the regulation of discourse (or abolish regulation altogether), the student movements produced only the most ephemeral of texts – graffiti and the leaflet – the former as important as an act of desacralisation as for its content, the latter functional to the extreme.[19] While professors preferred to point out the flaws of Marcuse and some students burnished their radical and intellectual credentials in the circles of the New Left, the cultural object most relevant to the majority of students was in fact one which itself just a few years earlier had generated talk of revolution: the paperback.

The Paperback Revolution

Many revolutions would be proclaimed in the course of the 1960s, political, cultural, or merely marketing. Already by the first year of that decade Robert Escarpit, founder of the *Centre de sociologie des faits littéraires* in 1960 and editor of *Le Canard Enchaîné* during the Algerian War,

---

[19] On the relation of 68ers to the printed word, see also Timothy Scott Brown, *West Germany and the Global Sixties* (Cambridge: Cambridge University Press, 2013), 123–127.

declared that 'a revolution was on the march'.[20] In a flourish of the Sixties' characteristic belief in imminent, unbridled transformation, he proclaimed 'the appearance of the mass-circulation book is probably the most important cultural development in the second half of the twentieth century'.[21] The *livre de poche* in France, the *tascabile* in Italy and the *Taschenbuch* in West Germany heralded, or so it appeared, a new cultural epoch, one in which knowledge and culture was freely available to all. High culture would never be the same again, Escarpit exulted: 'the whole of written culture as we have known it for two or three centuries past is directly challenged by mass-circulation books, and the cultivated classes of our time are only wrong in feeling disturbed over this development to the extent that such perturbation reflects a niggardly attachment to values which have become inadequate for the new dimensions of mankind'.[22] The democratisation of access to high culture would be accomplished by the paperback. As had the prophets of higher education's expansion, so too the apostles of the paperback predicted a new age of democratic civilisation. The arrival of the paperback unleashed a set of utopian and dystopian fantasies, images of revolution and crisis, which the new book format promised to realise.

There was, however, nothing novel about cheap books.[23] If most traced the modern paperback to the first Penguins, which appeared in the United Kingdom in 1935,[24] earlier incarnations were sought and found. In the Federal Republic of Germany, the *Reclam Universalbibliothek*, which began in 1867, provided a precedent and a contrast to the post-war *Taschenbuch*.[25] The late 1940s and early 1950s furnished further examples – Rowohlt's RoRoRo Taschenbücher in Germany, the Reclam-inspired *Biblioteca Universale Rizzoli* in Italy – in the traditional format of

---

[20] Robert Escarpit, *La révolution du livre* (Paris: Unesco and Presses Universitaires de France, 1965), 29.
[21] Robert Escarpit, 'The revolution in books', *Unesco Courier* 18.9 (1965), 4.   [22] Ibid., 6.
[23] On the history of the book and cheap editions, see David Finkelstein, 'The globalization of the book, 1800–1970', in Simon Eliot and Jonathan Rose (eds.), *A Companion to the History of the Book* (Malden MA: Blackwell, 2007); Adriaan van der Weel, 'Modernity and print II: Europe 1890–1970', in Eliot and Rose (eds.), *A Companion to the History of the Book*, 354–367; and Alistair McCleery, 'The return of the publisher to book history: The case of Allen Lane', *Book History* 5 (2002), 161–185.
[24] See McCleery, 'The return of the publisher'.
[25] See e.g. Heinz Gollhardt, 'Das Taschenbuch im Zeitalter der Massenkultur. Vom Bildungskanon zum "locker geordneten Informationschaos,"' in Georg Ramseger und Werner Schoenicke (eds.), *Das Buch zwischen gestern und Morgen: Zeichen und Aspekte* (Stuttgart: Deutscher Bücherbund, 1969), 122.

series of literary classics at low cost.[26] Both proponents and critics of the paperback readily admitted that the phenomenon of small, cheap editions did not constitute in itself something new. The publisher and bookshop owner François Maspero noted that the *poche* edition was sometimes more expensive than the existing one:

> *Native Son* by R. Wright ... costs 2,00F as a paperback ... the standard edition of the same book ... continues to exist at Albin Michel at the price of 1,50F. But in this case it is the more expensive edition that sells 30,000 copies. Likewise, Lenin's *Left-Wing Communism: An Infantile Disorder* costs significantly more in '10/18' than the Moscow publishers booklet distributed for years by Editions Sociale. However, the book in the 10/18 collection immediately finds dozens of thousands of new readers.[27]

In this instance, the democratisation of high culture imposed on its reader more expense than the old regime. The barrier breached by the paperback was not cost.

Neither the size nor the price was revolutionary. Rather, the large print run and the distribution in supermarkets, tobacco stores, newsagents and railway stations struck contemporary observers the most. This phenomenon, too, was not nearly as innovative as proclaimed. 'Penny dreadfuls' and detective stories sold in kiosks and railway stations in the nineteenth century.[28] Paperbacks, however, overcame the opposition between bookstore and kiosk, being sold in both. Escarpit expected book vending machines to further transform the market.[29] The book revolution would ensure the instant availability of any book, at any time, in any place. The pocketbook 'must be sold everywhere, yes, even in toilets, why not?' insisted one bookstore owner.[30] To its champions, the paperback form allowed knowledge to escape the archaic, forbidding and obstructive shell of the traditional book. Escarpit argued that 'our epoch ... returns the book to its true vocation, which is to be not a monument, but a vehicle'.[31] In words which would be echoed again with every new technological

---

[26] Alberto Cadioli, 'Esame di una collana universale', *Belfagor* 45 (1990), 467–480; Maria Iolanda Palazzolo, 'L'editoria verso un pubblico di massa', in Simonetta Soldani and Gabriele Turi (eds.), *Fare gli italiani: scuola e cultura nell'Italia contemporanea, vol II. Una società di massa* (Bologna: Il Mulino, 1993), 287–318; Giovanni Ragone, 'Editoria, letteratura e comunicazione', in Alberto Asor Rosa (ed.), *Letteratura italiana: Storia e geografia. III. L'età contemporanea* (Turin: Einaudi, 1989), 1047–1167.
[27] François Maspero, 'Livres de poche et culture de masse', *Partisans* 16 (1965), 66.
[28] Van der Weel, 'Modernity and print II', 356.   [29] See Escarpit, 'The revolution in books', 7.
[30] Jean Gaugeard, 'Le Phénomène du livre de poche en France: essai de synthèse d'une enquête', *Lettres Françaises* 1051 (29 October 1964), 2.
[31] Escarpit, *La révolution du livre*, 12.

development up to and beyond the Internet, he proclaimed a new era in cultural exchange: 'The diffusion, the unlimited and unceasingly renewed communication between all men – there is the proper function of the book.'[32] The purely functional form of the paperback abolished the barricades against access to high culture.

'Aristocratic culture is finished forever', wrote the philosopher and art historian Jean-Louis Ferrier, director of the *Médiations* pocketbook collection, in a paradigmatic expression of the paperback revolution's social impact. As with the university, the promoters of the paperback ascribed the transformation of the book market to the necessities of a modern economy: 'the scientific and economic situation of contemporary man demands a new participation in culture'.[33] This new cultural economy appeared to have been broached in the early 1960s as the paperback's market expanded beyond its base of literature to include all forms of scientific and intellectual production. Previous programs of cheap editions appealed either to sheer entertainment or a narrowly edifying imperative, much more hesitant in their embrace of the mass reader. In the 1850s, Louis Hachette proposed a 'railway library' to turn the 'forced free time (of train travellers) ... to the pleasure and instruction of all' which necessarily must omit any works that might incite 'political passions, as well as all writing contrary to morality'.[34] A century later, in the 1950s, the German editor Heinz Friedrich applauded Rowohlt's RoRoRo Taschenbücher that 'can smash a breach in the bulwark of bad taste'. Now the reader 'who earlier occupied himself with pulp fiction, will suddenly notice that good literature can be exciting, adventurous and amusing'. Nonetheless, it was 'naturally tragic' that an editor had to resort to such means to entice 'the battered person of today back out of the mire of his mental deadening'.[35] By contrast, the mass-circulation book of the late 1950s and early 1960s was conceived in a spirit of optimism, not as a didactic adaptation of dead time or a desperate recourse against the cultural bankruptcy of mass society, but as the instrument to fulfil the intellectual potential of the modern reader. The paperback of the Sixties rapidly moved beyond the traditional field of classic works of literature (preferably out of copyright). The launch (in 1962) of the *Idées* and *10/18* series in France, wrote Bernard

---

[32] Ibid., 163.
[33] Jean-Louis Ferrier, 'L'éducation permanente', *Les Temps Modernes* 227 (1965), 1735.
[34] Jean Mistler, *La librairie Hachette de 1826 à nos jours* (Paris: Hachette, 1964), 123.
[35] Heinz Friedrich, *Aufräumarbeiten: Berichte, Kommentare, Reden, Gedichte und Glossen aus vierzig Jahren* (Munich: Deutscher Taschenbuch Verlag, 1987), 107. See Reinhard Wittmann, *Geschichte des deutschen Buchhandels: Ein Überblick* (Munich: C. H. Beck, 1991).

Pingaud in 1965, 'marked a turning point. It then appeared that all books, whatever they are, can appear in pocketbook format and that, in the manner of standard editions, the *poche* is capable of satisfying equally well the taste for entertainment as that for scientific information or the most demanding reflections – something no-one would have dared to argue at the beginning'.[36] The same development occurred in West Germany, where pocketbook production initially consisted almost entirely – 94.4 per cent in 1950 by one estimate – of fiction. By 1957, however, fiction's share, excluding detective novels, had slumped to 45.6 per cent.[37] The readership of the paperback revolution was the population that simultaneously expanded into the institutions of higher education: students.

The democratisation of high culture and higher education, the book and the university, appeared to go hand in hand. Both drew on a vision of an old, aristocratic culture swept away not by political revolution but rather the inevitable demands of a technocratic, modernised economy. Both the mass university and the mass-circulation book responded to the perceived 'modern necessity for permanent education'.[38] As with the economy and the higher education system, the need for planning appeared urgent. A Franco-Italian conference agreed 'on the necessity to plan and scale the production' of the paperback.[39] Reading habits of nations were read as indicators of backwardness or progress, much like the numbers of university graduates were thought to guarantee economic growth. One French author noted nervously that 'three "*poches*" are sold per inhabitant of the U.S.A. to 1.6 in Great Britain, 1.4 in West Germany and only 0.9 in France'.[40] The mass university and paperback markets served the same constituency. University students proved to be the greatest consumers of pocketbooks. They accounted for 34 per cent of sales for the *livre de poche* (and, according to one survey, 70 per cent of all buyers were under 30 years of age).[41] In Italy, 'the young', of whom a large number must have been university students, constituted 30 per cent of the purchasers of the *tascabile*.[42] West Germans under 25 accounted for 35 per cent of the market. The greatest proportion of consumers – almost half – were

---

[36] Bernard Pingaud, 'Les livres de "poche"', *Les Temps Modernes* 227 (1965), 1730.
[37] Herbert G. Göpfert, 'Bemerkungen zum Taschenbuch', in H. Gonski et al. (eds.), *Der Deutsche Buchhandel in unserer Zeit* (Göttingen: Vandenhoeck & Ruprecht, 1961), 105.
[38] Ferrier, 'L'éducation permanente', 1735.
[39] 'Dibattito italo-francese sul "libro tascabile"', *Accademie e biblioteche d'Italia* 18.1 (1967), 65.
[40] Paul Morelle, 'Les collections de poche', *Tendances* 44 (1966), 2.
[41] Gaugeard, 'Le phénomène du livre de poche', 2.
[42] 'Un problema culturale e sociale: il libro economico', *Vita Italiana* 16 (1966), 749.

academics, university and school students, apprentices and members of the free professions.[43] Together, the two phenomena of the mass university and the mass-circulation book appeared destined to turn the cultural world upside down. But just as the project of increased access to higher education only unleashed a conflict over different conceptualisations of democratisation, so too the expansion of access to high culture through the paperback revolution merely set in motion a debate on the meaning of cultural democracy.

The Commodification of High Culture

'I am in favour of the democratisation of culture, for its greatest diffusion', affirmed Albert Memmi in reference to the *livre de poche*. 'Yes, there are risks. All human undertakings entail them. It is up to intellectuals to prohibit that popularisation means debasement.'[44] Like the student movements later in the decade, the paperback evoked visions both of cultural democratisation and cultural collapse, anticipation for a new age of enlightenment and forebodings of barbarism. In West Germany the negative comparison of the contemporary to the historical pocketbook was compensated somewhat by its juxtaposition to the United States:

> While the American pocketbook already performs the capitulation of the mind before the violence of the apparatus in its cover illustration, and packages the Bible or Homer just like Mickey Spillane or Superman in exactly the same bloodthirsty cover picture that would do honour to the masochistic half-nude blonde und the snarling SA-face of the hero of every comic-book, the German pocket book holds out against barbarism with the greatest tenaciousness.[45]

The Italian weekly *Espresso*, greatly overestimating the temperament of French intellectuals and exasperated at the avalanche of criticism of the *tascabile*, expressed the desire that Italians emulate the French debate 'in which no French writer sees a symptom of the decline of civilisation'.[46] Even those who rejected the apocalyptic picture evinced some unease. In France, Memmi admitted to a 'vague disgust', 'a sort of nausea in the face

---

[43] Hans Magnus Enzensberger, 'Analyse der Taschenbuch-Produktion. Teil III', *Neue Deutsche Hefte* 59 (1959), 251. Göpfert, 'Bemerkungen zum Taschenbuch', 106.
[44] Jean Gaugeard, 'Albert Memmi: "Notre société sera jugée sur ce qu'elle aura fait du livre de poche et des autres moyens de diffusion"', *Lettres Françaises* 1051 (29 Octobre 1964), 3.
[45] Enzensberger, 'Teil III', 249.
[46] As quoted by Herbert R. Lottman, 'Italia: rallenta il boom dei tascabili', *Giornale della libreria* 80.12 (1967), 172.

of the rise of the *livre de poche*.⁴⁷ All recognised in the advent of the paperback a symbol of consumer society, no less than the 'other products of industrial civilisation (refrigerators, cars, televisions, vacuum cleaners and other gadgets)'.⁴⁸ In the paperback, high culture achieved its greatest dissemination or capitulated to its commodification.

Critics charged that the paperback rendered the book a mere commodity. The German poet and essayist Hans Magnus Enzensberger (whose influence on 68ers in West Germany, according to one of them, 'can hardly be overestimated'⁴⁹) described how 'since the invention of the printing press the literary object was always a commodity, but first here, as a brand name product, does its character as commodity come into its own ... The lamination, the finish, the ephemeral aura of its virginity transfigures it into a pure consumer good'.⁵⁰ The new bookstore, Enzensberger claimed, functioned as 'literary supermarkets which, without changing the personnel, could be transformed overnight into food or tie stores based on the principle of self-service'.⁵¹ Bookstore owners themselves emphasised that the paperback collapsed the distinction between culture and commerce: 'At union meetings I'm obliged to fight bookstore owners to make them acknowledge that the *livre de poche* is merchandise, that it's not a piece of art ... one does not sell the *livre de poche* the way one sells other books. They must be sold like postcards.'⁵² Cheap editions subverted the illusion of books exempt from commercial considerations. Not only criticism of the pocketbook focused on the act of consumption and the book as a consumer article. Robert Escarpit linked the appearance of the first Penguins to the rise of the supermarket: 1935 was the year of the paperback, the Moscow metro, and the 'year of the store with multiple branches'.⁵³ But where Escarpit saw a positive development, others saw no possibility of reconciliation between culture and consumption:

> In almost no other example does the concept 'cultural assets' so drastically betray itself as with pocketbooks: in large supermarkets, where they have meanwhile penetrated, they appear as commodities like all the rest. The gulf between *Kultur* and *Zivilisation* ironically appears here to be closed – next

---

⁴⁷ Gaugeard, 'Memmi', 3. ⁴⁸ Morelle, 'Les collections de poche', 2.
⁴⁹ Peter Schneider, *Rebellion und Wahn. Mein '68: Eine autobiographische Erzählung* (Köln: Kippenheuer & Witsch, 2008), 194.
⁵⁰ Hans Magnus Enzensberger, 'Analyse der Taschenbuch-Produktion. Teil I', *Neue Deutsche Hefte* 57 (1959), 55.
⁵¹ Ibid., 53. ⁵² Gaugeard, 'Le phénomène du livre de poche', 2.
⁵³ Escarpit, *La révolution du livre*, 27.

to sausages and cheese the high-gloss lamination appears like transparent packaging.[54]

While the advocates of paperbacks celebrated the expanded availability of high culture through consumerism, its detractors discerned in the commodification of the book a fundamental challenge to the meaning and status of high culture itself.

Cheap books reduced culture to the act of buying, for paperback purchasers – or so their critics complained – did not actually read. They consumed. Food furnished the favourite metaphor. Bookstore owners joked at the equation of literature with comestibles: 'A salad and the latest Camus: one will buy books like that.'[55] Different series of books had to be decoded 'like the labels of new condiments'. A diagnosis of bulimia befell those who bought an entire collection of paperbacks.[56] The paperback market fed these abnormal appetites through visual stimulation: 'the pocketbook is tasted even before the spine is cracked. It is the triumph of the image.'[57] Commentators nervously noted that sales shrank if only the spine and not the full cover were presented to the consumer.[58] The paperback seduced its purchaser instead of being sought out, 'imposes itself by exposing itself: it is a book which is *shown* (qui donne à *voir*)'.[59] Less disparaging commentators like François Maspero nonetheless opined that

> a very large part of the buyers of paperbacks do not really read what they buy. The success of Lukács' *Theory of the Novel* is certain. It is, nonetheless, ultimately doubtful. Even if the reader who acquired it with ten other works had the firm intention of truly absorbing it – without allowing himself, like me, to be discouraged by the totally abstruse writing of Lukács – the following month, the following week, Lecomte de Noüy and ten others of the same importance come to solicit him.[60]

That the purchase of pocketbooks only satiated an unruly appetite for high culture instead of nourishing an enduring intellectual engagement found confirmation in the widespread assertion that 'the buyers of the *livre de poche* don't even keep them. They throw them away.'[61] Paperback

---

[54] Helga Märthesheimer, 'Kulturgut Taschenbuch – aufgezeigt am Deutschen Taschenbuch Verlag', *Frankfurter Hefte* 9 (1964), 485.
[55] Gaugeard, 'Le phénomène du livre de poche', 2.
[56] Georges Dupré, 'Va donc, petit livre, et choisis ton monde ...', *Les Temps Modernes* 227 (1965), 1757.
[57] Ibid.
[58] See Yvonne Johannot, *Quand le livre devient poche: une sémiologie du livre au format de poche* (Grenoble: Presses Universitaires de Grenoble, 1978), 110.
[59] 'Le livre-image', *Les Temps Modernes* 227 (1965), 1785. Italics in the original.
[60] Maspero, 'Livres de poche et culture de masse', 69.   [61] Gaugeard, 'Memmi', 3.

consumers did not, could not read, and did not even retain what they bought. The Situationist International merely reiterated this perspective in its caustic condemnation of the 'student' who 'like everyone else, is proud to buy paperback re-editions of a series of important and difficult texts which "mass culture" pours out at an accelerated rhythm. Only he does not know how to read. He contents himself by consuming visually.'[62] Subordinating the content to the cover and reducing culture to the act of purchase, the product sold via the paperback was the illusion of democratisation.

Indeed, the most sophisticated attack on the paperback charged that it produced and packaged the delusory promise of open access to high culture. The French philosopher Hubert Damisch, who launched a scathing attack on the *livre de poche* in the *Mercure de France*, insisted that 'it is first of all the access to aristocratic culture which pocket editions procures and guarantees',[63] a myth of egalitarianism, 'as if our good society accorded to everyone the right to pursue higher education, the lessons professed by the great teachers of the university ... '[64] The paperback sold the idea that high culture was available for a small price. Hans Magnus Enzensberger noted the irony of the slogan 'the knowledge of the world for 1.90DM',[65] while 'pocketbooks for the demanding reader' incited the ire of the *Frankfurter Hefte*, appalled how 'the "demanding" attitude in the choice of books is reduced to the subjective determination to practice it'.[66] High culture had been cheapened. For Damisch, the transaction was doubly treacherous, not simply reducing culture to the act of purchasing, but providing it only in abridged and edited texts. The *livre de poche* adulterated the original, 'dedicated to extracts, choice morsels, truncated texts'.[67] The consumer, unlike the reader, would never venture beyond the surface of the text:

> It is this dimension of the work which the *culture de poche* works to destroy and eliminate, better to reduce the reader to the status of consumer, better to enclose him in the space beyond the institution, offering him a little bit of the surface of all works all at once more surely to turn him away from the particular work upon which he could be tempted to linger ...[68]

---

[62] Internationale Situationniste, *De la misère*, 10.
[63] Hubert Damisch, 'La culture de poche', *Mercure de France* 1213 (1964), 488. On Damisch and the French debate, see also Douglas Smith, 'The Burning Library: The Paperback Revolution and the End of the Book in 1960s France', *French Studies* 72.4 (2018), 539–556.
[64] Damisch, 'La culture de poche', 488.   [65] Enzensberger, 'Teil I', 54.
[66] Märthesheimer, 'Kulturgut Taschenbuch', 488.   [67] Damisch, 'La culture de poche', 496.
[68] Ibid., 497.

Spatially, consumer culture provided only surfaces; temporally, merely moments. The paperback that promised access to high culture instead dispensed its simulacrum: cheap, quick and superficial.

The Disorder of Reading

The mass market thus threatened to redefine high culture according to the whims of the consumer. While West German booksellers debated whether it was economically rational to spend a lengthy amount of time providing thorough guidance to customers about cheaply priced books, they also noted that Taschenbuch buyers frequently did not even desire their advice.[69] Seduced by the power of the image, the reader might choose wrong:

> Many times I have paused in front of the little carts overflowing with 'pocketbooks' in front of newsagents or railway stations. And there, observing those attractive little volumes with the liveliness of their covers, were men, young people – students or not – and soldiers, who had little familiarity with the authors of fiction either contemporary or past, with which to orient themselves with some degree of awareness. They stand visibly uncertain as to their choice. Then, the hand is extended and usually falls not on the book of the most promising and interesting author, but on that with the most spicy title and illustration. These are people who previously went to seek the book, and now find themselves unexpectedly approached by a book which has sought them out, offering itself within reach and in a seductive manner, between newspapers and news magazines.[70]

Armando Petrucci has drawn a similar picture in his delineation of a crisis in the 'order of reading' – 'a unified, hierarchical repertory of texts both readable and "to be read"'[71] – in the late twentieth century. The 'reader-consumer' acts in an

> irrational manner ... He or she buys or does not buy, chooses or refuses to choose, prefers one type of book today and another tomorrow, is seduced on one occasion by a reduced price, on another by the graphic presentation

---

[69] Göpfert, 'Bemerkungen zum Taschenbuch', 107.
[70] Domenico Mondrone, 'Il chiasso attorno ai "tascabili"', *La civiltà cattolica* 2785 (1966), 60.
[71] Armando Petrucci, 'Reading to Read: A Future for Reading', in Roger Chartier and Guglielmo Cavallo (eds.), *A History of Reading in the West*, trans. Lydia G. Cochrane (Amherst: University of Massachusetts Press, 1999), 345–367, 362.

of the book, on still another by a passing interest or by a publicity blitz. In short, the reader too begins to lose all criteria of selection.[72]

This interpretation perpetuates a caricature of the consumer – irrational, easily seduced, image-oriented, dangerously unguided. Nor can it be said to be illogical to take price into consideration when purchasing. Yet the mass consumption of books fatally undermined previous modes of selection by daily demonstrating other criteria in action. Paperbacks did not so much serve to provide access to the cultural canon, but the opportunity to call it into question.

Petrucci's description of the crisis of the 'order of reading' draws upon Eugenio Montale's characterisation of reading transformed not in relation to paperbacks but the press and periodicals. Nonetheless, Montale's analysis of 1961 encapsulated all of the criticisms that would be directed at the paperback. 'The time of slow and meditated reading is now long gone', proclaimed Montale,

> ever fewer books are read, while the number of readers of periodical pages, newspapers, reviews, manifestos on walls, and other printed matter is quite high. But the readers of fleeting, daily publications do not read, they see, they look. They look with a comic-strip attention, even when they really know how to read: they look and throw away. Our rapid trains, arriving at their destination, are a cemetery of ephemeral publications.[73]

For Montale real readers were few in number ('an exiguous minority'), bought true books 'with few sales' that went to form a library ('the traditional book one reads and returns to the bookshelves') and thus were re-read, slowly, rather than thrown away. Instead, the real book 'is being substituted by the *Ersatz* of the false book: the product that burns one's fingers if it is not thrown in the ashtray like a cigarette butt'.[74] Montale's description furnishes a full definition of an 'order of reading' as conceived by intellectuals: an elite, minority readership – a clerisy – defined in part by their time to re-read, who formed a library (represented also in the bookstore, and, metaphorically, a canon of texts), completely divorced from economic considerations. Undoubtedly reality was different. Montale's ideal must be distinguished from the institutions it legitimated (the university, the library, the bookstore, the literary canon), and the reality of reading practices. But this 'order of reading' furnished a powerful image

---

[72] Ibid., 356.
[73] Eugenio Montale, 'I libri nello scaffale', in Eugenio Montale, *Auto da fé: chronache in due tempi* (Milan: Il Saggiatore, 1966), 96.
[74] Ibid., 98.

that legitimated a particular cultural regime, enforced through its organising oppositions of read/see, re-read/throw away and elite/mass, divisions instinctively mobilised by the paperback's detractors.

The caricature of the paperback market, that mass of easily seduced consumers who bought based on an image, did not read and threw away, reflected the values of their critics, their ideal (and idealised) 'order of reading', rather than actual behaviour. Critics assumed readers would passively follow the indications of the advertisers (or 'the American promoter'[75] as one commentator specified), but the pocketbook 'the book of consumption, destined ... to be thrown away after reading'[76] received no such treatment. Survey after survey revealed readers kept their paperbacks. Indeed, a new hierarchy could be discerned between those who kept their paperbacks and those whose distaste for the less prestigious form of the book compelled them to discard it. The Sorbonne sociologist and anthropologist Roger Bastide generalised from himself when he asserted 'One does not hesitate to throw away the *livre de poche*. My cleaning lady leaves at 4 o'clock. Each evening I empty my bin myself. Well, I can say that one finds *livres de poche* in the trash.'[77] Furthermore, the sales of the 'traditional' book proved to be anything but harmed by the advent of the disposable editions.[78] As Yvonne Johannot has noted, the convergence of ephemeral printed matter and books never completely arrived: the quality of cheap editions improved, bookstores continued to be important points of distribution and books almost never became important vehicles of advertising for anything other than other books.[79] Some editors such as François Maspero intended their paperbacks as durable and reasonably-priced, but of sufficient quality to 'permit them to be included long-term in a library'.[80]

If the opposition between enduring and disposable books owed more to the imagination than a newfound contempt for culture, the aspersion that pocketbook purchasers never read (or re-read) their books inflated the diligence of traditional 'true readers'. After all, as Jean-François Revel noted, 'one does not ask a young bourgeois who disposes of a large family library if ... he is worthy of the books which are at his disposal, nor even if

---

[75] Dupré, 'Va donc, petit livre', 1758.
[76] Michel Bouvy, 'Le livre de poche en France', *Bulletin des Bibliothèques de France* 8.11 (1963), 413–422. DOI: http://bbf.enssib.fr/consulter/bbf-1963-11-0413-001.
[77] Jean Gaugeard, 'Roger Bastide: "C'est le livre de poche qui fait rayonner la culture française à l'étranger"', *Lettres Françaises* 1051(29 October 1964), 3.
[78] See Göpfert, 'Bemerkungen zum Taschenbuch', 103.
[79] Johannot, *Quand le livre devient poche*, 155.   [80] Quoted in Ibid., 95.

he has read them'.[81] Escarpit agreed: '90% of the old books which clutter French apartments have never been re-read'.[82] That all sorts of readers now bought books they then proceeded to shelve and ignore extended a traditionally elite practice to the majority. At the turn of the century *Kulturverleger* produced beautiful books 'not necessarily bought to be read' but which functioned to distinguish 'the discriminating owner from those who merely read for entertainment'.[83] Indeed, the panic over the paperback and its lurid, alluring cover ignored that the book had always been an aesthetic object. 'Sobriety ... is an artifice like any other', as one author pointed out.[84] Furthermore, the allegation that pocketbooks only offered abridged editions was simply incorrect. A number of commentators sensibly pointed out that the 1950s and 1960s were hardly the first decades in which high culture could be read in shortened texts, or even that entire education systems were built on digested versions of 'great texts'.[85] Was not Damisch himself the author of a *poche* edition of the writings of the nineteenth-century French architect Eugène Viollet-le-Duc, one which reduced 10 volumes to 200 pages?[86] All too often, the criticisms directed at the paperback and its readers either exaggerated or could have been levelled at their more socially exclusive counterparts, if anyone had presumed to do so.

The caricature of the consumer who barely read and failed to retain the mutilated, eviscerated books foisted upon them corresponded not to reality but served to shore up the status of high culture as the possession of a few. Confronted by a crisis in the demarcation of elite and mass culture, some insisted the boundary be policed more effectively. Alberto Moravia demanded of publishers that 'the paperback must cease to be an article of consumption and return to being a book ... advertise both the paperback and normal books, placing the emphasis on the difference between the two. People must realise ... that the paperback one reads and throws away, while books normally go to form a library'.[87] Moravia was hardly likely to see real reading as a genuinely mass activity since 'the Italians are an infantile and easily influenced people'.[88] By definition, the masses could

---

[81] Jean-Francois Revel, 'Culture de poche contre vulgarisation', *Les Temps Modernes* 227 (1965), 1754.
[82] Jean Gaugeard, 'Robert Escarpit: "Il s'agit d'un veritable mutation"', *Lettres Françaises* 1051 (29 October 1964), 3.
[83] Van der Weel, 'Modernity and Print II', 357.
[84] Michel-Claude Jalard, 'De la réédition à l'édition', *Les Temps Modernes* 227 (1965), 1745.
[85] Revel, 'Culture de poche contre vulgarisation', 1754.
[86] Ferrier, 'L'éducation permanente', 1737.
[87] As quoted by Lottman, 'Italia: rallenta il boom dei tascabili', 172.   [88] As quoted in Ibid.

not accede to high culture. The Italian author Goffredo Parise concurred: 'Art and culture have been, are and will always be individual, artisanal and direct products ... consumed by intellectuals ... a society anything but numerous'.[89] Enzensberger's paperbacked pessimism ran just as deep. Against the plaintive hope that cheap editions might attract new interest from hitherto readerless social strata, he asserted that workers' 'erstwhile hunger for reading has flown; film, radio, TV and magazines have stemmed and channelled their spiritual potency'.[90] The white-collar functionaries who bought cheap editions merited no higher esteem: 'The boredom of their private and professional existence, their hunger for social prestige and their timidity before risk make these strata the ideal object of exploitation of the culture industry.'[91] To the assertion that high culture could only concern the few, defenders of paperbacks retorted that 'the figure of the intellectual was assuming little by little a more democratic profile'.[92] However, if by 'democratisation' advocates of mass culture believed paperbacks opened a path to those who did not read or to workers excluded from high culture, they were wrong. German surveys indicated a bare 3 per cent of paperbacks were sold to workers,[93] while French commentators glumly noted that non-readers remained a majority.[94] As with the expansion of the universities, the scale of the transformation proved more modest than anticipated.

Yet the limited demographic transformation of the reading public nonetheless marked a significant reconfiguration of high culture, a disordering of reading, one registered in the moral panic of so many critics of the paperback. The expansion of readership may have been relatively small, but it was enough to strip high culture of its hallowed status, demystified if not democratised. 'The little shock caused by the introduction on the sidewalk of an author remote only yesterday', proved fatal to the reverential disposition towards high culture and its exemplars.[95] The book – previously, as Memmi emphasised, 'an almost sacred object'[96] – now sold (in the words of Damisch) 'in the same conditions and following the same methods as any packet of detergent'.[97] Wrenched from the sanctuary of the university and bookstore, deposited in the street and supermarket, scientific and literary culture had lost its lofty status. No longer elevated and unattainable, high culture was no longer high. The decline in social

---

[89] 'Un problema culturale e sociale', 746.　[90] Enzensberger, 'Teil III', 251.　[91] Ibid., 252.
[92] 'Un problema culturale e sociale', 746.
[93] Göpfert, 'Bemerkungen zum Taschenbuch', 106. See also Enzensberger, 'Teil III', 51.
[94] Dupré, 'Va donc, petit livre', 1760.　[95] Gaugeard, 'Le phénomène du livre de poche', 2.
[96] Gaugeard, 'Memmi', 3.　[97] Damisch, 'La culture de poche', 485.

altitude fostered a new attitude to books, their anointed guardians, and the knowledge and culture they conveyed.

Rather than the democratisation of access to the undisputed good of high culture, the paperback revolution instead undermined the old regime of elite culture. The book had become 'an object of current consumption. It has been "desacralised."'[98] As the West German journal *Merkur* noted, 'technical reproduction dissolves the passive attitude and enables critical approaches'.[99] Anyone could create their own library, on almost any category of selection, radically and rudely dislodging the cultural authorities who had defined the cultural canon. Those critics contrasted the coherence of traditional culture and *Bildung* to modern 'information'.[100] Yet in the choice between 'the canon and the endless process of information',[101] the former was not always favoured over the latter. Even if defenders of mass culture had little idea of how it might function, the information age appeared to signal the end of a paternalistic conception of culture. Hans Schmoller, a German Jewish émigré and the director of Penguin Books, wrote 'the earlier need for instruction and guidance has been joined by an appetite, now sharp, now a little more relaxed, for information which we pluck out of the uncoordinated yet somehow benevolent chaos of paperbacks in an age of mass culture'.[102] If the new culture disoriented, the 'tradition' now seemed restrictive. Whatever the style of the new reading, the passive and deferential attitude to culture vanished into air:

> Even if this process throws up at first nothing other than a bare accumulation of knowledge and information, which it is not yet possible to see how it should be ordered and in what way it can be subjected to critical judgments, then it would already be an advance over the reception of literature – or more generally of printed matter – under the constraints of hard norms and principles of those times which were equipped with an aesthetic, moralistic and politically castrated concept of literature.[103]

---

[98] Morelle, 'Les collections de poche', 2.
[99] Dieter Wellershoff, 'Literatur, Markt, Kulturindustrie', *Merkur* 21 (1967), 1014.
[100] Hans Magnus Enzensberger, 'Analyse der Taschenbuch-Produktion. Teil II', *Neue Deutsche Hefte* 58 (1959), 162.
[101] Wellershoff, 'Literatur, Markt, Kulturindustrie', 1020.
[102] Hans Schmoller, 'The Paperback Revolution', in Asa Briggs (ed.), *Essays in the History of Publishing in Celebration of the 250th Anniversary of the House of Longman 1724–1974* (London: Longman, 1974), 318. Cf. Arnold Gehlen, 'Die gesellschaftliche Situation in unserer Zeit', in Arnold Gehlen, *Die Seele im technischen Zeitalter und andere soziologische Schriften und Kulturanalysen* (Frankfurt: Vittorio Klostermann, 1978), 444.
[103] Gollhardt, 'Das Taschenbuch im Zeitalter der Massenkultur', 128–129.

Whether they envisioned the new cultural economy as magical and superficial, chaotic but benevolent, or simply a vacuum, cultural observers of the early 1960s concurred that the pocketbook 'revolution' heralded a new practice of reading and a redefinition of culture. Just a few years later, the student movements, composed of members from the most important demographic for the paperback market, sought a similar upheaval in intellectual relations. Claiming the mantle of a new critical, democratic culture, students stormed the barricades of high culture already undermined by the mass market in books. 1968 constituted the second paperback revolution of the decade.

CHAPTER 4

'Knowledge Is Over'
The Intellectual Politics of 1968

The student protests rode the wave of cultural democratisation epitomised by the paperback revolution. In this, they participated in a Sixties revolt in the sphere of cultural production much broader than among university students.[1] At times, the result appeared as one of 'cultural liberalisation . . . and affirmation of participatory and democratising demands.'[2] Yet the rebellion against cultural authority played out in a wide variety of forms, not all of them innocuous. In roughly chronological order, student protesters pursued access to high culture, sought to radically revise its content, or aimed to abolish it altogether. These goals were mutually incompatible. Each contained its own contradictions. The political dynamic, moreover, impelled the movement to ever more radical postures that meant the abandonment or denigration of previous aims. In this way, one terminus of the readers' revolt was the impasse of anti-intellectualism.

A Readers' Revolt

The radicals of 1968 were undoubtedly paperback readers, although often of particular publishers. The 68er and later publisher Karl Dietrich Wolff remembered that 'with "Suhrkamp-Kultur" we first discovered the specific mix of critical theory, psychoanalysis and literature with which we armed ourselves; had I read any books in the last few years which did not appear in the series?'[3] Similarly, when in 1969 students at the first Italian Faculty of Sociology at Trento developed a bibliography of twenty-eight titles on

---

[1] Timothy Scott Brown, *West Germany and the Global Sixties* (Cambridge University Press, 2013), 152.
[2] Adelheid von Saldern, 'Markt für Marx: Literaturbetrieb und Lesebewegungen in den Sechziger- und Siebzigerjahren', *Archiv für Sozialgeschichte* 44 (2004), 178.
[3] Karl Dietrich Wolff, '1968: Ein freischwebender Gruß', in Christoph Buchwald (ed.), *Verleger als Beruf: Siegfried Unseld zum fünfundsiebzigsten Geburtstag* (Frankfurt am Main: Suhrkamp, 1999), 143. See also von Saldern, 'Markt für Marx', 158.

their subject, all had been published or republished that decade, twenty-one between 1967 and 1969.[4] These dates suggest (re-)publication occurred often with the students movements as much as before. The protests latched on to this publishing phenomenon, appropriating in expansive fashion the intellectual heritage made available in paperback format. They began by 'chewing many books, eating books as if they were carrots ... national, international books, smashing any sort of cultural provincialism that was oppressive in that period'.[5] One Italian student remembered how 'people walked round with books of Lukàcs and Rosa Luxemburg in their pocket',[6] in a very literal manifestation of the term pocketbook that symbolised personal, immediate access. As Timothy Scott Brown has argued, 'it was not necessary ... to have *read* a particular book in question; rather, books represented badges of membership in one or more of the radical transnational publics that helped constitute 1968.'[7]

Yet students of 1968 did not simply constitute a market for paperbacks: they read with a speed and the style expected of pocketbook readers – 'browsing for analysis, the *aperçu* for knowledge'.[8] The acceleration of reception only intensified in the maelstrom of the revolts. When he arrived at the student hotbed of Trento in late 1968 as the new rector, the Italian sociologist Francesco Alberoni found that 'the rate of combustion of ideas is dizzying, authors like Marx and Freud are demolished in a few days – today it's Marcuse, tomorrow Korsch – no-one can follow this radical-destructive orgy'.[9] The German sociologist Theo Pirker remembered the same speed of reception at the Free University of Berlin: 'What was absorbed yesterday was no longer there the day after tomorrow.'[10] Rossana Rossanda noted that 'the relation to texts, even revolutionary ones, is scorching and allusive and has little to do with study, discussion and citation' and is marked by 'certain simplifications as much Manichaean as mobilising'.[11] Such observations came not merely from outsiders. New students who entered the revolutionary process discovered the same phenomenon: 'ideas and names of authors whom we didn't know passed over

---

[4] CMR B.3 f.8 (Fondo Movimento Studentesco G. Palma), 'Indicazioni Bibliografiche.'
[5] Mauro Rostagno, 'Una vita di lusso', *MicroMega* 4 (1988), 105–112, 106.
[6] Aldo Ricci, *I giovani non sono piante* (Milan: SugarCo, 1978), 85.   [7] Brown, *West Germany*, 153.
[8] Jean Gaugeard, 'Le phénomène du livre de poche en France: essai de synthèse d'une enquête', *Lettres Françaises* 1051(29 October 1964), 2.
[9] CMR B.1 f.5 (Fondo Movimento Studentesco G. Palma), Francesco Alberoni, 'Documento di lavoro n.2.'
[10] Siegward Lönnendonker (ed.), *Linksintellektueller Aufbruch zwischen 'Kulturrevolution' und 'kultureller Zerstörung'. Der Sozialistische Deutsche Studentenbund (SDS) in der Nachkriegsgeschichte (1946–1969). Dokumentation eines Symposiums* (Wiesbaden: Westdeutscher Verlag, 1998), 118.
[11] Rossana Rossanda, *L'anno degli studenti* (Bari: De Donato, 1968), 28.

our heads at an incredible speed'.[12] The intensifying politicisation of the movements did not favour a slow, studied intellectual engagement, but the frenzied consumption of culture also reflected the 'benevolent chaos of paperbacks' that loosed an almost limitless diet of ideas from the hierarchy of tradition. The protests of 1968 pursued each of the goals of cultural democratisation already identified for the paperback: the opening of access, the desacralisation of high culture in favour of a critical, democratic ethos and the construction of an alternative canon.

Protesters imitated as well as exploited the publication of paperbacks. Indeed, in the Federal Republic of Germany, radicals supplemented the paperback market with their own production of pirate editions. The *Raubdrucke* (as they were known in West Germany) imitated and attempted to displace the paperback market.[13] They were of low quality and cheap (by 1972, one study estimated that around 20 per cent of the editions were unreadable and only 45 per cent were in good or excellent condition).[14] They ranged in cost from 50 Pfennigs to around 6 Deutschmarks, with a few exceptions.[15] Initially, the texts reproduced were ones otherwise difficult to obtain. One student from Berlin remembered driving to Amsterdam to collect originals.[16] Wilhelm Reich, Max Horkheimer, Herbert Marcuse, Georg Lukács and others featured among the first authors, appearing mid-decade 1965, their works frequently republished in the commercial market just a few years later.[17] In the *Raubdrucke*, students and radicals sought to control both production and consumption of the text, playing the roles of readers and printers as well as editors, with introductions and critical bibliographies. Indeed, beyond providing texts that were difficult or expensive to obtain, lay an attack on the monopoly on property rights held by large publishing houses.[18] More mundane reasons also existed for the production of illegal editions. The money from the sales often aided other militant or radical causes, whether these be the socialist kindergartens of the late 1960s and early

---

[12] Ricci, *I giovani*, 197.
[13] See Brown, *West Germany*, 127–128, and von Saldern, 'Markt für Marx', 154.
[14] See Albrecht Götz von Olenhusen and Christa Gnirss, 'Schwarze Kunst und Rote Bücher. Zur Produktion von Raubdrucken in der Bundesrepublik', *Gutenberg-Jahrbuch* (1972), 280.
[15] See Albrecht Götz von Olenhusen and Christa Gnirss, *Handbuch der Raubdrucke 2: Theorie und Klassenkampf. Sozialistische Drucke und proletarische Reprints. Eine Biographie* (Pullach bei München: Verlag Dokumentation, 1973), 270.
[16] APO 68er Interviews Berlin A-H, I. 'Interview mit Lisa Binger am 4.2.1998 in Berlin'.
[17] See von Olenhusen and Gnirss, *Handbuch der Raubdrucke*.
[18] As quoted in von Olenhusen and Gnirss, 'Schwarze Kunst und Rote Bücher', 274.

1970s[19] or simply the funding of everyday existence during full-time political militancy. The early 1970s witnessed a number of attempts to create small publishers whose books were socialist in content, cost and mode of production, although few developed a market large enough to sustain such operations long-term.[20]

Pirate editions provided the most comprehensive attempt to control the circulation of culture, but cultural access, for most university students, meant surmounting the obstacles to the book held in the university library. One commentator in 1965 had optimistically proclaimed that 'the paperback puts an end to the traditional system of the library and its sacerdotal privileges'.[21] But the university library retained its restrictive reputation in 1968. Thus one demand of protesters at Nanterre simply called for the 'creation of a true lending library'.[22] Another noted that of the seventy-one books to be read in various French courses, the library held a mere seventeen.[23] Students expressed a similar commitment to 'books for all' that had once served the marketing of paperbacks: 'direct access to books for all scholars (students and teachers)' as Italian students demanded.[24] In the context of the paperback market, any limitation or control over access to knowledge and books became politicised. Thus French students argued, in an echo of complaints about the exclusionary nature of the traditional book, that 'the lack of available books in the lending library ... is inscribed within the politics of exclusion from the university of the least well-off students'.[25] The paperback revolution encouraged a sense of entitlement to open access to books, anything short of which smacked of authoritarianism and elitism. Yet the perceived limitations lay not solely in the lack of books but in the constricted, conditional access to those the libraries held. Robert Escarpit had lauded how 'by systematically introducing the paperback at the university, the Americans have managed to strip the library of its character as museum, conservatory, and to transform it into a site of consumption where the student is placed at the very heart of the living

---

[19] APO 68er Interviews Berlin, S-Z, III. 'Interview mit Rüdiger Stuckart und Helga Rauch am 27.11.1997'.
[20] On the effervescence of publishing in the 1970s in West Germany, see von Saldern, 'Markt für Marx' 149–180, particularly 152–153. See also Brown, *West Germany*, 146–152.
[21] Michel-Claude Jalard, 'De la réédition à l'édition', *Les Temps Modernes* 227 (1965), 1745.
[22] BDIC F delta 813(9), 'MARC 200' Nanterre, le 30 janvier 1969.
[23] BDIC F delta 813(3), 'Réclamations et revendications sections lettres modernes'.
[24] CMR B.4 f.3 (Fondo Movimento Studentesco Riccardo Scartezzini), 'Ai Chiarissimi Professori Marcello Boldrini Norberto Bobbio Beniamino Andreatta componenti il Comitato Ordinatore dell'Isituto Superiore di Scienze Sociali di Trento. Trento 18 marzo 1968'.
[25] BDIC F delta 813(3), 'Les bibliothèques'.

world of books and can dialogue with them daily'.[26] So too, students in 1968 envisioned a radical democratic reconfiguration of the library. The 'library commission' at Trento demanded an 'American-style' library – 'horizontal development – maximum development of the man/book relation – no intermediary – all the books on the walls and within hand reach – maximum simplification of the bureaucracy ... – no stairs, or elevators or ups and downs: every form of verticalism complicates, rather than eases, consultation'.[27] The personal relationship to books that characterised the sale of paperbacks and the American library became the ideal of the students, one which dispensed with the guardians of culture – whether bookseller, librarian or professor.

The demand for a genuine lending library that facilitated rather than obstructed access to books assumed the absolute value of high culture, but by bringing books to hand it also targeted their hitherto exclusive status. The same development characterised the other institution of the professorial lecture. The lack of space in amphitheatres elicited calls for lectures to be written down and duplicated, both as an alternative to crowding and to allow working students to access the transcripts. The 'formation of a photocopying centre, free and open to all students',[28] ran one typical demand. 'Lectures must be duplicated and edited in book format', went another.[29] Yet these demands did not simply aim at overcoming the physical obstacles to professorial knowledge, but at dismantling dutiful and deferential student attitudes. Thus at Nanterre, students of psychology insisted that the 'lectures are photocopied well before meetings', in order to create the conditions for 'debates ... where dialogue will be established between professors and students'.[30] One West German author explicitly stressed the goal was not 'a new, well functioning university, but rather fewer students submissive to authority'.[31] The professorial lecture inculcated a passive consumption of knowledge, a function made all the more obvious by severe overcrowding. The student newspaper in West Berlin, the *FU Spiegel*, portrayed this as a decline of both ancient and Humboldtian ideals of pedagogy: 'In the mammoth courses in which today the bulk

---

[26] Robert Escarpit, 'Le livre de diffusion de masse', *Communication et langages* 5 (1970), 93.
[27] CMR, Fondo Marco Boato, Busta Trento Sociologia Anno 1963–1968, fascicolo 'Commissione per la Biblioteca', 'Verbale di seduta. Dicembre 1966'.
[28] BDIC F delta 813(1), 'Charte revendicative des étudiants de philo, psycho, socio. premier cycle'.
[29] A. Deledicq (ed.), *Un moi de mai orageux: 113 étudiants parisiens expliquent les raisons du soulèvement universitaire* (Privat: Toulouse, 1968), 87.
[30] Alain Schnapp and Pierre Vidal-Naquet (eds.), *Journal de la commune étudiante: textes et documents. Novembre 1967–juin 1968*, édition augmentée (Paris: Seuil, 1969), 126.
[31] APO Privatbesitz Sigrid Fronius 67 Hochschulref 'Möglichkeiten studentischer Basisarbeit'.

of study takes place, a Socratic dialogue between student and teacher can no longer take place.'[32] At Nanterre, the verdict was more lapidary: 'an hour of class = an hour of steno'.[33] Lectures involved the training of force-fed geese, as one pamphlet famously described it, rendering the student 'no more than a scribe who copies down the dull words of the teacher, copies precious to him, since he will produce them, almost to the comma, on the exam as the teacher demands'.[34] The self-conception of high culture had contrasted the active, vocal, critical ability of a minority to the passive, silent consumption of the majority: 'Opposite the sovereign professor and his forms of expression (lecture, authoritarian program, examiner's jury ...) the student is reduced to docile resignation and a passive "consumption" of the speech of the master, without participation, without discussion, without critique.'[35] In the teeming university lecture hall, students uncomfortably placed in the second position turned the condemnation of passivity away from themselves towards the structures of higher education itself.

The documents and tracts of the student movements are thus replete with initiatives and suggestions to foster the critical capacity of students. At Turin books 'were digested, "remade" in bibliographical cards, – the fruit not only of reading, but also of the collective discussion – then duplicated, that is "published", and distributed'.[36] A similar attempt to produce digested versions of texts and simultaneously insert the reader into the book occurred in France: 'Readings can be proposed by the teacher, and put by students into reading cards. The student can then talk of these readings and analyse the process of a text rather than summarising it.'[37] By simplifying access to lectures and books, the basis for critical dialogue would be established. The printing and circulation of lectures would facilitate discussion, while open-book exams would test 'the capacity for intellectual initiative, the power of analysis and depth of reflection, and not as now a simple, sterile and elementary mnemonic ability'.[38] In each instance, students assumed that the traditional format of the book or the

---

[32] 'Öffentliche Kritik von Lehrveranstaltungen – Anmaßung einer arroganten Ignoranz?' *FU Spiegel* 50 (February 1966), 15.
[33] BDIC F delta 1961(10) – VI, 'Des réformes!! Pourquoi?'.
[34] Schnapp and Vidal-Naquet, *Journal*, 126.
[35] Centre d'histoire sociale du XXe siècle [CHS] Fonds II/V(11), 'Qu'est ce que l'université de contestation'.
[36] Movimento Studentesco (ed.), *Documenti della rivolta universitaria* (Bari: Laterza, 1968), 230.
[37] CHS II/V(11), 'Commission forme et contenu de l'enseignement Français. Mercredi 30 mai – 16h'.
[38] Schnapp and Vidal-Naquet, *Journal*, 126.

lecture inculcated a passive, uncritical reception and demanded widespread reproduction and the integration of the reader (or auditor) into the original. At the Free University of Berlin, the student paper, the *FU Spiegel* announced in February 1966 a series of critical reviews of lectures, conceived as an 'inducement to further discussion', to replace the disappearance of Socratic dialogue in the lecture hall itself.[39] The student Hartmut Häußermann noted that a draft of the FU constitution from 1948 had proposed to institute reviews of lectures and that they sought to serve the 'community of teaching and learning' of the German university.[40] Others noted that such reviews commonly occurred in the United States. Yet if reviews of lectures aimed to restore critical dialogue to the lecture hall of the mass university, the project immediately had to reorient itself to criticism of smaller, more advanced seminars, since the older students the paper judged qualified and competent to assess the mass lectures simply did not attend them.[41] The intellectual justification of critical dialogue gave way to its desacralising drive.

The response to the reviews confirmed to the students their effectiveness as a 'fundamental assault on the paternalistic-unpolitical climate and hierarchical order of the university'.[42] One professor dismissed his reviewer as an 'anonymous muckraker', while the political scientist Ernst Fraenkel sought the support of the Free University's Senate to ban seminar reviews.[43] Others simply evoked the intellectual apathy and incapacity of the authors. In France, the psychology professor Robert Francès dismissed the summary of his lecture as 'not only a caricature of a simplification but full of serious errors'. The poverty of the production accounted for poor grades, along with the 'extreme passivity of certain students I've often been surprised to see not taking any notes in the class'.[44] Indeed, one student who evaluated the reviews of the *FU Spiegel* rated their 'critique' as 'at worst, trivial', 'only hinted at' or 'one-sidedly limited to problems of method and techniques of teaching and learning'.[45] When the *FU Spiegel* surveyed the 40 students who had taken Ernst Fraenkel's seminar, only one of the 22 who returned the survey judged the review to be 'factual and

---

[39] Wolfgang Nitsch, 'Vorlesungsrezensionen als Hochschulkritik: zur Problematik studentischer Rezension von Lehrveranstaltungen mit einem Vorwort von Ernst Elitz sowie Literaturhinweisen', in Stephan Leibfried (ed.), *Wider die Untertanenfabrik: Handbuch zur Demokratisierung der Hochschule* (Köln: Pahl-Rugenstein Verlag, 1967), 221.
[40] Hartmut Häußerman, 'Lieber Leser', *FU Spiegel* 51 (May 1966), 3.
[41] *FU Spiegel* 50 (February 1966), 14.   [42] Nitsch, 'Vorlesungsrezensionen', 222.
[43] See 'Der Akademische Senat verbot diese Rezension', *FU Spiegel* 57 (May 1967), 12.
[44] ADHS 1208W/180, Letter of Francès to Beaujeu, 14 March 1968.
[45] Wulf Hopf, 'Schlimmstenfalls Trivial', *FU Spiegel* 58 (June 1967), 12.

objective'.⁴⁶ None agreed with its allegation of dogmatism. The practice of reviews revealed a tension between criticism of pedagogical form and intellectual content. Instead of producing the passivity assumed by its critics, the mass consumption of culture slowly stripped the professor of authority. The mass lecture was unmasked as a mechanism to promote passivity rather than diffuse knowledge. Mass consumption thus ultimately invited rather than stifled criticism, but it also favoured criticism directed at the weakest point of the university – professorial authority – rather than fostering the self-reflexive critical intellectual engagement idealised by all. Students proved much more successful at deflating the status and authority of professors than engaging their ideas, while professors preferred to fight on their favoured terrain of knowledge. Mass consumption created critical possibilities, but nothing guaranteed they would be used wisely.

The desacralisation of high culture did not stop at the demolition of deference to the book, the professor and the lecture, but invested the hierarchy of culture itself. In another imitation of the paperback market, students expanded the definition of literature to include every text available. Thus students in France declared:

> We are studying '*Lettres*', but where does one study classified adverts, sport or other reporting, medical expenses claim forms from social security, crosswords, tax returns, traffic laws, school books, how-to manuals, the rules of the game of advertising? These texts, however, are read by more people than whatever literary text; there are some which everyone is obliged to read; why do our studies not speak of this everyday reality?
>
> In the domain of literary text, that is to say those which do not have any practical utility, and above all those which appear to have no utility at all, the greatest part of what is read is left to one side: detective novels, children's books, adventure and romance novels ... photo-stories (which are the only 'novels' for a lot of people who do not read *La Princesse de Clèves* or *Madame Bovary*), serialised novels of newspapers and reviews, etc. ....⁴⁷

Such heterogeneity and juxtaposition of texts without regard for their quality was precisely what shocked about the paperback revolution. 'Where the filter of the past is missing', wrote Enzensberger in 1959, 'it is evidently no longer possible to differentiate what is important from third-rate ... Faulkner next to Agatha Christie, Hofmannsthal next to Horst Wolfram Geißler ... Here it comes to a reciprocal flattening that is

---

[46] Klausjürgen Schroeder, 'Echt wissenschaftlich', *FU Spiegel* 59 (July 1967), 18.
[47] BDIC F delta 813(14), 'Journal du Comité de Lutte Lettres'.

characteristic of all expressions of the culture industry.'⁴⁸ The thought of studying the most popular texts never occurred to the hesitant well-wishers of the pocketbook. In 1963 Michel Bouvy in the *Bulletin des bibliothèques de France* expressed some unease that while indeed more copies sold of Antoine de Saint-Exupéry's *Night Flight* or Albert Camus' *The Plague*, 'to take only texts of indisputable quality' that nonetheless meant 'only 35,000 copies per year while one can sell 500,000 copies of *La Foire aux cancres* in a year and more than a million copies are regularly sold of each volume of *Tintin*, and not all of them for children'.⁴⁹ By the end of the 1960s, some students dismissed the distinction between 'third rate' and 'important' as mere ideology, at least as regards what should be studied. The radicals of 1968 turned what was a facet of the paperback market into a political project, one that radically contradicted inherited ideas of literary worth or quality. The assertion of textual equivalence reflected the collapse of cultural authority, one that reduced the hierarchy of high and low culture to the expression of a particular class. The guardians of high culture emphasised its elite, minority status. Democratisers sought its widest diffusion. Some desacralisers reinstated the boundary between high and low, but as a marker only of class and not inherent quality, the idea of dissemination rejected as paternalism.

Anti-Intellectualism

If the intention of facilitating access to books imperceptibly slipped into the cultivation of a critical attitude to the idea of high culture, so too its desacralisation slouched towards its dismissal. 'We quickly realised that books are almost as authoritarian as lecturers', explained the Torinese student leader Guido Viale.⁵⁰ The protest dynamic radically devalued the authority of written culture, threatening to reduce it to its social uses and misuses. Readers bought books not to read but to display in craven submission to the market: 'the cult of the book has become in recent years ... one of the goals and primary occupations of students and young couples. In the place of the family altars ... the new levers of neocapitalism

---

[48] Hans Magnus Enzensberger, 'Analyse der Taschenbuch-Produktion. Teil II', *Neue Deutsche Hefte* 58 (1959), 164. Cf. Armando Petrucci, 'Reading to Read: A Future for Reading', in Roger Chartier and Guglielmo Cavallo (eds.), *A History of Reading in the West*, trans. Lydia G. Cochrane (Amherst: University of Massachusetts Press, 1999), 356.
[49] Michel Bouvy, 'Le livre de poche en France', *Bulletin des bibliothèques de France* (November 1963).
[50] Guido Viale, 'Contro l'università', in *Università: l'ipotesi rivoluzionaria. Documenti delle lotte studenteshe Trento, Torino, Napoli, Pisa, Milano, Roma* (Vicenza: Marsilio Editori, 1968), 110.

construct altars, designated as bookcases, or even chapels called studies, where the book fetish reigns uncontested, content to submit to private adoration.'[51] In the early 1960s, commentators celebrated how the paperback had 'broken through the book ideology which fetishised the book as object and sanctified its contents',[52] but the results were more unpredictable. The abundance of cheap editions served as much to diffuse as to destroy the fetishisation of books, albeit redirected to the constitution of a library rather than the individual book. Students excoriated the library builders and self-consciously performed their emancipation from the fetishised object. At Turin the book was literally dismembered in, as one student put it, 'the ultimate liberatory act in confrontation with the god-book: the cutting up of books being read for the distribution of five pages to each member [of the group]'.[53] Such an act presupposed a paperback market: the destruction would not have been so happily embarked on if cheap, identical copies were not readily available. The student slaying of the 'god-book' drew upon the work of the paperback market in the prior years.

Another form of demonstrative disengagement from the book-as-object lay in theft. Students and protesters attacked the notion of the book as private property or part of a personal library:

> For a while, with the diffusion of the critique of capitalism, the criticism of the private ownership of books was applied. To return loaned books (whether from private persons or institutional libraries) went out of fashion for a time – not only out of slovenliness or forgetfulness, but as an act of emancipation from petit-bourgeois values. At the end of the Sixties, it was clear to everyone who hosted a party at their house that their collection of books would be a little thinned out the next morning.[54]

Theft could also be interpreted as another affirmation of the free circulation of books, although thefts from institutional libraries undoubtedly impeded the access of others to the same book, unless they too could find a copy to borrow or steal. The critique of the book as private property damaged bookstores in particular. In France, the publisher François Maspero closed his bookstore at the end of 1970, no longer economically viable partly as a result of fines imposed by the French government for

---

[51] Viale, 'Contro l'università', 112.
[52] Gollhardt, 'Das Taschenbuch im Zeitalter der Massenkultur', 125.
[53] Viale, 'Contro l'università', 113.
[54] Hartmut Häußermann, 'Das Berliner Milieu und die Stadtforschung', in Heinz Bude and Martin Kohli (eds.), *Radikalisierte Aufklärung: Studentenbewegung und Soziologie in Berlin 1965 bis 1970* (Weinheim and Munich: Juventa Verlag, 1989), 43–70, 45.

prohibited publications but also due to the increase in thefts from the far Left. 'For some', he remembered 'it was revolutionary to "steal at Masp"'.⁵⁵ In a leaflet of 1969, the bookstore pleaded vainly with those who accused it 'of "making money on the back of the revolution" and being "capitalist traders" and then resell the books they have stolen from us'.⁵⁶ Here, the revolution devoured its parents. Editors and publishers such as Maspero in France, Feltrinelli in Italy or Suhrkamp in West Germany played an important role through the 1960s in promoting access to texts unavailable, untranslated or merely hard to find.

Yet desacralisation touched not just the book as object, but its content as well. If the purchasers of books bought them to display rather than read, the authors of such superficial objects exhibited motives no less mercenary. Academic publications, one Italian student wrote, 'are not born from the stimulus aroused by certain political or social problems, but solely from the need to print a certain number of pages to win positions and wages. The culture of book-learning exists solely for the fact that books exist and must be sold.'⁵⁷ Thus one student commission, instead of dismembering the book, proposed to prohibit its use altogether. Here the desacralisation of books culminated in the total dismissal of written culture. The wholesale rejection of 'book-learning' drew on multiple sources: the rejection of examinations that demanded rote-learning, the abrupt devaluation of the cultural authority derived from knowledge and the increasing politicisation of the protest movements that derided university politics as elitist, to be abandoned for the real struggle in the factories. The repudiation of the book was consummated in the extreme fetishisation of the little red one of Mao, more of a catechism to be recited than a book to be read.⁵⁸ Two phrases of Mao – 'the correct ideas come from social practice', and 'no investigation, no right to speak' – served to further diminish the value of knowledge gleaned from books. The desacralisation of the book entailed a fetishisation of experience. As one member of *Lotta Continua* recalled, the

---

⁵⁵ François Maspero, *Les abeilles & la guêpe* (Paris: Seuil, 2002), 221. On Maspero and other publishing houses see Philippe Olivera, 'Les livres de Mai', in Damamme et al. (eds.), *Mai–Juin 68*, 144–157, 152–154.

⁵⁶ BDIC F delta res 612(15), 'L'ensemble des travailleurs des librairies et des Éditions Maspero vous informe'.

⁵⁷ Viale, 'Contro l'università', 110–111.

⁵⁸ On the little red book, see Alexander C. Cook (ed.), *Mao's Little Red Book: A Global History* (Cambridge: Cambridge University Press, 2014). For serious intellectual engagement with the little red book, see in particular Julian Bourg, 'Principally contradiction: The flourishing of French Maoism' in Alexander C. Cook (ed.), *Mao's Little Red Book*, 225–244. See also Julien Hage, 'Les petits livres rouges (1966–1976)' in Philippe Artières and Michelle Zancarini-Fournel, *68: Une histoire collective 1962–1981* (Paris: La Decouverte, 2008), 457–461.

Maoist aphorisms 'had a brute, literal application. ... almost a disdain for reflection, for reading books. When in the group someone was seen to be too dedicated to reading books he was told "go do an investigation, go do social practice."'[59] Anti-intellectualism could be either apologetic, dismissive or aggressive, as when one group from the Socialist German Student League (SDS) broke into a share-house in Frankfurt, 'threw books and records out the window and painted on the wall: "Theorists to the concentration camp [*Theoretiker ins KZ*]!"'[60] Such actions took the attack on the content of books into a dead end.[61]

Thus, student movements that had begun with a voracious and expansive attitude towards knowledge turned at times to the most reductionist interpretation of knowledge as nothing more than an expression of social power. As one 68er recalled, 'we came out of '68 with the fixation that to write a book, sign one's name to a book, was a betrayal'.[62] In the early 1970s, in one of the first feminist texts to emerge from the Italian student movement the authors felt obliged to apologise for its very status of being 'a *book*': that is, 'an instrument only ever for intellectuals, and that is, for few women: while all women can write their history because they make it; they write it in fact from the moment in which they begin to come together'.[63] The gulf between elite and popular culture re-emerged. To apologise for the act of creating a book was to assert implicitly that the paperback market had failed to bridge the gap between books as objects for intellectuals and books as objects for all. The declaration that books were 'only ever for intellectuals' tolled the defeat of attempts to democratise them. Political radicalism here converged with the conviction of the most conservative defenders of high culture that intellectuals could only ever be a tiny minority. Those sympathetic to the desacralisation of high culture found themselves disconcerted. The scholar of working-class literacy Richard Hoggart argued 'courses in literature for people from working-class backgrounds which invite them to read professedly and explicitly working-class literature only and reject or deny their opportunity to grapple with King Lear, on the grounds that it is bourgeois, are simply

---

[59] Roberto Niccolai (ed.), *Parlando di rivoluzioni: Ventuno protagonisti dei gruppi, dei movimenti e delle riviste degli anni '60 e '70 descrivono la loro idea di mutamento sociale* (Pistoia: Centro di documentazione Pistoia Editrice, 1998), 154.
[60] Wolff, '1968: Ein freischwebender Gruß', 144.
[61] On the fall of the left-wing readers' movement, see von Saldern, 'Markt für Marx', 171–177.
[62] Ricci, *I giovani*, 279.
[63] Luisa Abbà, Gabriella Ferri, Giorgio Lazzaretto, Elena Medi and Silvia Motta, *La coscienza di sfruttata* (Milan: Gabriele Mazzotta Editore, 1972), 8.

stupid.'⁶⁴ In retrospect, some students resented that it was the well-read student leaders who denounced the culture of learning. One grumbled that Mauro Rostagno, the most charismatic leader and orator of the movement at Trento, 'said that books were going to be thrown in the shithole but did not say that he had read a few thousand'.⁶⁵ The denunciation of high culture from a position of cultural privilege could appear long-term as merely the most audacious form of exclusion.

Discontents of a Democratised Culture

'A global challenge to the civilisation of writing', Renato Curcio described 1968 twenty years later, 'so much so that it was the faces of the walls, rather than the paper of books, which received our messages'.⁶⁶ Yet anti-intellectualism was not the last word of the student movements, only one response to the desacralisation of high culture. Many currents of the protest movements continued to pursue the expansion of access to knowledge and the liberation of the intellectual content from the constrictive confines of the book as object. But the political radicalisation of the late 1960s shifted the cultural argument away from proposing increased access to knowledge and books, to a sceptical, critical disposition towards high culture, to one in which intellectual books merited no more attention than any other texts, and even warranted an apology when contrasted with the actions of ordinary people. Democratisation, conceived as the liberalisation of access to high culture, proved paradoxical, beholden to the assumption that high culture was an easily identifiable thing that only required the greatest possible diffusion. The mass dissemination of high culture did not simply make it available, but rather undermined the traditional relationship between books and readers and the concept of high culture itself. Access thus unfolded as both the most naïve and most radical form of cultural democratisation. Despite the Situationist International's dismissal of students who bought texts and consumed them 'visually', the desacralised attitude towards books, inculcated by the paperback and transferred to the seminar and the lecture hall, was one reason why the defences of 'high culture' crumbled so quickly when the most radical students attacked the edifice of the university. The profusion of texts undermined an old

---

⁶⁴ Richard Hoggart, '1968–1978: The student movement and its effect on the universities', in Stewart Armstrong (ed.), *Decade of Change?* (Guildford: Society for Research into Higher Education, 1979), 8.
⁶⁵ Ricci, *I giovani*, 198.
⁶⁶ CMR, B.14 f.1 (Fondo Calì), A Trento Vent'Anni Dopo. 'Amici'. Lettera dal Renato Curcio.

regime of revered books and a clear demarcation between high and popular culture, just as the mass university, however restricted it still remained, no longer resembled an aristocratic sanctuary cut off from society. The novelty and power of the paperback lay not so much in its cost, distribution or print run, but this blurring of the divide between high and low culture, the consequent desacralisation of the book, the destabilisation of the canon, the clerisy who interpreted it and the elite university that educated them.

Yet if democratisation as access seemed simple, almost naïve, by 1968, the desacralisation of high culture, the attempt to replace a deferential, hierarchical culture with a critical, democratic one, held no fewer pitfalls. As the project of writing critical reviews of professorial lectures made clear, the hierarchies within the lecture hall and the university expressed both a structure of social power and an intellectual justification. Democratisation via desacralisation succeeded somewhat in disentangling the two hierarchies but, scandalised by their students' insolence, professors all too frequently resorted to assertions of authority rather than engaging their critics on academic grounds. In similar fashion, students found in the status of professors their most vulnerable point, and the criticism of culture could veer into anti-intellectualism. While the protests most frequently aimed to hold university life to its regulative ideal of critical dialogue and evidence-based argument, a current of anti-intellectualism abandoned that internal critique for a crude reduction of intellectual culture to the expression of social hierarchy. Anti-intellectualism was the most illusory form of democratisation, one that beneath a façade of anti-elitism abandoned the arduous democratic task of disentangling truth from power.

The sudden disappearance of an old idea of culture accounts for the intoxication and terror of 1968 for many of its participants. Sanctified knowledge appeared dead, displaced by talking: a free, chaotic flow of speech. The authority of high culture, the book and the professor surrendered its once self-evident status. Yet the new cultural regime contained its own hierarchies. After all, the movements of 1968 typically threw up leaders whose mastery of language and speech, grounded in their familiarity with high culture, distinguished them from their fellow students. Yet, crucially, their charismatic authority appeared personal, not institutional. Indeed, the collapse of a clear distinction between high and low culture and the blurring of issues of access made the political frontlines of culture harder to identify. After the deluge of 1968, a cultural barrier no longer separated those who could afford books, and built a personal library, from those who could not buy. Rather, the division lay between those who read the books they bought and those who did not, or between those who laboured to understand books and those with the prized ability to talk about them without having read them at all. Finding the time in which to absorb the content of books proved a greater obstacle than access to them. Similarly, the university with its broadened access no longer appeared as an impenetrable fortress; the greater the number of students admitted, the more their failures appeared individual rather than institutional.

The political freight of the book declined somewhat after the charged decade of the 1960s. The events of 1968 themselves produced an immediate, enormous and best-selling literature.[67] 'It is unlikely', wrote Michel de Certeau in a familiar criticism, that these books 'were really *read*. For many it was no doubt enough to have *paid* for them'.[68] Yet the opposition between consumers and readers that underlay the imagery of written culture in crisis in the early 1960s no longer reigned after 1968. De Certeau himself set out to elaborate the idea of 'reading as poaching', to question the 'assimilation of reading to passivity'[69] and explore a space of freedom in consumption – metaphors that no longer implied cultural collapse or vulgarity: 'to read is to wander through an imposed system (that of the text, analogous to the constructed order of a city or of a supermarket)'.[70] So, too, Enzensberger, who in 1959 depicted the reader as bludgeoned into intellectual apathy by the culture industry, in 1976 celebrated the reader's freedom to snub received interpretations and do whatever she wished with the text:

> the reader is always right and no one can take away the freedom to make whatever use of a text that suits him. This freedom includes the right to leaf back and forward, to skip whole passages, to read sentences against the grain, to misunderstand them, to reshape them, to spin sentences out and embroider them with every possible association, to draw conclusions from the text, of which the text knows nothing ... to forget it, to plagiarise it and to throw the book in which it is printed into the corner at any time he likes. Reading is an anarchic act. Interpretation, especially the single correct one,

---

[67] See Olivera, 'Les livres de Mai'.
[68] Michel de Certeau, *The Capture of Speech and Other Political Writings*, trans. Tom Conley (Minneapolis: University of Minnesota Press, 1997), 42.
[69] Michel de Certeau, *The Practice of Everyday Life* (Berkeley: University of California Press, 1984), 169.
[70] Ibid.

exists to frustrate this act. Its expression is consequently always authoritarian, it produces either subordination or resistance.[71]

No doubt the transformation of the irrational, seduced, consumer into the free-wheeling, poaching, inventive reader is a necessary, salutary correction to the assumptions of the pre-paperback order of reading. Yet Enzensberger's anarchic reader sits uncomfortably alongside his prior figure of a passive, manipulated consumer and the critical visions sought by 68ers.

While the critical, irreverent reader conforms to the desacralising drive of 1968, 68ers always understood reading as a social act. Where once reading expressed relations of social power, it now reflects nothing other than itself. Readers of the sacralised book sought entry to the privileged world of high culture. The reader of the desacralised book is imagined to have escaped social and cultural hierarchy altogether. If the reader is always right, they are only ever right for themselves. To contrast the free act of reading to the authoritarian one of interpretation obscures that interpretation is merely a reading with authority, with validity for more than the individual. The liberty of the anarchic reader is thus the freedom of the powerless. The revolts of 1968 sought to democratise the construction of authority, not abolish it altogether. Yet authority proved easier to unmask than to reconstruct in radical democratic fashion. Despite the often rigidly politicised reading of texts during and after 1968, the power of an official interpretation, including radical ones, entered a long-term decline. The institutional power to impose interpretations receded, to the profit of a perceived individual liberty. The single, sacral book in the sanctum of the library to be interpreted correctly gave way to the multitude of demystified, easily accessed copies which supported a number of readings. Yet 68ers did not seek the freedom of the anarchic reader. They demanded access to the book (or to culture), desacralisation (an assumption of an active, critical, at times instrumental approach to texts) and a re-ordering of the canon. The last thing 68ers sought to destroy was the legitimacy of their own official interpretations. When speech was captured in 1968, the students had stormed the Bastille, only to find it empty.

---

[71] Hans Magnus Enzensberger, *Mediocrity and Delusion*, trans. Martin Chalmers (London: Verso, 1992), 11. Cf. Petrucci, 'Reading to Read', 365–366.

PART II

The Politics of Revolt

CHAPTER 5

'The Space of Autonomy Must Be Created'
The Politics of Democracy

An enormous wave of politicisation and political activism defined the late 1960s. Yet just a few years, and sometimes only months, before the explosion of revolt commentators diagnosed a widespread political apathy. Students, in particular, appeared unconcerned with or incapable of politics. A 1967 French government study asserted that young people 'feel little concerned by that which is beyond their probable reach'.[1] An analysis of West Berlin university politics in 1965 argued that the basis for a significant student opposition simply did not exist. Students would probably not even notice a severe reduction of their rights: 'Supposing student representation was limited or dissolved by an administrative act, the protest of the committed few would probably meet no significant response from their fellow students', ran the conclusion.[2] In February 1968, the treasurer of the main French student union warned the organisation could no longer pay the wages of four typists. Their positions expired on 1 May, mere days before a student revolt sparked the largest strike in French history.[3] A year before, the student union's congress concluded that 'a favourable balance of power is not conceivable in the immediate future on the fundamental aspect of our orientation: the reform of university structures and the control of

---

[1] Ministère de la jeunesse et des sports, *Rapport d'enquête sur la jeunesse française: analyse des études et opinions exprimées 1966–1967*. No pagination.
[2] Heribert Adam, *Studentenschaft und Hochschule: Möglichkeiten und Grenzen studentischer Politik* (Frankfurt: Europäischer Verlagsanstalt, 1965), 41, 70, 71, 77. For an analysis of politicisation of West German students in the 1960s see Boris Spix, *Abschied vom Elfenbeinturm? Politisches Verhalten Studierender 1957–1967. Berlin und Nordrhein-Westfalen im Vergleich* (Essen: Klartext Verlag, 2008). For a brief overview of France, see Robi Morder, 'Années 1960: crise des jeunesses, mutations de la jeunesse,' *Matériaux pour l'histoire de notre temps* 74 (2004), 62–69.
[3] Alain Monchalbon, 'L'UNEF avant mai. En attendant le miracle', in Geneviève Dreyfus-Armand et Laurent Gervereau (eds.), *Mai 68. Les mouvements étudiants en France et dans le monde* (Nanterre: Bibliothèque de la Documentation Internationale Contemporaine, 1988), 87.

these by those concerned by them'.⁴ Powerlessness and apathy appeared the hallmarks of student politics.

This dismal verdict on the prospects for politics was not entirely wrong, despite subsequent developments. The major student organisations did not form the backbone of the revolts, which emerged instead outside the traditional structures. As Louis Gruel argued, 'the period is marked less by depoliticisation of youth than by disaffection for the terms in which alternative politics was proposed to them.'⁵ The explosion of 1968 was a radical response to political suffocation, with the aim, first and foremost, of making politics possible. As Italian students argued in 1966, 'the structure of power does not consent to any effective form of contestation ... The space of autonomy is given unilaterally by the authorities: that space only allows abstract and unrealistic operations. The space must be created.'⁶ Faced with the inadequacies and insufficiencies of electoral politics and representative democracy at both the national level and within the university, the protest movements sought to wrest politics from its distant, unattainable status, the domain of politicians and parties, and bring it down to daily life. Politics belonged not just periodically at the ballot box or confined to national parliaments, but everywhere, at all times. The student movements demanded autonomy and self-government at all levels of society. This demand for democratisation was also directed against the parties that traditionally monopolised political power (particularly those of the Left that self-consciously championed greater democracy). The crisis of institutional authority that engulfed the university in 1968 already existed in both political and religious institutions – parties and churches – in the mid-1960s. The perceived gap between their goals and what they delivered undermined their ability to command consent from their youth organisations, impose party discipline, and compel adherence to the official interpretation of party ideology. The decline of youth politics was a necessary precursor to its spectacular explosion.

A space for student protest emerged at the conjunction of a profound disappointment in the politics of democracy at the national level and in

---

⁴ As quoted by Jean-Philippe Legois, Alain Monchablon and Robi Morder, 'Le mouvement étudiant et l'université: entre réforme et révolution (1964–1976)', in Dreyfus-Armand et al. (eds.), *Les Années 68. Le temps de la contestation* (Brussels: Editions Complexe, 2000), 285.
⁵ Louis Gruel, *La rébellion de 68: Une relecture sociologique* (Rennes: Presses Universitaires de Rennes, 2004), 120.
⁶ CMR B.4 f.1 (Fondo Movimento Studentesco Riccardo Scartezzini) 'Perché facciamo "occupazione"'.

the traditional organisations of student representation. As had happened with the expansion of the universities, so too the politics of the 1960s raised unrequited hopes for political democratisation in the younger generation that flocked to the university. The gap between the rhetoric of democracy and the reality of political compromise created a significant crisis of legitimacy for the major political parties. That crisis was if anything even more acute for the student organisations, whose best days were usually behind them by the late 1960s. Despite the differences in national politics and student organisations, whatever aspirations existed earlier in the decade for greater autonomy and democracy within youth politics had been suffocated by the late 1960s in all three states. The first consequence was the attenuation of student politics, and the subsequent diagnosis of apathy and apoliticism. Yet the asphyxiation of official student politics ultimately only served to displace the dynamic into organisations and groups with even less connection to the national political parties. Having been excluded from the political arena, they sought to create the space themselves. The aspirations for greater democracy and autonomy re-emerged, but outside the control of the major political parties, in forms characterised by provocation and protest.

The National Politics of Democracy

The return of parliamentary democracy to western Europe in the wake of the Second World War appeared relatively successful by the mid-1960s. Despite the political turbulence of the decade, the Sixties only confirmed the democratic consensus. Unlike the 1920s or 1930s, and with the exception of Greece and to some extent Italy, most European conservatives ultimately strengthened their embrace of electoral democracy in response to the radicalism of the 1960s and 1970s. However, western Europe's long-term attachment to democracy emerged only in retrospect, strengthened by the social conflict of the Sixties. Contemporaries understood democracy during that decade as a fragile conquest that could all too easily unravel, a postwar promise yet to be completely fulfilled. Furthermore, for many in the early 1960s, the need to deepen democracy was urgently required in defence against a resurgent radical Right.

In West Germany, the success of the neo-Nazi National Democratic Party of Germany (*Nationaldemokratische Partei Deutschlands*, NPD) in state elections raised the spectre of the return of Nazism. Founded in 1964, the NPD won 7.4 per cent of the vote in Bavaria and 7.9 per cent in Hesse in 1966, reaching a height of 9.8 per cent in Baden-Württemberg in 1968.[7] At the beginning of 1967, just a few months before left-wing protests entered a phase of rapid expansion and mass mobilisation, the philosopher Georg Picht pointed to how 'a new wave of German nationalism slowly rises'.[8] Fritz Thielen, the head of the NPD, concurred, declaring 'the national idea's time of suffering is over'.[9] The NPD never made an impact at the national level, achieving 4.3 per cent of the vote in the 1969 elections and failing to breach the 5 per cent barrier for representation in the Federal Parliament, but its ability to exploit an authoritarian groundswell amid the first economic downturn of the postwar era in 1966–1967 raised questions about the depth of democratic sentiment in postwar West Germany. After all, in one West German survey 50 per cent of the general public agreed that 'National Socialism had been a good idea badly carried out'.[10] West Germany's attachment to democracy appeared only slightly more substantial than that of the NPD, which formally adhered to democracy in order to avoid a constitutional ban.

More disturbing than the relatively minor electoral success of the NPD was the response. Conservative politicians responded to the far Right's resurgence as reflecting a failure of the mainstream Right to effectively represent German nationalism. The Christian Socialist Franz Josef Strauss read the NPD's success as 'the answer to years of ridicule and mockery of the Federal Republic, to years of dragging in the filth whatever is German and national'.[11] Left and liberal critics interpreted the NPD's success instead as the failure of democratisation. The political scientist Kurt Sontheimer wrote that 'the democratic "substance," of the German people is, contrary to the expectations of the time between 1945 and 1949, only marginally established. The continuity of a political thought, adapted to democracy but tendentially authoritarian, oriented to the idea of the state and its power of decision, to security, calm and order, has proven stronger.'[12] The Spiegel Affair of October 1962 confirmed this impression.

---

[7] On the role of the Nazi Past in the 1960s, see Torben Fischer and Matthias N. Lorenz (eds.), *Lexikon der 'Vergangenheitsbewältigung' in Deutschland: Debatten- und Diskursgeschichte des Nationalsozialismus nach 1945* (Bielefeld: Transcript Verlag, 2007). See also Norbert Frei, *1968: Jugendrevolte und Globaler Protest* (Munich: Deutscher Taschenbuch Verlag, 2008), 79–88.
[8] Georg Picht, 'Grundlagen eines neuen deutschen Nationalbewußtseins', *Merkur* 226 (1967), 1.
[9] 'Wer Adolf Will', *Der Spiegel* 49 (1966), 37.
[10] See Nick Thomas, *Protest Movements in 1960s West Germany: A Social History of Dissent and Democracy* (Oxford: Berg, 2003), 26–27.
[11] 'Wer Adolf Will', 34.
[12] Kurt Sontheimer, *Antidemokratisches Denken in der Weimarer Republik. Die politischen Ideen des deutschen Nationalismus zwischen 1918 und 1933*, expanded edition (Munich: Nymphenburger, 1968), 333–334.

Police occupied and searched the offices of *Der Spiegel* on the accusation of treason, arresting its publisher and the author of an article about the preparedness of the West German army to defend the Federal Republic. The rise of the radical right, however weak it ultimately proved, placed the meaning of democracy at the centre of West German politics in the 1960s. Did democracy begin and end at electoral legitimacy? Was the mid-1960s the 'end of the postwar era', as the Chancellor Ludwig Erhard proclaimed in November 1965, or the opportunity to finally accomplish the unfulfilled democratisation of 1945?

The role of parliamentary democracy, and the place of other forms of democracy, took on greater importance in the context of the 'Grand Coalition' between the two major political forces, the Christian Democratic and Christian Socialist Unions and the Social Democratic Party (*Sozialdemokratische Partei Deutschlands*, SPD) in December 1966. The CDU/CSU coalition had held power, at times in coalition with the small, liberal Free Democratic Party (*Freie Demokratische Party*, FDP), uninterrupted since 1949. The failure of West German democracy to produce an alternation of government thus gave way to one with no significant parliamentary opposition. The Grand Coalition comprised over 90 per cent of the deputies in the Federal Parliament. The coalition government marked a decisive step for the Social Democrats in their quest to prove the party's legitimacy to govern at the federal level. The SPD sought to exit the electoral cage of just under one-third of the vote to which it remained confined in the 1950s. The CDU/CSU coalition obtained an absolute majority in 1957, despite the SPD having managed to increase its vote in each successive election.[13] The new SPD Basic Program, adopted at its 1959 Congress in Bad Godesberg, omitted Marxism and any program of nationalisations. The traditional distinction between short-term reformist goals and the revolutionary end-goal of socialism disappeared. The SPD now presented itself as a 'people's party' rather than the party of the German working class.[14] Contemporaries ascribed the de-ideologisation of the national political scene to affluence and the necessity of forging electoral majorities.[15] While the strategy proved effective for the SPD,

---

[13] The SPD obtained 29.2 per cent of the vote in the federal elections of 1949, 31.8 per cent in 1957, 36.2 per cent in 1961, 39.3 per cent in 1965 and 42.7 per cent in 1969.
[14] See Donald Sassoon, *One Hundred Years of Socialism*, revised edition (London: I. B. Tauris, 2010), 249.
[15] See Otto Kirchheimer, 'The transformation of the Western European party system', in Joseph LaPalombara and Myron Weiner (eds.), *Political Parties and Political Development* (Princeton: Princeton University Press, 1966), 177–200.

whose vote increased from 31.8 per cent in 1957 to 42.7 per cent in 1969, it also created discontent with the compromises of the electoral democracy and proclaimed 'end of ideology'.

The presence of a small but symbolically important neo-fascist Right, concerns of deficient democratisation, as well as the search for legitimacy and the exercise of power by a socialist Left, also characterised Italian national politics in the 1960s. In Italy, however, neo-fascism existed as an electoral force well before the Sixties. Founded by former Fascists in 1947, the Italian Social Movement (*Movimento Sociale Italiano*, MSI) had already achieved more than 5 per cent of the vote in the mid 1950s. Resentful of international criticism of the success of the NPD a decade later, the West German journalist Dieter Gütt complained 'it is repugnant, that every second Italian newspaper behaves like Garibaldi's household rag towards us, while they have long tolerated the neo-fascists in Rome'.[16] The MSI's vote hovered consistently around the 5 per cent mark in the 1960s (and, indeed, until the end of the Cold War), with a high of 8.7 per cent in 1972. But while the far Right's electoral impact did not expand, the government of Christian Democrat Fernando Tambroni that began in March 1960 only managed to win its initial vote of confidence through reliance on the parliamentary votes of the MSI and the monarchists. The decade of the 1960s thus appeared to herald a new legitimacy to neo-fascist politics. Instead, the provocative choice of the MSI to hold its 1960 congress in Genova, a bastion of the anti-fascist Resistance, brought the swift demise of the government. Mass demonstrations and street battles between protesters and police forced the abandonment of the congress. Tambroni's attempt to assert order by authorising police to shoot in emergency situations led to several deaths and a general strike. The Christian Democratic leadership promptly procured his resignation. Instead of relying on support from the far-Right, Italian Christian Democracy began a cagey, cautious opening to the Left.

As in West Germany, the Christian Democrats had held power continuously, in a variety of coalitions, since the return of free elections in 1946. Unlike the Federal Republic, they would remain part of the government until the end of the Cold War and the disintegration of the entire Italian political spectrum in corruption scandals in the early 1990s. The presence of western Europe's largest Communist Party provided the other major contrast to West Germany (where Communism was embodied in an alternative state). The *Partito Comunista Italiano* (PCI) would

---

[16] 'Wer Adolf Will', 34.

unsuccessfully pursue the path of seeking legitimacy in the 1970s that the SPD had in Germany a decade earlier. Instead, the smaller Italian Socialist Party (*Partito Socialista Italiano*, PSI) fulfilled the role of the coalition partner in the early 1960s, first abstaining from voting against the reformist Christian Democrat Amintore Fanfani in 1962 and then entering government alongside the Christian Democrats in the Prime Ministership of Aldo Moro in December 1963. This was already too great a compromise for a significant minority of the party, which broke off to form the Socialist Party of Proletarian Unity (*Partito Socialista Italiano di Unità Proletaria*, PSIUP). The centre-left governments of Italy in no way presaged a future left-liberal coalition as it did in West Germany. The Italian Socialists always held a weaker position in the Italian political scene than the SPD, one that deteriorated with the formation of PSIUP. The failure to achieve any significant reforms only further discredited the tactics of parliamentary coalition building and the parties involved in them.

The centre-left coalition's scant results left unfulfilled the democratic impetus from the popular rejection of a government reliant on neo-fascist support in 1960. The democratisation of Italian society implicit in the new Constitution promulgated in 1947 remained equally incomplete. As the philosopher Norberto Bobbio wistfully noted, Italy had not become the country dreamed of during the Resistance to Nazi-Fascism.[17] Others pointed to the 'conflict between the democratic Constitution and the considerable amount of legislation of fascist mark'.[18] To moderate critics in the mid-1960s, the persistence of neo-fascism merely highlighted the widespread authoritarianism in the institutions of the state. In 1966, a scandal broke over the detailed files maintained by the military's secret service (*Servizio Informazioni Forze Armate*, SIFAR) on leading politicians. The following year, the radical weekly *Espresso* claimed that General Giovanni de Lorenzo (once head of SIFAR, by 1967 Chief of Staff of the Army) planned a coup d'état at the moment when the Socialists were about to enter government. Whether 'Plan Solo' was an unsuccessful coup d'état along the lines of the colonels' seizure of power in Greece in 1967 or merely a more limited and successful cowing of the Socialists, the scandals reinforced the sense of shallowness to Italian democracy.[19] Democratisation remained a project, not an accomplishment. The problems of Italian

---

[17] Norberto Bobbio, 'Resistenza incompiuta', *Resistenza, Giustizia e Libertà* 20.3 (1966), 1.
[18] Mario A. Cattaneo, 'S'ispira a principi autoritari la nuova legge di polizia', *Resistenza, Giustizia e Libertà* 21.8 (1967), 1.
[19] For a recent analysis, see Mimmo Franzinelli, *Il Piano Solo: I servizi segreti, il centro-sinistra e il 'golpe' del 1964* (Milan: Mondadori, 2010).

society appeared to be not the 'flaws of an imperfect democracy but the indisputable proof that democracy is distant because there is no interest in realising it'.[20] The historian Nicola Tranfaglia questioned how 'a democratic order was realisable in a society dominated by authoritarianism in its major institutions'.[21] The contrast between the formal trappings of democracy – elections, parliament, multiple political parties – and its substantive content led to a focus on democratisation from below, 'not merely at the level of political representation, but in the principal human institutions, in the factory, in the school, in the formation of public opinion'.[22] As in West Germany, desires and dreams of greater democracy searched for expression beyond elections and political parties.

French politics differed from West German and Italian. Despite its roots in French history, the fascist Vichy regime was the product of military defeat and lasted nowhere near as long as the neighbouring dictatorships. Democratisation did not appear as a historical task imposed by the experience of fascism. But authoritarianism and paternalism were deeply rooted in French politics of the 1960s. Unlike the other two states, France also remained a major imperial power and the crises of its postwar politics stemmed from its colonial wars in Vietnam and Algeria.[23] In 1958, the French military and right-wing settlers in Algeria, increasingly worried about the will of the French parliament to repress Algerian nationalism, carried out a coup d'état in Algiers, demanding the appointment of Charles de Gaulle to form a government in Paris. Neither condemning nor condoning the military coup, de Gaulle declared himself willing to assume power, to rescue a France 'in the grip of problems too severe to be solved by the regime of the parties'.[24] The French Communist Party (*Parti communiste française*, PCF) offered the only solid opposition to his investiture, organising a demonstration of half a million in Paris, while Corsica submitted to military control and paratroopers prepared the seizure of Paris. Placed between military insurrection and Communist militancy, most French politicians scurried to the ostensibly legal assumption of power by de Gaulle. The socialist Guy Mollet perceived the choice as

---

[20] Cesare Mannucci, 'Università e "vera" democrazia', *Resistenza, Giustizia e Libertà* 22.2 (1968), 1.
[21] Nicola Tranfaglia, 'Le ragioni d'una lotta', *Resistenza, Giustizia e Libertà* 21.12 (1967), 1.
[22] Ibid.
[23] On the importance of Algeria to May 68, see Kristen Ross, *May 68 and its Afterlives* (Chicago: University of Chicago Press, 2002). For Vietnam, see Salar Mohandesi, 'Bringing Vietnam home: The Vietnam War, internationalism and May '68', *French Historical Studies* 41.2 (2018), 219–251.
[24] Jean Lacouture, *De Gaulle. The Ruler, 1945–1970*, trans. Alan Sheridan (New York: W. W. Norton, 1991), 169. On De Gaulle, see Julian Jackson, *A Certain Idea of France: The Life of Charles De Gaulle* (London: Allen Lane, 2018).

one between 'a de Gaulle government or a colonels' *pronunciamento*'.²⁵ Despite some hesitancy parliamentary democracy in France ceded its power to de Gaulle, whose accession won acclamation by 80 per cent of the electorate. The compromises of parliamentary politics and incompetence of political parties thus appeared already to have provided an authoritarian solution in the first presidential regime in France since the 1848 election of Louis-Napoléon Bonaparte.

In France, therefore, authoritarianism appeared not as the legacy of an unmastered fascist past but the embodiment of a modernising, technocratic government, incarnated in the figure of the French Resistance, Charles de Gaulle. Parliamentary politics receded in the face of plebiscitary presidentialism. De Gaulle tended to view himself as France, presented himself as above politics and parties, and disdained to campaign in elections. The outlook for the Left appeared bleak. The French Communist Party remained in an electoral ghetto. The entry of socialist parties into power-sharing arrangements in the 1960s in West Germany and Italy raised as many hopes for reform as they did fears of compromise and failure. But in France, the Socialists (*Section française de l'Internationale ouvrière*, SFIO) had enjoyed a share of power in the 1950s, executing a miserable and disastrous policy over Algeria that split the party and created the breakaway Unified Socialist Party (*Parti socialiste unifié*, PSU). The SFIO then wavered between opposing and participating in the governments of de Gaulle, before its permanent exclusion as an irrelevance. The French Communist Party's opposition to the Gaullist regime was more certain. But the PCF both underestimated de Gaulle and remained a Stalinist party incapable of distancing itself from the Soviet Union. The candidacy of François Mitterrand for the presidency in 1965 forced de Gaulle into a second round, and even necessitated a television appearance by the General, but the prospects for effective expression of opposition to the 'Republican monarchy' appeared slim. Not only had the parties been bypassed, but de Gaulle had effectively appropriated the plebiscite – a tool elsewhere seen as a potential direct democratic alternative to parliamentary representation. In France, however, the referendum operated not to democratically assert the popular will on a single issue but to sanctify the sovereignty of an individual.

---

²⁵ Guy Mollet, letter to a Belgian comrade, 29 May 1958, in Mollet, *13 mai 1958–13 mai 1962* (Paris, Plon, 1962), 10–11, as quoted by Robert Gildea, *The Past in French History* (New Haven: Yale University Press, 1994), 84.

In all three states, persistent fears of latent (or not-so-latent) authoritarianism, disappointed hopes for democratisation and disillusion with the compromises made by Left-wing parties under the conventions of electoral democracy created a potent matrix for a new politics. Yet in none of these states did the traditional student organisations prove capable of expressing these fears and desires. In each state, the student organisations found their attempts to express a democratic and radical politics suppressed by party hierarchies and government. By the late 1960s, this reaction rendered them irrelevant other than as training grounds for future politicians. The result was that the potential for mass mobilisation lay submerged beneath the appearance of apolitical apathy. The decline of student organisations narrowed the space for expression of youth politics. When politics suddenly re-emerged, it bore the marks of this rejection.

West Berlin: The Rise of SDS

The compromises of parliamentary politics, the ominous if liminal presence of the far Right, and stalled democratisation that characterised West German federal politics created a potent political mix at the local, university level. The path to political power of the SPD influenced most the trajectory of the German Socialist Student League (*Sozialistische Deutsche Studentenbund*, SDS) that formed the core of the West German student movement. Although SDS always enjoyed a formal autonomy from the Social Democratic Party, prior to the Sixties it was 'a student association that conformed to the SPD, with opportunities to rise in the party apparatus'.[26] In the late 1950s, SDS and the SPD campaigned together against arming the West German military with tactical nuclear weapons, which Chancellor Konrad Adenauer had infamously referred to as 'nothing more than the further development of artillery'.[27] Yet whereas the SPD abandoned its opposition when faced with defeat in parliament and in the Federal Constitutional Court (which declared unconstitutional the local referenda on nuclear armament promoted by the SPD), SDS refused to compromise, or in its own words, 'to suppress for reasons of opportunism

---

[26] Tilman Fichter and Siegward Lönnendonker, *Kleine Geschichte des SDS: Der Sozialistische Deutsche Studentenbund von 1946 bis zur Selbstauflösung* (Berlin: Rotbuch Verlag, 1977), 14–15.
[27] Cited in Andreas Altenhoff, 'Bunte Chronik der Fünfziger', in Dieter Bänsch (ed.), *Die Fünfziger Jahre. Beiträge zu Politik und Kultur* (Tübingen: Gunter Narr, 1985), 434.

the continuation of the struggle against atomic weapons'.[28] The tension between principle and compromise began to take the form of an opposition between parliamentary party and youth organisation.

The failed experiment with referenda also shaped the growing divide as one between parliamentary and extra-parliamentary, representative and direct democracy. The Social Democratic Party redirected its energies towards the conquest of political power through parliamentary elections. The reasons for compromise were clear. In the Federal election of 1957, the Christian Democrat and Christian Socialist coalition won an absolute majority of the vote, while in 1958, at the height of the campaign against nuclear weapons, the CDU also won an absolute majority in state elections in Nordrhein-Westfalen, turning out a social-liberal coalition after just two years in power. While SDS moved with the rest of the *Kampf dem Atomtod* ('Against Atomic Death') movement into the Easter marches of the early 1960s, the SPD boycotted them. The SDS became defined by its resistance to the compromises of electoral strategy.

The Nazi past and the recognition of the Oder-Neiße line created further friction.[29] On the latter issue, the SPD prevailed upon SDS to expel the left-wing *konkret* faction that most vigorously promoted the recognition of Poland's postwar western border. However, in the debate over the 'Ungesühnte Nazijustiz' ('Unexpiated Nazi-Justice') exhibition that highlighted the National Socialist judicial activity of judges in the Federal Republic (using copies of documents from Czechoslovak and Polish archives), the party leadership could not force SDS to abandon the project entirely. When, in November 1959, the SPD adopted the Godesberg Program, SDS did not follow suit. The following February, the SPD announced it would support organisations other than SDS should they recognise the new Party Program. The Social-Democratic University Union (*Sozialdemokratische Hochschulbund*, SHB) rapidly emerged as a rival to the right of SDS. Then, in November 1961, the SPD ruled that membership in SDS was incompatible with membership in the SPD. While the SPD addended no reasons to the *Unvereinbarkeitsbeschluß*, the divergences had continued to multiply. One student testified that 'it played a large role in the Berlin situation ... that at that time SDS

---

[28] As quoted in Willy Albrecht, '"Unter den Talaren ..." Studentenbewegung und Sozialdemokratie bis 1968', in Dieter Dowe (ed.), *Partei und soziale Bewegung: Kritische Beiträge zur Entwicklung der SPD seit 1945* (Bonn: Verlag J. H. W. Dietz Nachf, 1993), 64.

[29] The West German government only recognised the Oder-Neisse line in December 1970 under the Left-liberal coalition of Willy Brandt.

organised a demonstration and documentation against the Algerian War'.[30] Despite its prominence in the late Sixties, SDS began the decade threatened with extinction. Deprived of a significant source of funds and its members facing expulsion from the party, the student organisation appeared destined to disappear. Indeed, one SDS member recalled, 'we had all decided, should the *Unvereinbarkeitsbeschluß* come, to stay in the SPD, to dissolve SDS and give it up. Only we didn't ...'[31] SDS would indeed disband itself, but not until 1970. The SPD action did not destroy the student organisation, but rather transformed it.

SDS now exploited the autonomy from the Social Democratic Party it had always formally enjoyed. For the decade after Godesberg, while the SPD first sought to establish its electoral viability, then (from December 1966) to demonstrate its responsibility in governing through the Grand Coalition, before reaching its goal in a left-liberal coalition from October 1969, SDS occupied the space of radical opposition. Ever since the German Communist Party had been banned by the Federal Constitutional Court in 1956, those who would have entered that party's student organisation had found a place in the left wing of SDS. However, despite its perceived radicalism, in the late 1950s the student organisation was, at least in West Berlin, as one of its members recalled, 'a rather sedate association'.[32] 'A Marxist academic debating club', Bernd Rabehl described SDS at the moment in which he, Rudi Dutschke and other members of the anti-authoritarian group 'Subversive Aktion' joined it in 1965, although one 'open to diverse aspects of theoretical and political discussion'.[33] Set adrift from the SPD, SDS now became even more attractive for other parts of the radical Left critical of the social democratic tradition. The *Unvereinbarkeitsbeschluß* hardened the distinction between the SPD and SDS over practical and principled, parliamentary and extra-parliamentary politics, compromise and rigor, careerism and activism. While the SPD sought power, SDS pursued the role of theoretical avant-garde. In November 1963, the new head of SDS defined it 'as the organisation of young socialist intelligentsia', in a clear 'break with the hitherto self-understanding of the association as a part of the social democratic workers' movement led by the SPD'.[34] Four years after SDS's expulsion from the SPD, the student organisation housed a pluralist

---

[30] Siegward Lönnendonker, *Linksintellektueller Aufbruch zwischen 'Kulturrevolution' und 'kultureller Zerstörung'. Der Sozialistische Deutsche Studentenbund (SDS) in der Nachkriegsgeschichte (1946–1969). Dokumentation eines Symposiums* (Wiesbaden: Westdeutscher Verlag, 1998), 77.
[31] Ibid., 78.   [32] Ibid., 146.   [33] Ibid., 40.
[34] Fichter and Lönnendonker, *Kleine Geschichte*, 76.

radical Left in which traditional socialists, various Marxisms, anarchists and anti-authoritarians commingled.

SDS embodied a particular dissatisfaction with electoral democracy and an ongoing search for alternatives. In the early 1960s, students in SDS authored a treatise on the role of the university in democracy, published in 1965 as *Hochschule in der Demokratie* with an introduction by Jürgen Habermas. Already at the beginning of the decade, the organisation demanded a conceptualisation of democracy 'not satisfied with the current reduction of the concept to the political methods and formal apparatus of majority decisions and periodic rotation of office, but the social preconditions of the construction of a rational political will via the medium of free public discussion and information'.[35] Democratisation of the university demanded the 'minimisation of authority'.[36] The analysis elaborated early in the decade served as an ongoing basis for projects of democratisation within the university.

However, much of the charge to the politics of SDS in the mid-1960s came not from the old guard that had studiously developed their theses on education in democracy but the provocative tactics of Situationist-inspired students such as Rudi Dutschke and Bernd Rabehl. Those groups debated 'whether the parliamentary system and its public sphere was only the façade of a subtle form of dictatorship or whether remnants of a democratic public sphere existed in the parties and press',[37] and sought through provocation to either increase awareness of the dictatorial nature of contemporary society or expose its contradictions. While scepticism about the possibilities of democratisation increased with the politicisation of the protest movement, the tensions between the tactics of provocation and the ideal of a rational will constructed through open debate initially proved productive. Despite reservations of many in SDS, provocation proved particularly appropriate for an organisation marginalised by the politics of majority decisions.

Members of SDS shared the self-consciousness of an orphaned association representing a political minority. One student remembered how 'in the Fifties the Left remained ... inside the whole student body an isolated fringe group. In my opinion this minority position clarifies the behaviour of the SDS at the end of the Sixties. We always had the consciousness of

---

[35] Wolfgang Nitsch, Uta Gerhardt, Claus Offe and Ulrich K. Preuß, *Hochschule in der Demokratie* (New York: Arno Press, 1977), 102.
[36] Ibid.
[37] Bernd Rabehl, *Am Ende der Utopie: Die politische Geschichte der Freien Universität Berlin* (Berlin: Argon Verlag, 1988), 197–198.

being a minority, and this even still at a time, when we had long become the majority.'³⁸ Left-wing students felt only too aware of the widespread conservative disposition that had impelled the SPD towards the political centre. Indeed, the decade had begun with the publication of Jürgen Habermas' *Student und Politik: Eine soziologische Untersuchung zum politischen Bewußtsein Frankfurter Studenten*, in which only 30 per cent of students at Frankfurt were classified as democratic, while 39 per cent were perceived as formally democratic, 22 per cent as authoritarian and 9 per cent as indifferent.³⁹ Knut Nevermann, the leader of the student body at the Free University of Berlin in 1966, described the historical task of democratisation, compelled by the historical burden of student Nazism and left unfinished after 1945:

> The student representation of the Free University has sought for a long time to draw the (according to empirical investigations) for the most part politically disinterested students out of their system-stabilising lethargy. This task is determined on the one hand by the historical findings about German fascism, in particular the fact that not only the professors, but also the students fell early for National Socialism and paved its way; on the other hand, by the evaluation of the Federal Republic, the reactionary development of which has led to the repression of those postwar impulses which wanted to assemble and develop a social and democratic constitutional state.⁴⁰

Nevermann belonged not to SDS but its rival the SHB, created to more faithfully follow the SPD party-line, but whose political positions gradually converged with SDS despite the attempts of Social Democratic politicians to hinder its radicalisation, or at least its public expression. A mere five years after its creation, the SHB espoused precisely the views on the Godesberg Program that provoked the SPD to enforce the *Unvereinbarkeitsbeschluß* with SDS.⁴¹ Unexpectedly and suddenly, the university emerged as the site for a Left-wing politics abandoned at the federal level. The SDS, loosed from the control of a political hierarchy and largely disinterested

---

³⁸ Tilman Fichter, 'Vom linken Offiziersbund zur Revolte: Vier SDS-Generationen', in Jürgen Seifert, Heinz Thörmer and Klaus Wettig (eds.), *Soziale oder sozialistische Demokratie? Beiträge zur Geschichte der Linken in der Bundesrepublik. Freundesgabe für Peter von Oertzen zum 65. Geburtstag* (Marburg: SP-Verlag, 1989), 18.
³⁹ Jürgen Habermas et al., *Student und Politik: Eine soziologische Untersuchung zum politischen Bewußtsein Frankfurter Studenten* (Neuwied: Luchterhand Verlag, 1961), 147.
⁴⁰ Knut Nevermann, 'Politik und demokratische Reform', *FU Spiegel* 54 (1966), 3.
⁴¹ See Hartmut Häußermann, 'Das Berliner Milieu und die Stadtforschung', in Heinz Bude and Martin Kohli (eds.), *Radikalisierte Aufklärung: Studentenbewegung und Soziologie in Berlin 1965 bis 1970* (Weinheim: Juventa Verlag, 1989), 43–70, 50. The SHB called for a recognition of the Oder-Neiße line in the summer of 1964.

in electoral politics, was best placed to mobilise the leftward-moving student body.

The transformation of SDS reveals a set of typical features for the incubation of student revolt. Disavowed by the powerful party hierarchy, financially constrained, its organisational monopoly broken by the advent of a tame rival organisation, SDS was effectively marginalised. In other historical circumstances, extinction may have quickly followed. But in the Sixties there existed a reservoir of democratic aspirations to tap, an ever-expanding student body to mobilise, and in the university an institution much less adept than political parties at smothering dissent. Instead of extinction, the distance from electoral politics and party hierarchies allowed SDS to pursue a politics of principle unhindered by consideration of political 'realism'. Lack of accountability to any hierarchy further created the opportunity for a politics of provocation. The convergence of multiple ideological currents within SDS forced the more traditional members to embrace (somewhat reluctantly) a politics of provocation alongside their attachment to the politics of public reason. Despite, or rather because, of its minority status, SDS stood positioned both to provoke and capture the moment of mass mobilisation.

France: UNEF in the Wake of Algeria

The exclusion of SDS from the Social Democratic Party occurred over highly charged symbolic issues: the Nazi Past, the Oder-Neiße Line, nuclear weapons, the abandonment of Marxism in the Godesberg Program, and the charge that on these issues SDS did '*das Geschäft Pankows* [the business of the Communist East Germany]'. In France, the trouble was Algeria. The response of the National Union of French Students (*Union nationale des étudiants de France*, UNEF) to the Algerian war marked both its triumph and the start of its decline. Unlike SDS (an explicitly political organisation), UNEF was a student union. In a slow and halting engagement, first the leadership, then the union as a whole, shifted from an apolitical to a politically progressive position on the Algerian War (all the while condemning torture). At its April 1960 Congress, UNEF called for 'negotiations with the National Liberation Front on the basis of a ceasefire and guarantees of self-determination'.[42] The restoration of

---

[42] As quoted in Alain Monchablon, *Histoire de l'UNEF de 1956 à 1968*, (Paris: Presses Universitaires de France, 1983), 109. In part, the radicalisation over Algeria was directly linked to the possibility of being called up to the army.

relations with the Union of Algerian Muslim Students (*Union générale des Etudiants musulmans algériens*), broken off in 1956 after the latter demanded UNEF take a position on the war, soon followed. The political impact of the stance was all the greater as UNEF represented the entire French student body. At the beginning of 1960 the union had reached a record number of members, with one student in two enrolled in the organisation.[43]

The Algerian campaign culminated in the first major demonstration against the war, called by UNEF on 27 October 1960. The protest united the two major unions, the CFDT (*Confédération française des travailleurs chrétiens*) and the FEN (*Fédération de l'Education nationale*) but, unable to overcome its hesitancy, not the Communist CGT (*Confédération générale du travail*). This success momentarily placed the student union in the political vanguard on Algeria, and far in advance of the PCF. The prominence of UNEF demonstrated the failure of the French Left. The socialists were unable to emerge from the mire of their abysmal Algerian policy, and the Communists were too timid to contradict the nationalism of their own voters. However, the students struggled to maintain the achievements of October 1960. Having alienated the CGT, UNEF had little chance of again playing the role of organiser and arbiter between unions. The government retaliated by withholding UNEF's funding. In June the following year the National Federation of French Students (*Fédération nationale des étudiants de France*, FNEF) emerged from the faculties of medicine. FNEF took the state financial support and despite remaining small in size, stripped UNEF of its monopoly on student representation.

As in West Germany, the political activism of a student organisation – in this case, UNEF – brought retribution in the form of financial sanctions and political isolation. The repercussions for UNEF's activism reflected not just Gaullist paternalism and authoritarianism. The crisis of hierarchy extended across the political spectrum and was particularly apparent on the Left. At the height of UNEF's influence and success, in the protest over the Algerian war, the Catholic student organisation, the Christian Student Youth (*Jeunesse Étudiante Chrétienne*, JEC), formed the core of its leadership. However, the political activity of the JEC, whether about Algeria or university reform, brought it into conflict with the hierarchy of the Catholic Church, who pressured the student leadership to abandon its political engagement. In Catholicism, as in other social spheres, 'the crisis

[43] Ibid., 102.

of authority ... precedes 1968'.[44] For the Catholic Church, 'the activity of the JEC occurs in close connection with the Church hierarchy ... its purpose is not the same as those of unions and political parties', insisting that 'the JEC, as a movement of Catholic Action, will refrain from any political or syndical position'.[45] The Church explicitly welcomed the individual political engagement of Catholic students, but not of the organisation as a whole. Confronted by this choice, the JEC leadership tendered their resignations. In parting, they questioned whether 'the Church will conserve so decisively its links with the bourgeoisie, confusing the purity of the Gospels with the safeguarding of interests to be defended or whether it will have the audacity to become the Church of the poor'.[46] The resignees immediately formed a new organisation, the Christian University Youth (*Jeunesse Universitaire Chrétienne*, JUC). By 1967 the JEC had no presence at the university level, being an association almost exclusively of secondary school and vocational education students. The failed student demand for greater autonomy meant a diminished presence of both the hierarchy's approved association and its independent rival.

Institutional fission and the diffusion of political energies also characterised the Communist Left. In the reflux from the mobilisation over Algeria, and the passing of that generation of students, UNEF moved leftward and the Union of Communist Students (*Union des étudiants communistes*, UEC) became its animating force.[47] The most visible manifestation of the turn was the deployment of Marxist theory. One delegate complained that 'one cannot follow the debates in the congress unless one's read *Capital* ...'[48] Theorising the student as a 'young worker in training', the UEC sought to mobilise students to contest their work conditions.

---

[44] On the long crisis of the Catholic youth in France, see Denis Pelletier, *La crise catholique: religion, société, politique en France (1965–1978)* (Paris, Editions Payot & Rivages, 2002), 73–75, 75; Grégory Barrau, *Le mai 68 des catholiques* (Paris: L'Atelier, 1988); Denis Pelletier, 'Catholiques français de gauche et d'extrême gauche à l'épreuve du "moment 68"' *Histoire@Politique* 30.3 (2016), 114–127. For a wider perspective, see the rest of the dossier and Gerd-Rainer Horn, *The Spirit of Vatican II: Western European Progressive Catholicism in the Long Sixties* (Oxford: Oxford University Press, 2015).

[45] As quoted by Massimo Olmi, 'La crisi della "Jeunesse Étudiante Chrétienne" di Francia', *Humanitas* 20 (1965), 537.

[46] Olmi, 'La crisi della "Jeunesse Étudiante Chrétienne"', 540.

[47] On the UEC, see Frédérique Matonti and Bernard Pudal, 'L'UEC ou l'autonomie confisquée (1956–1968)', in Dominique Damamme et al., *Mai–Juin 68* (Paris: Editions de l'Atelier, 2008), 130–143.

[48] *Le monde* 2/4/1964, as quoted in Daniel Baggioni, 'Le discours syndical étudiant (1962–1967)', in Bernard Gardin, Daneil Baggioni and Louis Guespin, *Pratiques linguistiques, pratiques sociales* (Paris: Presses Universitaires de France, 1980), 84.

Emphasising the increasing importance of the university in a technocratic society, the student body could be ranked amongst the revolutionary forces. Yet, while dominating the debates at annual congresses, and often providing the only proposals for discussion, the Communist UEC never commanded the whole of UNEF. Its bastion remained the Sorbonne, where its most spectacular action also marked its peak.

Taking advantage of an official visit by the Italian President Antonio Segni to the Sorbonne in April 1964, the UEC-controlled local UNEF bureau announced five demands – 'the doubling of the number of assistants, the tripling of the number of classes in the format of small seminars, the creation of a photocopy centre, official recognition of the union in the Faculty, the opening of negotiations on study grants' – and threatened to occupy the building and bar access if unsatisfied.[49] In the event, the occupation was abandoned, under pressure from the national bureau of UNEF, just before the police entered to clear the premises. The recourse to tactics of direct action, in this instance an occupation, petered out in the face of pressure from the union hierarchy. Amid a massive police presence in the Latin Quarter, Segni visited an empty Sorbonne. One student was arrested and sentenced to eight days of prison for having knocked off a policeman's képi, eliciting large demonstrations of solidarity from the student body. But having failed to negotiate and then having aborted the occupation, the students had dared simultaneously too much and too little. Not only was their theoretical sophistication and Marxist ideology ever more at odds with the vast majority of students for whom, as one president had noted, UNEF 'is the canteen',[50] the UEC was itself split into hostile camps. The French Communist Party, smarting from the independence shown by the UEC when it supported UNEF's stance on the Algerian war, excluded the moderate 'Italian' Communists who dared call for the formal independence of the UEC from the PCF in 1965. The Trotskyists (who had colluded in the exclusion of the 'Italians') followed later in the same year, with the Maoists (seemingly victors of the prior two operations) exiting in 1966.[51] As had occurred with the SPD in West Germany and the Catholic Church in France, so too in the Communist Party a schism between party hierarchy and independent-minded student organisations left an increasing number of student activists consigned to

---

[49] Monchablon, *Histoire de l'UNEF*, 156. [50] Ibid., 201.
[51] See Didier Fischer, *L'histoire des étudiants en France de 1945 à nos jours* (Paris: Flammarion, 2000), 317–321, or, for a perspective from the later JCR: Daniel Bensaïd, and Henri Weber, *Mai 68: une répétition générale* (Paris: Maspero, 1968), 38–50.

the dustbin of university politics, neither beholden to the greater party nor capable of wielding its influence.

Compared to the SPD's botched exclusion of SDS from its patronage, French parties and hierarchies appeared very successful in rendering impotent the recalcitrant members of their youth organisations. Small political sects – *groupuscules* – proliferated. The *Jeunesse Universitaire Chrétienne* regrouped those who had left the JEC. The Trotskyist Revolutionary Communist Youth (*Jeunesse communiste révolutionnaire*, JCR), founded in 1966 and most influenced by the Belgian Ernest Mandel, competed with the more literal and dogmatic 'Lambertist' Trotskyist Liaison Committee of Revolutionary Students (*Comité de liaison des étudiants révolutionnaires*, CLER), founded in 1961.[52] Maoists made their debut in the Union of Marxist-Leninist Communist Youth (*Union des jeunesses communistes marxistes-léninistes*, UJCml), founded in 1966. All the while, the UEC continued, weak in numbers but loyal to the PCF. After the implosion of the UEC, a more moderate UNEF gained little traction against a hostile government that had opened a new faculty at Nanterre, postponed some of its reforms and poured more money into the university system. UNEF declined steadily in size, funding and effectiveness. From 809 delegates at its 1961 congress (when the student body was just over 200,000), the 1968 congress attracted a mere 170 despite student numbers more than doubling in the interim. In this context, the union decided to let go its typists come May 1968. They concluded no successful political struggle was imminent.

Despite the major differences between West Germany and France, a very similar decline and disintegration of youth politics marked the two states. Political and financial pressure from party or church hierarchy, the expulsion of insubordinate factions and individuals, and the creation of docile rival organisations characterised both situations. If anything, such operations proved more successful in France than West Germany. There existed in France no single organisation such as SDS, which housed multiple ideological currents. UNEF was a shadow of its former self, while the *groupuscules* remained isolated, more interested in asserting their ideological differences than engaging with each other. It was instead the campus of Nanterre that played the role no single organisation could accomplish. At Nanterre, the success of UNEF's Algerian struggle 'existed

---

[52] On JCR politics, see Mohandesi, 'Bringing Vietnam home', 219–251.

only by hearsay'.[53] While the Nanterre chapter initially gathered a higher number of members than elsewhere, it rapidly stagnated. The *groupuscules* dominated the political scene. Elsewhere, this entrenched their irrelevance. But at Nanterre, the campus forced together the various political groups, in the need to combine to fight off occasional attacks from the right-wing Occident group,[54] and simply in the sense of belonging to the new university: 'what was specific to Nanterre, was the *feeling of belonging*. One might well be JCR, anarchist or militant in the Vietnam Base Committees . . . one is furthermore *from* Nanterre'. In France, the campus of Nanterre served the function that SDS fulfilled in West Berlin. UNEF might be 'atypical, bloodless if envisaged as a union, but relatively large as a site of confrontation between ideologies and political strategies'.[55] Whereas SDS could harness the revolt in West Germany, in France, the campus of Nanterre brought together the disparate pieces of student activism to forge an entirely new movement.

Italy: The Crisis of UNURI

Italian student politics featured neither *groupuscules* nor a single organisation such as SDS poised to collect the fruits of discontent. The Italian Communist Party was not as authoritarian as its French counterpart, nor did it feel compelled to exclude radicals to consecrate its electoral legitimacy as did the SPD. Nonetheless, the same disappointment with national politics and the repression of any attempt at autonomy from youth organisations marked the Italian scene. As in France, the major student organisation in Italy, the National Representative University Union (*Unione nazionale universitaria rappresentativa*, UNURI), entered the late 1960s already in deep crisis, incapable of imposing itself in the perennial question of university reform and stifled by a political system characterised above all by immobilism. UNURI, unlike UNEF, was not a union, but rather a parliament in which all local Italian associations were represented. Indeed, its transformation into a student union along the lines of UNEF was one proposed solution to its 'crisis'. However, the parliamentary model proved no more capable than student union in escaping the confines of national politics.

---

[53] Jean-Pierre Duteuil, *Nanterre, 1965–66–67–68. Vers le movement du 22 mars* (Paris: Acratie, 1988), 14.
[54] Which in the Latin Quarter occurred in ritualised encounters in precise locations not involving the majority of the student population.
[55] Duteuil, *Nanterre*, 22.

Youth organisations in France and West Germany found themselves punished for agendas that contradicted those of their national hierarchies. In Italy, the failure of reform within UNURI directly reflected the breakdown in national politics. The two major associations were the Catholic University Accord (*Intesa Universitaria Cattolica*) and the Italian Student Union (*Unione goliardica italiana*, UGI). These represented respectively the Catholic and left-wing students. Until the 1960s, the presence of the Communists in the left-wing UGI hampered the development of any progressive platform. However, after the December 1963 advent of the centre-left in the national parliament, so too inside UNURI, a joint Catholic–Left-wing program attempted to engage the problems of the university with a reformist agenda. In contrast to the isolation of the Communists at the national level, the shared executive of UNURI included a single Communist representative. In its first statement, the Intesa–UGI committee declared necessary a 'profound renewal of the structures of university representation' to create 'the movement of the mass of university students through new and more advanced forms of democracy'.[56] The program of the shared council (*giunta*) included the democratisation of the university with students' participation in all areas from administration to teaching and research, and a long-term plan for the realisation of the right to study. This program was nonetheless publicly rejected by the major Catholic organisations, not for the content of the proposed program, but the alliance with UGI, perceived as the instrument of the Italian Communist Party.[57] UNURI's opposition to the proposed university reform (the Piano Gui), had some success mobilising students, with large demonstrations in 1964 and 1965, although all to no avail. As in France and West Germany, the traditional institutions of student representation promoted a politics of democratisation and reform but failed to find effective means to realise that program.

The search for autonomy for youth organisations held particular importance for the Catholic student organisation Intesa. For while the left-wing students grouped in UGI could align themselves with the Communist Party, the Socialist Party or the PSIUP, there existed just one political party of Catholic orientation. Intesa included the young Christian

---

[56] Giovanni Orsina, 'Universitari, partiti e politica dal dopoguerra al 1968', in Gaetano Quagliariello (ed.), *La politica dei giovani in Italia: 1945–1968* (Rome: Libera Università Internazionale degli Studi Sociali Press, 2005), 175–218, 210.

[57] Such as FUCI, the *Federazione universitaria cattolica italiana*. Note here the difference between FUCI and Intesa. See also Roberto D'Agostino, Mario Natali and Giorgio Sarto, 'La Giunta Intesa-U.G.I. all' U. N. U. R. I. e le associazioni universitarie cattoliche', *Questitalia* 8 (1965), 7–30.

Democrats, but it was not the youth organisation of the DC. In 1961, it formally affirmed its autonomy from the Catholic youth organisations that founded it. This reflected broader trends within Catholicism. When Trento's new bishop, Alessandro Maria Gottardi, arrived in 1963 from Venice (where he had been pro-vicar to Giuseppe Roncalli, later Pope John XXIII), one of his first actions was to sell the shares of the local newspaper *L'Adige*, owned by the Curia but run by the Christian Democrats, to the Christian Democratic Party. The new bishop thereby demarcated more clearly the autonomy of the Catholic Church from the political party. The Neapolitan student Paolo Sorbi drew the consequences in 1963 for his fellow Catholics at Trento:

> From 1955 on, events like the Hungarian revolution, de-Stalinisation and, gradually, the politics of peace and international détente developed by the two great powers and the openness of spirit at a global level of Pope John [XXIII] gave many Catholics the possibility to detach themselves from the D.C. [the Christian Democratic Party].[58]

As early as 1963, the Catholic students clearly posed the question 'why there still exists only one Catholic political party in Italy today'.[59] Even the most moderate assertion of autonomy thus brought into question both the political monopoly of the Christian Democratic Party over Catholics and its permanent monopolisation of power. However much the assertion of autonomy, and the desire to escape Cold War political alignments, appeared consonant with other changes within Catholicism in the 1960s, collaboration with left-wing students failed within UNURI, as it did at the national level.

The local remained the last outlet for aspirations of an autonomous, democratic politics. Trento served a similar function in Italy to the campus of Nanterre in France. The novelty of the institution meant that the local student associations adopted from the outset the most progressive ideals of their respective national associations. The small size of the institute and the shared interest in sociology also fostered collaboration beyond the usual political divisions. The perceived 'modernity' of sociology ensured that students sought in the institute a more progressive form of student politics. As happened in France, the conflict dissolved the existing organisations and created its own. SDS thus remained the exception to the rule of student mobilisation in the late 1960s – a pre-existing organisation that

---

[58] CMR B.4 f.5 (Fondo Movimento Studentesco Riccardo Scartezzini): Paolo Sorbi, 'Sulla unità politica dei cattolici', *Ut Vivat* (Natale 1963), 10–11, 10.
[59] Ibid.

managed to capture rather than be by-passed by the revolt. However, the contradictory impulses of the revolt would mean that it too could not help but ultimately find itself overwhelmed.

In all three states, disappointment with the national politics of democracy raised profound political aspirations both in national politics and in the sector of higher education. Invariably, student and youth organisations sought to practice a politics autonomous from their party or church hierarchies to fulfil these aspirations. The most common experience, however, was repression and marginalisation. Democratisation proved illusory both at the national level and within political parties. Radical students found themselves effectively excluded from the space of national politics while politics within the university appeared relegated to a preoccupation of the tiniest minority, incapable of making even the most minimal impact. There was nothing new or unusual about conflict between youth or student organisations and their parent bodies.[60] Yet the demand for autonomy resonated particularly deeply and widely in the political moment of the mid-1960s as a necessary element of post-war democratisation. Furthermore, the institutions of higher education, already in difficulty due to demographic pressure, proved especially susceptible to the tension between base and hierarchy, autonomy and administrative power. The demands for democracy and self-government, repressed elsewhere, re-emerged, not so much as issues of national politics, but rather as demands made of the university itself.

---

[60] As Morder notes, it was the rule rather than the exception. See Morder, 'Années 1960', 63.

CHAPTER 6

'We Represent Nothing'
The Crisis of Representation

The student movements of the late 1960s emerged amid a deep crisis of representation. This crisis was threefold. First came the failure of national institutions to effectively express desires for democratisation and political change. Representative democracy did not represent, but rather repressed, its troublesome youth organisations. The attempt to practice an autonomous political line by youth and student organisations the early 1960s provoked reprisals from those with political and financial authority. As a result, student politics stagnated. Independence, where it existed, came at the expense of influence. The repression thereby extended the crisis of representation to student and youth organisations themselves. They languished, neither able to effectively represent the student body, nor even representative, as declining numbers sapped their credibility. The failures of student representation proved all the more spectacular because of a third crisis of representation: that of the interests of students within the university itself. Students held almost no institutional power and perceived a lack of autonomy in both their academic studies and political expression within the university. Such a situation took on new meaning when many assumed that a new, mass, 'democratised' university meant a devolution of power within the institution. Suspicion of representative democracy led directly towards the more radical direct democratic aspirations of the occupation and general assembly.

The student movements thus incarnated a double critique of representation: firstly, of the university's repression of student expression, particularly on political issues, and secondly of student organisations' own lack of representativeness. The movements proved most successful challenging the university when they bypassed the traditional forms of student representation. University administrators invariably and unsuccessfully sought to confine the protest to official organs. Even more important than their ability to disconcert and destabilise the university, however, the occupation and assembly provided protesters with an experience of politics that traditional student elections and forms of representation simply could not sustain. They delivered an experience of democratic politics in which the action of students mattered, or at least felt as if they mattered. Participation in occupations and protests indelibly marked the experiences of student protesters in the 1960s. Yet they heralded no utopia of direct democracy but contained their own contradictions and hierarchies. Abolishing traditional forms of representation, the new movements proved susceptible instead to male charismatic authority.

The Berlin Model

The Free University of Berlin boasted a form of student representation to which other movements in West Germany and Europe could only aspire. The 'Berlin Model' included student self-government in many affairs and student representation, including voting rights, on almost all bodies of academic governance including the Board of Regents.[1] Its progressive reputation enticed students from West Germany to the isolated enclave of West Berlin. The Free University boasted a student parliament, *Konvent*, with yearly elections. The *Konvent* then elected a president of an executive steering committee, the *Allgemeiner Studentenausschuß* (AStA) with a legally recognised role in the functioning of the university. The student movement at West Berlin thus began with what for other movements constituted their final goal. For the students at the Free University, however, the Berlin Model merely 'counted as the first step on the path to a democratically oriented university reform'.[2] As a result, the early debate at West Berlin revolved around the constitutional limits of student autonomy rather than the attempt to create it.

Just as many students saw a failure to deliver the promise of democratisation implicit in the immediate postwar period, so too they complained that 'even the first steps for realising the Berlin Model were ever more hollowed out in the unmethodical development of the FU'.[3] One observer described how student parliaments 'suffer from a lack of

---

[1] For a detailed history, see James F. Tent, *The Free University of Berlin: A Political History* (Bloomington and Indianapolis: Indiana University Press, 1988).
[2] Knut Nevermann, 'Zum Selbsverständnis der Studentenvertretung', *Blätter für deutsche und internationale Politik* 12 (1967), 709.
[3] Ibid.

meaningful topics and consequently from lack of interest and participation by the delegates'.[4] Furthermore, despite its institutionally progressive allure, the student body in the late 1950s at the Free University conformed to the conservatism evident in the federal political scene. In December 1959, the right-wing won an absolute majority in *Konvent*, echoing the electoral performance of the conservatives in the Bundestag. But rather than replicating the SPD's march to the centre, the university milieu proved much more amenable to radical politics.

The student body at the Free University demonstrated an aversion to the Right just three years after having elected its conservative parliament. Controversy erupted in December 1962 when the student parliament, the *Konvent*, elected as the head of its executive steering committee (AStA) the law student Eberhard Diepgen, later mayor of Berlin and at that time a member of the Savaria fraternity. The *Korporationen* (fraternities), widely perceived to have been bastions of Nazism, had been banned from the FU until October 1958 when the Courts ruled the prohibition unconstitutional.[5] Put to a referendum in mid-1963, Diepgen's presidency of AStA was rejected and the Konvent that elected him dissolved. The new student parliament marked no radical political shift, retaining a conservative majority. But it demonstrated the limits to right-wing politics in the student body.[6]

The clear rejection of the fraternities contrasted sharply with the federal scene. The same year as the referendum at the FU, the leadership of the Social Democratic Party sent a telegram of greetings for the first time in the postwar era to the yearly congress of the *Korporationen*. While the SPD policed its Left flank by expelling SDS and softened its attitude towards the Right, the students at the Freie Universität refused to accept a member of the *Korporationen* at its head while retaining a firm liberal-conservative orientation. The university itself found its ban on the Union of German Students Berlin-Leipzig (*Verein Deutscher Studenten Berlin-Leipzig*, VDSt) twice overturned by the Constitutional Court of Berlin.[7] The VDSt, a

---

[4] Kurt Sontheimer, 'Student Opposition in Western Germany', *Government and Opposition* 3.1 (1968), 55.
[5] See Tent, *Free University*, 214–218.
[6] On Diepgen and other Christian Democratic students, see Anna von der Goltz, 'Other '68ers in West Berlin: Christian Democratic students and the Cold War city', *Central European History* 50 (2017), 87–112, 97–98.
[7] See APO, FU Allgemein Akademischer Senat 1966–1969, Attachment to 'Protokoll der ordentlichen Senatssitzung am 8. Oktober 1966', 2.

student association that dated to the anti-Jewish agitation in the 1880s and had long maintained nationalist and anti-Semitic views, obtained official recognition in February 1968.

The very different boundaries drawn at federal and local level reflected primarily the difference between representative and direct democracy. The Constitutional Court blocked the recourse to referenda at the federal level, depriving the SPD of any plebiscitary alternative to parliamentary calculations. That option remained (for the moment) at the FU. The success of the referendum in mobilising a constituency to reject the Right suggested the broader student body might not be quite so apathetic as the radical fringe assumed. The widespread diagnosis of a deficient democratisation of society, epitomised in the apathy of university students, found an apparent remedy in the development of new forms of politics. In the case of the Free University, any perceived gap between direct democracy and representation soon closed as, first, *Konvent* elected SDS member Wolfgang Lefèvre its head in 1965 and then the student parliament as a whole shifted to the Left.[8]

The presence of a student parliament with a defined representative role within the university, capable of reflecting shifts in the political orientation of the student body, meant that the debate at the Free University focused on the limits of student self-government. The problem was not new. In 1958, to the disappointment of the AStA, while the Senate allowed a collection for refugee Algerian students, it barred it from occurring in the university lecture halls. The following year, the FU Senate (as had the SPD) distanced itself from the congress against atomic armaments, stressing that the FU had only rented its rooms for the occasion and had no other link to the event. A month later, in February 1959, faced with a request to organise on the FU campus a petition to the Bundestag concerning the Nazi past of some judges (again, an issue on which the SPD and SDS had diverged), the rector and Senate commissioned a special committee to examine the limits of political expression within the university. The committee concluded that 'political open-mindedness and activity of teachers and students as individuals as well as by student groups are to be welcomed and promoted'. However, 'organs of the self-government of the F.U. can only take a position on political questions within the limits of their responsibilities that are part of the responsibilities of the entire

---

[8] In the 1966 Konvent, composed of 78 seats, 46 were won by the Left and 22 by the Right, with 10 representatives having no affiliation.

university'.[9] For the university, the institutionally recognised position of the student body meant an equivalent limitation on the autonomy of that body. The student parliament found itself in a similar position in relation to the university as that of the youth organisations of political parties in their attempts to express themselves politically. The rector further sought to be informed well in advance of any 'political' expression by part of the university.[10]

For the rector and Senate of the Freie Universität the distinction was quite simple: 'The "student body" is a member of the corporation of the university. Its duties and responsibilities cannot therefore exceed the university'.[11] Exceeding the bounds of their autonomy they would 'violate the law'.[12] The student parliament (*Konvent*) and its elected executive committee (the AStA), could take stances on all questions concerning teaching or the university, but no broader political issue. The rector and Senate of the FU consistently adhered to this definition of the limits of political engagement within the university throughout the early 1960s. The students – whether on the Left or not – just as consistently opposed the limited, corporatist definition. In an age when so many public intellectuals and politicians stressed the economic function of the university, the boundary between educational and high politics blurred. The search for democratisation rejected any such delimitation of spheres. As Knut Nevermann noted, 'even if [student representatives] want solely to represent students' university interests, [this] simultaneously means a struggle against authoritarian, not rationally justified structures of authority, that ultimately can only be successful through a democratisation of all social areas'.[13] The university milieu thus reproduced two features of the broader crisis of political representation: the degree of autonomy of a junior organ within a corporation and the limits of official politics to encompass a demand for democratisation of all aspects of life.

---

[9] APO FU-Berlin Allgemein 2 2098 2 Politische Meinungsäußerung 'Freie Universität Berlin 3.8.59 An Se. Magnifizenz den Rektor der Freien Universität Berlin ...' There are two narratives in English of the student movements at the Free University: Tent, *Free University*, and Nick Thomas, *Protest Movements in 1960s West Germany: A Social History of Dissent and Democracy* (Oxford: Berg, 2003), who stresses the arbitrary power of the rector and the provocation tactics of SDS. The best and most comprehensive account is provided through the chronology and the documents in the multivolume *Hochschule im Umbruch*.

[10] APO FU-Berlin Allgemein 2 2098 2 '3.8.59 An Se. Magnifizenz den Rektor der Freien Universität Berlin ...'

[11] APO FU-Berlin Allgemein 2 2098 2 Politische Meinungsäußerung 'Tgb.Nr. 6976/59'.

[12] Ibid.   [13] Nevermann, 'Zum Selbstverständnis der Studentenvertretung', 709.

The limitations on political activity to purely education issues proved impossible to maintain even by the university itself, let alone the students. In 1959, the Senate committee discussed which themes the student parliament and its executive could pronounce upon, insisting 'that the FU may deliver a statement on the freedom of Berlin and the Soviet plans and claims that threaten the existence of the FU'.[14] In 1962, the FU Senate rejected the proposal for a collection for Algerian refugees and students in February, and declined a petition against British actions in Hong Kong towards Chinese refugees, but endorsed a collection for 'fellow students in the SBZ [*Sowjetische Besatzungszone*, Soviet Occupation Zone]' in June. The rector furthermore promoted the collection through a circular to the deans of the faculties, lauding the students who thereby sought to 'practice not only with words, but also through deeds the consciousness of their political responsibility'.[15] Despite disclaimers that such endorsement 'was neither an exception, nor to be interpreted as the beginning of a new practice',[16] *Konvent* interpreted the past political activity of Berlin students not in its specific content, but its universal implications, demanding 'to become politically active in the name of their democratic responsibility for freedom and rights'.[17] This understanding of political rights within the university was not the sole concern of radical students. The then chairman of AStA pointedly insisted 'that he does not identify himself with the content of the protest, but that he is of the opinion, that the spontaneous expression of political opinion within the student body should be given free development'.[18] The differences between the student body and the university hierarchy at the Freie Universität were thus clearly expressed at the very beginning of the 1960s. Yet while the *Konvent* and AStA verbally protested the decisions of the rector and Senate, the disagreement of opinion never became an open conflict. That changed by mid-decade.

The Berlin Model, while serving as a lightning rod for discontent with the pace of democratisation, nonetheless functioned efficiently to channel the protest. The student parliament, *Konvent*, was not swept aside by the

---

[14] APO FU-Berlin Allgemein 2 2098 2 Politische Meinungsäußerung 'Protokoll der Sitzung des Senatsausschusses für politische Meinungsäusserung akademischer Gremien am 16. Juni 1959'
[15] APO FU-Berlin Allgemein 2 2098 2 Politische Meinungsäußerung.
[16] APO FU-Berlin Allgemein 2 2098 2 Politische Meinungsäußerung 'An den 1. Vorsitzenden des AStA'. Letter of 25.6.1962.
[17] APO FU-Berlin Allgemein 2 2098 2 Politische Meinungsäußerung FUB '15.2.1962' 1. Vorsitz AStA to Rektor Heinitz 15.2.1962.
[18] APO Archiv FU-Berlin Allgemein Rektoratsakten Politisches Mandat Teil 1.2. 2098 2 1950 – August 1967. 'Kurzprotokoll der 7. (ao.) und 8. (ao.) Sitzung des 13. Konvents am Mittwoch, dem 6. Juni 1962'.

general assembly. Until late 1968, SDS absorbed the radical challenges and practices of direct democracy and provocation rather than being destroyed by them. The Berlin Model and *Konvent* protected SDS from reprisals. The Free University's Senate determined (by 10 votes to 9) in May 1967 that SDS no longer deserved recognition by the university but found no support for such a move in the student parliament. Far more than at Nanterre or Trento, the existing institutional structures proved capable of representing the revolt. This did not prevent the eruption of protest, but it did ensure a significant presence of more traditional student leaders, the ability of SDS to impose long-held goals onto the movement and explains in part how at West Berlin the protest movement could embark on a project as complex as the *Kritische Universität*.

Nanterre: The Movement of March 22.

In contrast to the Free University of Berlin, disaggregation marked the political organisations at Nanterre. Groups that in West Berlin coalesced inside SDS all formed separate, miniscule organisations in France – the *groupuscules*. The interaction of anarchist and Marxist ideologies in particular marked the milieu. A small but significant group of anarchists existed alongside the various Marxist *groupuscules*, as well as the local branch of the Situationist International (who would call themselves *enragés*, a name often erroneously attributed to the whole of the student movement in 1968).[19] These organisations each counted only a few militants. At the beginning of the 1967-68 academic year, the main Trotskyist group boasted some 25 militants, the two anarchist groups 15 and 40, the Maoists, Lambertist Trotskyists and Situationists seven or eight each, with two or three members of the socialist student organisation.[20] Each *groupuscule* could mobilise more, but most understood the decline of UNEF as demonstration of the futility of representative politics based in electoral mobilisation characteristic of mass political parties.

While the campus of Nanterre ultimately helped to fuse these diverse political groups, at first most politically active students could only observe

---

[19] The anarchists were called the *Liaison des étudiants anarchistes* (LEA, founded 1964), which transformed itself in the *Tendance syndicale révolutionnaire fédéraliste* (TSRF) in 1966.

[20] According to Jean-Pierre Duteuil, co-founder of the anarchist Liaison of Anarchist Students (LEA): Jean-Pierre Duteuil, *Nanterre, 1965–66–67–68. Vers le mouvement du 22 mars* (Paris: Acratie, 1988), 21. The socialist student oragnisation was the ESU (*Etudiants socialistes unifiés*, the student organisation of the *Parti Socialiste Unifié*),

the inefficacy of UNEF and the consequent ideological fragmentation. The union itself admitted its weakness. The problems of university reform festered, but the UNEF branch at Nanterre envisioned intervening 'only on minimal demands bearing on the weak points of the reform' in November 1966.[21] Goals such as *travaux pratiques* (small seminars) limited to thirty students, and student-faculty committees to be established in each department, had little chance of success: 'the teaching corps' reaction was brutal, including the professors known for their left-wing opinions and union activism who tenaciously defended their cast privileges in the face of our demands'.[22] UNEF railed against 'the industrialisation of the university',[23] but its political position was confined to verbal protests. The Trotskyist JCR condemned how 'for two years, UNEF has only been the locus of factional debates and groupuscular activities that permit only an already politicised miniscule minority to take part'.[24]

More ideologically radical groups did not necessarily achieve greater impact. The Trotskyist JCR, which sought to adopt the traditional role of vanguard, aimed to 'radicalise these struggles, to give them a political dimension their original objectives do not always have'.[25] The JCR had carefully studied the Berkeley revolts and the formation of the Vietnam Day Committee in the United States.[26] At Nanterre, they identified three areas of engagement – Vietnam, the university residences and university reform. The JCR aimed to work within the representative organs[27] to promote 'precise and realistic objectives'[28] that might lead towards 'the reconstruction of a revolutionary Marxist party'.[29] However, this tactic proved no more successful than UNEF's activism on university reform. The Trotskyists retrospectively admitted that 'the "university line" was erroneous in principle ... The student milieu ... was not unionisable. There were no homogeneous interests to defend.'[30] The student body appeared impossible to mobilise either with syndical demands or for revolutionary purposes.

The context of demobilisation suited most the anarchists who sought not to represent the students but rather to expose the hypocrisy of representation. While the leadership of UNEF lamented its decline and

---

[21] BDIC. F delta 813(1), 'Programme d'unité syndicale'.   [22] Ibid.   [23] Ibid.
[24] Duteuil, *Nanterre*, 31.   [25] Ibid.
[26] Salar Mohandesi, 'Bringing Vietnam Home: The Vietnam War, Internationalism and May '68', *French Historical Studies* 41.2 (2018), 219–251, 224.
[27] (AFGEN and ARCUN – the *Association des residents de la cité universitaire de Nanterre*).
[28] Duteuil, *Nanterre*, 31.   [29] Ibid.
[30] Daniel Bensaïd, and Henri Weber, *Mai 68: une répétition générale*, (Paris: Maspero, 1968), 36.

the Trotskyists sought to infiltrate the structures of representation to create a revolutionary Marxist party, the anarchists at Nanterre rejected the traditional structures of student governance altogether. Arguing the union had become 'the work of a few specialists, professionals of the student movement, whom the students are led to rely upon', they declared 'LET US BREAK with all forms of collaboration with power'.[31] For the student organisations, the anarchists demanded 'statutes that avoid scheming, the practices of corridors, bureaucratic manoeuvres'. They called for 'regular meetings of militants with large political debates (amphitheatre committees, general assemblies) ... proportional representation at all levels'.[32] Regarding the university, the anarchists envisaged a more vigorous politics than the 'realistic' but unachievable demands of either UNEF or the Trotskyists. Castigating the UNEF bureau for having 'refused, especially at Nanterre, to see in the administration a government agent charged with putting into practice the Fouchet reform',[33] the anarchists planned 'direct actions (not verbal denunciations, petitions, etc.) likely to produce creative situations: the occupation of the university canteen, the girls building of the university residences, and a host of other actions which we haven't thought of but which it is for the students themselves to decide on'.[34] The anarchists spurned the traditional forms of protest – demands, marches and manifestos – and took up more spectacular and provocative tactics. This inventiveness, in contrast to UNEF, stemmed from their disinterest for mass mobilisation. The occupation – the action that had divided UNEF in 1964 – better suited an organisation that neither held nor sought legitimacy as representative of the entire student body.

The anarchists did not seek the mantle of majority acclamation, vaunting their own minority status and deriding the vast bulk of students as right-wing: 'by their social origin, as in their acceptance to become the salaried employees of different authoritarian apparatuses (state, enterprise, advertising firm, etc. ...) the majority of students are already conservatives'.[35] The Situationists and anarchists typically engaged in the electoral and representative institutions only in order to demonstrate their democratic illegitimacy. In May 1966, students inspired by the Situationist International took advantage of the poor participation in UNEF elections to win control of the local branch in Strasbourg.[36] They used the funds to

---

[31] BDIC. F delta 813(1), 'Programme de la tendance anti-corporatiste'. [32] Ibid.
[33] Duteuil, *Nanterre*, 67. [34] Ibid., 68. [35] Ibid., 190.
[36] The Association Fédérative Générale des Etudiants de Strasbourg, which was affiliated to UNEF.

commission a Situationist text on the student milieu,[37] then closed the Office of Psychological Assistance. At Nanterre in January 1967, the anarchists again exploited student apathy, capturing the Philosophy, Sociology and Psychology UNEF office by four votes to three[38]: 'Thanks to the profound interest manifested by the majority faction ... (*completely absent*) we are now the legitimate, statutory, recognised as publicly useful, vaccinated, etc., representatives of the 120 members of UNEF in philosophy-sociology-psychology'.[39] Renamed the 'Bogus-Office [*Bureau-Bidon*] of Philosophy-Sociology-Psychology', and insisting 'we represent nothing; we will soon be overthrown by people who are no (or only a little bit) more representative than we are',[40] they called for a public meeting against exams. Criticism of examinations represented no radical new departure in university politics. UNEF's 1964 manifesto for democratic reform of education condemned the system of examinations and derided their tendency to foster memorisation rather than independent judgment.[41] But this meeting gathered around 200 instead of the 50 usual suspects.

The rally against exams suggested the political problem lay in the inability of representative organs to channel protest rather than the apathy of the student body. Instead of the traditional bodies, a series of ad hoc committees arose to organise protest. In mid-1967 the Faculty of Arts at Nanterre informed 55 psychology students that because of the university reform they must retake an exam they had already passed. Around half failed their second attempt. A 'Committee for the Defence of the 55' formed to contest 'the validity of the exam results'.[42] This improvised form of representation, however, only grudgingly won acknowledgement from the institution. Seeking to send a delegation to the dean, the committee was told 'that he would only agree to receive three individuals and demanded their names!'[43] The gulf between representative politics and direct action became even more evident in the November 1967 strike over the Fouchet reforms. UNEF attempted to contest the reforms, and gathered around 5,000 protesters in the Latin Quarter on

---

[37] Membres de l'Internationale Situationniste et des étudiants de Strasbourg, *De la misère en milieu étudiant, considérée sous ses aspects économique, politique, psychologique, sexuel et notamment intellectuel et de quelques moyens pour y remédier*, 2nd ed. (Paris: Ch. Bernard, 1967).
[38] Of a possible 18 votes. [39] Duteuil, *Nanterre*, 89. Italics underlined in original. [40] Ibid.
[41] National Union of Students of France (UNEF), *Manifesto for the Democratic Reform of Higher Education* (Prague: International Union of Students, 1965), 17. See also Dominique Damamme, 'Laboratoires de la réforme pédagogique' in Dominique Damamme et al., *Mai–Juin 68* (Paris: Editions de l'Atelier, 2008), 246–247.
[42] BDIC. F delta 813(3), '55 etudiants frustrés de leur examen'.
[43] BDIC. F delta 813(3), 'Que Faire? Comité de defense des 54'.

9 November – the largest such demonstration since 1963. At Nanterre, on 7 November, their call collected about 400. But this moderate mobilisation was dwarfed by the much more successful movement that emerged from the department of sociology. The leaders there were neither UNEF nor the *groupuscules*, but left-wing Catholics and a number who adhered neither to the groupuscules nor even were members of the union.[44]

The November 1967 strike committee, using strikes and general assemblies to place pressure directly on the university administration, proved again the obsolescence of UNEF. The student union, condemned perpetually to document its increasing insignificance, recognised that 'the strike cruelly illuminated the relatively weak capacity for intervention of AFGEN [the Nanterre branch of UNEF] militants, the total deficiency of information ... due in part to the absence of real union structures and ... of a minimal material infrastructure'.[45] Nonetheless, they tried to preempt the '"launch" of a completely different militant structure which will moreover have neither possibility nor reason for being without a real life [of the union]'.[46] Equally undesirous of having to deal again with a strike or general assembly, the Council of the Faculty expressed the wish 'that the students define, in a precise and lasting manner, the procedures for choosing their representatives',[47] and declared itself 'favourable to the consolidation or creation of organs of liaison between teachers and students interior to each department'.[48] The strike thus opened new avenues of representation, all the while suggesting direct action was the most effective form of protest.

The results of the November strike proved illusory in terms of the concessions won, but enduring in its reconfiguration of politics at the University of Nanterre.[49] The crisis of student politics deepened. The newest form of representation, the participation of students in the Departmental Councils (*Conseils des Départments*), revealed itself nugatory. Students complained the meetings 'give free rein to the demagogy of the professors', were often not instituted, and when they were, held little power: 'these councils are in no way authoritative. In the last instance,

---

[44] See Paul Christophe, 'Mai 1968 et l'Eglise de France', *Ensemble* 41.2 (1984), 97–104, 98. For a contrasting view on the importance of Catholic students at Nanterre, see René Rémond, '"La révolution de mai 68", l'évolution des moeurs, l'Église et les jeunes', *Revue de l'institut catholique de Paris* 22 (1987), 195–202, 197.
[45] Duteuil, *Nanterre*, 112.   [46] Ibid., 113.   [47] Ibid.
[48] ADHS 1208W/2, 'Conseil de faculté de Nanterre, le 25 Novembre 1967'.
[49] See René Lourau, 'Nanterre 1968: La transe institutionnelle', in *L'instituant contre l'institué* (Paris: Anthopos, 1969), 155.

it's the head of the Department who decides'. The primary result, they concluded dejectedly, was 'to co-opt the students to administrative decisions, to neutralise their demands, to suffocate the struggle in embryo'.[50] The delegates to the Departmental Councils, 'conscious of their powerlessness', voted the 'dissolution of their organisation'.[51] The achievement of a recognised place in administrative structures – the point from which revolts in West Berlin began – only revealed the depth of the problem of effective political representation.

Most ominously for the future peace of the faculty, but hardly surprising in the context of the administration's own protestations of impotence, the students observed 'the flight of decision-making authority, this professor deferring to the departmental council, that deferring to the faculty council, or to the dean, he deferring to the minister'.[52] The lack of democracy appeared symptomatic of the entire political system:

> in certain periods, the authorities, rather than accepting power-sharing and the concessions it implies, prefer to decide alone, feeling strong enough to risk the trial of strength with the working class. The Gaullist regime is one of these periods: for ten years, it has liquidated the existing power-sharing organisms ... and sought to concentrate in its hands all the centres of decision-making.[53]

In this, students merely identified something professors themselves bemoaned. At the erection of barricades in Paris in May 1968, the deans of the faculties of arts and social sciences complained that 'the authorities have got into the habit of dialoguing with itself in the persons of its representatives'.[54] The failure of representation at the local level was intimately tied to the authoritarian and hierarchical structures of French society, symbolised in the figure of de Gaulle.

The failure of representation perceived by both faculty and students led the university hierarchy to demand in May 1968 a functional representative democracy: 'the general administration, the financial management, and the organisation of teaching must be devolved ... to particular organisms where students and teachers will be represented, in the person of their democratically elected delegates'.[55] However, such a reassertion of representative democracy came at least a year too late for most in the

---

[50] BDIC. F delta 1961(10) – VI, Nanterre Information. Journal de l'association fédérative des groups d'études de Nanterre. A la MNEF votez UNEF. Bureau sortant.
[51] Duteuil, *Nanterre*, 103.   [52] BDIC. F delta 1961(10) – VI, Nanterre information.
[53] Alain Schnapp and Pierre Vidal-Naquet, *Journal de la Commune Étudiante: textes et documents. Novembre 1967–juin 1968*, edition augmentée (Paris: Éditions du Seuil, 1969), 118.
[54] BDIC F delta 1056(2)(4), 'Déclaration des Doyens, 13 mai 68'.   [55] Ibid.

student movement. Moreover, students had early declared the goal of 'the democratisation of university life at all levels' rather than merely a more functional representation.[56] While the deans demanded elected representatives, the student movement insisted on 'direct democracy', and thus 'the suppression as soon as possible of intermediary representation and, therefore, of elections at multiple levels'.[57] The student vision of devolution went much further than the deans', extending 'the right of initiative, permitting all groups on condition of sufficient number to take action, whatever it may be, on its propositions without following hierarchical paths'.[58] Neither UNEF, nor any of the groupuscules, adequately incarnated such a demand. Instead, the occupation of the administrative tower at Nanterre on 22 March 1968 forged a new movement from the previously fragmented political groups. Initially calling itself the 'Movement of the 144' after the number of occupants, a name rendered obsolete within days by the flood of new recruits, the Movement of 22 March declared itself politicised (that is, not concerned solely with 'corporatist' demands), 'a minority and conscious of it',[59] and wielded a set of tactics designed to bypass traditional political forms: 'improvised meetings in the faculty, the occupation of rooms to hold our debates, interventions in classes or lectures, boycotting of exams, political posters and panels in the hallways, seizure of the microphone monopolised by the administration, etc'.[60] This was a movement forged in a crisis of representation: it neither claimed to be representative, nor sought representative democracy, but rather the greatest autonomy of action possible at all levels. Its mode of action aimed to institute that freedom in practice, but its ability to ensure freedoms long-term were undermined by its suspicion of institutionalisation.

Trento: Power of the Powerless

Students at Trento demanded a democratisation of representation in their organisations well before the outbreak of protest. The founding motion of the Catholic Intesa at Trento stressed both the importance of autonomy in relation to society and a more democratic and effective political organisation. The goal of university education was to be 'the training of

---

[56] BDIC. F delta 813(1), 'Communiqué des résidents de Nanterre'.
[57] Bibliothèque Nationale de France [BNF], 'Les tracts de mai 68'. 1205 'Convention nationale des universités de France. Paris. Nanterre 20–21 juin 1968'.
[58] Ibid.   [59] Schnapp and Vidal-Naquet, *Journal*, 149.   [60] Ibid., 150.

a graduate as an intellectual-professional, able to assert an autonomous critical judgement in relation to the system in which he inserts himself'.[61] Within student politics, the Trento Intesa sought 'a greater democratic validity of representation, avoiding a top-down, consequently unrealistic and ineffective, approach'.[62] Autonomy implied a critical conception of society, as well as distance from the religious and political hierarchies. In 1965, Marco Boato, the major figure in Intesa at Trento, addressed the national conference with the argument that '*Intesa does not derive its political ideology directly from Christian inspiration*; rather it refers to Christian inspiration solely as its *basic orientation*.'[63] As a consequence, there could be more than one group of Christian inspiration, and all students, not just Catholic ones, could adhere to the organisation.[64] This openness extended to political alliances, a highly charged position in a society where Christian Democracy's alliance with the most moderate socialists proved difficult, controversial and unrewarding.

The foundation of the Trentino University Left (*Sinistra Universitaria Trentina*), the local version of the left-wing UGI, demonstrated a determination equal to the Catholics for a more democratic self-governance, both for itself and within the university. The left-wing students outlined among their key objectives to 'conduct inside the Student Movement the transformation of representation by overcoming the leadership-base dichotomy' and the 'democratisation of university structures, understood as co-responsibility and informed participation in the management and in the self-government of each single faculty'.[65] Similarly, the students expressed a deep suspicion of the role of political parties within the university milieu: 'the attempt to automatically transpose party models into the university world has never produced positive results'.[66] That suspicion extended to the national political leadership of UNURI. After all, the association functioned as 'an important breeding ground of the

---

[61] CMR B.4 f.1 (Fondo Movimento Studentesco Riccardo Scartezzini), 'Mozione costitutiva del Gruppo Democratico Intesa Universitaria'.
[62] Ibid.
[63] CMR B.4 f.1 (Fondo Movimento Studentesco Riccardo Scartezzini), 'Gruppo Democratico Intesa Universitaria Trentina. Un rinnovato Movimento Universitario per lo sviluppo dell'Università e della società italiana. (Contributo per il Congresso Nazionale di Trieste, elaborato dal Segretario ed approvato dall'Assemblea del GDIUT) Trento 1965'. Italics underlined in original.
[64] Ibid.
[65] CMR B.4 f.1 (Fondo Movimento Studentesco Riccardo Scartezzini), 'Mozione costitutiva della Sinistra Universitaria Trentina'.
[66] Ibid.

political class'.[67] As one student put it, 'in general... the student leader at the national level is today a young man who has foregone the experience of cultural elaboration and civic engagement in order to manage power'.[68] Students at Trento (even the leaders) began with little or no trust in their representatives.

When the national leadership of UNURI visited Trento to lend its support for the first occupation, the local leadership responded warily: 'Already in the preparatory phase for these meetings, Mauro [Rostagno] trembled: be aware, he told us, these are sons of bitches coming here to instrumentalise and divide us, and instead it must be we who instrumentalise them, using their structures and availability to generalise our struggle'.[69] The Faculty, by contrast, insisted on dealing with representatives of the traditional organisations. The founder of the Institute, Bruno Kessler, declared himself willing to journey to Rome to lobby for the *laurea* in sociology. He requested a delegation of students, but 'on condition that they are the official representatives of ORUT [the Trentino University Representative Organisation, *Organizzazione Rappresentativa Universitaria Trentina*]'.[70] However, the struggle for the recognition of a degree in sociology rather than political science rapidly bypassed the traditional student organisations and had hit upon the occupation and student assembly. As the students themselves put it, the movement operated 'outside the political crystallisations',[71] fusing the Catholic and left-wing students, who now adopted the title of the Student Movement of Trento, a name at times prefaced by 'Anti-Authoritarian'. They therefore rejected any return to previously elected representatives. Instead, 'the assembly of the occupiers is to be considered the only effectively representative organism' and would choose the delegation.[72]

Thus at Trento a movement emerged very early that bypassed the traditional forms of representation, welding together a set of previously

---

[67] Giovanni Orsina and Gaetano Quagliariello, 'L'Unuri e la formazione della classe politica italiana', in Giovanni Orsina and Gaetano Quagliariello (eds.), *La formazione della classe politica in Europa (1945–1956)* (Rome: Piero Lacaita Editore, 2000), 334.
[68] G. Lovato, 'Una rappresentanza da riformare', *Il Mulino*, 5–6, maggio-giugno 1967, 399–416, 402 as quoted by Marco Boato, *Il '68 è morto: viva il '68! Prima del '68: origini del movimento studentesco e della nuova sinistra; dopo il '68: abbiamo 'sbagliato tutto'...?* (Verona: Bertani Editore, 1979), 119.
[69] Marianella Sclavi, 'Le origine del '68 a Trento: come si creano e come si distruggono una, due tre, tante fantasie', *I Giorni Cantati* 1.1 (1981), 75–83, 83.
[70] '"No" al compromesso' *Alto Adige*, 3 February 1966, 4.
[71] CMR B.4 f.1 (Fondo Movimento Studentesco Riccardo Scartezzini), 'Perché facciamo l'occupazione'.
[72] '"No" al compromesso', 4.

disparate ideological currents through the practice of the occupation. As in France and West Germany, this occurred first through mobilisation around a very specific goal – at Trento, the successful struggle for the recognition of the degree in sociology, then the conflict over the statute and curriculum of the Institute. The small size of the faculty facilitated the emergence of a distinct and coherent student movement much earlier than at Nanterre or West Berlin. The success of its first struggle, however, ultimately depended on the eventual cooperation of the major political parties. Without the student occupation the degree in sociology would not have been won. The students acerbically noted the speed with which the university administration changed its letterhead to acknowledge the degree in political science as soon as the proposal for sociology encountered difficulties.[73] Nonetheless, however decisive the occupation, without the support of the national political parties the degree in sociology could not have triumphed. The success of the first struggle only confirmed the relative impotence of students in the questions that concerned them.

Equally evident was the reluctance of those who held power to devolve it. The student assembly won recognition from the faculty of sociology as the representative body by sheer weight of numbers. However, the Ministry of Education froze the funds dedicated to student organisations, an action denounced by the students as one designed 'to boycott the activity of the Student Movement and to influence the students to reconstitute new representative organs, characterised by mechanisms of delegation and a consequently reformist line of union-demands'.[74] This response to activism once more reminded students of the financial and political limitations imposed on their politics.

The opposition of not only the local university administration but also the national government validated the nascent student movement in the assertion that 'a struggle made for all the students must be by all the students, a mass mobilisation that refuses to remain caged in the traditional bureaucratic forms of student representation, the easy object of sanctions and the paternalism of those who actually hold power'.[75] Students conceived the problem of authoritarianism as both national and local: 'the absence in our country of a real democratic participation highlights the incapacity of social groups to establish themselves as a

---

[73] CMR B.2 f.1 (Fondo Movimento Studentesco G. Palma), No Title.
[74] CMR B.1 f.6 (Fondo Movimento Studentesco G. Palma), 'Finanziamento del M.S.'.
[75] CMR B.1 f.2 (Fondo Movimento Studentesco G. Palma), 'Che cosa significano le lotte studentesche'.

moment of formation of a political will.' However formally democratic the structures of representation, they failed to function effectively and instead produced 'the state of disaggregation that characterises Italian society'.[76] The Italian students thus arrived at a similar diagnosis to those at West Berlin and Nanterre: representative democracy functioned to dissipate progressive politics.

Despite rejecting delegation, the student movement nonetheless demanded representation within the university hierarchy in the debate over the statute and curriculum of the university. Students sought a place in both the Consiglio di Amministrazione (the Administrative Council, the governing body of the Institute) and the Consiglio dei Professori (the Council of Professors, which regrouped the professors *di ruolo* and *fuori ruolo* – tenured and untenured professors – with representation from the other teaching ranks).[77] In this instance, the statute of the Faculty of Sociology, although it foresaw only one student representative with an advisory vote, placed itself at the forefront of institutional reform among Italian universities (although not as advanced as the 'Berlin Model'). Mario Volpato, the first director of the institute, frustrated by student accusations of a regressive constitution, retorted that 'the proposals anticipate the presence of students and assistant [professors] in the Administrative Council, experiments that will create difficulties in the seat of approval'.[78] The new institute guaranteed presence, but not power, to the students in the government of the university. Nonetheless, the ability of students to hear, report and publicise the discussions held within closed doors ruptured a strongly held institutional taboo.

The concession of representation (with or without voting rights) failed to satisfy the student movements' demands, which had early focused on the goal of autonomy. In the first occupation over the title of the degree, the students had asserted the need for autonomy 'above all from the political parties', where real power was held: 'The Student Movement depends strictly on the political context in as much as one has power, the other not. ... the space of autonomy is given unilaterally by power;

---

[76] CMR B.4 f.1 (Fondo Movimento Studentesco Riccardo Scartezzini), 'Gruppo Democratico Intesa Universitaria Trentina. Mozione Politico-Programmatica del G.D.I.U.T. per il rinnovo dell'organismo rappresentativo', 5–6.
[77] The council regrouped the *Professori di ruolo* and *fuori ruolo* with representation from the *professori aggregate*, the *assistenti* and *professori incaricati provvisto di libera docenza*.
[78] CMR Archivio Marco Boato, Busta Trento Sociologia Anno 1963–1968. f. 'Trento 1966–67 2ª occupazione. Statuto e piano di studi. Boato Documentazione. Condensato riunione student docent per esame bozza statuto e piano di studi. 8 dicembre 1966'.

that space only allows abstract, unrealistic operations. The space must be created.'[79] The occupation became the privileged instrument for creating this space. This goal underlay each of the successive occupations at Trento, becoming ever more explicit. Even at the very beginning of the student movement, the students declared that they were 'occupying the university ... not ... solely to see recognised a degree that is due them by right, but to pose in a serious way the problem of their non a priori integration'.[80] Instead, the students conceived the occupation as 'an indispensable moment ... which permits [students] to feel their autonomy not as a transcendent beyond or as an indeterminate future, but as the horizon of a practice already in operation'.[81] By the third occupation of January 1968, the creation of an autonomous space of politics moved to the forefront.

Whereas the first two occupations at Trento primarily concerned specific demands – the recognition of a degree in sociology, and the elaboration of a different curriculum and more democratic statute – the third occupation began not with demands but rather the decision to create them. The occupants outlined four broad goals: the struggle against 'academic authoritarianism and the development of "student power"', the contestation of the proposed university reform 'through agitation organised from below', the 'political organisation of the student movement' and the development of a 'charter of demands'.[82] Instead of mobilising over a particular issue, the student movement now set itself and its autonomy as its primary cause, identified the 'fundamental moment of struggle in its own political force',[83] the 'organisation of the mass of the student population as principal object of the movement as the only objective that cannot be integrated'.[84] In a manner very similar to France and West Germany, tensions over particular issues of curriculum and speech revealed an underlying impasse over the lack of self-government in the university and in democratic society.

In February 1968, the Faculty of Sociology at Trento hosted a convention of the student movements in Italy. They passed a joint resolution that

---

[79] CMR B.4 f.1 (Fondo Movimento Studentesco Riccardo Scartezzini), 'Perché facciamo l'occupazione'.
[80] Ibid.   [81] Ibid.
[82] CMR B.5 f.4 (Fondo Movimento Studentesco Gabriella Ferri), 'Caro collega'.
[83] Marco Boato, 'Il Movimento Studentesco Trentino da Forza Corporativa a Forza Sociale', *Il Cristallo* 10 (1968), 16.
[84] CMR B.3 f.4 (Fondo Movimento Studentesco G. Palma), 'Documento della Commissione Studenti Medi'.

aimed to encapsulate the struggles within the university, and once again focused on the theme of autonomy. The new movements began from the 'generalised and diffuse comprehension of the non-autonomy of the structures of education from those of production', and asserted the need to establish 'autonomy ... be it from oppressive scholastic structures, be it from the bureaucratised structures of traditional representation'.[85] The establishment of autonomy would proceed 'experimentally in a series of forms differentiated by place (counter-courses, collective seminars, groups of political work, etc.)', to be cultivated in '"structural spaces" inside the Faculty'.[86] The slogan of 'student power' thus meant the power of students to govern themselves, the 'refusal of every hypothesis of co-government and participation in the current or reformed structures'.[87] At the national level the movement similarly 'refused every exhaustive parliamentary mediation and develops a global contestation of the current structure of political, academic and economic power at every level'.[88] In Italy, as elsewhere, protesters emphasised democratisation not as the achievement of representation but rather the tangible experience of self-government. Yet the practical detail of such autonomy was often vague, negatively defined in opposition to a pointless and enervating bureaucratic political process. At best, it implied an open endorsement of experimentation. Much rode on the how the actually existing structural spaces of student autonomy operated and how they could be maintained in the absence of bureaucratisation and institutionalisation.

Contradictions of the New Student Movements

The search for a democratic, autonomous form of politics did not end in the occupation. The overthrow of representation and the enactment of politics on the theatrical stage of the student assembly produced new political leaders and new hierarchies. In retrospect, students often castigated the assembly as an even more undemocratic, because demagogic, political structure. 'The democracy of assemblies also proved itself fascistising and manipulatory', wrote the Brigatista Renato Curcio in the 1980s.[89] The leaders of the student movements dominated. Few female

---

[85] CMR B.1 f.2 (Fondo Movimento Studentesco G. Palma), 'Mozione Conclusiva del Convegno Sulle Lotte Studentesche', 6 febbraio 1968.
[86] Ibid. [87] Ibid. [88] Ibid.
[89] CMR B.14 f.1 (Fondo Cali), A Trento Venti'Anni Dopo. 'Amici' Lettera dal Renato Curcio. On assemblies and charisma see also Gianfranco Pasquino, 'Il '68 e il sistema politico italiano', in Aldo Agostini et al., *La cultura e i luoghi del '68* (Milan: FrancoAngeli, 1991), 344–359, 349.

voices were heard. The Italian philosopher Norberto Bobbio remembered at Trento 'two official orators ... Boato and Rostagno: all the rest were in reality a passive mass'.[90] Such a judgment unfairly characterises as apathetic the large numbers of students actively engaged in the occupations. Nonetheless, the growing criticism of assemblies revealed their limited lifespan. The stimulus of disruption faded and the assembly congealed into informal but enduring power structures.

The most striking feature of the movements for many observers was the emergence of a new set of student leaders, characterised first and foremost by their oratory, incarnating the protest and capable of commanding the student assemblies. At Nanterre Daniel Cohn-Bendit came to prominence: 'this red-headed boy, face sprinkled with freckles, very blue eyes, clothed in a jacket, sweater and a chequered coloured shirt, open, combined with a conviction and temperament of a "leader", a perfect casualness and a pronounced taste for funny provocation'.[91] In West Berlin, Rudi Dutschke rapidly achieved the status of celebrity. Journalists wondered what stood before them: 'Is he a Maoist, Trotskyist, Marxist, even a Liebknechtist, or else simply an ordinary beatnik who provocatively enters into discussions ... in the uniform of today's protesting youth: in jeans, a sweater, an overgrown shock of raven hair'.[92] At Trento, Mauro Rostagno dominated proceedings: 'thick beard and long hair, Rasputin-like look, a knowing charisma of sulphurous fascination'.[93] However much outside observers fastened onto their appearance, hair or clothing, the ideological radicalism combined with a casual demeanour, they each possessed an unquestionable intellectual ability. Part of Rostagno's mystique came because 'he didn't give a damn about the university but he did well at it ... always the highest grade and then knew more than anyone on the level of general analysis'.[94] Dutschke and Cohn-Bendit equally elicited academic testimonials.

Despite their newfound prominence, none of these figures were political novices. Cohn-Bendit described the influence of his brother, 'who passed

---

[90] CMR B.14 f.2 (Fondo Calì), Norberto Bobbio.
[91] Philippe Labro et al. (eds.), *Ce n'est qu'un début* (Paris: Éditions et publications Premiéres, 1968), 24.
[92] Paulina Bren, '1968 East and West: Visions of Political Change and Student Protest across the Iron Curtain' in Gerd-Rainer Horn and Padraic Kenney (eds.), *Transnational Moments of Change: Europe 1945, 1968, 1989* (Oxford: Rowman and Littlefield, 2004), 119–136, 124.
[93] Filippo Barbano, 'La sociologia di Trento. Il mio coinvolgimento', in Fabrizio Cambi, Diego Quaglioni, and Enzo Rutigliano, *L'Università a Trento, 1962–2002* (Trento: Università degli studi di Trento, 2004).
[94] Ricci, *I giovani*, 116.

through all the groups of the far-Left after having been excluded from the Communist Party',[95] and was steeped in journals of the heterodox Marxist Left such as *Socialisme ou Barbarie*. Dutschke entered SDS from 'Subversive Action', a small group influenced by the Situationist International. Rostagno arrived at Trento direct from the experience of *Quaderni Rossi:* 'I was already Marxist and very prepared. I had known [Raniero] Panzieri and was part of *Quaderni rossi*, at that time the only extra-parliamentary and anti-union Left'.[96] Another student remembered the influence with less romanticism: 'He spoke to us of the experience of *Quaderni Rossi* at Torino with the manner of one who through the keyhole had watched the grown-ups thinking.'[97] A formidable political background thus underlay the apparent ease with which such students commanded the student assembly. This background and training distinguished the leaders from the mass of students suddenly politicised in 1968 who had no such heritage on which to draw.

The importance of such leaders should not be overstated. For every charismatic chief of the student movement sanctified by the media, there existed numerous others much more traditional in their behaviour. At Trento, opposite Mauro Rostagno 'an odd guy, full of ideas that continuously ran away from him as he jumped from one to the other'[98] and possessed of an impressive belch,[99] stood the leader of the Catholic students, Marco Boato, who remained the entirety of the student revolts in shirt, tie and jacket, and led a group of students that 'expressed seriousness, rectitude, responsibility'.[100] Many more student leaders moved from one end of this spectrum to the other across the course of the revolts. In West Berlin, Knut Nevermann remembered how 'I used to keep a suit and tie in my office ... and when I went over to see Rector Lieber, I would throw them on because it was expected of students addressing the rector'.[101] He soon ditched the deference. In West Berlin in particular, one set of leaders from the student movement emerged relatively seamlessly from the traditional student organisations. SDS retained, or tried to retain, its intellectual and political seriousness, opposite an alternative pole of revolt embodied in the Communes that exhibited protest in lifestyle. The most successful leaders embodied both ends. The most celebrated individuals to emerge were, as the sociologist Alain

---

[95] Labro et al. (eds.), *Ce n'est qu'un début*, 28.   [96] Ricci, *I giovani*, 117.
[97] Sclavi, 'Le origine del '68 a Trento', 77.   [98] Ibid.   [99] Ricci, *I giovani*, 108.
[100] Boato himself arrived at Trento with background in the Catholic journal *Questitalia*.
[101] Tent, *Free University*, 319.

Touraine described Daniel Cohn-Bendit, a 'man of revolt, not of organisation. He was not a manager, but a leader.'[102] Numerous managers and organisers nonetheless existed, albeit in less spectacular fashion. One Italian student remembered how 'beyond the "big ones" there were intermediate cadres like Gianni Lodi, Vittorio Tavolato, Piero Manganoni, Ettore Camuffo, Gigi Chiais, Checco Zotti, etc. ... each of these could, in the space of a few minutes, organise at least 25 men for whatever purpose, be it political or cultural. This was the true force of the movement, not the leaders.'[103] For all the novelty of the student movements, they relied on such individuals, most frequently nameless, not possessed of any great charisma, managing the operations of the movement in a manner much more like traditional organisers of student politics.

The prominence of the leaders of the movements thus needs to be set into the context of the nameless figures who populated the second tier of politics and the masses of students who, if unable to speak equally in assemblies, can hardly be qualified as an amorphous passive mass. The leaders that emerged did so not because they won a particular number of votes or had risen by bureaucratic prowess to the head of an organisation but because they managed most successfully to capture the feelings of an assembly. The most celebrated leaders incarnated a particular attitude that fostered a sense of identification much more easily than the traditional, bureaucratic authority of the student leader. Observers at the time, as well as students in retrospect, ascribed to them the ability to intuitively lead the student movements, placing themselves inside and following the broader movement. Mauro Rostagno 'was a leader of undoubted capacity for intuition and analysis that no-one else had inside them, he had this sixth sense that permitted him to manage whatever assembly or gathering of persons'.[104] He was the figure 'who you "felt" was on your side even when you didn't agree.'[105] So too, Cohn-Bendit, 'has quick comebacks and an extraordinary sense of the public's reactions. He speaks in a direct manner, simple and without ever seeking to "impose himself".'[106] Rudi Dutschke, wrote Bernd Rabehl, 'proved himself as interpreter and agitator of the anti-authoritarian revolt:' 'Dutschke had addressed, articulated and theorised what many students sensed, felt: the pressure to achieve, de-registration, examinations, careers, for what?'[107] Rostagno himself described his role as

---

[102] Alain Touraine, *Le mouvement de mai ou le communisme utopique* (Paris: Seuil, 1968), 115.
[103] Ricci, *I giovani*, 123.   [104] Ibid., 108.   [105] Ibid., 121.
[106] Labro et al. (eds.), *Ce n'est qu'un début*, 24.
[107] Bernd Rabehl, *Am Ende der Utopie: Die politische Geschichte der Freien Universität Berlin* (Berlin: Argon Verlag, 1988), 260.

having 'a bit the function of father that obliged me to always move first. That is, I had to legitimate behaviours that were not legitimate'.[108] The leaders of the movement did not lead by determining a political strategy but by incarnating and legitimating the attitudes and behaviours of the majority.

For all the preponderance of the leaders, they most frequently articulated the viewpoint of the majority, so much so that the leaders themselves authored tracts criticising their dominance: 'few speak and it's always the leaders. The others terrorised and intimidated, take notes or fall asleep or leave. They feel themselves passive, manipulated.'[109] The emergence of individual leaders, almost celebrities, sanctified by the media as the embodiment of revolt, created a contradiction for movements that conceived themselves in opposition to the delegation of representation and all hierarchies. Cohn-Bendit liked to refer to himself as the 'loudspeaker'[110] of the movement, claiming somewhat unconvincingly that 'anyone can replace me'.[111] The growing media fascination with the leaders increasingly affected their role within the movements. SDS found the attention granted it by the mainstream media unprecedented, but it came with a price: 'most delegates on the first day were rather annoyed by the cult of personality carried on by the journalists with Rudi Dutschke. The cameras whirred almost only when Rudi spoke.'[112] A few weeks before the assassination attempt on Dutschke, the SDS considered a proposition to expel him for having taken money for an interview with the newspaper *Capital*, where he appeared on the cover. After his shooting, the SDS hierarchy explained to *Der Spiegel* that the organisation had spoken to Dutschke about the 'cult of personality' surrounding him and if he returned it would be 'not as chief ideologist because we have no use for one'.[113]

The protest movements began in an attempt to overthrow the structure of representation, leadership, and hierarchy characteristic of political parties, whether at the national or university level. While the occupation initially appeared to correspond to that goal, it produced a set of leaders whose dominance contradicted the democratising drive of the movements. This deepened the student movements' distaste for the mainstream media and led to much reflection on the hierarchies of the student assembly.

---

[108] Ricci, *I giovani*, 92.
[109] Renato Curcio and Mauro Rostagno, *Fuori dai denti* (Milan: Gammalibri, 1980), 25–26.
[110] Labro et al. (eds.), *Ce n'est qu'un début*, 28.   [111] Ibid., 32.
[112] Tilman Fichter and Siegward Lönnendonker, *Kleine Geschichte des SDS: Der Sozialistische Deutsche Studentenbund von 1946 bis zur Selbstauflösung* (Berlin: Rotbuch Verlag, 1977), 116.
[113] 'Ohne uns wäre es viel schlimmer gekommen', *Der Spiegel* 17 (1968), 36–43, 43.

'We Represent Nothing' 153

A much larger and more intractable contradiction emerged in the transformation of the protesters from a small minority into a mass movement. To be sure, the explosion of 1968 marked the end of the traditional organisations. UNEF redefined itself in December 1968 as a 'mass political movement' regrouping the 'students of the struggle'[114] and ceased to exist as a union. UNURI's fate was even more definitive. In the same month as UNEF's metamorphosis, the Italian 'little parliament' acknowledged it was 'totally surpassed politically and institutionally' and dissolved itself.[115] But the sudden expansion of the student revolts and their extension beyond the university overwhelmed not just the old student organisations but also the new ones. In Germany, new recruits swamped SDS: '1968 meant for us first of all dissolution'.[116] The socialist student union lasted until March 1970, before it too dissolved itself. In early June 1968, the French government dissolved the Movement of 22 March, itself in the midst of a debate over its future. New organisations took their place.

From the moment of their expansion, the protest movements began to pose the problem of organisation. As one SDS member put it, since 1967 'we did not know any more what to do with so many people. There was always the discussion of how to build a mass organisation that was simultaneously socialist, radical-democratic anti-authoritarian.'[117] The movements had begun largely by aiming at devolution of political power and representation. Some continued to pursue this agenda: 'after the mass onrush of new members the SDS largely gave up the comfortable, *bündisch* organisational layout and set up different working groups and initiatives that related to each other in a loose assemblage'.[118] However, in the absence of actual autonomy, and of power, the drive to reconstitute a more structured organisation capable of seizing and holding it reasserted itself. At its February 1968 convention, the Italian movements raised 'the

---

[114] Jean-Philippe Legois, Alain Monchablon and Robi Morder, 'Le mouvement étudiant et l'université: entre réforme et révolution (1964–1976)', in Geneviève Dreyfus-Armand et al. (eds.), *Les Années 68. Le temps de la contestation* (Brussels: Editions Complexe, 2000), 293.

[115] Marco Boato, 'Origini istituzionali, caratteristiche ideologiche e crisi politica del movimento studentesco 'rappresentativo' prima del '68' in Marco Boato, *Il '68 è morto: viva il '68! Prima del '68: origini del movimento studentesco e della nuova sinistra; dopo il '68: abbiamo 'sbagliato tutto'...?* (Verona: Bertani Editore, 1979), 110–149, 143.

[116] Ute Kätzel, *Die 68erinnen: Porträt einer rebellischen Frauengeneration* (Berlin: Rowohlt, 2002), 187.

[117] Siegward Lönnendonker (ed.), *Linksintellektueller Aufbruch zwischen 'Kulturrevolution' und 'kultureller Zerstörung'. Der Sozialistische Deutsche Studentenbund (SDS) in der Nachkriegsgeschichte (1946–1969). Dokumentation eines Symposiums* (Wiesbaden: Westdeutscher Verlag, 1998), 321.

[118] Rabehl, *Am Ende der Utopie*, 260.

problem of a party'.[119] At this stage, the students attempted to reconcile the anti-hierarchical drive with the organisational conundrum presented by a mass movement by insisting that the construction of a new movement and party must come not from above or outside, but 'must rather come from inside, from the base'.[120] The Movement of 22 March began to debate 'the problem of a revolutionary organisation',[121] which revealed a split. Cohn-Bendit and the more anarchist-inspired wing argued 'this initiative appears to us today premature as it has not yet been the object of in-depth discussion at the base'.[122] Others declared they 'do not make of disorganisation a permanent principle',[123] and 'it's a question of regrouping the avant-garde militants'.[124] For some the radical democratic, anti-hierarchical chaos of the student revolts was merely a moment on the way to the organisation of a new, revolutionary political party. To others, there was no point to a revolutionary party that was not anti-hierarchical and radical-democratic.

The revolutionary and anti-bureaucratic drives of the movements diverged. Frequently, the former returned to quite traditional forms of political parties. At the national level, the election results in France in June 1968 and Italy in May 1968 demonstrated the extent to which the protest movements had little electoral impact, had they wanted one. The West German elections a year later delivered a similar confirmation of the parliamentary system's resilience, while also ending the Grand Coalition that had left virtually no opposition within parliament. Within the university, elected representation in the administrative hierarchy was the most rapidly conceded demand. In France, the Gaullist government, proclaiming a newfound desire for 'participation' throughout society, organised elections within the university system, boycotted by the most radical protesters as a form of co-optation. The demands for autonomy and democratisation did not disappear but found themselves blocked at the institutional level.

---

[119] CMR B.1 f.2 (Fondo Movimento Studentesco G. Palma), 'Mozione Conclusiva del Convegno Sulle Lotte Studentesche' 6 febbraio 1968.
[120] Ibid.   [121] Schnapp and Vidal-Naquet, *Journal*, 408.   [122] Ibid., 409.   [123] Ibid.
[124] Ibid., 411.

CHAPTER 7

'We Began to Talk'
The Seizure of Speech

The protests of the late 1960s evoked a grand spectacle of global conflict and revolution. Vietnam, capitalism, the Third World and the threat of fascist dictatorship recurred constantly in the vocabulary of demonstrators. Frequently, however, conflict erupted after festering in the most mundane relations. Rather than the world-historical events that coursed through the revolutionary lexicon, it was living arrangements, dormitories, control of the classroom – the regulation of speech and space – that provided the material basis for discord. Yet for many protesters the global situation was writ small within the university. Protesters mapped Vietnam over the space of the university in 1968. Students at Trento drew a line between the half of the building they occupied and the other half, patrolled by police. They named the division the 17th parallel. The layering of university, society and globe was not merely symbolic. When debates about Vietnam could close the gates of the university, students counted themselves justified in discerning an inherent connection. Both conflicts revolved around the control of a population of the space in which it lived, of autonomy and democracy at the international and local levels. The language of global struggle, apparently at odds with the quotidian character of the conflict, testified to the politicisation of daily life. The politics of speech and space drove the radicalisation of the university, short-circuiting global and local politics.

The struggle for space in higher education was simultaneously literal and symbolic: the search for control of a physical location for student activism, and the place of politics within the university. The conflict thus concerned both the internal regulation of the physical realm of the university and the symbolic boundary between university and society. Administrators and faculty members liked to conceive of the university as a privileged precinct, set apart from society, to be defended from any incursion of politics. They administered the space inside the university, but they preferred not to emphasise their role in governance. The administrative domain, however, provided protesters with a fertile field for their challenge to authority. Occupations appealed as a tactic to groups attempting to bypass the traditional hegemony of political organisations. They also manifested in practice the appropriation of university space by students for their own ends rather than those created by administrators or professors. They reduced faculty to the role of administrators of space rather than the dispensers and guardians of knowledge.

The protest movements spurned the image of the university as a protected apolitical realm, just as they derided the idea of objectivity. They sought, in various forms, a politicisation of the university. In the first instance, this demand operated as a debunking of the professorial or administrative claim to the university's sovereign independence from society: an unmasking of the university as already politicised. The charge of hypocrisy proved especially easy to level in the 1960s as questions of reform, curriculum and access inevitably emphasised the university was a part of society, not some independent appendage.

However, protesters and students criticised the politics of the university not on the assumption that the university ought to be apolitical, but that it could not avoid its imbrication in the wider world. They discarded altogether the cherished ideal of an academic sanctum severed from society to demand instead political engagement within the university. This politicisation of intellectual space meant, initially, the subjection of politics to rational intellectual debate. Instead of an unconscious, because unarticulated, subordination of intellectual life to politics, the acknowledgement of politics within the university would lead to a consciously critical political and intellectual discussion. But the appeal to an idealised world of a politics tamed by rational debate merely replaced one fantasy with another. In practice, the goal of academic debate (for example, about the war in Vietnam) often gave way to less intellectualised forms of politics, based on the mobilisation of student numbers within the university. For politicisation of the intellectual space of the university also meant the self-conscious perception of relations within the university as historical and political, rather than founded in apolitical, purely academic rationales. Once this view was established, and in the midst of escalating conflict, protesters found it increasingly difficult to distinguish between the demand for politics inside the university (a politics subject to the rules of academia) and the politicisation of the university (an academia subject to the rule of politics). The growth of contention undermined the original goals of protest.

1968 brought the university to earth, democratised in the sense that it could no longer maintain the illusion of its isolation from politics and society. The university had never been as detached from social pressures or politics as its advocates imagined. There was no golden age of splendid isolation. But the Sixties laid bare the social functions of higher education. Greater numbers of students exposed a contradiction between curricula and teaching styles developed for the select few rather than the still selective 'mass' and new disciplines emphasised their social utility instead of their centrality to the hallowed tradition of high culture. Faculty leaders thus discovered themselves in the unfamiliar, unwanted and hitherto unconsidered role of administrators. The classroom openly emerged as a politicised space, one in which power could be challenged and seized. The democratisation of the university stripped the lecture hall of its image as a space of access to and diffusion of knowledge. Instead, it appeared as merely a locus of authority. Indeed, it was and always had been both. Students developed a consciousness of the university as an administered space that required their consent to function. 'Academic and social authoritarianism', wrote students at Trento, 'takes root not just in a series of structures, but also and especially in the consent of those who submit to these structures'.[1] Conflict escalated over issues of space and speech precisely because all that was required was the withdrawal of student compliance. The protest's prime target was student passivity. Where faculty discovered themselves in a role of governance, students discovered themselves as (hitherto) unreflectively obedient. Primarily through the creative use of speech and space, they sought to make a virtue of disobedience.

The nexus between authority, consent and speech is one reason why, when the revolts began, they unleashed a torrent of words. The hierarchical organisation of speech that marked the traditional university gave way to the chaotic and effervescent assemblies of student protest. Endless discussion, the demand for debate, and repeated challenges to the speech of authority figures constituted the daily diet of protest. Words as much as actions appeared to be the revolts' major events. 'From the beginning to the end, speech is what has played the decisive role', wrote Michel de Certeau.[2] The prominence of talking in 1968 led some to dismiss the

---

[1] CMR B.3 f.9 (Fondo Movimento Studentesco G. Palma), 'Carta Rivendicativa – Trento Schema di massima'.
[2] Michel De Certeau, *The Capture of Speech and Other Political Writings*, trans. Tom Conley (Minneapolis: University of Minnesota Press, 1997), 6. See also the brief comments of Philippe

revolutions as entirely symbolic. Raymond Aron explained the 'utmost joy' of talking in 1968 as an emotional release from the solitary crowd, not a political revolt but a psychodrama.³ But revolutions are always also psychodramas. An emotional element did accompany the release of words in 1968. The intoxication of speech came precisely from the collapse of authority and the promise of a new subjectivity built on the ashes of conformity and consent.

The best evocation remains that of de Certeau, who described how speech was seized or, rather, imprisoned speech liberated: 'Everyone finally began to talk: about essential things, about society, about happiness, about knowledge, about art, about politics. A permanent drone of speech spread, like fire ... It changed spectators into actors, confrontation into dialogue, information or apprenticeship in "knowledge" into impassioned discussions about options involving life itself'.⁴ De Certeau elaborated on this image to analyse a crisis of representation, the denial of legitimacy to contemporary knowledge and politics, a demand for a society in which speaking stood for 'the right of being a human, and no longer a client destined for consumer culture or instruments useful for the anonymous organisation of society'.⁵ Suddenly, for many, and for the first time, their speech mattered.

Memoirs demonstrate the experience of talking was a defining moment for many participants, the outward sign of a subjective transformation, the move from spectator to actor (or at least speaker). 'We began to speak. It seemed as if it were for the first time', said de Certeau.⁶ One female student wrote that, 'most important about 1968 was that I learnt to articulate myself'.⁷ The importance of speech should perhaps not be so surprising. Universities prize articulacy. If anything, the ability to talk would be more highly valued in the new professions to which the mass university led students. The revolts established what the education system proclaimed but failed to do. Little wonder that the transformation of

---

Artières, '"Je crie, j'écris." Quand la revolution passe par la prise de la parole et de l'écriture', in Philippe Artières and Michelle Zancarini-Fournel (eds.), *68: Une histoire collective 1962–1981* (Paris: La Découverte, 2008), 373–377. On the 'prise de la parole', see also Anna-Louise Milne, 'Decentring the Events' in Julian Jackson, Anna-Louise Milne and James S. Williams (eds.), *May 68: Rethinking France's Last Revolution* (Basingstoke: Palgrave-Macmillan, 2011), 172–173.
³ Raymond Aron, *La révolution introuvable: réflexions sur la revolution de mai* (Paris: Fayard, 1968), 35. Henri Lefebvre also used the term, rephrasing it as a 'social therapy'. Henri Lefebvre, *L'irruption de Nanterre au sommet* (Paris: Éditions Syllepse, 1998), 108.
⁴ De Certeau, *The Capture of Speech*, 13. ⁵ Ibid., 11. ⁶ Ibid., 23
⁷ Bärbel Danneberg, Fritz Keller, Aly Machalicky and Julius Mende (eds.), *Die 68er: Eine Generation und ihr Erbe* (Wien: Döcker Verlag, 1998), 15.

apathetic students into actively engaged protesters astonished professors, especially those who had themselves vainly sought to stimulate student participation.[8] In the revolts, however, students captured speech for and by themselves. Many experienced 1968 as the discovery of their subjectivity, marked in the first instance by speech. As de Certeau put it: 'The capture of speech ... consists in stating, "I am not a thing"'.[9] Thus Gerd-Rainer Horn has rightly pointed out, 'far left activism was first of all experienced as a fulfilling, pleasurable, and meaningful way of life'.[10]

Yet although the seizure of speech defined '68 to many of its participants, and indeed, drove much of the conflict that stimulated the expansion of revolt, its position in most accounts of the revolts remains descriptive. If anything, the prominence of debate about 'free speech' serves the narrative of the 'growth of tolerance' in the 1960s: the arrival of a more permissive era amid the dissipation of a stuffy 1950s conservatism, or the triumph of a critical rather than consensual public sphere.[11] Some aspects of the Sixties correspond to this image. Boundaries of acceptable political speech shifted leftwards through the sheer weight of the numbers of protesters. The same activists sought consistently, with some success, to delegitimise the speech of the far-Right. The contradiction between political positions held to be legitimate by students and protesters and illegitimate by the press, politicians or administrators generated much of the conflict in the 1960s. The spectrum of political speech expanded as a result, although nothing guaranteed the permanence of such a mutation.

The revolts fostered a broad liberalisation in another sense, by targeting forms of censorship, particularly within the university. Indeed, speech owed its prominence in the revolts partly to the relative lack of restrictions that made attempts to close down debate and political discussion all the more egregious. Restrictions on speech appeared as the most emblematic use or misuse of authority. The declining legitimacy of professorial and administrative authority in the university gave more space to speech. Yet outside the institutions of higher education the balance sheet was less clear.

---

[8] See for example, Bertrand de Jouvenel, 'L'explosion estudiantine', *Analyse et Prévision* 6 (1968), 561–582, 567.
[9] De Certeau, *The Capture of Speech*, 12.
[10] Gerd-Rainer Horn, *The Spirit of '68: Rebellion in Western Europe and North America 1956–1976* (Oxford: Oxford University Press, 2007), 162.
[11] For example, Michael Seidman, *The Imaginary Revolution: Parisian Students and Workers in 1968* (New York: Berghahn, 2004), 279. See also Christina von Hodenberg, 'Mass media and the generation of conflict: West Germany's long sixties and the formation of a critical public sphere', *Contemporary European History* 15.3 (2006), 367–395.

The French government banned short-wave radios during the student protests but allowed them again for the pro-government demonstration at the end of May.[12] Political movements were disbanded, disciplinary measures invoked. Governments found broad tolerance and intermittent censorship quite compatible.[13]

Protest raised a series of more intractable problems about speech. Censorship swelled the numbers of student supporters but acts of protest also courted controversy. When students seized the microphone from faculty to impose their own voices, was this a triumph of free speech, or as administrators increasingly complained, also a form of censorship? Such actions required the justification of urgent protest. They did not establish an enduring basis for the politics of speech. However, they also conformed to the long-term shift in the university from more to less hierarchical modes, whether voluntarily as in the radical introduction of dialogue into the lecture theatre, or not, as in the case of interruptions and interjections. Faculty and professors clearly lost the most in this transition, their speech no longer representing the diffusion of knowledge but the prompt for students' demonstration of their subjectivity. The growth of tolerance was the counterpart to the decline of professorial power.

Whose words held power formed the crux of the politics of speech. Debate on speech in the late 1960s revolved not merely around censorship, the legitimacy of Left-wing political positions or the right to protest. Protesters demanded that their speech matter. From the very beginning, they sought not merely to speak (or abolish the restrictions on speech), but to be heard. Gerd-Rainer Horn has framed the explosion of discourse as part of the flowering of participatory democracy or the 'democratisation of debate'.[14] So it did seem, with the collapse of authority in the late 1960s. 'Everybody wanted to express themselves, to take matters into their own hands. That's what socialism is all about' proclaimed Jacques Sauvageot in a characteristic conflation of words and deeds. Such was indeed the experience of many. But the seizure of speech was simultaneously profound and short-lived. Interrupting a professor for the first time was intoxicating.

---

[12] Philippe Labro et al. (eds.), *Ce n'est qu'un début* (Paris: Éditions et publications Premières, 1968), 135.

[13] On the lack of accommodation to the challenge, see also Anne Rohstock, *Von der 'Ordinarienuniversität' zur 'Revolutionszentrale'? Hochschulreform und Hochschulrevolte in Bayern und Hessen 1957–1976* (Munich: R. Oldenbourg Verlag, 2010), 410. For the liberalising narrative, see Ulrich Herbert, 'Liberalisierung als Lernprozeß. Die Bundesrepublik in der deutschen Geschichte – eine Skizze', in Ulrich Herbert (ed.), *Wandlungsprozesse in Westdeutschland. Belastung, Integration, Liberalisierung 1945–1980* (Göttingen: Wallstein Verlag, 2002), 7–49.

[14] For a discussion of speech and participatory democracy, see Horn, *Spirit of '68*, 162, 216–217.

After the tenth it was boring or pointless. As de Certeau noted, in France speech was rapidly recaptured. As with the revolts more generally, the challenge of democratised discourse proved more complex than first appeared in its glorious storming.

Between Vulgarity and Opacity

The politics of speech followed three distinct, if overlapping, and at times contradictory modes between which protesters oscillated: desacralisation, the demand for debate and provocation. These reflected the wider social transformation of an increasingly informalised social hierarchy, the traditional liberal goal of debate as the precondition for politics, and a more radical attempt to overthrow cultural authority and awaken the wider population from its undemocratic apathy.

The decline of deference that accompanied the disintegration of authority and desacralisation of high culture marked protesters' patterns of speech. The old regime had been simultaneously more intimate and more formal, more personal and more hierarchical. Ekkehart Krippendorff remembered the 'intimacy and distance between teachers and learners'[15] in the *Ordinarienuniversität*, how 'the so elevated Professors could establish such personal contact in the small seminars that students had the feeling of being taken seriously, and they were'.[16] He also remembered requests to help with the shopping. The growth of numbers undermined this dialectic of authority and intimacy, rendering the latter in particular more difficult and creating the demand for alternative ways of developing subjectivity, of being 'taken seriously'. The intimate induction into a culture of high status transformed into a less rarefied process of mass socialisation into expert knowledge. Professors no longer taught a tiny, elite minority but a much broader middle-class demographic, however much it remained the upper echelons of society. More broadly, social status and identity increasingly referred less to professional categories. A more informal regime of speech appeared to confirm a democratic effacement of hierarchy. The new forms of speech both reflected this social transformation – a democratisation, for want of a better word – and had practical, immediate uses that were at times far from democratic. Various modes of speech – informalisation,

---

[15] Ekkehart Krippendorff, *Lebensfäden: Zehn autobiografische Versuche* (Heidelberg: Verlag Graswurzelrevolution, 2012), 124.
[16] Ibid., 125.

vulgarity, verbal violence and opacity – reconfigured rather than abolished authority.

The new 'mass' university fostered an informalisation of speech. Most typically, this levelling thrust was expressed in the collapse of deference towards authority figures, whether professors, parents or politicians. Distinctions that previously existed between how one spoke to one's peers, or inferiors, and how one spoke to superiors disappeared in the short term and were attenuated in the long. Students revelled in the charge created by addressing professors in the informal, disrespectfully, or merely by daring to challenge them. Many professors, indeed, experienced this as the collapse of their personal authority. One West German professor demanded legal action for libel after being called a professorial idiot.[17] Others rapidly adapted to the situation. When the new rector Francesco Alberoni arrived at the Faculty of Sociology at Trento, students labelled him 'Franz von Alberon' and painted his green Alfa Romeo Spider with a swastika, but Alberoni merely paid students to clean his car.[18] He accepted being addressed in the informal, adopted the language of students, and sat on the floor in assemblies, quickly attaining a charismatic allure to rival those of the student leaders.[19]

Thus, faculty who took up the challenge of a democratised discourse could frequently impose themselves. Instead of invoking the traditional authority of the professor and demanding student deference, they dispensed with the requirement of submissiveness and adopted (when useful) a demotic speech from a position of power. The ability to move seamlessly between these registers of speech divided those faculty members who adapted to the crisis of traditional authority and those left forlorn. Similarly, while the diminution of deference swept through student speech, leaders tended to be those who were equally capable of approximating the traditional diction of high culture. The losers in the linguistic struggle were the groups least capable of moving between high and low.

The levelling drive in speech led to the deliberate employment of vulgarity. Swearing marked the speech of many protesters – the deployment of a particular image of uneducated speech and a posture of transgression that generated much pleasure. 'Everything was interposed with the words *cazzo*, *figa* and surrounded by curses', remembered one Italian student. 'The Trentini: "But what violent language these sociologists use,"

---

[17] APO FU-Berlin Allgemein 2 2098 2 Politische Meinungsäußerung 'Prof. Dr. Hermann Blei 28.11.1966'.
[18] Aldo Ricci, *I giovani non sono piante* (Milan: SugarCo, 1978), 185.   [19] Ibid., 186.

and us: "violence is the continual mystification of reality, to say that workers don't want to work, that is violence ... not the word *cazzo*".[20] The charge came from the use of a particular form of speech previously accepted between peers now transposed to a very different community. Vulgarity demonstratively rejected 'proper' codes of conduct. Swearing also functioned as provocation. By the deliberate deployment of informal speech students demonstrated their contempt for a linguistic hierarchy, their escape from the strictures of polite speech. Vulgarity gave the impression of democratisation, or at least an informalisation of language that blurred the linguistic markers of social hierarchy.

Of course, the ostentatious rejection of codes of deference did not dispense with hierarchy altogether, either within the university or within the protest movements. Aggressive, violent, provocative or vulgar speech could quite easily be appropriated to impose new regimes of dominance, to dismiss and dispose of alternative voices. This, after all, was its initial, primary value – to disconcert and defeat faculty. The Berlin sociologist Gerhard Grohs, sympathetic to the students, nonetheless admitted that 'the "verbal brutalism" that led everyone to *duzen* [use the familiar] and label opponents as "pig", "idiot", or "opportunist" was difficult to bear, above all for those who were over fifty. But one had to get through it to the question's serious core'.[21] Yet nothing ensured that aggressive speech would be used only for the purposes of overturning authority.

The levelling informalisation of speech created many opportunities for expressing and generating conflict with authority on all sides of politics. Even severe critics of the protesters such as Michel Crozier admired the laughter that greeted Communist trade unionists at Nanterre: 'the last taboo had been lifted. One dared laugh at the Communist Party and even the working class. The world would never be as before'.[22] Many observers remarked on the novelty of the protest language, its distance from the traditional, rigid ideological speech of political opposition; 'Finally', thought the Italian sociologist Alessandro Pizzorno, 'an opposition movement, non-conformist, in revolt, not prisoner of the stiff ideological language ... of the Marxist vulgate. ... I was happy when I read manifestos, flyers, graffiti, in everyday language, with airy, sometimes poetic

---

[20] Ibid., 66.
[21] Gerhard Grohs, 'Arbeitserfahrungen als Entwicklungssoziologe', in Karl Martin Bolte and Friedhelm Neidhardt (eds.), *Soziologie als Beruf. Erinnerungen westdeutscher Hochschulprofessoren der Nachkriegsgeneration* (Baden-Baden: NOMOS Verlagsgesellschaft, 1998), 303–314, 310.
[22] Michel Crozier, *Ma belle époque: Mémoires* (Paris: Fayard, 2002), 329.

images, fantastic slogans. That style, as we know, did not last long.'[23] Indeed, informality and desacralisation were just part of the transformation of relations in language.

If informalisation marked student speech, so did opacity. SDS members 'spoke a language, that outside of a few, no-one could understand. It sounded like a secret language', remembered Gretschen Dutschke-Klotz.[24] The language of protesters in 1968 could be articulated in both informal, direct, speech and a dense, turgid, ideological discourse that demanded an intimate familiarity with a set of complicated theoretical texts. As one Italian student put it, 'the typical illness was essayism. We were all affected ... you had to read essays because they were much quoted and if you didn't read, you didn't quote... that is, you didn't speak.'[25] Despite the enormous informalisation of speech (particularly that directed towards figures of authority), speaking (within the protest movements) meant mastering a complex lexicon, difficult to obtain and wield with ease. One West German student went so far as to suggest in retrospect that 'I don't represent 68ers because of my inadequate knowledge of theory'.[26] A fellow traveller of SDS remembered how 'if one participated in the discussion as a politicological layperson, one would be laughed at ... a few chief ideologists dominated with their sociological jargon. I didn't trust myself to say, "let me talk – at least I speak plainly."'[27] Just because plain, vulgar or undeferential speech ruled the interactions of students with their social or cultural superiors, the same was not always true of the internal regulation of the movements themselves. The ideal student leader deployed vulgarity when necessary but equally demonstrated intellectual sophistication (or its approximation) at others, and could move between these registers with ease, rather than being confined to one or the other.

The triumph of intellectual jargon was nonetheless one form of democratisation. The mass university produced a large audience for intellectually sophisticated (or pseudo-sophisticated) discourse. Student protest thus drew on two forms of linguistic democratisation: the levelling, downward thrust of informalised speech that stripped authority figures of the

---

[23] Alessandro Pizzorno, 'Tra accademia e movimento negli anni Sessanta (Amarcord la sociologia)', in Renate Siebert (ed.), *Il piacere della Sociologia. Essere e diventare sociologi. Trent'anni dopo il Sessantotto* (Catanzsro: Rubbettino, 1998), 15–42, 38.
[24] Gretschen Dutschke-Klotz, 'Jemanden zu lieben war irgendwie falsch', in Ute Kätzel, *Die 68erinnen: Porträt einer rebellischen Frauengeneration* (Berlin: Rowohlt, 2002), 277–296, 281.
[25] Ricci, *I giovani*, 198.
[26] Annette Schwarzenau, 'Nicht diese theoretischen Dinger, etwas Praktisches unternehmen', in Kätzel, *Die 68erinnen*, 58–59.
[27] Elke Regehr, 'Für viele Männer des SDS war die Psyche Weiberkram', in Kätzel, *Die 68erinnen*, 85.

deference they once assumed, and the ascent of large numbers who now accessed and adopted academic, theoretical jargon. Both modes depended on the greater student numbers in the 'mass university'. However, while the first was instrumental, designed to undermine the power of professorial discourse, the second emerged less consciously and betrayed the limitations of the drive towards a democratic discourse.

The preponderance of intellectual and political jargon created a hierarchy both within the protest movements and between the larger numbers at university and those who remained excluded. Student leaders were themselves unnerved by the gap between the protests against opaque language and the opaque language of protesters. Cohn-Bendit, whose gift for pithy statements made him one of the less incomprehensible orators of 1968, wrote that

> The problem of language is fundamental; the works of philosophers, sociologists, professional politicians ... present a danger that we wish to avoid at all costs: that of being formulated in such a way that it remains incomprehensible to the workers and peasants for whom, in any case, they are not written. This danger also awaits the analyses and texts of far-Left groups who want the leadership, the cadres of a workers' movement to whom they do not even know how to speak.[28]

Such a stance contained numerous contradictions. Many of the works of philosophers or others, as Cohn-Bendit admitted, did not aim at a lay audience. A difficult language could both reflect the complexity of a topic, disdain for any unsophisticated audience, a revelling in deliberately obtuse language, poor writing, and a self-serving refusal of clarity. It could be all of those. The assumption of incomprehensibility to workers or peasants partook of a populism that could shade into condescension. However, much of the time the charge of cultural elitism through obfuscation masked as intellectual sophistication was directed at students by themselves, and signified a rejection of a university system that prized linguistic brilliance in and of itself as a marker of elite status. Thus in Italy Marco Boato wrote how 'the problem of language has been – and in many cases remains – central, in a negative sense, to the political experience of the MS [Student Movement], inasmuch as it is seriously weighed down by its own cultural class conditioning ... and many times rendered incomprehensible

---

[28] Daniel Cohn-Bendit and Gabriel Cohn-Bendit, *Le gauchisme: remède à la maladie senile du communism* (Paris: Seuil, 1968), 13.

to non-student forces, because it is still too abstract and too often heavy with ideological and intellectualistic lucubrations'.[29]

There was little new about such denunciations, which constituted a trope of the literature on university politics that effectively criticised student politicians for too obviously being students. No less a figure than Louis Althusser (hardly a model of clarity) proffered the same criticism for texts written in a 'dense, deliberately elliptical, deeply cultivated language, full of rhetorical figures, and overloaded with an esoteric vocabulary. I doubt that any worker comrade could read this text easily, or at all. ... That is, in my opinion, already a serious political fault'.[30] The charge of elliptic expression put students in their place in the same way that at other times they might be derided as too unsophisticated. Yet the revolts of 1968 and after raised the contradiction to new heights, as when two students working in the factories believed they had each discovered in the other the avant-garde of the proletariat, before realising that neither of them was in fact working-class.[31] One ex-Maoist remarked, 'one of the workers with whom I remained friends confessed to me two years later, that when I spoke at the time, he understood absolutely nothing of what I said'.[32] The mass university brought a heightened awareness of language as a cultural barrier, leading to inevitable self-denunciations of student discourse on the one hand and a posture of aggressive simplicity on the other.

The Politicisation of Speech

The ongoing tension between the linguistic goals and practices of the student movements stemmed from the different style and purpose of intellectual and political speech. The first, attuned to complexity, subject to the rules of academic debate, sought a relatively limited audience and, less charitably, was self-consciously concerned with its sophistication. The second aimed to mobilise, often as widely as possible, and thus rather than concern itself with complexity, preferred a posture of self-evident simplicity. Leaflets, graffiti and slogans required a reductive form of

---

[29] Marco Boato, 'Unità e diversità nel nuovo ciclo di lotte del movimento studentesco italiano', *Questitalia* 11 (1968), 14, n6.
[30] Althusser, 'A propos de l'article de Michel Verret sur "Mai Etudiant"', *La Pensée: revue du rationalisme moderne* 145 (1969), 3–14, 4.
[31] Jean-Pierre Le Goff, *Mai 68: l'héritage impossible* (Paris: La Découverte, 1998), 213.
[32] Bruno Giorgini (ed.), *Que sont mes amis devenus? (Mai 68 – été 78, dix ans après...)* (Paris: Savelli, 1978), 50.

expression. So too did most protest meetings. As one female student in Trento noted, 'the assembly demanded of whoever wanted to speak a mechanism of very heavy simplification'. This explained for her the relative absence of female voices since 'women take more of an interest in subtleties'.³³

Indeed, the discourse that emerged was decidedly gendered in its practice. One male militant described how 'as I didn't know how to express myself in a theoretical language, to overcome people's irony ... I always spoke in an aggressive tone. ... The first time I managed to speak for a half-hour was at a meeting of women'.³⁴ This student thus identified three sources of authority – theoretical sophistication, lacking which he opted for aggression or the privilege of gender. This was a distinctly undemocratic capture of speech, reliant in each instance on exclusion. To be sure, a number of women successfully adopted the speech of protest. The historian Luisa Passerini described how 'my language reflected cynicism and bitterness; I used strong terms, terse or biting expressions, I was hypercritical, derisory, cutting'.³⁵ The Trento student Marta Losito remembered how she made a great effort to find an 'assembly voice', and sometimes managed to achieve it: 'a tone of voice *imbonitore* [a barker], a tone of voice of someone who makes things happen, of someone who wants to be a protagonist'.³⁶ The assembly emerges, at least in retrospect, as much as a field of domination as liberation.

Female protesters typically remember that few women spoke successfully in student assemblies. Yet there are just as frequently recollections of exceptions: 'At the time I did not at all dare to speak in a political assembly at the FU where the great theoreticians of SDS debated. And most other women also did not dare. There was however one student, Hanna Kröger, whom I much admired, because she did not let herself be intimidated by anyone. She could speak well and was never discouraged'.³⁷ The student representative to the FU Senate, Sigrun Anselm, remembered the Argument-Club and SDS as a formative experience: 'never had so many opportunities been given to me to do something. Here I learnt to speak'.³⁸

---

³³ Ricci, *I giovani*, 106.   ³⁴ Giorgini (ed.), *Que sont mes amis devenus?*, 41.
³⁵ Luisa Passerini, *Autoritratto di gruppo* (Florence: Giunti, 1988), 75.
³⁶ CMR B.14 f.1 (Fondo Calì), A Trento Venti'Anni Dopo. Assemblea. Marta (Losito).
³⁷ Elsa Rassbach, 'Ich fand es wunderbar und schockierend, dass eine Frau so etwas macht', in Kätzel, *Die 68erinnen*, 65–66.
³⁸ As quoted by Henrike Hülsbergen, 'Wir wollten etwas Neues, anderes ... : Studentinnen an der Freien Universität während der Studentenbewegung', in Frauenbeauftragten der Freien Universität Berlin (ed.), *Selbstbewusst und Frei: 50 Jahre Frauen an der Freien Universität Berlin* (Königstein: Ulrike Helmer Verlag, 1998), 155.

The methods for silencing female speech were no more sophisticated than that aimed at professors. At Trento, one student recalled how 'Marianella [Sclavi] succeeded in speaking until she was Mauro's woman and then there was Elena Medi – dedicated and devoted to Boato – but even she was silenced with sentences such as "Elena, Elena, you'll be burnt at the stake."'[39] Sclavi herself remembered how, when the student movement at Trento met with national student leaders whom they viewed with suspicion, she 'expressed my dissent in my own way, different to the "party line" of seeing the question. The national representative, it hardly needs to be said, supported my intervention. Boato, interpreting the paralysing looks that were trained on me, rapidly closed the meeting, saying, "these disagreements, you and Mauro, resolve them in family"'.[40] The demands of politics favoured simplified sloganeering and welcomed neither dissent nor disagreement. They promoted not a democratic discourse but male charismatic authority.

The politicising and democratising drive of the revolts in 1968 tended to render academic speech ever more suspicious. The student movements effectively stripped professors of the automatic authority of academic speech, a triumph of a political and democratic impulse over the authority and autonomy of the academy. The consequences were not always expected. The old regime stuttered, but new forms of order and authority took their place. Charismatic speech, unstable and intangible, vanquished institutional authority, staid and tarnished. Students tended to reproduce the hierarchies characteristic of intellectual language (all the while rejecting them). In an intellectual sphere where authority supposedly derived from knowledge and expertise, anti-authoritarianism easily became populism or anti-intellectualism. Furthermore, the unmasking of the political and authoritarian dimensions to academic speech – so effective in silencing seemingly all-powerful professors – threatened to reduce all arguments to the political power to mobilise. Faculty were dethroned by displacing the authority of intellectual expertise by the power of the multitude – students outnumbered the professor in the classroom. To be sure, the most successful provocateurs in the lecture theatre were the best read and capable of challenging the professor on intellectual grounds. Nonetheless, challenges were as often to the authority of the lecturer as to their expertise.

---

[39] Ricci, *I giovani*, 106.
[40] Marianella Sclavi, 'Le origine del '68 a Trento: come si creano e come si distruggono una, due tre, tante fantasie', *I Giorni Cantati* 1.1 (1981), 83.

Indeed, much conflict over speech targeted not the content and formality of speech so much as its control, exemplified in the interruption, the interjection, the demand for debate. Different agendas jostled behind these actions. The interruption of professors reflected the decline of intellectual authority and the flagging of a conceptualisation of education as the diffusion of knowledge, as passed from one generation to the next, from professor to student. Disruption of academic authority was the first element of an attempt to democratise the control of speech. Much more complicated was the problem of what democratic speech in a lecture hall should look like. The student assemblies sometimes approached an ideal of democratic debate, but often not for very long, dominated instead by charismatic male students. At Trento, Mauro Rostagno denounced his own domination of a forum 'where you are free only to raise a hand to approve what the others have thought, analysed and decided for you. Or, at limit, free not to approve'.[41] The negative sides of the student assembly should not be exaggerated. Emphasised in retrospect, many were initially oblivious to the problems. Observers such as the French psychoanalyst Didier Anzieu insisted: 'in all the general assemblies I attended, not merely at Nanterre . . . the minority could always make itself heard'.[42] However, minority opinions had to contend with interruptions, whistles, and various forms of the verbal intimidation. The transcript of one West German assembly in June 1967 shows the style of debate, as one student questioned the value of demonstrating against a ban on demonstrations:

> It will be said that the death [of Ohnesorg] is being exploited . . . (disquiet, interjections: by whom? By whom?) It was earlier further stated that everything will be postponed, a policeman will be sacrificed to us, but nothing changed in the fundamentals. I believe we have to defend ourselves against this. (Disquiet. Laughter) Explain that you detest the use of such means for a democratic demonstration as inappropriate. (Whistles, interjections. Booing. Interjection: your tie's not straight!) Secondly, I would like to propose to vote to prevent the repetition of such events, that we adopt the following proposal . . . (rhythmic clapping, whistles, interjection of the chair Hameister: get this resolution quickly out of the way.)[43]

Small wonder that many of the movements' orators demonstrated a mastery of aggressive simplification or dense theory. A speaker had to

---

[41] Mauro Rostagno, 'Anatomia della rivolta', *Problemi del socialism* 28–29 (1968), 283.
[42] Epistémon, *Ces idées qui ont ébranlé la France. Nanterre, novembre 1967–juin 1968* (Paris: Fayard, 1968), 86.
[43] Frank Wolff and Eberhard Windaus (eds.), *Studentenbewegung 1967–1969: Protokollen und Materialen* (Frankfurt: Verlag Roter Stern, 1977), 33–34.

contend with laughter, whistling, booing, interjections, ironic clapping and applause. In one sense, such a forum was distinctly democratic. Certainly, the audience was far from passive. Yet this democracy also made the assembly an arena of intimidation and exclusion.

The Silence of Others

The assembly was the typical product of the student revolts, its multiple speakers and rowdy interactions in stark contrast to the professorial lecture. The assembly appeared to offer the best response to the persistent demand for debate. However unusually this demand was expressed, the rationale behind it – to create a rational political will through public debate – was very old. In *The Structural Transformation of the Public Sphere*, Jürgen Habermas had pointed out that 'publicity once meant the exposure of political domination before the public use of reason; publicity now adds up the reactions of an uncommitted friendly disposition'.[44] While Habermas understood this image of the public sphere as out-dated, the major press controversies of the 1960s focused on censorship, and the exposure of government authority before the reading public. A perceived lack of free speech formed an important element of the authoritarian heritage demonstrators identified and despised. The Spiegel Affair of 1962, when the police raided the offices of the magazine *Der Spiegel*, drove home the potential limits of freedom of the press in the Federal Republic of Germany.[45] In Italy, the 1966 scandal over the Milanese student newspaper *La Zanzara* that published a story on sexual education only to find its editors charged by the government with obscenity and corruption of minors, epitomised the conflict between freedoms of speech and the claims of custom and morality.[46] The French government reflexively responded to the problems of the Algerian wars with censorship. The vicious suppression of the October 1961 demonstration in Paris that resulted in many dead found little echo in the press. The editor François Maspero regularly complained of censorship.

---

[44] Jürgen Habermas, *Structural Transformation of the Public Sphere. An Inquiry into a Category of Bourgeois Society*, trans. Thomas Burger (Cambridge, MA: MIT Press, 1989), 195.

[45] See von Hodenberg, 'Mass media and the generation of conflict'. See also Christina von Hodenberg, 'Konkurrierende Konzepte von "Öffentlichkeit" in der Orientierungskrise der 60er Jahre' in Matthias Frese, Julia Pauls and Karl Treppe (eds.), *Demokratisierung und gesellschaftlicher Aufbruch: Die sechziger Jahre als Wendezeit der Bundesrepublik* (Paderborn: Ferdinand Schöningh, 2003), 205–226.

[46] See Guido Nozzoli and Pier Maria Paoletti, *'La Zanzara'. Cronache e documenti di uno scandalo* (Milan: Feltrinelli, 1966).

These controversies usually pitted the freedom of the press against interests of state, and the formal imposition of restraints on speech remained an important issue in the 1960s. 'Reasons of state', while not disappearing completely, could no longer claim automatic assent, any more than professorial authority. However, the protest movements rarely viewed the major organs of the press as valiant defenders of free speech, but rather as complicit in the conformity of the majority of society, and particularly egregious in their reporting of the rise of protest. The students certainly opposed censorship. Within the university, this meant the rejection of speech not in terms of print columns but through withholding the space and right to speak. Some of the first protests evoked the spectre of censorship within academia, in conflicts not over the intellectual work of faculty but the suppression of political discussion. The clumsiness of university administrators provided an enduring source of scandal in the first stage of protest, an important motor of student mobilisation and solidarity.

Yet while they opposed censorship, of equal if not greater concern were seduction and apathy. For many students, the problem was increasingly not freedom of speech but effective speech. As the German student Peter Schneider proclaimed in his speech 'We Have Made Errors': 'we informed in all seriousness about the war in Vietnam, however we experienced that we could cite the most unimaginable details of American politics in Vietnam without moving the imagination of our neighbours'.[47] The protest movements simultaneously articulated the Berkeley demand to be able to speak 'on any subject at any time in any place', but also complained that while they could speak as much as they liked, their words had little to no effect. The model of a public sphere held to account by the critical use of reason confronted the realisation that criticism could be all too easily ignored, dismissed or disparaged. Thus while the demand for freedom of speech never disappeared, equally if not more urgent became the very different project of creating a space in which speech might actually matter. To rouse the majority from their undemocratic slumbers required disruptive acts, not measured speech. As Schneider proclaimed, 'is it about doing away with calm and order, it is about undemocratic behaviour'.[48] As Dutschke put it, 'without provocation we wouldn't be noticed at all'.[49]

---

[47] Peter Schneider, *Ansprachen: Reden, Notize, Gedichte* (Berlin: Verlag Klaus Wagenbach, 1970), 12–13.
[48] Ibid.
[49] David Caute, *The Year of the Barricades: A Journey through 1968* (New York: Harper & Row, 1988), 98.

Thus the most visible and controversial uses of speech in the late 1960s did not reflect a model based on reason, of rational debate, but rather of provocation. The speech of provocation both embodied the collapse of deference and directly attacked what many found to be the illusions of the model of a functional public sphere: the inefficacy of criticism and the implied equality of public individuals, as if the speech of a student and a professor held equal weight. This explains why student movements could simultaneously ritually demand 'dialogue' yet be very wary of it in practice. As the Cohn-Bendit brothers argued, 'the rejection of a premature dialogue with professors is just a protective measure before having the necessarily theoretical base'.[50] Provocation trumped dialogue, as the latter appeared merely a more pleasant façade of equality. The professorial lecture required the silence, for the most part, of the audience and one of the early insights of protesters was that such silent consent could easily be withdrawn by a small minority.

Above all, provocation broke the bonds of passivity that protesters perceived as central to their subordination. Italian students argued that 'we are all victims of a despotic system which dishabituates us from debate and political struggle and imposes on us its politics, that is, authoritarianism and subordination'.[51]

> The student doesn't talk, he has never been taught to, rather the entire structure and institutions of the system have repressed this basic human right. We need therefore to relearn to talk... and to do this we need to find ourselves among equals.[52]

Provocations sought to silence the professor to create a space in which other voices could be heard. Many members of the student movement only hesitantly embraced this aggressive mode of speech, but it proved the most productive in humiliating professors, provoking retaliation and producing situations that increased student solidarity. Thus, while students often invoked the Berkeley-inspired demand to speak on any subject, at any time, in any place when it suited them and concerned their own freedom of speech, many of the most successful provocations did not demand the right to speak but withdrew that right from others. As Pierre Bourdieu noted, freedom of speech 'is always freedom from the speech of

---

[50] Cohn-Bendit, *Le gauchisme*, 34.
[51] CMR B.1 f.2 (Fondo Movimento Studentesco G. Palma), 'Documenti per le agitazioni'.
[52] CMR B.1 f.7 (Fondo Movimento Studentesco G. Palma), 'Controcorso di psicoanalisi e società repressiva'.

others, or rather control of their silence'.[53] Despite declarations of the absolute principle of free speech – 'the prior condition of all revolutionary action is the right to speak for all'[54] – no such absolute freedom existed. The proclamation of free speech was deeply ambiguous and obscured a fundamental question of power. Faculty were often silenced in practice; so were many in the audience of the assembly, alternative, dissenting and female voices. Fascists were explicitly excluded – 'these freedoms are not for fascists', one paper quoted Rudi Dutschke.[55] Daniel Cohn-Bendit found the most felicitous formula for both hearing and silencing opponents: when students prevented the French mathematician and socialist Laurent Schwartz from speaking, Cohn-Bendit insisted he 'is certainly a scoundrel, but he must be allowed to talk, and no-one will be deprived afterwards of letting him know that he is a bastard'.[56]

Speech and space formed the frontiers of cultural democratisation. The politics of transgression, the trespass of boundaries and the rupturing of taboos undermined the voice of traditional authorities and opened a space in which students sought to define a more democratic regime of speech. Against the administrative regime of the university, students demanded a policy of self-regulation. They embarked on a long experimentation with forms of space and speech. In a trajectory similar to that of the vision of democratised education, the protesters initially focused on issues of access – of censorship and of the right to speak. Yet very rapidly, the form of speech came into play – informalisation, vulgarity, laughter, verbal violence and opacity – both reflecting and shaping a new hierarchy. In response, some protesters sought new spaces they hoped would reproduce neither the passivity of the lecture hall nor the political theatre of the student assembly. They discovered no definitive resolution to this problem. Some found it difficult to recapture the thrill from the sudden devaluation of professorial power and embarked on an elusive search to recover that feeling of freedom. The inventive element of provocation soon turned to deadening repetition. The demand for dialogue seemed paramount only until it was granted. The politicisation that created space for debate threatened to subordinate speech to the perceived necessities of political mobilisation.

[53] Pierre Bourdieu, *Homo Academicus* (Stanford: Stanford University Press, 1988), 192.
[54] BDIC. F delta 813(7), 'Compte rendu de l'AG de 1 juin' 22 mars.
[55] Richard Kaufmann, 'Der Aufstand der Söhne', *Christ und Welt* (22 March 1968), 21.
[56] Jean-Pierre Duteuil, *Nanterre, 1965–66–67–68. Vers le movement du 22 mars* (Paris: Acratie, 1988), 196. On Schwartz, the key figure in the Comité Vietnam National, see Salar Mohandesi, 'Bringing Vietnam home: The Vietnam War, internationalism and May '68', *French Historical Studies* 41.2 (2018), 219–251, 223.

As with any revolution, the conformity of the past was no doubt exaggerated. The revolts enabled a simplified contrast of active protesters with the passive students of yore. Yet after the deluge of speech, the limits and practices did not return to the status quo ante. The revolts accelerated the making of a new subjectivity marked by the ability to speak. Although such a facility had always been valued, it was now consecrated by a broader market instead of the intimate approbation of authority. The protesters sought less to be taken seriously by the demi-Gods of the professoriate than the raucous audiences of the assembly. The revolts drove the making of a new university-educated elite, with a subjectivity self-conscious of its active scepticism of authority and marked by the striving for authenticity, epitomised above all in speech.

PART III
Crisis of the University

CHAPTER 8

'Question, Doubt and Criticise'
Free Speech at the Free University

Speech in all its guises – provocative, desacralising, charismatic – marked student protests everywhere in the Sixties. But the Free University of Berlin offers the most extended case-study in how the politics of speech could generate institutional crisis in the university. The particular prominence of speech in West Berlin reflected the advantages of the 'Berlin Model', which officially sanctioned representation within the university hierarchy. Official recognition created a space in which the legitimacy of student speech was not questioned, only its limits. The institutional entrenchment of student politics offered more opportunities for conflict. The 'Berlin Model' furthermore allowed protest in West Berlin to proceed as the preservation of existing rights as much as the establishment of new ones. The Nazi past and unfulfilled hopes for the democratisation of the university and West German society added historical weight to arguments about free speech. Finally, the frontier status of West Berlin, so self-consciously an outpost of freedom in the Cold War, ensured aspirations for democratisation held a special charge. Thus the Free University, located in the quiet, leafy, middle-class suburb of Dahlem in the isolated outpost of West Berlin became a focal point for the politics of protest.

The student movement crystallised through a series of 'affairs' that to its protagonists appeared trivial in retrospect. Debates over speech paled in comparison to the violent conflict to come, the deaths and assassination attempts that haunted the mass mobilisation of 1967 and 1968. Yet these early events – the 'Kuby Affair', the 'Krippendorff Affair', the egging of the Amerika Haus in West Berlin – were momentous, indices of a tectonic shift in student culture and revealing a new dynamic of protest. Students at the Free University not only asserted a democratic vision of the university but sought to establish it. In doing so, they very successfully framed the struggle as one of democracy versus authority. The nascent revolt counterposed students' rights of speech to the rector's administration of space. Two assertions of autonomy opposed each other: that of the university as corporation and that of the student body as a democratic self-governing entity. Claims of 'free speech' were, as always, in fact claims about power, in particular that of the rector within the university realm. Censorship provided students a powerful framework within which to cast the new controversy to the detriment of the rector. Furthermore, by conducting their disagreements with the university administration through the student and local press, the protest movement subjected the university to unfamiliar and unwanted public scrutiny. However, the democracy of protest was not confined to assertions of self-government and appeals to public opinion but included more aggressive assaults on traditional authority. Provocative speech quickly rivalled censorship scandals for its ability to mobilise, targeting above all the ideology of objectivity, apoliticism, reputation and dignity in which administrators and faculty cloaked themselves. The conflict pushed the university ever more into the unwelcome role of administrative police and censors. The dynamic of confrontation between administration and democracy escalated without resolution until wider society displaced the university as the focus of revolt.

The 'Kuby Affair'

If the 'Kuby Affair' in 1965 was the moment that 'brought the democratic credentials of the university into question',[1] that was not because the event was unprecedented. Rather, student protest swelled over an incident that had occurred thrice already. In July 1958 the journalist Erich Kuby had called into question the 'free' part of the university's title. Ironically, Kuby's comments targeted the university's politicisation: 'the name [Free University] expresses a large measure of unfreedom. . . . in the words "Free University" is fixed an inner, antithetical connection to the unfree university on the other side of the Brandenburg Gate . . . that is, to my mind, plainly incompatible with the scientific and pedagogical task of the university'.[2] For this statement, the rector of the FU refused to provide rooms for any event to which Kuby was subsequently invited. In July 1960, far from

---

[1] Nick Thomas, *Protest Movements in 1960s West Germany: A Social History of Dissent and Democracy* (Oxford: Berg, 2003), 55. See also James F. Tent, *The Free University of Berlin: A Political History* (Bloomington: Indiana University Press, 1988), 291–298; Peter Müller, 'Wie frei ist der Freie Universität Berlin', in Rolf Seeliger (ed.), *Braune Universität: Deutsche Hochschullehrer gestern und heute. Dokumentation mit Stellungnahmen IV. Westberlin* (Munich: Verlag Rolf Seeliger, 1966), 6–26.

[2] Pressestelle der FU Berlin (ed.), *Hochschule im Umbruch: Teil IV: Die Krise (1964–1967)* (Berlin: Pressestelle der FU Berlin, 1975), 198.

stoking the fires of left-wing revolt, the conservative *Ring Christlich Demokratischer Studenten* demanded that the Protestant church, which had allowed the Evangelische Gemeindehaus Dahlem to host the event, not allow itself to be 'misused by activities of left-radical interest groups'.[3] A further two events to which student associations invited Kuby took place off-campus in December 1961 and May 1962.[4] Only the fourth instance, in 1965, sparked an 'affair'. Had it not, a scandal would surely have erupted at the fifth. In 1965, the rector (by then biology professor Herbert Lüers) confirmed the *Redeverbot* when students invited Kuby to contribute to a planned May 1965 podium discussion on 'Restoration or New Beginning: the Federal Republic Twenty Years On'. The Kuby Affair had begun.

What made an event previously so unremarkable suddenly so controversial? One reason lies in the changed political climate. In 1965, unlike 1960 or 1962, the Right no longer held a majority in the Konvent. The chief executive of AStA, Wolfgang Lefèvre, was a member of SDS. The Leftwards political shift constituted the primary novelty of this situation, although students did not always perceive this. The *FU-Spiegel* could write in February 1966 that 'up to May 1965 the University administration in no way practiced censorship in the allocation of rooms for political meetings. Then came the Kuby Affair...'[5] The perception of decline was an illusion. Student assumptions had shifted, not the practice of administrative power. Indeed, the RCDS proved itself much more consistent (albeit less assertive), describing the rector's actions as 'unfortunate', but entitled to 'make use of his authority'.[6] The changed political climate primarily meant one where the rector's authority could be questioned.

The international context further facilitated the controversy. The Berkeley Free Speech Movement had begun late the previous year. As has often been noted, West German students in the United States helped transfer protest ideas from the United States to the Federal Republic.[7] The SDS

---

[3] Pressestelle der FU Berlin (ed.), *Hochschule im Umbruch: Teil III: Auf dem Weg in den Dissens (1957–1964)* (Berlin: Pressestelle der FU Berlin, 1974), 27. On the RCDS see Anna von der Goltz, 'Other '68ers in West Berlin: Christian Democratic students and the Cold War city', *Central European History* 50 (2017), 87–112.

[4] In December 1961, Kuby spoke in the Studentenhaus at Steinplatz in an event organised by the LSD and SDS. It is not clear whether in the second and third instances the associations even bothered to seek a room on campus for the event.

[5] 'Form oder Inhalt', *FU Spiegel* 50 (Februar 1966), 10.

[6] Pressestelle der FU Berlin (ed.), *Hochschule IV*, 202.

[7] Doug McAdam and Dieter Rucht, 'The Cross-National Diffusion of Movement Ideas', *Annals of the American Academy of Political and Social Science* 528 (July 1993), 56–74. See also Martin Klimke, *The Other Alliance: Student Protest in West Germany and the United States in the Global Sixties*

journal *Neue Kritik* published a short dispatch on the Free Speech Movement in February 1965, just two months before the Kuby Affair.[8] Yet the protest at the Free University did not result simply from the diffusion of the model of Berkeley. Indeed, some students thought the situations in Berkeley and West Berlin had little in common.[9] After all, the revolt at Berkeley took off from the withdrawal of the right to collect money on campus by political organisations. In West Berlin, Kuby's invitation to the podium discussion came from AStA, the representative of all students, acting in its mandated role of political education.[10] The divergences mattered not. Reports of the Free Speech movement arrived in a situation that could have been designed for them. The appeal to the United States resonated in West Germany more than the other Western European states due to the Cold War and invoked a legitimate tradition of protest assumed absent from the German past. More than the other protest movements in Western Europe, therefore, the West Germans framed their demands as echoes of the United States.[11] Prior to the podium discussion in May, a broad coalition of student groups demanded the right (in German and English) 'to hear any person speak in any open area on campus at any time on any subject except when it would cause a traffic problem or interfere with classes'.[12] They called for public protest.

Despite the conflation of Berlin and Berkeley, the protest at the Free University, unlike California, did not emerge from censorship of political activity. There had been recurrent debates over political activity within the university – over nuclear weapons (in 1959) and over the Algerian war – but the Kuby Affair did not fall into this tradition. While the rector would

---

(Princeton: Princeton University Press, 2010). For reports on Berkeley prior to the Kuby Affair, see Michael Vester, 'Die Strategie der direkten Aktion', *Neue Kritik* 6.30 (1965), 12–20.

[8] Günter Amendt, 'Die Studentenrevolte in Berkeley.' *Neue Kritik* 6.28 (1965), 5–7. The article focused on the relation of the Berkeley revolt to the civil rights movement and the tactics of non-violence, and does not mention the slogan to be re-used by the students in Berlin, to hear anyone speak, at any time, in any place.

[9] Ludwig von Friedeburg et al., *Freie Universität und politisches Potential der Studenten: Über die Entwicklung des Berliner Modells und den Anfang der Studentenbewegung in Deutschland* (Luchterhand: Neuwied und Berlin, 1968), 256.

[10] The invitation had been made by the outgoing president Wolfgang Roth, affiliated with the SHB, but it would be up to Wolfgang Lefevre (SDS) to deal with the affair.

[11] Other student movements appear to have had fewer personal contacts than the West German groups to the United States. See also Timothy Scott Brown, *West Germany and the Global Sixties* (Cambridge: Cambridge University Press, 2013), 366 for how the West German movements in particular constructed their 68 via global connections.

[12] The groups were: the SDS, SHB, the Liberaler Studentenbund Deutschlands (LSD), the Gewerkschaftliche Studentengruppe, Evangelische Studentengemeinde, Deutsch-Israelische Studiengruppe, Argument-Klub and Humanistische Studentenunion. Pressestelle der FU Berlin (ed.), *Hochschule IV*, 199.

indeed complain that students misinterpreted his position as political, that the *Redeverbot* occurred not because of Kuby's political views but because of his defamation of the university,[13] this self-serving representation of the situation obscured the fundamental issue. The Kuby Affair opened the era of protest not because it concerned politics but because it pitted the administrative prerogatives of the rector against the democratic self-conception of the student body. This conflict had already been foreshadowed. Administrative moves to forcibly deregister students had begun in late 1964, although that controversy would not take off until the following year, in February 1966. The 1964 debate over the *Bildungskatastrophe* emphasised the problem of a democratic higher education system. The growing contradictions between administrative and democratic visions of the university only deepened when the rector's initial openness to student representation on a committee to deal with the revision of the university's constitution dissipated after consultation with professors. The fourth exclusion of Erich Kuby occurred in the midst of debate over the meaning of a democratic university.

The Kuby Affair demonstrated the marginality of student representation. Aware of previous issues with Kuby, AStA had sought confirmation from the rector's office of any prohibition and had received approval for the invitation. The rector's subsequent intervention contradicted the previous advice and, furthermore, was taken without any consultation with the students. Crucial to the growth of controversy was the use of administrative power to make rooms unavailable rather than allow any debate over the judiciousness of the invitation. In a public letter to the rector, AStA criticised above all the 'administrative measures' used to prevent debate at the FU, deploring that 'the means of internal campus administration, that normally serves to keep away unreliable and doubtful elements from the university, are used against student representation'.[14] In opposition to the administrative power of the rector, the student associations appealed not to other parts of the university but rather to public (student) opinion. A flood of leaflets ensued – 'hardly a single statement given in relation to the "Kuby Affair" remained unpublished'.[15] The controversy called the administrative powers of the rector to account before the student body.

Despite the rhetoric, therefore, the conflict concerned not so much freedom of speech as the freedom of the student organisation to decide,

---

[13] See von Friedeburg et al., *Freie Universität*, 249.
[14] Pressestelle der FU Berlin (ed.), *Hochschule IV*, 200.
[15] Von Friedeburg et al., *Freie Universität*, 253.

democratically, for themselves what was legitimate. Yet both sides often preferred to debate the topic in the language of a universal right to speech – the students for its clarity and international resonance, the administration for what they perceived as its evident irrelevance. Lüers was adamant: the use of rooms at the FU was his prerogative, and 'there can be no talk of a violation of the basic right of free expression of opinion. A basic right so understood does not exist.'[16] In a letter to Lefèvre, Lüers restated the long-held position of the Freie Universität hierarchy: 'the rector represents the university and ... must prevent the university from becoming a stage for events that are not compatible with the tasks or the dignity of a university'.[17] The students retorted that the refusal to allow Kuby to speak itself damaged the reputation of the FU.

The 'dignity' of the university was a poorly articulated rationale, easily debated, and entirely dependent on the beholder. Yet all agreed that there was no basic right of freedom of expression. Few if any of the students protesting the censorship of Kuby argued for the rights of fascists to speak on the university grounds – quite the opposite. In June 1965 most students strongly opposed the recognition of the right-wing fraternities that would give those associations access to university facilities. The student representation wanted the right to decide for itself who could or could not be invited onto campus for discussion and debate. They recoiled from the arbitrariness of a personal authority, embodied in the rector and exercised through a supposedly apolitical control of space. As the student newspaper, the *FU-Spiegel* noted 'how a meeting is evaluated depends on the character of the particular rector'.[18] This probably overestimated the leeway for a rector's individuality but focused on the problem of how rectorial authority was justified. The rectors tried to limit the problem to the sole question of whether or not that authority existed – 'Do you want to say that the university has absolutely no right to make available its rooms according to content?' asked Lüers' successor, Hans-Joachim Lieber.[19] However, the debate had already shifted. Students did not simply assert the right to self-governance but sought to subject the rector's authority to democratic scrutiny. One open letter described the change: 'so far we have allowed the impression of a conflict between *Hausordnung*

---

[16] Pressestelle der FU Berlin (ed.), *Hochschule IV*, 201.
[17] APO FU-Berlin Allgemein Rektoratsakten Politisches Mandat Teil 1. 2. 2098 2 1950 – August 1967. 'Abschrift der Rektor der Freien Universität Berlin an den Vorsitzenden des AStA Herrn Wolfgang Lefèvre 20.5.1965'.
[18] 'Form oder Inhalt', *FU Spiegel* 50 (Februar 1966), 10.   [19] Ibid.

and student rights. In truth, it's about a conflict between clear student rights and an exceedingly doubtful interpretation of *Hausordnung* from a democratic point of view.'[20] Students thus interpreted democracy to mean, in addition to self-government, the standard by which to measure the rector's actions.

The Kuby Affair revealed both the student will to debate the rector's use of his authority and the determination to contest the rector's decisions with an array of protest forms. The podium discussion itself, displaced to the Technische Universität, occurred with little controversy. The content of the event was its least contentious aspect. However, a demonstration against Rector Lüers' decision mobilised some 500 students. Over 3,000 signed a petition for Berkeley-style freedom of speech. A number of professors and numerous assistants expressed their opposition to any *Redeverbot*, although rarely endorsing the universal right demanded by the students. On 17 May, ten days after Kuby's speech had come and gone, the student representatives of the politics department, along with SDS and SHB, called for a 'lecture strike' (*Vorlesungsstreik*) at the Otto Suhr Institute (OSI, the institute for political science at the FU). The following day only 10 per cent of students attended lectures at the OSI. Most professors did not bother to hold their classes. George Kotowski, CDU representative in the West Berlin Parliament, lectured to a residual forty. Yet political affiliation did not necessarily determine the attitude to protest. The SPD member and vice-Rector Ernst Heinitz warned student associations might have their privileges withdrawn should teaching be disturbed by demonstrations.[21]

A general assembly of some 600 politics students debated the 'Kuby Affair' and re-endorsed their representatives. Even this relatively sedate protest brought forth the ire of the Springer Press, which denounced the demonstrations as 'not freedom ... but anarchy'.[22] More sympathetic observers such as the head of the Institute, Kurt Sontheimer, criticised the strike on the grounds it would only serve to garner publicity.[23] Indeed, none of these actions were likely to have any effect on the policy or administration of the university. The rector pointedly stated that such methods were not the way to achieve change in university regulations, which would have to be considered by the university Senate. The petition,

---

[20] 'Offener Brief der Fachschaft Politologie vom 17. Mai 1965', as quoted in von Friedeburg et al., *Freie Universität*, 261.
[21] 'Freie Universität: Berliner Blockade', *Der Spiegel* 22 (26 May 1965), 134.   [22] Ibid.
[23] Pressestelle der FU Berlin (ed.), *Hochschule IV*, 28.

strike and assembly, did, however, reinforce the solidarity of students around the idea of their democratic self-governance.

The protests successfully established the framework of democracy and self-government, not merely for the students, but increasingly as a means to undermine the authority of the university administration: 'The idea that the democratic spirit of the university can be protected through the authoritative exercise of the disciplinary power of *Hausrecht* alone betrays a mistrust of democratic supervisory bodies', declared the Konvent. 'The student body demands no suspension of the rights of individual parts of the university, but the confirmation of its right to democratic self-government.'[24] After considering a referendum (used successfully two years previously to overturn the election of the *Burschenschaftler* Eberhard Diepgen to the head of AStA), the student parliament drafted a proposal for its members of the academic Senate to put forward: that approval for the use of university rooms 'cannot be made dependent on either the theme of the event or the political opinions of the invited speakers'.[25] The Senate quickly rejected the proposal, considering it irrelevant, restating once again that the demand that 'any person desired by [the student body] speak on any subject at any time, in any place whatsoever is incompatible with the statutory authority of the rector'.[26] Thus neither petitions, nor protest, nor the proposal to the Senate proved effective in establishing a public debate over who could speak at the Free University. Yet while the 'Berlin Model' yielded little satisfaction to the protesters, it provided them seats on the stage and the opportunity to address the new students at the *Immatrikulationsfeier* (matriculation ceremony) to take place two days later.

The ceremonial occasion substituted for the absence of a public debate. Rector Lüers gave his version of the Kuby Affair. Wolfgang Lefèvre followed. Controversy over one use of speech thus culminated in another. Previous forms of protest served to mobilise students as a democratic force. Now Lefèvre's speech targeted the symbolic authority of the rector in an explicit withdrawal of the presumption of student consent. The speech began a process of desacralisation that would culminate in 1967 when the *FU-Spiegel* printed a picture collage in which the student representative Sigrun Fronius displayed her naked backside to the incoming rector.[27] Noting that many of the new students may have chosen the Freie Universität for the renowned 'Berlin Model' of student co-government, Lefèvre accounted for the sorry state of student rights and condemned the 'patriarchal oversight of the rector'. Throwing the rector's arguments

[24] Ibid., 206.   [25] Ibid., 205.   [26] Ibid., 207.   [27] See Tent, *Free University*, 340.

about reputation back in his face, Lefèvre insisted that 'it is in no way consistent with the reputation of the university if one labels critical comments about the university as slander and thereby forbids a discussion'.[28] The Senate, he declared, had 'behaved creatively in an ambiguous legal situation'[29] – at which point several faculty members interrupted the speech. Karl August Bettermann, professor of Law and one of the key members of the committee that had sat in 1958 to delineate the limits of the students' political mandate, protested 'We are not here at a political meeting.'[30] He appealed to the rector: 'Your Magnificence, if you do not intervene now, I will leave the room.'[31] Lüers accepted the invitation with alacrity and led Lefèvre away from the podium amid general tumult. As his speech ended, Lefèvre proclaimed that 'this beautiful unity that you see before you, where teachers and taught sit beside each other, rather *with* each other on the podium – this beautiful unity deceives'.[32] He need hardly have mouthed the words. No unity of '*Lehrende* und *Lernende*' was visible.

The controversy of the *Immatrikulationsfeier* demonstrated the dissipation of the rector's authority had just begun. Many of the new students appeared to side with the rector, at least regarding the appropriateness of the festivities as the moment to articulate the differences between student representation and the administration.[33] Yet they rejected less the criticism than the radical desacralising thrust of the performance: 'when the Professor who gave the commemorative speech likewise spoke critically about the Berlin Model, the students applauded him. Clearly they were ready to accept the exact same criticism if it was made by a Professor with scientific and personal authority'.[34] Collegial criticism was acceptable. The radical reversal of student deference was not. The representatives on AStA, however, had moved beyond such distinctions. The student body would soon follow, although this was not obvious at the time. Erich Kuby, asked about the rejection by students of Lefèvre's speech, argued in terms that mere months later would look outdated: 'this generation' he thought 'is not characterised by a special will to generational rebellion. . . . already at the

---

[28] APO FU-Berlin Allgemein Rektoratsakten Politisches Mandat Teil 1. 2. 2098 2 1950 – August 1967. 'Rede des 1. Vorsitzenden des Allgemeinen Studentenausschusses der Freien Universität Berlin, Herrn Wolfgang Lefèvre, anläßlich der Immatrikulationsfeier am Freitag, dem 28. Mai 1965'.
[29] Ibid.   [30] Pressestelle der FU Berlin (ed.), *Hochschule IV*, 223.   [31] Ibid., 30.
[32] APO FU-Berlin Allgemein Rektoratsakten Politisches Mandat Teil 1. 2. 2098 2 1950 – August 1967.
[33] See von Friedeburg et al., *Freie Universität*, 267.   [34] Ibid., 268.

Abitur they see everything as civil servants and they behave themselves that way'.³⁵ In the part of his speech left undelivered Lefèvre reported how 'Konvent has put the question to the Senate if it believes the freedom of the university is guaranteed by democratic organisation', to which question the Senate had merely offered 'legal demarcations'.³⁶ This depiction – democracy against administration – would prevail. In the meantime, the debate festered in rival press releases. The rector's office reported that Lefèvre was 'prevented from speaking further by the students and members of the academic Senate on the basis of his irrelevant remarks'.³⁷ AStA complained that 'after banning an outside critic now the freedom of speech for the elected representatives of the student body has also been restricted'.³⁸ For the student representatives, for whom the 'Berlin Model' meant a community of teachers and learners on equal terms, the inability of Lefèvre to complete his speech was another case of censorship that gave the lie to the illusion of student self-government.

The Kuby affair catalysed a new understanding of student politics. In the Konvent debate on Lefèvre's speech, the talk still revolved around the 'Berlin Model'. Some argued that 'the present motions are not positive for the Berlin Model'. Others insisted it 'functions well, as long as the student body would be accepted as an equal partner', and others that 'the Berlin Model was driven to absurdity by the behaviour of the Professors at the matriculation ceremony'. Lefèvre himself justified his conduct as unavoidable 'as the Berlin Model was at stake'.³⁹ Whether or not the 'Berlin Model' had ever really functioned as an equal partnership of students and faculty, the members of the 1965 *Konvent* saw themselves as acting within that tradition. However, they imbued the Berlin Model with a much more radical democratic ethos and endorsed previously unthinkable tactics to express it. The strike at the Otto-Suhr Institute constituted an unusual action (in the Federal Republic of Germany). The appropriation of the matriculation-day event was unprecedented. The students may have thought of themselves as defending their traditional rights, but Lefèvre's speech marked a stark discontinuity with past student behaviour. When Konvent supported Lefèvre's actions by 35 votes to 18, with 6 abstentions, it marked a new beginning. Within the continuity of an emphasis on

---

³⁵ Pressestelle der FU Berlin (ed.), *Hochschule IV*, 212.
³⁶ 'Rede des 1. Vorsitzenden, dem 28. Mai 1965'.
³⁷ Mitteilung der Pressestelle des Rektors vom 28. Mai 1965 as quoted in von Friedeburg et al., *Freie Universität*, 269.
³⁸ Pressemitteilung des AStA vom 29.5.1965 as quoted in von Friedeburg et al., *Freie Universität*, 269.
³⁹ Pressestelle der FU Berlin (ed.), *Hochschule IV*, 209.

student self-government lay a turn to a public use of criticism, one that no longer deferred to the authority of the rector and led increasingly to a demand for a democratisation of all forms of authority.

Without always recognising it, the student representatives had supplemented the defence of their own self-government with the criticism of university authorities on the basis of 'democracy'. Administrators reacted with incomprehension to the challenge of student politics. Public criticisms by professors generated bewilderment 'that a member of the corporation takes a public position against their highest representative (elected by them), without beforehand making an attempt to discuss this viewpoint with him'.[40] Rectors continued to insist on vague invocations of the dignity of the university and the corporate responsibility of students. The failure to understand the challenge only entrenched the critique of authority. The student newspaper wrote the following year 'long overcome anti-democratic alternatives are revived, such as pure science versus agitatory politics; daily or party politics versus state politics, that is unhesitating, uncritical alignment with existing relations and established powers'.[41] The Berlin Model of co-governance may have proved itself an illusion, but so too the ceremony of the hallowed university was hollow. Whether welcome or not, the rector's authority was now to be subject to ongoing public criticism, and there would be no respite.

The Krippendorff Affair

The Krippendorff Affair revealed the contrast between an authoritarian and democratic mentality appealed well beyond a small minority of students. The controversy took off directly from the Kuby incident.[42] Ekkehart Krippendorff was an assistant at the Otto-Suhr Institute at the FU and ex-member of SDS. Inspired by the example of academics in the United States (where he had studied), he authored a regular column for the *Spandauer Volksblatt*, a small daily. He thereby staked out a position in the public sphere as well as the university. In his rundown of the Kuby Affair, Krippendorff endorsed the actions of the students, lamenting that 'we have in Germany no tradition of civil disobedience against limitations on

---

[40] Ibid., 27.   [41] Peter Müller, 'Es wird was geschehen', *FU Spiegel* 53 (Juli 1966), 5.
[42] On the Krippendorff affair, see Peter Szondi, *Über eine Freie (d.h. freie) Universität: Stellungnahmen eines Philologen* (Frankfurt am Main: Suhrkamp, 1973), 11–16. Krippendorff's analytical recollections can be found in Ekkehart Krippendorff, *Lebensfäden: Zehn autobiografische Versuche* (Heidelberg: Verlag Graswurzelrevolution, 2012). See also von Friedeburg et al., *Freie Universität*, 279–291.

freedom by the authorities. Demonstrations and 'the street' have here, unfortunately, the odium of disturbing the peace of citizens, and yet it is in such behaviour and actions that a living democracy is made'.[43] The Nazi past further informed Krippendorff's approval: 'We were once, 20 years ago, freed from outside; now it is up to us to defend and enlarge on the freedom obtained at that time.'[44] But Krippendorff also moved beyond the Kuby Affair. Insisting the issue was not the character of Kuby, but the principle of freedom of speech, Krippendorff wrote: 'By all accounts, already as great a scholar as Karl Jaspers could not speak or rather be invited to the 8 May 1945 [events] at this Free University, because the rector does not share his view on the German question.'[45] Public criticism of the rector from an untenured assistant was unheard of, another dent in the rector's prestige, and another airing of university issues in a public forum.

The rector's response proved more damaging than the original accusation. Writing to the *Spandauer Volksblatt*, Rector Lüers criticised the implication of political censure as 'grotesque and slanderous'. He quoted a letter from Jaspers responding to an invitation to speak and declining due to health reasons.[46] Krippendorff, having learnt of his error, had already printed a correction and apologised. But the rector, not in the least appeased, informed Krippendorff in June that as his 'behaviour is incompatible with your contractual duties', the FU would not renew his position after the end of September. Indeed, only the imminent end of his contract had obviated 'a summary dismissal'.[47] Having courted the spectre of censorship through the withholding of space in the Kuby Affair, the rector now appeared to practice it through the withdrawal of employment. Instead of political censure by refusing to invite Jaspers, Lüers faced the same charge by not renewing Krippendorff's contract. Crucially, the divisions now emerged between faculty members of the university.

The faculty of the Otto-Suhr Institute found itself in the same position as had AStA in the Kuby Affair. Lüers acted without consulting either Kurt Sontheimer, the director of the institute that employed Krippendorff, or Gilbert Ziebura, the professor to whom he was assistant. Sontheimer and Ziebura interpreted Lüers' action 'as a grave breach of the customary relations of loyalty within the university between rector and his colleagues'.[48] The severity of the response must mean 'the end of the academic career of Herr Krippendorff. The rector's goal of an 'instructive

---

[43] Pressestelle der FU Berlin (ed.), *Hochschule IV*, 202. [44] Ibid. [45] Ibid., 201–202.
[46] Ibid., 206. [47] Ibid., 216. [48] Ibid., 219.

effect' appeared designed to make an example of assistants 'who expose themselves politically'.[49] Yet Krippendorff's left-wing orientation was probably not the problem. The rector criticised his disregard for truth: 'one should demand and expect a striving for truth from a prospective academic (*Wissenschaftler*), that he is informed before a publication and not after'.[50] More importantly, the rector interpreted the article as personally defamatory, and as damaging to the reputation of the university, using much the same language that justified the rejection of Erich Kuby as speaker. In the wake of that affair, the rector probably felt the need to curtail further public criticism. However, he only succeeded in further undermining his authority.

The impression of political censorship found further confirmation in yet another instance of controversial speech in June 1965. The Law Professor Karl August Bettermann had interrupted Lefèvre's speech at the commencement ceremonies. A year later he would insist that students who did not finish their studies rapidly had only themselves to blame and diagnosed the need for a 'depoliticisation of the university'.[51] In June 1965, he attended the national conference of the *Burschenschaften* (the student fraternities). So, too, did Rector Lüers, a move hardly likely to win him more admirers in a university where, three years previously, the students had overturned the election of a *Burschenschaftler* as the head of AStA. But Bettermann's speech, a transcript of which soon circulated at the FU, courted much greater controversy:

> *Meine Herren*, as long as the words 'Honour, Freedom, Fatherland' stand on your flags, you cannot expect that all students or the mass of the population celebrate them. (Applause). Who says honour, demands honour and defends honour in these times must know that he finds himself in the minority. (Applause). And he who takes the word Fatherland so strongly and dutifully must yet work decades until all Germans are infused by the love of Fatherland and are ready to sacrifice themselves for this Fatherland. (frenetic applause).[52]

Referring to the prior weeks' troubles at the FU that 'happened in non-academic forms, that are not dignified and bring the Free University into disrepute', Bettermann expressed the opinion 'that these conflicts are misused for the purpose of making a row, to create a racket'. He ended with a call to restore order to the university: 'make a new beginning, bring our university once again to order (strong applause). In this sense, I call:

---

[49] Ibid. [50] Ibid., 216. [51] 'Berliner Modell', *Der Spiegel*, 28 February 1966, 34.
[52] APO FU-Berlin Allgemein 2 2098 2 Politische Meinungsäußerung 1965-7-26.

'*Burschen heraus!*' (continuing applause)'.⁵³ Where Krippendorff (and the students) contrasted civil disobedience and authoritarianism, Bettermann did the same with anarchy and order (as before him had the Springer Press). While the former sought to overcome the heritage of Nazism, the latter's language echoed that of the far Right. The political divide between disorderly democracy and orderly authority increasingly determined the meaning of individual actions.

The Burschenschaften did not come out at Berlin. Bettermann's critics did. In *Die Welt*, Otto von der Gablentz, professor at the Otto-Suhr Institute, summed up the Kuby and Krippendorff affairs, with one eye on the Bettermann speech, and criticised both the rector and the university in stinging terms: 'That a considerable proportion of the professors approve the standpoint of the rector testifies to a disposition as subject, that is only the obverse of the naive adoration of the authoritarian state'.⁵⁴ In a similar diagnosis to Krippendorff, von der Gablentz noted an enduring democratic deficit in West Germany and the university: 'None of the parties involved can be accused of a National Socialist past or disposition. But their mindset is characteristic of that "state consciousness" with which the Germans acquiesced in National Socialism, because it was ostensibly legitimate and "maintained order"'.⁵⁵ The students formulated their objections in a more lapidary manner: 'Better no man than Bettermann'.⁵⁶ The FU Senate censured von der Gablentz, but not Bettermann. The former had besmirched the reputation of the rector and university, the latter had not. At the July meeting of the Konvent, the student parliament took a unanimous stand on the Krippendorff affair. If Krippendorff had been careless, so had others; had he been disloyal, the charge could also be levelled at the rector; if he had damaged the university's reputation, Bettermann had done worse. They gave no credence to notions of honour: 'concepts such as "academic dignity", "academic custom" and "academic decency" … are 'not derived from the tasks of the university … but correspond to an antiquated corporate mentality'.⁵⁷ At a plenary meeting of all faculties at the FU on 16 July, calls were raised for the rector's resignation. Lüers brushed these aside, but their mere articulation showed how far his prestige had been tarnished. The Kuby affair affronted the

---

⁵³ APO FU-Berlin Allgemein 2 2098 2 Politische Meinungsäußerung 1965-7-26.
⁵⁴ Pressestelle der FU Berlin (ed.), *Hochschule IV*, 224.   ⁵⁵ Ibid.
⁵⁶ Karol Kubicki and Siegward Lönnendonker (eds.), *50 Jahre Freie Universität Berlin aus der Sicht von Zeitzeugen* (Berlin: Zentrale Universitätsdruckerei, 2002), 132.
⁵⁷ APO Berlin FU Allgemein Konvent 1965 7.–14. Sitzung 25 Juni–31 Dezember 'Antrag zum Tagesordnungspunkt 5) der 8. (o.) Sitzung des Konvents am Dienstag, dem 13. Juli 1965'.

students. The Krippendorff case underlined the assistants' subordinate status. Only the professors could be reliably expected to back the rector, and they included prominent dissident voices.

The divisions within the faculty once again became public at the end of July with the publication of the letter the rector had sent to Kurt Sontheimer, the head of the Otto-Suhr Institute, over the latter's invitation to Karl Jaspers to speak at the FU – the non-event which Ekkehart Krippendorff had speculated was due to political reasons. Jaspers indeed declined due to health reasons. But, Lüers wrote to Sontheimer, 'in the case of an acceptance, the Academic Senate ... authorised me to attempt to revoke your invitation ... In such a case, I would doubtless have proposed to the Academic Senate your replacement as the Senate's Designee for Political Education'.[58] Sontheimer had been censured for having the temerity to invite Jaspers without receiving official sanction from the rector (he had misunderstood a verbal communication from the rector's office as a go-ahead for the invitation). The Senate decided 'that the Free University would not conduct an official event on the day of capitulation' (what Krippendorff had described in the *Spandauer Volksblatt* as the moment when Germany was 'freed from outside'). Among other arguments, it was emphasised that 'January 30th [i.e. the appointment of Hitler as Chancellor] provided a more meaningful date for a critical self-appreciation and reckoning'.[59] Fortunately for Lüers, his term as rector ended in the summer. Instead of the usual rotation, which demanded a member of the Faculty of Medicine to step forward, Hans-Joachim Lieber, a professor of sociology who had taught classes on Marxism, was deemed better suited to deal with the crises of the Freie Universität.

The idea that Lieber might prove more amenable to the students and return a degree of calm to the FU was not naïve. Despite the entrenched positions in which the students and Lüers repeatedly found themselves in the summer of 1965, the students had by no means converted en masse to political radicalism. The Kuby, Krippendorff and Bettermann affairs were all interpreted within the framework of the 'Berlin Model'. Indeed, as soon as September 1965, the *Konvent* distanced itself from the chairman of AStA, Wolfgang Lefèvre, and his deputy, Peter Damerow, for having signed a petition calling for peace in Vietnam sponsored by a committee close to the East German Communist Party (SED). The same *Konvent* which had backed Lefèvre over his speech at the *Immatrikulationsfeiertag* now voted him out of office. No one interpreted this as a limitation on free

---

[58] Pressestelle der FU Berlin (ed.), *Hochschule IV*, 190.   [59] Ibid.

speech, but rather as an unrepresentative action by the leader of the entire student body. Above all, it was the students themselves who decided, for themselves, what was or was not acceptable.

Nonetheless, the willingness to adopt unusual forms of protest – strikes, demonstrations, the undermining of university ceremonies – to condemn perceived censorship by the rector indicated a clear shift in the nature of politics at the FU. The Berlin Model of student participation did not function. Students and rector no longer agreed on the limits of student self-government. The latter emphasised the student body's location within the university corporation with an emphasis on the institution's honour, dignity and reputation. Student representatives prioritised democratic self-government and rejected any restrictions as appealing to outdated and authoritarian ideologies. Furthermore, in the event of a clash between student self-governance and the rector's authority, students applied explicitly democratic criteria to judge an office that was never really conceived as such. In the growth of this conflict, the influence of SDS was paramount, although more through its individuals than as an organisation. Wolfgang Lefèvre and Ekkehart Krippendorff, two of the key figures in the mid-year crisis, were both members of SDS. Krippendorff's willingness to criticise the rector in the press, and Lefèvre's speech at the *Immatrikulationsfeiertag* pushed the limits of what was previously acceptable politics. SDS also played an important role in promoting the strike at the Otto-Suhr Institute. In all these cases, however, students reacted to an already existing situation: the *Redeverbot* for Kuby, the Jaspers invitation, or Bettermann's speech to the Burschenschaften. After mid-1965, the initiative came from SDS.

The Administration of Politics and Politics of Administration

The Free University stood precariously poised in mid-1965. The events of the previous year revealed a basic contradiction between a view of the university as a corporation, headed by the rector, to whom the other parts of the corporation owed fealty, and an alternative understanding of autonomy that emphasised the self-government of the corporation's constituent parts. Already ill-equipped to deal with public criticism and demands for democratisation, the Free University faced the problem that a significant minority of students and their sympathisers understood the talk of autonomy and dignity as fig-leaves for political censorship and exclusion. At the time of the Kuby Affair, the rector himself clearly understood the reputation of the university as reliant on the exclusion of certain sorts of politics, without which 'the university is in danger of becoming a tribune of right- and left-radical extremists'.⁶⁰ The concern with 'reputation', and the assumption that whatever went on inside the university could be identified with it, lent itself to censorship. SDS now promoted its views more aggressively, inviting the equivalence of administration and censorship, tipping the university administration into a treacherous administration of politics.

The conflation of politics and administration accelerated in December 1965, when Rector Lieber rejected an SDS proposal for an exhibition on the Vietnam war in the entrance hall to the Henry Ford Building. Lieber justified the rejection in purely administrative terms: the building regulations not allowing any exhibitions in the space, an argument sufficiently plausible to win over the head of AStA. But a number of student groups protested the decision, pointing to other exhibitions that had previously taken place in the building: 'Is it really only the building regulations being enforced here? Why are these regulations suddenly taken so seriously after ten years? ... Is not here rather an uncomfortable political event prevented?'⁶¹ The administrative limit on politics was followed by the administrative limit on the right to study when the Law Faculty announced in February 1966 its intention to de-register students who had not completed their degree by nine semesters.

Critical forms of speech continued to evoke the rector's disapprobation. In its February edition, the *FU-Spiegel* announced it would print critical reviews of Professors' lectures, a move designed to shift students from passive consumers to active participants in the creation of knowledge, able to 'question, doubt and criticise'.⁶² Lieber, in what students perceived as yet another restriction on student speech, criticised the paper, declaring seven professors had as a result requested a premature retirement while others would undoubtedly leave the FU for other universities. The faculty experienced the prospect of critical reviews as an affront, a direct, desacralising assault on the authority of the professor. Other student actions aimed more at provocation than critical reflection. On the night of 3 February, the 'Anschlag-Gruppe' based around Rudi Dutschke and Bernd Rabehl put up posters across the city of West Berlin in which the Federal Chancellor Erhard was indicted for supporting murder in Vietnam – 'Murder through Napalm! Murder through poison gas! Murder through atomic bombs?'⁶³ A number of the persons engaged in the action were

---

⁶⁰ Brief des Rektors vom 20.5.1965 as quoted in von Friedeburg et al., *Freie Universität*, 262.
⁶¹ Pressestelle der FU Berlin (ed.), *Hochschule IV*, 53.   ⁶² Ibid., 259.   ⁶³ Ibid., 66.

arrested, among them four students of the FU, whose names were passed on to the university. In addition to that provocation, on 5 February around 2,500 students protested against the US war in Vietnam. At the end of the demonstration, some 500 continued to the 'Amerika Haus', took down the US flag and threw five eggs against the façade. The *Bild-Zeitung* thundered with outrage: 'Shameful! Unthinkable! Short-sighted – scathing criticism of student demonstration'.[64] Rector Lieber expressed his regret to the US military commander in Berlin. Willy Brandt, as mayor, wrote how 'the great majority of the people of Berlin is not willing to allow the city's repute to be put in danger by irresponsible minorities. ... Such groups bring shame to Berlin'.[65] The recurrent concern for reputation, similar to that articulated by the rector of the Free University, cemented the student impression that reputation really meant conformity.

The Amerika Haus egging diverged the furthest yet from rational public criticism. Its model of democracy was not that of the formation of a rational will, but the unruly undermining of sacred symbols. Provocation called forth the greatest reaction and increased the solidarity of students. A counter-demonstration by more conservative students took place a few days later.[66] One remembered 'it was a completely spontaneous action. But those harmless eggs called forth a massive reaction. Although everyone saw the atrocities and crimes happening in Vietnam. Finally, one thought: "they are nuts, not us." Through this hatred, created by the media, one was step-by-step confirmed in attitudes that at first one only tentatively adopted'.[67] That an egging outside the campus could be punished through disciplinary action by the university on the request of the West Berlin administration also lent credence to the belief that little difference existed between political authorities, university hierarchy and police. At the Academic Senate meeting of 16 February, the rector announced disciplinary procedures against seven students 'in connection to the poster action and the incidents at the America House'.[68] Provocation served student solidarity and forced the university hierarchy to choose between indulgence or overreaction.

As the university policed politics outside academia, the problem of political meetings inside the FU returned. At the end of January, an explosive had gone off outside a meeting about Vietnam organised by

---

[64] See Ibid., 68.   [65] Ibid., 68.   [66] See von der Goltz, 'Other '68ers in West Berlin', 95.
[67] Susanne Schunter-Kleemann, 'Wir waren Akteurinnen und nicht etwa die Anhängsel', in Kätzel, *Die 68erinnen: Porträt einer rebellischen Frauengeneration* (Berlin: Rowohlt, 2002), 108.
[68] APO Berlin FU Allgemein Akademischer Senat 1966–1969 'Protokoll der ordentlichen Senatssitzung vom 16.2.1966'.

the *Sozialistischen Jugend*. The rector, who had approved an SDS meeting about Vietnam for a few days later, consulted with the Berlin Senators for Internal Affairs and Sciences and Art, both of whom counselled against maintaining the planned exhibition. Failing to convince SDS itself to cancel the event, the rector decided to refrain from a ban. No incidents occurred, but the rector received approval from the Senate, 'henceforth not to make available rooms in the Free University for such events at which a disruption of the orderly functioning of the university must be feared'.[69] While the Senate had recommended the rector allow, for even-handedness, a Vietnam Discussion by the Christian Democratic RCDS, Lieber banned the event 'so that possible damages to property and persons are avoided, but above all because the dignity, repute and autonomy of the university is most seriously endangered by such events that make police measures necessary'.[70] The decision drew criticism not only from the students – AStA considered 'such a practice an extreme endangering of the autonomy of the university'[71] – but also from Kurt Sontheimer of the Otto-Suhr Institute and the Senate Delegate for Political Education, once again uninformed of the rector's decision and doubtful of its wisdom.

Faced with disruption, the university sought to exclude politics, a decision guaranteed to elicit further protest. The Senate, on the advice of its constitutional committee, withheld all FU facilities, apart from the cafeterias, for students' political gatherings. The cafeterias, it was also known, 'cannot regularly be put at disposal for other purposes'.[72] The blanket ban marked the triumph of the constitutional committee over Kurt Sontheimer as Senate Delegate for Political Education. The latter, ignored once again as the Senate passed its new guidelines, strongly criticised the regulations; so did the AStA, which tendered its resignation. At a press conference Lieber called to clarify matters, he found himself contradicted in public by Sontheimer, whose resignation as Senate Delegate for Political Education was soon demanded and received.[73] Lieber's insistence that no rights had been taken from students, since rooms of the FU remained available for 'scientific' purposes mollified no one. As Sontheimer had pointed out early in February, the chief problem was that

---

[69] Ibid. [70] Pressestelle der FU Berlin (ed.), *Hochschule IV*, 65.
[71] APO Berlin FU Allgemein AStA Protokolle 1966–69 '1. Vorsitzender - 4.2.1966'.
[72] Pressestelle der FU Berlin (ed.), *Hochschule IV*, 72.
[73] On Sontheimer and his shift to criticism of the protest movement, see Riccardo Bajav, 'Turning "liberal Critics" into "Liberal-Conservatives": Kurt Sontheimer and the Re-coding of the Political Culture in the Wake of the Student Revolt of "1968"', *German Politics and Society* 27.1 (2009), 39–59.

'a sharp division between university and general political expressions comes up against more difficulties'.[74] Even the West Berlin Senator for Sciences and Art suggested 'that the Academic Senate's recommendation be reconsidered'.[75] In early March, Lieber provided an interpretation of the guidelines for student expression, distinguishing between 'political education and one-sided political agitation'.[76] His example of the latter was the demand 'anyone in the university be able to speak on any topic at any time in any place'.[77] Less than half a year after taking on the position of rector, Lieber found himself in a similar position to that of Lüers in mid-1965. Yet while the language of university 'reputation' and the maintenance of 'order' was the same, a shift had occurred. Lüers had focused his censorship on those who, to his mind, had defamed the university. Lieber had begun a doomed attempt to distinguish legitimate from illegitimate political discussion. The Senate, furthermore, had embarked on an equally futile and foolish attempt to exclude all politics from the university as unscientific. Protest and provocation had pushed rector and Senate into ever more dubious rationales that only laid the basis for further conflict.

The threatened *Zwangsexmatrikulation*, which focused the conflict between rector, Senate and students after February, brought forth an even sharper clash between forms of administration and the political expression of the student body. Forced deregistration appeared to the students as yet another example of their lack of self-determination and the tendency of the university to respond to problems with administrative measures rather than structural reform. Dematriculation was further understood as a politics of a deliberately underfunded education system in which 'defence and economy are financed primarily as pillars of government politics. Science is only interesting insofar as it directly serves both these spheres.'[78] The student representatives of the Law Faculty, hardly a radical institution, tendered their resignation in April. In May, a full meeting of the Law Faculty unanimously demanded the lifting of the restriction. That same month, the Medicine Faculty proposed to limit the number of semesters in which students could complete their degree. At this point *Konvent* sought a referendum in which students would vote on the resolution: 'The student

---

[74] APO Berlin FU Allgemein Akademischer Senat 1966–1969 'Protokoll der ausserordentlichen Senatssitzung am 4.2.1966'.
[75] Pressestelle der FU Berlin (ed.), *Hochschule IV*, 272.   [76] Ibid., 282.   [77] Ibid., 282–283.
[78] APO Berlin FU Allgemein Konvent 1966 18. Konvent 'Konventsdrucksache Nr. XVIII/26a Memorandum des Hochschulausschusses zur Frage der befristeten Zulassung'.

body of the Free University of Berlin rejects any form of forced deregistration from its university.'[79] The student body now challenged the corporation with the politics of direct democracy.

A university reluctant to embrace political speech could hardly countenance the direct expression of student politics on a matter of university administration. Lieber expressed the opinion that 'the planned referendum [was] a violation of the constitution of the student body'.[80] The students dismissed the objection as merely another attempt to limit their rights with 'formalistic arguments'. They pointed to a previous referendum in 1958. The rector responded that unless 'that referendum is abrogated or changed ... so too that referendum would be invalid according to the constitution of the student body'.[81] When students persisted with their plans to hold the plebiscite, the rector informed them that no rooms would be put at their disposal. Once again, the administration had resorted to its control of space. Once again, the *Immatrikulationsfeiertag* was due to occur.

The 1966 ceremony became the stage for an explicit condemnation of the contemporary university. In 1965, Wolfgang Lefèvre had placed the 'Berlin Model' in the foreground. A year later, Knut Nevermann, AStA's new chairman, also emphasised 'the hardening of hierarchical structures, the roll-back of the postwar period's impulses, built upon the concept of a social and democratic constitutional state, also reflected in the Berlin Model'.[82] However, the Berlin Model now served as prologue to a broader critique:

> society is on the way to standardisation and discipline ... the university, integrated in this formation process, is becoming a rationally functioning business, a factory of academics ... with the task to produce the cheapest possible specialised functionary. The political activity of students – so often dismissed as 'disorderly conduct', or 'politicisation' and 'radicalisation' – must be understood against this background, namely as a powerless attempt to arrest the infantilisation of the individual and to create a critical consciousness.[83]

---

[79] Pressestelle der FU Berlin (ed.), *Hochschule IV*, 94.   [80] Ibid.
[81] APO Berlin FU Allgemein Akademischer Senat 1966–1969 'Abschrift. Der Rektor der Freien Universität Berlin. Berlin, den 2.6.1966. An den 1. AStA-Vorsitzenden Herrn Knut Nevermann ...'.
[82] Pressestelle der FU Berlin (ed.), *Hochschule IV*, 331.
[83] Ibid. 'Gleichmachung und Formierung'; 'Formierung' seems to be a clear reference to the 'formierte Gesellschaft', which could be translated as the formed, aligned or disciplined society, as proposed by then-West German Chancellor Ludwig Erhard.

The similarity to the language of students at Trento is striking. The latter articulated a critique of the university as an assembly line of blind, managerial impulses. That formulation emerged from debates over the nature and purpose of the degree in sociology. In West Berlin, the same vision sprang from a series of conflicts over university space and speech. The end result was the same. Both student movements had found their way towards an articulation of a subjectivity defined by autonomy, critical thinking and disorderly politics as the basis of democracy.

What courted controversy the year before now evoked acclamation. Nevermann provided the rector with an advance copy of his speech. Lieber shared the content with the Senate, who decided not to attend. After Nevermann read his speech, Lieber explained the absence of the professors, arguing the speech contained half-truths and untruths. At that point, in a reversal of what had happened the previous year, Nevermann and the members of AStA left the room to the applause of the students. As in 1965, a plenary meeting of all faculties followed. The year before, calls for Lüers' resignation were made. This time, no confidence was voted in Karl August Bettermann, who a few days earlier suggested that whoever 'is not finished after nine semesters creates the suspicion that something is not right with his studies, and not in the institutional sphere of the university but rather in his individual realm'.[84] The student representative in the Senate (and SDS member) Sigrid Rüger, proposed a protest for the following day, at the same time as the next Senate meeting. Another SDS member 'reminded the assembled students of the new forms of demonstration of the Californian students at Berkeley and invited them to carry out a "sit-in"'.[85] Over 3,000 students gathered the following day.

The sit-in symbolised in the starkest manner the gaping divide between student body and Senate. Two assemblies sat alongside each other. The Academic Senate deliberated in one room, while the massed students outside passed resolutions thereafter sent via delegation to the Senate. In addition to long-standing demands for the lifting of restrictions on the use of rooms and the abolition of any limitation on the length of study, the student assembly formulated a demand for '*Drittelparität*' or tripartite parity in the university, with equal power to be held by professors, assistants and students. Leaving the Senate meeting to speak to the assembled students, Lieber refused to take an immediate position on the demands but promised to discuss them with student representatives within the following ten days. His request to end the demonstration in order to

[84] Pressestelle der FU Berlin (ed.), *Hochschule IV*, 101.   [85] Ibid.

avoid 'disagreeable consequences' received a chorus of boos and whistles. The sit-in continued for the remainder of the day, ending at 12:45 the next morning after the remaining 2,000 students passed a final resolution:

> We are fighting not just for the right to study a longer time and to be able to express our opinions more strongly. That is only half of it. The point for us is that decisions that concern students are taken democratically and only with the participation of students. What is happening in Berlin, just as in society, is a conflict whose main object is neither longer study nor more holidays but the dismantling of an oligarchic rule and the realisation of democratic freedom in all areas of society.[86]

No reference to the 'Berlin Model' remained. The students had passed beyond the defence of what they perceived to be their traditional rights and had begun a process of elaborating their vision of what a democratic university structure ought to be. The call for *Drittelparität* furnished the first draft for a new institution, not the preservation of an old one, and provided yet another point on which future conflict with the rector and Senate appeared likely. The rector's promise to consider the demands merely postponed the oncoming confrontation to another day.

Democracy and Desacralisation

The growth of conflict subtly shifted the ideas and practices of both students and administration. The former now articulated their ideas of democratic self-governance much more strongly and backed it up with plebiscites, general assemblies and public criticism. The latter leaned ever more towards a narrow apoliticism as the foundation of the university, enforced through administrative powers. Each disagreement only widened the gulf between them. That dynamic escalated as some students began to adopt more aggressive tactics. The movement had begun when it appealed to public opinion and democratic debate to contest the rector's decisions. That act simultaneously established a democratic political process and undermined the authority of the rector. Democratisation and desacralisation reinforced each other. While never parting company entirely, methods of undermining authority quickly emerged that only partially appeared democratic, but effectively pushed administration into ever starker and ever more undemocratic affirmations of their authority.

[86] Ibid., 333.

Student protesters now approached the university with the expectation of further friction. In October 1966, the AStA laid out its conception for the winter semester, expecting confrontations over politics (particularly the emergency laws), over reviews of lectures, 'the disciplinary rights of the authoritarian state' and the social position of the student.[87] Minor disagreements occurred over the composition of a committee to study university reform and over the theme for the *Universitätstage* of 1967 – the students preferred 'University and Democracy' while the Law Faculty promoted the topic of 'Authority and Freedom in State, Society and University'. The real conflict restarted, once again, over speech. In November Rector Lieber had agreed to meet with students to discuss their concerns. Students saw in the meeting the fulfilment of the promise from the June sit-in to debate their demands. However, Lieber insisted he turned up only in his personal capacity and not as rector. The misunderstanding led to fruitless discussion, interrupted by a group calling themselves the 'Provisional Committee for the Preparation of a Student Self-Organisation', (a fraction of SDS which had formed the Kommune I), who distributed a flyer entitled 'We have nothing to expect from this conversation'. The rector's insistence he attended in his personal capacity made the charge more plausible. Instead of a conversation or debate, the committee seized speech in the most literal manner:

> I stood up, went in the growing tumult to the stage, took the microphone from His Magnificence's nose (later they said it was wrested and captured in a struggle; but at that time professors were far too shocked by such acts of rebellion against sacrosanct authority to be able to physically react). I mechanically read the text of the flyer. The microphone was shut off. I bellowed out the text ...[88]

The flyer itself displayed little respect for the rector and the university, complaining of 'poor work conditions, miserable lectures, stupefying seminars and absurd exam assignments'. Only the promise of a degree prevented the refusal to 'be trained as useful idiots by professorial idiots'.[89] The leaflet simply restated a common opinion among students, but the action proved more controversial.

The seizure of the microphone marked a significant shift away from the promotion of critical discourse towards the silencing of speech. Most student groups condemned the action for 'poor political style' but insisted that 'several of the themes in the flyer [are] worthy of discussion'.[90] The

---

[87] Ibid., 354.   [88] Ibid., 364.   [89] Ibid., 363.
[90] APO FU-Berlin Allgemein 2 2098 2 Politische Meinungsäußerung 'Ein Wort zum Samstag'.

ambivalent reaction, however, in no way prevented unanimous condemnation of the administrative response. Insisting that the event 'inflicted severe damage on the repute of the Free University and particularly the reputation of the student body in public opinion', the rector demanded first of AStA, then of SDS the names of the perpetrators.[91] Faculty reaction did not stop at disciplinary measures within the university. One professor requested of the rector a libel suit against the students: 'We cannot anymore let ourselves be slandered in the public sphere by a group of extremist students. I consider a disciplinary action to be inappropriate in this case'.[92] Four ex-rectors of the FU (Heinitz, Hirsch, Lüers and Schenck) began proceedings against 'unknown' for libel. The administrative recourse to disciplinary measures now extended to the courts.

Protest increasingly adopted more aggressive forms of disruption as the taboos on disorderly politics fell away along with the rector's authority. In December 1966, two rival sessions on Vietnam took place. SDS showed the film *The Time of the Locust*, while the *Ring Christlich Demokratischer Studenten* discussed the war with the South Vietnamese ambassador.[93] SDS proposed the two events be held together, an offer the RCDS rebuffed. SDS then sent a delegation of two students to the RCDS meeting with the ambassador to ask him some questions. The ambassador consenting, some 600 students from the SDS gathering joined the hundred or so at the RCDS discussion. SDS protests escalated when they discovered questions could only be posed in writing, then read by the RCDS moderator. The call rang out of 'to the microphone'. Rudi Dutschke 'stormed to the podium and the Ambassador had no choice but to cede to him the right to speak'.[94] A few days later, in another demonstration against the war, came further evidence of the willingness to transgress the traditional limits to protest. A large contingent of SDS students departed from the route prescribed by the police in an attempt to break the constraints on protest: 'The "democratic public" silently swallows every protest without effort. Demonstrating becomes posters that libel no one, chanting that no one hears on streets that, far away from the rhythm of the busy "free world", do not hinder order and functioning'.[95]

---

[91] APO FU-Berlin Allgemein 2 2098 2 Politische Meinungsäußerung '28.11.1966 2250 8667/66. An den Vorsitzenden des AStA Herrn Knut Nevermann'.
[92] APO FU-Berlin Allgemein 2 2098 2 Politische Meinungsäußerung 'Prof. Dr. W. Wöhlke to S. Magnifizenz dem Rektor der Freien Universität'.
[93] On this event see von der Goltz, 'Other '68ers in West Berlin', 88.
[94] Pressestelle der FU Berlin (ed.), *Hochschule IV*, 374.
[95] APO 2 Privatsammlung Nitsch 1967 'Entwurf II'.

The police attacked the demonstrators, the violence further polarising West Berlin, with a furore in the press and further protests from all students. Provocation proved spectacularly successful in both inciting the overreaction of the forces of order and the solidarity of students.

Provocation very successfully created an equivalence between political repression outside and inside the university. In another demonstration on 17 December, small groups of students (mainly from SDS) engaged Christmas shoppers in discussion on the Kurfürstendamm. The police again responded with violence and the indiscriminate arrest of students as well as passers-by (including the editor of *Die Zeit*). Jacob Taubes, professor of philosophy at the FU, who also happened to be passing, wrote to the mayor of West Berlin 'shocked that an action by students conducted in civil form within the rules of democracy was met by police action that as an eyewitness I can only label as brutal and provocative'. The overreaction was all the more egregious in a state where 'not so long ago the bearers of state uniforms carried out the worst crimes'.[96] In this context of violent police repression of political demonstrations outside the university, police raided the headquarters of SDS in January 1967, taking the organisation's membership cards. The search occurred due to the charges brought by the four previous rectors of the FU for libel. Even the RCDS vehemently protested the police action:

> Since when is the political police responsible for libel actions? By what right were the SDS membership cards confiscated? We do not agree politically on any point with SDS, but we will campaign with all our strength that their right and possibility of free political expression is not restricted.[97]

In fact, at the beginning of January the FU Senate authorised the rector to withdraw the rights of SDS as an organisation within the university should they plan or carry out an action that created disorder at the FU. That incident occurred when police raided the Kommune I (largely composed of SDS members), and arrested them for having 'met in conspiratorial circumstances and in this connection planned attacks against the life or health of the American Vice-President Hubert Horatio Humphrey with bombs, plastic bags filled with unknown chemicals or with other dangerous instruments such as stones, etc'.[98] 'Bomb-attack on US Vice President'

---

[96] APO FU-Berlin Allgemein 2 2098 2 Politische Meinungsäußerung 'Freie Universität Berlin Philosophisches Seminar Professor Dr. Jacob Taubes 20. Dez. 1966. An den Regierenden Bürgermeister von Berlin Herrn Heinrich Albertz'.
[97] Pressestelle der FU Berlin (ed.), *Hochschule IV*, 398.   [98] Ibid., 151.

was the headline of the *Bild Zeitung*. The 'unknown chemicals' were soon revealed to be flour, pudding and dye and the 'bombs' to be smoke-candles. Heinrich Albertz, the Mayor of Berlin, passed the names of those involved to the university.

In addition to the imminent banning of SDS and the disciplining of the would-be pudding-bombers, the FU Senate prepared to act on the ongoing reviews of lectures and seminars in the student newspaper. Ernst Fraenkel, having unsuccessfully sued the *FU-Spiegel* not to publish its review, turned to the Senate, arguing that 'the publication of the planned review is unconstitutional in the university', undermining the 'confidential character' of his seminar and contradicting a tradition of over 100 years at the German university.[99] The Senate declared seminars could not be reported due to their 'special character', and demanded a statement from SDS on their involvement in the events of the previous weeks. Meanwhile, around 2,000 students, pre-empting the Senate, had already gathered for their own discussion of seminar reviews, the likely banning of SDS and the 'initiation of disciplinary measures on the basis of blacklists passed on to the rector by the incumbent Mayor'.[100] Protest and provocation had effectively reduced the Senate to its disciplinary function.

Once again, two forms of government opposed each other within the Henry-Ford Building of the Freie Universität. Beginning in the Auditorium Maximum, the students moved to the lobby to listen to music and poetry. The administration cut the electricity, deploying their control of space in the most mechanical manner. Moving to the hallway, the meeting continued as a protest against the Senate, which was frequently interrupted with delegations. The rector demanded that the students return to the Auditorium Maximum and finish their gathering by 11:00 p.m. The latter refused, insisting they had democratically chosen to continue their protest in the hallways. Threatened by the rector with police intervention, AStA officially closed the meeting, but the assembled students voted to continue the protest as a sit-in. Just before midnight, Lieber called the police. Knut Nevermann advised the students to resist passively. The clearing began, but not only did the 70 or so police tire carrying out some 1,000 students, those removed from the premises simply turned around and re-entered the building. After twenty minutes, the police gave up. The students continued their occupation until they abandoned the sit-in of their own accord around 1:00 the following morning.

[99] Ibid., 155.   [100] Ibid.

The students appeared triumphant. Certainly, Lieber would be reluctant to call upon the police in the future. The appeal to the police was the culmination of the various failed attempts to discipline the student body. Yet success in occupying the university buildings did not translate into any change in university policy. Lieber instituted disciplinary proceedings against the AStA leaders and Rudi Dutschke. Professors had been reduced to administrators, but they nonetheless remained the administrators of power. The student movement was not successful in transforming the official structure of the university, but it had created itself. The protesters could no longer be dismissed as a discontented fringe minority. Furthermore, faculty now lived in a fundamentally desacralised landscape. Interruption of lectures, contestation of the curriculum, satirical and scathing public criticism, the shouting down of professors became part of their daily experience. The desacralisation of authority proved enduring, but it was less clear that the results would be a more democratic university. For the moment, the student demand for *Drittelparität* remained, as well as plans to develop a parallel 'critical' university. But these were complex goals for a movement built on moral outrage, provocation, administrative overreaction and the consequent solidarisation.

In West Berlin 'free speech' and the 'Berlin Model' formed the apparent origins of conflict, just as the degree in sociology did in Trento. In both instances, an unusual configuration fostered protest earlier than elsewhere. The earlier the outbreak of dissent, the more local was the ostensible basis of dispute. Yet in both instances the circumstantial reasons for conflict drew meaning from the broader context in an emerging struggle over self-government, autonomy and democracy. The degree in sociology held significance well beyond the careers of students at Trento, a symbol of modernisation and democratisation of society. So too, the Berlin Model stood as the most progressive and democratic vision of the West German university. Regardless of the specifics of conflict at the moment of origin, the protests detached themselves from those circumstances, framed in ever more general terms as politicisation proceeded apace. At the Free University, this process of generalisation was crystallised by events outside the university. At the meeting of 19 April 1967, the theology professor Helmut Gollwitzer had telegrammed the students: 'A soup needs salt, the FU the SDS. Otherwise, the Shah will confuse Berlin for Tehran'.[101] At the beginning of June 1967, the Shah of Iran visited Berlin. Students

---

[101] Ibid.

protested and the police responded. Benno Ohnesorg, student at the FU and onlooker at the protest, was shot in the back of the head by the police.[102] The resultant polarisation, student politicisation and mobilisation, laid the ground for an even more aggressive conflict between students and faculty at the FU and between students and the state in West Berlin.

[102] The best description in English of Ohnesorg's shooting is contained in Thomas, *Protest Movements*, 107–111. For the wider context see Quinn Slobodian, *Foreign Front: Third-World Politics in Sixties West Germany* (Durham: Duke University Press, 2012). In German, see Eckard Michels, *Schahbesuch 1967: Fanal für die Studentenbewegung* (Berlin: Christoph Links Verlag, 2017) and Uwe Soukup, *Der 2. Juni 1967. Ein Schuss, der die Republik veränderte* (Berlin: Transit Verlag, 2017). As is now well known, the policeman who shot Ohnesorg was also a spy for the German Democratic Republic. For some sensible discussion, see Brown, *West Germany*, 1–2.

CHAPTER 9

'Student Power'
Vietnam at Trento

In West Berlin, the generalisation of conflict occurred through the shooting of Benno Ohnesorg in June 1967. In France, confrontation with police in the Latin Quarter and the building of barricades in May 1968 signalled another such moment that transformed student protest into social conflict. At Trento, no single event altered the protest movement in the same way. Trento lacked the opportunities that Paris and West Berlin provided for broader social mobilisation, and the size of the institute meant the limits of student mobilisation were reached in the first occupations. The institute had just 622 enrolments in the 1965–1966 academic year – the moment of the first occupation – and many of those students commuted. There was no broader mass to mobilise other than the new students who arrived each academic year, whose numbers rapidly dwarfed those present at the first protests. The institute's student population nearly doubled in 1967, to 1207; in 1967–1968 it rose to 1,762 and in 1968–1969 it reached 2,813.[1] New recruits swamped the veteran protesters. Small wonder that entering students in these later years recalled an intense process of politicisation on arrival, one that demanded they declare their politics, assimilate to the culture of protest and work for its perpetuation.[2]

The relatively small size of the town and institute created other possibilities for the expansion of revolt in contrast to West Berlin or Paris. It was far easier for the students at Trento than elsewhere to provoke the entire surrounding population. But the conflict at Trento nonetheless developed without an abrupt transformation such as June 1967 in West Berlin. To be sure, students in Italy drew inspiration from the events in Paris. Longer term, the bombing at Piazza Fontana in Milan in November 1969 would be a watershed moment. But the protest at Trento that had

---

[1] The numbers are in Istituto Superiore di Scienze Sociali di Trento, *Dieci anni di vita 1962/1963–1971/1972* (Trento, Libera Università degli Studi di Trento, 1976), 108–125.
[2] See the comments in Aldo Ricci, *I giovani non sono piante* (Milan: SugarCo, 1978), 203–204.

begun in 1965 and entered its third year in 1968 expanded without any equivalent moment of rupture as in France or West Germany. Instead, the revolt within the university played itself out to a stand-off that paralysed the institute for months.

The student movement at Trento demonstrates the way in which student protest evolved in ever more general terms even absent an event that radically fused university and social protest. Regardless of the specific events that sparked the initial revolt, a social movement emerged in search of protest rather than responding to events. As in West Berlin, the student movement at Trento was initially defensive in nature, coming into being in order to preserve perceived rights against attacks. The first occupation at Trento fought for, and won, the recognition of the degree in sociology, threatened with relegation to a minor within political science. Even the second occupation, which demanded a greater say for students in the construction of the university curriculum and a 'historical-critical' rather than a 'technocratic-statistical' orientation, presented itself as adhering to the novelty of the institution and the degree, defending its innovativeness against attempts to make sociology conform to the traditional structures of the Italian university. The conflict that emerged in Trento over 1965 and 1966 was self-consciously innovative only in its method – the occupation, which deliberately bypassed the traditional organs of student politics and representation. In practice, the occupations always served not only whatever immediate demands were formulated, but to create a new political form for the realisation of student goals.

The birth of the protest movement and the move from an essentially reactive to proactive struggle raised new problems. What specific goals would the movement pursue? Could it be sustained absent a steady drip of authoritarian provocations? The initial insight of protesters was the fact of powerlessness: in West Berlin, the bypassing of student government via the rector's authority and in Trento the dismissal of student representation first by the legislative rejection of sociology and then the professorial disregard for student input on curriculum. In both instances, the defining experience of students was impotence when confronted with an imposed policy. The disruptive style of protest sought primarily to counter this irrelevance. But how viable was the occupation long-term? How was a democratic self-government of the university to be organised once the movements moved beyond the rejection of specific measures? The escalation of revolt in West Berlin and Paris obscured that little had been achieved by the protesters within the university, other than the deep, if often temporary, disorientation of faculty and administrators. In Trento the endurance of confrontation meant the absence of a long-term resolution could not be avoided. Ultimately, the student movement at Trento found in the local population the same opposition that other movements found in clashes with the police.

In the Space of Vietnam

The police entered the Freie Universität in April 1967. At Trento, the rector had made the call in March, just one month earlier. The appeal to police represented a failure of university administration, reduced by student protest to its disciplinary dimension. While the maintenance of order undoubtedly remained an irreducible element of university government, the use of police could only be successful if the broad mass of students saw the action as legitimate. Lacking that credibility, police intervention only served to exemplify the university's lack of democratic credentials. Students, police intervention made clear, did not hold power in the university. Administrators often found themselves pressured to restore order by more powerful constituencies – faculty or politicians.

The expulsion of protesters by police provided the most explicit image of the university's rejection of student revolt, but administrative curbs on unruly student self-expression dated from the very beginnings of the movement. In the first occupation of January 1966, university officials sought to insist that neither the student assembly nor its delegation, but rather the traditional organs, represent the students. Yet the administration found it impossible to enforce their preference for representative over direct democracy. Student disregard for traditional procedure was matched by the administrative adaptation of routine measures for the purposes of restoring order. There surfaced a number of claims of reprisals. For the male students, 'the secretary who worked inside the institution ... refused to release the certification of registration to a student who, if he did not obtain it, would be obliged immediately to start military service'. For the female students, 'the families of women who participated actively in the occupation and therefore slept inside the institute were telephoned'.[3] This gendered appeal to family or military facilitated the conflation of all forms of authority. Similar measures continued after the second occupation, in November 1966, when students won representation with a seat and consultative vote in the Collegio Commissariale. Marco Boato, the first

---

[3] 'I Partiti hanno detto sì', *Alto Adige*, 4 February 1966 in CMR B.5 f.5 (Fondo Movimento Studentesco Gabriella Ferri).

student to sit with the university hierarchy, found his free accommodation at the university withdrawn.[4] As in West Berlin, students rapidly concluded that the administrative power of the university served to impose authority and conformity. Apparently anonymous and anodyne administrative measures became deeply politicised. The withdrawal of space, of accommodation, reflected an unstated but consistent application of a patrimonial principle that rewarded loyalty and conformity. Such reprisals proved counterproductive, undermining an authority that relied on student consent and revealing it as personal and capricious rather than bureaucratic and rational.

Administrative pressures failed to curtail protest. To the contrary, they tended to sap the legitimacy of university hierarchies. But it would take some time for the administrators to turn to police – an action so at odds with the self-conception of the university as a free space of teaching and learning. Police interactions more typically and naturally occurred in social protest outside the university. As students' demonstrations and demands moved beyond the definition of sociology, clashes with police became increasingly common, and in 1967 the two fields of protest began to converge. In Trento, at the end of January 1967, some twenty sociologists protested the celebrations of the twentieth anniversary of the neo-fascist MSI. The confrontation led to charges of organising an unauthorised demonstration and interfering with traffic. As with the response of the university, the students perceived the forces of order as primarily concerned with clamping down on democratic protest, those struggling for 'the principles of liberalism and democratisation in national institutions'. They condemned the attempt to 'strike the democratic students, even (perhaps above all) brutally, overlooking rather the open, documented provocations of neo-fascists'.[5] Students in West Berlin invoked the Nazi Past as part of a failed democratisation of German culture; so too Italian students evoked the ongoing presence of neo-fascists and the behaviour of police to indict a similar democratic deficit. If initially police did not enter the university, student protesters already understood the forces of order as part of a general repression of protest. When the administration finally did call on the police, it confirmed higher education's place within this broader framework of the repression of democratisation.

---

[4] CMR Marco Boato, Busta Trento Sociologia Anno 1963–1968. f. 'TN 1966. Sociologia 1966'.
[5] CMR B.2 f.1 (Fondo Movimento Studentesco G. Palma), No title. Il Movimento Studentesco Trentino 15 febb. 1967.

By 1967, student protest at Trento no longer occurred within the local setting of the Faculty of Sociology. A national context began to place incidents in Trento in a much broader framework. At Pisa, the chemistry and physics faculties had been occupied since 27 January 1967.[6] The Faculty of Letters and the La Sapienza building followed on 6 February and 8 February, respectively. The occupations coincided with the National Conference of rectors held at Pisa. For the first time, on 11 February, a rector called the police to clear the university. Seventy-seven occupants (including twelve students of other universities) were photographed by police and charged. Following the example of Pisa (where, after all, the various rectors of Italian universities had been present) police interventions multiplied. The University of Napoli followed on 16 February. A few days later, at Viareggio, the arrest of students demonstrating in solidarity with the Pisan occupation sparked a large protest from the city, with some 6,000 descending on the piazza. For the students at Trento, these events coalesced into a coherent whole: 'Faced with ... the systematic and ever greater awareness of students of the need for an effective democratic restructuring of the university system, local and national politicians respond with police brutality.'[7] Before the forces of order entered the Faculty of Sociology, students perceived a unity of police action in the piazza and within the university. In March, a month after the police had cleared the occupation at Pisa, it was the turn of Trento.

The other Italian occupations concerned the reform of the university. At Trento, students turned to the topic of Vietnam. If the conflict at Trento already took place in a national (even European) context of 'democratisation' and reform, the Vietnam war added an international dimension. A committee composed of citizens of Trento and students of sociology called for a week of protest for Vietnam: 'the intervention of the Americans in Vietnam – as the students at Berkeley have stated – transcends political disputes'.[8] Echoing the West Berlin posters about 'murder by poison gas', the Vietnam committee demanded that the Italian government disassociate itself from the 'acts of extermination that the USA carries out daily'.[9] A contestation begun over the degree of sociology now embraced Berkeley

---

[6] For the student movements at Pisa, see Giovanni Nardi, *L'immaginazione e il potere: cronache del '68 a Pisa* (Pisa: Nistri-Lischi, 1982).
[7] CMR B.2 f.1 (Fondo Movimento Studentesco G. Palma), No title. Il Movimento Studentesco Trentino 15 febb. 1967.
[8] CMR B.3 f.1 (Fondo Movimento Studentesco G. Palma), 'Documento politico del comitato permanente per la pace e la libertà nel Vietnam'.
[9] Ibid.

and Vietnam. Yet the distance from the United States to Trento and to Vietnam was not so great. 'America' had already appeared in the student imagination as the home of a certain sort of sociology, modernity and of capitalism. To these could be added or even equated the war in Vietnam, while the Berkeley protests offered an alternative. Mauro Rostagno evocatively connected the dots between Vietnam, Auschwitz and objectivity:

> Scientific 'neutrality' drips with ideology ... The student 'Cadum soap' ... can be placed on the market, sold and consumed. What does not appear is what really forms the soap. The crematory oven it comes from is a long way away. One does not smell the burning. The Mekong Delta is 10,000 miles off. Science flies like angels, its capitalist use does not appear.[10]

The turn to Vietnam marked a clear escalation of student protest. The contestation was simultaneously conceived as local, national and global. Where previously protesters framed problems of teaching and learning in global terms (of democratisation or modernisation), they now contested global politics (the Vietnam War) within institutions of higher education. The politics of protest thus no longer revolved around specific aspects of education and learning, but rather the role of politics itself within the university, the very question that proved so troublesome at the Free University.

The student assembly at Trento (again bypassing the traditional representative structures) voted to adhere to the program of the Vietnam Committee. Christian Democratic youth groups and the *Associazione goliardi indipendenti* (a liberal group born from a split with the left-wing UGI) opposed the move – seeing Vietnam as a 'purely political issue' rather than one that 'concerns the students as such'.[11] But the dissenters were a minority. The Vietnam Committee envisaged actions across the city: an exhibition in the piazza, a theatrical happening in which the war was represented and a public talk by a Vietnamese bonze (meant to be held in Piazza Duomo, but due to the refusal to authorise the demonstration ended up in the local pub). In addition, they planned a two-day strike at the university and a demonstration that interrupted traffic and ended at the Italian Communist Party's offices asking them to declare war on the US by the Geneva conventions (the PCI response: 'let's talk a bit')[12]. The strike ended with the planned projection of a film on the Vietcong at 3:00 p.m., replacing (pointedly) a lecture on methodology in the social sciences.

[10] CMR B.1 f.7 (Fondo Movimento Studentesco G. Palma), 'Università come istituto produttivo'.
[11] CMR B.5 f.5 (Fondo Movimento Studentesco Gabriella Ferri), *Alto Adige*, 17 March 1967.
[12] Ricci, *I giovani*, 63.

The rector, Mario Volpato, expressed his opposition: 'The administration does not intend to contest the right of anyone to express their opinion on any issue, even politically. However, the demonstration must not happen inside the university in order not to disturb the normal course of studies for those who wish to continue'.[13] The majority of the students adhered to the strike. About 100 began to watch the documentary around 3:30 p.m. The administration cut the electricity (as would the FU hierarchy just two months later at the sit-in of 19 April 1967). Unable to continue the film, the students transformed the event into a round-table discussion. At 6:00 p.m. the police arrived. After a couple of hours of negotiation, with the students refusing to budge, the police began, one by one, to carry out the remaining seventy who resisted passively and whose names and photographs were taken. The action, the newspaper *L'Adige* recorded, was described as a 'cleaning'.[14] The following day, Volpato closed the university indefinitely.

By the standards of later clashes, the clearing of the Institute was a decidedly polite affair. Nonetheless, the 'Vietnam Week' sharpened the opposition between a majority of the active students and the university administration. Volpato had fallen into the role of political censor, as had the rectors of the Free University of Berlin. His authority, already challenged by the student assembly, had been reduced first to control of the electricity supply, then the police. Ousting the students from their institution of study literalised the charge of an institution ruled in the last instance by police authority. Protesters hung a sign on the closed door: 'Yankee University: Director Volpato lackey of the US aggressors'[15] The Faculty remained closed for just two days. Upon reopening, Volpato called all seventy students to him individually, beginning with the newest and working his way up, demanding they sign a statement in which they admitted 'to "have acted irresponsibly"'.[16] This exercise of paternalistic authority could not possibly hope to contain the revolt. Volpato took no further action, although the students were fined for not obeying a police order, as well as 'seditious calls'.[17] To Volpato's demand if they knew of his prohibition on political meetings, and, if they knew, why they had continued, the students answered: 'Because Vietnam concerns us as students and sociologists'.[18] The ongoing struggle to define sociology at

---

[13] Quoted in Concetto Vecchio, *Vietato obbedire* (Milan: Rizzoli, 2005), 60–61.
[14] 'La polizia all'Università', *Alto Adige*, 15 March 1967, 4.
[15] 'Volpato ordina di chiudere', *Alto Adige*, 16 March 1967. CMR B.5 f.5 (Fondo Movimento Studentesco Gabriella Ferri).
[16] Ricci, *I giovani*, 89. [17] Vecchio, *Vietato obbedire*, 66. [18] Ibid., 65.

Trento, begun over the title of the degree and continued in the elaboration of the curriculum, now encompassed the politics of the war in Vietnam. Yet the conflict only apparently still revolved around the meaning of the discipline. In reality, the subtext of student powerlessness had become explicit. By locating the university in the mental space of Vietnam, students generalised and globalised the conflict. Placing Vietnam within the university meant the dispute focused ever less on curricular or academic questions and more on the question of power. Vietnam Week stripped whatever credibility remained of Volpato's paternalistic authority. The students sought to fill the vacuum.

Student Power

Police intervention marked a turning point in the student movement, one that starkly symbolised the direct confrontation of authority and anti-authoritarian protest. That opposition now featured in all aspects of the Institute's existence. The Istituto Universitario at Trento conferred its first degrees in sociology in July 1967: seven men and three women received the *laurea*. 'This event', proclaimed Mario Volpato, 'marks an epoch for Italian university students'.[19] As with similar ceremonies in West Berlin, the graduation also served to allow the student movement to publicly express its rival understanding of the new degree, adding another dent to the public prestige of the rector: 'today closes just the first phase ... of [the Trento Student Movement's] political-cultural activity, while another passage of this story will open with the beginning of the next academic year'.[20] Demanding the 'renewal of an old and sclerotic university – classist and autocratic, damagingly academic, at times ridiculously Arcadian, corporatist, socially absent or irresponsible', the student movement summed up its goals: new degrees in social sciences, funding for research, the realisation of the right to study, a curriculum characterised by 'the maximum elasticity and possibility of choice', and above all, 'the primary and absolutely irrevocable realisation of an authentic self-government of the university, in which the participation of all components of the university would guarantee that autonomy does not degenerate into an inadequate corporatism'.[21] The central demand here was this last one.

---

[19] Ibid., 67.
[20] CMR B.1 f.1 (Fondo Movimento Studentesco G. Palma), 'Intervento del rappresentante del movimento studentesco trentino durante la cerimonia del 22 luglio 1967 nell'aula dell'istituto superiore di scienze sociali di trento per il conferimento delle prime lauree di sociologia'.
[21] Ibid.

Most of the others followed from that principle. As had occurred in Berlin, the students contrasted a genuine with a false autonomy, the self-government of all members of the university with authoritarianism or corporatism. To be sure, 'participation of all components of the university' could encompass very different models of university government. However, none of them included the current arrangements of paternal authority.

Open forms of opposition thus marked the second half of 1967. The events of 'Vietnam Week' had left Mario Volpato an object of ridicule. One document wondered whether 'Professor Volpato expelled the students … out of solidarity with General Westmoreland or in the name of an absurd idea of the neutrality of the social sciences, or to avoid the wear and tear of desks or whatever other reason', typically equating Vietnam, objectivity, and the concern for 'order' and property.[22] As confrontation within the university hardened, so too student actions outside the university took the form of overt displays of dissent. In May, charges against two students for having burnt the US flag were dropped. A complaint against another was filed in July for having shouted 'long live China' as the Italian flag was raised. When the conservative journalist Indro Montanelli arrived at Trento to present his latest book, a female student approached him with a copy 'asking with the utmost seriousness "will you sign it for me?" After which, to the applause of her comrades, she tore it to pieces laughing contentedly'.[23] In the new academic year of 1967–1968, the faculty encountered the same forms of protest, along with some 700 new students.

Open conflict, the students had decided, was the only way to impose change. The greatest revelation furnished to the students by the struggles at Trento was their powerlessness: 'as students we have no power, we cannot therefore influence in any way the decisions that concern us, we can only obey and bow our heads; only by forms of agitation can we create the power that structurally we lack'.[24] Powerlessness was not just a structural feature of the hierarchical organisation of the university. Rather, it was also a personal attribute inculcated in students by the education system: 'students in the university are the exemplification of impotence.

---

[22] CMR B.2 f.1 (Fondo Movimento Studentesco G. Palma), 'L'Istituto Universitario di Scienze Sociali di Trento'.
[23] Piero Agostini, *Mara Cagol: Una donna nelle prime Brigate Rosse* (Venice: Marsilio-Temi, 1980), 76.
[24] CMR B.2 f.1, 'L'Istituto Universitario di Scienze Sociali di Trento'.

Like Pavlovian dogs, they are slowly taught to salivate. The reward is a job'.[25] The turn to political agitation simultaneously sought to redress the lack of political power of the student body within the university and overcome the personal passivity students discovered in themselves. Through protest, students recovered a sense of themselves as active subjects that the education system no longer delivered. A search for forms of politics that would redress this powerlessness dominated the beginning of the academic year. A month-long strike paralysed the institute with the demand (with direct reference to Berkeley) to have the right to discuss politics within the university. At the end of January 1968, the students at Trento occupied the faculty once again – no longer with a specific goal such as recognition of the degree or the nature of the curriculum, but in order to redefine the student movement itself. After having diagnosed themselves with the affliction of powerlessness, they now hung a banner on the façade of the faculty with the slogan *potere studentesco*: 'student power'.

The occupation of 1968 differed markedly from its predecessors. Begun on 31 January, it lasted until the end of March, longer than the previous two occupations combined. Where the prior occupations responded to particular incidents – the problem of the title of the *laurea* and the discovery of a full draft of the curriculum prepared without consultation of the student body – the third occupation took off from a confrontation between the rector, Mario Volpato, and the students in his mathematics class who refused to split the class in two (as had been customary). The exchange that followed exemplified in its petty threats and name-calling the precipitous decline in academic authority:

VOLPATO: 'Hey, you, why do you protest and don't want to do as usual? You should be smacked!'
STUDENT: 'Try and slap me. I couldn't care less about the director!'
VOLPATO: 'Give me your card'
STUDENT: 'I won't give it to anyone. ... I don't give a damn about the director.'
VOLPATO: 'You're a fool not to give it to me.'
STUDENT: 'You're the fool'.[26]

Such a confrontation left little possibility of resolution. The sheer exuberance of student defiance signalled the total collapse of Volpato's authority.

---

[25] CMR B.4. f.2 (Fondo Movimento Studentesco Riccardo Scartezzini) 'Trento 1967. 'Manifesto per una università negativa', 3.
[26] For the full description see Vecchio, *Vietato obbedire*, 86.

Nothing new prompted the occupation except the student movement's own need to move forward.

The third occupation at Trento began with no specific demand, but instead outlined four broad goals: the struggle against 'academic authoritarianism and the development of "student power"', the contestation of the proposed university reform 'through action organised from below', the 'political organisation of the student movement' and the development of a 'charter of demands'.[27] The students themselves stressed the difference: the past occupations sought 'circumscribed objectives even if of great importance'.[28] Now the task at hand was the analysis of the relations of power in the Italian university, the creation of 'forms of struggle – no longer, as previously, episodic, but continuous (year by year, course by course, exam by exam)' and 'new forms of organisation of the student forces in struggle'. Effectively, the movement posed the problem of its perpetuation, of how to institutionalise its struggle beyond ad hoc responses to the latest crisis. The university administration equally faced a conundrum of how to deal with the protest without resorting to tactics that would only encourage greater participation. The faculty of the university issued a statement in support of Volpato but decided against calling the police. They declared themselves open to dialogue on the condition that the occupation ceased. Such a deal hardly appealed to students who felt their only power lay in the paralysis of the institute and whose previous experiences of 'dialogue' led them to expect little from such an exercise. The protest movement insisted any negotiation come before rather than after the cessation of occupation. A stand-off ensued. In fact, police did enter the university building, but only to safeguard passage to the Trentino Museum of Natural Sciences on the third floor (presumably deemed to be at risk from sociologists). The students demarcated their side of the corridor with a line over which they wrote 'North Vietnam, 17°' and (in English) 'GO HOME'.

The generalisation of the revolt took further impetus from the national context. In contrast to previous occupations, Trento was no longer alone. University revolts existed throughout Italy. Indeed, on 6 February 1968, the occupied Faculty of Sociology hosted representatives of the other Italian student movements.[29] The joint resolution passed at the conference summarised the state of the struggle, returned to the twin themes of autonomy and power, and revealed a growing problem of political tactics.

---

[27] CMR B.5 f.4 (Fondo Movimento Studentesco Gabriella Ferri), 'Caro collega'. [28] Ibid.
[29] This convention was the second. The first was held at Turin in January, the third in Milan in March.

There was no consensus on how best to establish such autonomy, and the logical outcome was an endorsement of a wide variety of tactics. The student movements sought 'larger "structural spaces" inside the Faculty',[30] – in other words, semi-permanent forms of student power within which an autonomous development of the struggle could continue. Some at the conference clearly sought to take the student movement in a more formalised direction: to begin 'construction of a mass political movement' and posed the 'the problem of a party'.[31] However, others countered the institutionalising impulse in the insistence that any new party or organisation must not be imposed from the outside, but 'must rather come from inside, from below, through a series of political initiatives'.[32] The resolution of the student convention at Trento recapitulated the experience of the student struggles. It did not serve as a guide to the future, indeed deliberately avoided prescriptions. While the question of a 'party' was posed, there would be no immediate moves to create one. The resolution of the student convention finely balanced two competing drives: that towards politicisation, tending towards the creation of a political party that potentially would abandon the university altogether for full-time political activism, and that seeking to transform the university into a genuinely self-governing institution.

The tension between transformation of the university or exit from higher education into a broader field of social and political struggle intensified across 1968 and 1969. In early 1968, however, after the end of the convention and the departure of radicals from other universities, with no event yet to fuse social and student protest, the movement at Trento returned to the elaboration of its charter of demands and inevitably focused on the Faculty of Sociology itself. The task of analysis flourished under the occupation at Trento: 'counter-courses' took place on the social function of the sociologist, psychoanalysis and repression. Seminars examined the social figure of the sociologist, society and repression, imperialism, and the university and the region. 'Work groups' commissioned by the general assembly researched student movements, authoritarianism and the right to study, while 'political commissions' reached out to high school students, working students and the factories. The result was a set of analyses of the university, the roles of the professor and the student in entrenching authoritarian social relations.

---

[30] CMR B.1 f.2 (Fondo Movimento Studentesco G. Palma), 'Mozione Conclusiva del Convegno Sulle Lotte Studentesche' 6 febbraio 1968.
[31] Ibid.   [32] Ibid.

The greatest object of criticism from the perspective of '*potere studentesco*' remained the figure of the professor and methods of teaching: 'one-way professorial explanations, superficial individual learning, arbitrary supervision; these are the fundamental components of education when one strips it of all the surrounding mystifications'.[33] The protests divested the university of its pretension to educate. The experience of superficial learning taught students that the real content of education was not the 'knowledge' conveyed, but the style of teaching that inculcated passivity, isolation and authoritarian supervision. Not only did the intellectual content of education appear increasingly irrelevant compared to the authoritarianism of its delivery, but so too was the personal and political attributes of individual instructors: 'It doesn't matter if the professor is fascist, Catholic or on the "Left" ... whatever content prepared through university teaching ... carries within it the traces of the authoritarian ideology of power'.[34] Even a university which was free with a universal salary for students would remain authoritarian if it did not touch the relations of power and teaching practices within the university, 'since what is truly classist in the university is the authoritarian student-teacher relation, the professorial lecture, the grade, the exam that makes of students an impotent imbecile who must consume the alienated culture imposed on him'.[35] The students of the 1960s were certainly not the first, nor the last, to indict the lecture and the exam in the name of 'active' rather than 'passive' learning. Yet they developed that critique further than most of their predecessors or successors, who most frequently understood the exam and lecture as poor delivery of academic content. Instead, the protesters of 1968 identified social control as the fundamental purpose. That analysis reflected a severe crisis in academic legitimacy and professorial power, due in part to the expansion of the student body. The paternal authoritarianism of some professors was no longer mitigated by their personal relationship with a small body of students.

The depersonalisation of professorial power led the students to set as their goal to 'destroy the fundamental institution of the current order, the figure of the professor – not, obviously, as individuals, but as a category,

---

[33] CMR B.4 f.3 (Fondo Movimento Studentesco Riccardo Scartezzini), 'Un contributo alla discussione', 11 February 1968.
[34] Ibid.
[35] CMR B.1 f.7 (Fondo Movimento Studentesco G. Palma), 'Alcuni dati sui mutamenti della struttura scolastica italiana'.

that is in the role the current structure attributes to him'.[36] Similarly identified for destruction was the lecture, to be replaced by seminars and collective research projects. Faculty 'should not be our bosses but participate in seminars and research on a basis of parity, putting their competence at the disposal of the study group'.[37] The result would be the emergence of a new figure: 'the professor, no longer the authoritarian distribution centre of empty notions, no longer the monitor of the efficient subordination of other people, will thus become the 'expert', with a specific function of coordination'.[38] By substituting the professor with the expert, real inequalities in knowledge would no longer justify spurious inequalities in power. Despite the wholesale condemnation of the notion of objectivity elsewhere, students here embraced the idea of a knowledge divorced from power. They could hardly do otherwise without abandoning the university or intellectual life altogether. However, the result was not a technocratic vision of apolitical expertise, but rather the empowerment of individuals as part of a collective in full consciousness of the political import of research. The protesters pinpointed the possibility of knowledge least contaminated by power in the structure of the university rather than the supposed neutrality of the individual or the exclusion of politics from the university. Such a proposal faced enormous obstacles – the structural transformation of the university needed to support it, the containment of the politicising drive that could indeed condemn all intellectual operations as elitist or irrelevant, the willingness of professors to place themselves 'at the service of the group', enduring inequalities in knowledge, and not least the willingness and ability of students themselves to pull off such a model.

For all the focus on transforming the role of the professor, the real object of analysis was the students themselves. After developing a critique of the lecture, the exam system and the control of attendance, the protesters at Trento identified 'the main instrument of control in the hands of professors, the only one that permits them to use the others, is the COLLABORATION of the students. Without the collaboration of the students the professor is nothing'.[39] This conclusion drew in part on the experience of protest where the withdrawal of student consent caused a crisis in the functioning of the university. Crucially, however, the identification of

---

[36] CMR B.4 f.3 (Fondo Movimento Studentesco Riccardo Scartezzini), 'Un contributo alla disscussione'.
[37] CMR B.1 f.2 (Fondo Movimento Studentesco G. Palma), 'Documenti per le agitazioni'.
[38] CMR B.4 f.3 (Fondo Movimento Studentesco Riccardo Scartezzini), 'Un contributo alla disscussione'.
[39] CMR B.2 f.1 (Fondo Movimento Studentesco G. Palma), 'Studente'.

student complicity reflected as much the experience of the student assembly as it did the lecture hall. The revelation that, even absent professors, most students fell into a structure of passive compliance demonstrated that their collaboration in their own domination went well beyond the acceptance of professors' authority. If in the student assemblies the majority sat passively while the leaders spoke, the reason was because 'we are all victims of a despotic system that dishabituates us from discussion and political struggle, and that imposes on us its politics, that is authoritarianism and subordination'.[40] In the assembly, as much as the lecture, student protesters discovered themselves as passive, inarticulate and manipulated.

Students thus invented themselves as inarticulate, subordinated and repressed. There can be no doubt that the feeling of having internalised an authoritarian mentality was genuine. Yet it was also a discovery that occurred retrospectively. The general assembly appeared initially as a liberating phenomenon. Over time, its authoritarianism – its privileging of charismatic leaders – became evident, yet this does not mean the initial sense of liberation of the student assembly was misplaced. Similarly, while few defended the lecture, protesters exaggerated their socialisation into passivity. As one document noted, students had listened 'allowing ourselves some hidden smiles', slyly but not openly challenging professors.[41] The rejection of academic authority was no longer covert but explicit, no longer ironic but serious. If 'academic and social authoritarianism establish their roots not just in a series of structures but also and especially in the consent of those who submit to these structures',[42] the transformation of oneself formed the first logical step away from this self-imposed immaturity. Not for nothing was the Maoist slogan 'to rebel is justified' a favourite of the protest movements. Protesters invented the figure of the passive student in order to create a new subjectivity. They turned from general assemblies to counter-courses and small commissions 'where finally the word collective begins to have a meaning, where preconstituted positions dissolve into contrasts between individuals. A concrete method to begin negating oneself as a product and discover oneself as a "comrade."'[43] Small groups aimed to be the space in which individuals could finally 'talk' and

[40] CMR B.1 f.2 (Fondo Movimento Studentesco G. Palma), 'Documenti per le agitazioni'.
[41] CMR B.1 f.2 (Fondo Movimento Studentesco G. Palma), 'Abbiamo commesso degli errori.' This document is a re-writing of Peter Schneider's speech at the Free University of Berlin.
[42] CMR B.3 f.9 (Fondo Movimento Studentesco G. Palma), 'Carta Revendicativa – Trento schema di massima'.
[43] Mauro Rostagno, 'Anatomia della rivolta', *Problemi del socialismo* 28–29 (1968), 283.

reinvent themselves as active subjects, while simultaneously inventing a collective subject.

The anti-authoritarian structure sought by protesters proved a moving target, shifting from the introduction of dialogue in the lecture hall to the student assembly to the small group. However great the collapse in professorial authority, genuine egalitarianism only appeared possible in ever-smaller arenas. Yet this in no way implied a total abandonment of the student assembly, which as a collective embodiment of the protest movement remained the only forum capable of challenging the university as a whole. Although some forms of authority inevitably existed in the small groups and political commissions, the major tension stemmed from whether the trajectory of devolution would in fact undermine the protest movement as a collective. The assertion that in small groups one discovered oneself as a 'comrade' aimed to avoid that dilemma. Equally possible, however, was that the pressure to conform to the role of comrade would undermine the experience of liberation: 'whoever wasn't in line was a fascist,' one student noted in retrospect.[44] After all, if students had discovered themselves as inarticulate, they had simultaneously discovered themselves as a mass movement. If one urgent task concerned learning to talk and think actively rather than passively, another required the maintenance of the movement itself.

Two dangers threatened – cooptation or pacification on the one hand and hierarchisation and institutionalisation on the other. Mauro Rostagno identified the key problem as being 'how a subversive mass movement could maintain itself as such in its two aspects of subversion and mass, maintaining itself as a movement, that is without institutionalising itself'.[45] His solution was to refuse any offers of student co-government or even self-government of the university and to envision an eternal contestation: 'The movement must therefore aim at the management of the *permanent crisis of the university.*'[46] For this, 'physical and political spaces ("structural spaces") need to be opened inside the university in which it can work politically, continue counter-courses and commissions'.[47] This demand for space (simultaneously literal and metaphorical) underpinned the 'charter of demands' elaborated by the students occupying the Faculty of Sociology. In addition to demands to be able to co-determine the courses for study, the readings therein, and the nature of assessment, the student movement sought to define the 'structural spaces' that would provide the

---

[44] Ricci, *I giovani,* 203.   [45] Rostagno, 'Anatomia della rivolta', 287.   [46] Ibid., 288.
[47] Ibid.

basis of an autonomous political movement continually able to contest the institution without ever pretending to govern it.

The student charter thus demanded actual space (lecture halls free for political activities), a floor of the institute for the movement, financial autonomy, and the abolition of disciplinary controls: of attendance in particular, with disciplinary procedures discussed before the assembly.[48] For all the rhetoric of student power, these were a relatively limited set of demands. Indeed, it embodied an explicit rejection 'of seizing power. Rostagno summed up the program in the slogan '*The control of the university to the bureaucrats* (professors, administrators, etc.) *The control of the movement to the students*. In between there is no space for reformist participation, nor for enlightened co-government.'[49] '*Potere studentesco*' thus rejected both the 'syndical hypothesis' (which demanded a more efficient and technocratic university, with improved professional formation) and the 'reformist hypothesis', which could conceive a university open to everyone with a generalised salary but which never touched the power relations within the institution, to stress the 'revolutionary hypothesis' in which the student movement identified itself as 'the sole object incapable of co-optation'.[50] Student power emerged as a solution to the tension between the demand for change to the university and the fear of being undermined by superficial concessions, as an attempt to turn an episodic and events-driven conflict into an enduring protest capable of perpetuating itself, and a compromise between the those determined to reform the university (and hence tempted by 'reformism' or 'enlightened co-government') and those who felt a new political movement needed to go beyond (if not abandon) the university to enter the political sphere.

Resolution and Anti-Lent

Students elaborated their charter of demands, but there was little hope of their recognition by the university. Police intervention had been ruled out, but neither faculty nor administrators seriously considered conceding to all the student demands. *L'Adige*, the newspaper of the Christian Democratic boss Flaminio Piccoli, actively opposed the notion of 'student power'. The autonomy of the university applied above all to the professor: 'we hold the

---

[48] CMR B.3 f.9, 'Carta Rivendicativa – Trento schema di massima'.
[49] Rostagno, 'Anatomia della rivolta', 288.
[50] Marco Boato, 'Il Movimento Studentesco Trentino da Forza Corporativa a Forza Sociale', *Il Cristallo* 10 (1968), 17.

liberty of the teacher an essential, primordial element of liberty of culture'.[51] The liberty of the student 'does not consist in refusing teaching and the teacher ... [but] the right to examine in depth, which is different to the right of ignorance or scholastic anarchy that is ultimately being preached'.[52] The founder of the university, Bruno Kessler, sought a compromise and turned to Rome, where the Minister for Public Education named a 'committee of control' composed of Beniamino Andreatta, Marcello Boldrini and Norberto Bobbio. As the latter recalled, 'In a Catholic-DC environment like Trento there had to be one who was secular. There were two Christian Democrats: Andreatta... and then Boldrini ... I arrived at Trento ... as the non-Catholic, non–Christian-Democratic representative.'[53] Typically, the first problem arose around the legitimacy of student representation. The committee requested a delegation from the student assembly, which refused, demanding the 'coordinating committee' come to them: 'only the general assembly has the right to negotiate with the committee on the basis of the current phase of political consciousness of the Trentino and Italian student movement'.[54] Contrary to expectations, the committee indeed visited the assembly at the end of February but with no results. The administration could only offer collaboration on the curriculum. Students wanted more, dismissing a 'collaboration that sees the students devoid of power' as 'now surpassed by the current phase of organisation of the Movement'.[55] In mid-March the students proposed a public discussion with the 'coordinating committee' before the general assembly, but they received no response. Instead, events outside the university dragged the students and university alike into crisis.

Catholic politics had played an important role at Trento since the inception of the institute. Now the Catholic Church entered the orbit of contestation.[56] In February 1968, at the beginning of the occupation, nine priests enrolled in the faculty of sociology issued a statement in support of the occupation, for 'the distortions inexorably produced by the capitalist system and denounced by Paul VI are ever more generalised and extended even at the university level'.[57] Almost two months later, after 55 days of occupation, the contestation hit the Catholic Church with full force. The

---

[51] 'Una strada per l'anarchia', L'Adige, 1 February 1968, 4.   [52] Ibid.
[53] CMR B.14 f.2 (Fondo Calì), untitled document.   [54] Vecchio, Vietato obbedire, 97.
[55] 'Conversazione cordiale, ma inutile', Alto Adige, 26 February 1968, 3.
[56] On Catholicism and '68 in Italy, see Guido Verucci, 'Il '68, il mondo cattolico e la Chiesa', in Aldo Agostini et al. (eds.), La cultura e i luoghi del '68, (Milan: FrancoAngeli, 1991), 381–399.
[57] CMR B.1 f.2 (Fondo Movimento Studentesco G. Palma), 'Solidali con gli occupant i preti iscritti a sociologia'.

Franciscan monk Igino Sbalchiero arrived at Trento to celebrate Lent. Listening in the audience to his homily was Paolo Sorbi, a Neapolitan student who had come to Trento with political experience of Christian base groups that had protested conditions in shanty towns in the early 1960s. Two very different visions of Catholicism thus confronted each other in the Cathedral at Trento. The bishop of Trento, Alessandro Maria Gottardi, later admitted 'that preacher raised some reservations in myself who was present, there's no doubt – even before the young ones'.[58] Sbalchiero's homily began to touch on the war in Vietnam and the speech of Cardinal Francis Spellman[59] or, according to another account 'was attacking the USSR and its camps',[60] when Sorbi rose to his feet, interrupted the friar and said 'Padre, this is not true, I would like to speak …'.[61] Having captured speech in the university, Sorbi now sought to do the same in the church.

While the action at the Cathedral did not appear coordinated by the student movement, the inspiration was West Berlin. The actions of 'Rudi Dutschke who had interrupted the Christmas ceremonies in the protestant Cathedral in Berlin about Vietnam … incited me to do the same at Trento'.[62] The reaction also echoed West Berlin. Some of the congregation attempted to silence Sorbi. Others escorted him swiftly to the door, or as the charge against Sorbi stated, 'a few faithful, indignant at his behaviour, expelled him from the Church'.[63] The contestation in the cathedral scandalised Trento. Sorbi defended his actions to the press in terms very similar to those levelled at professorial and academic power: 'it is impossible to continue with such mystificatory preaching that has nothing to do with the gospels and continues to betray the liberatory message of the Council'.[64] Little remained of the legacy of the Vatican Council, 'There is only a false renewal that does nothing to substantially change the apparatus of authority of the hierarchy of bishops and priests, who continue in their deafness, and do not live the word of God as

---

[58] Paolo Ghezzi (ed.), 'Questi 24 anni con voi' in Editors of Vita Trentina (eds.), *60 anni di Vita Trentina: 1926–1986, supplemento al n.50* (Trento: Vita Trentina, 1986), 69.

[59] Armando Vadagnini, *Trento: città del '68* (Trento: Reverdito, 1988), 74.

[60] See Vecchio, *Vietato obbedire*, 104, and Roberto Beretta, *Il lungo autunno: controstoria del sessantotto cattolico* (Milan: Rizzoli, 1998), 76.

[61] CMR B.3 f.4 (Fondo Movimento Studentesco G. Palma), 'Procura della repubblica presso il tribunale di Trento. Ordine di comparizione emesso dal P.M.'

[62] Beretta, *Il lungo autunno*, 76.

[63] CMR B.3 f.4, 'Procura della repubblica presso il tribunale di Trento. Ordine di comparizione emesso dal P.M.'

[64] 'Quaresimale con la questura', *Alto Adige*, 28 March 1968, 4.

testimony of service to the poor and the exploited'.[65] The Anti-Lent (*il controquaresimale*) had only just begun. The day after his intervention, Sorbi returned to the Cathedral with a number of the Catholic students of sociology (and several police agents in plain-clothes).

The second evening, instead of interrupting the Franciscan's homily, some 15 students rose silently 'at the first piece of bullshit expressed by the abbot'[66] and exited the cathedral. Outside on the piazza, they read passages from the radical priests Ernesto Balducci, don Lorenzo Milani, Arturo Paoli or the Gospels. When the Franciscan friar finished his speech, the students re-entered the cathedral and the mass continued without any disturbance. The same occurred the following evening. The Bishop apparently affirmed that 'if the young people want, they can continue even ten years'[67] but soon released a document criticising 'a clear intention of subversion'.[68] The letters page of the Christian Democratic paper *L'Adige* went further, with demands for police intervention, or 'perhaps, the citizen has to defend himself directly from these brutes who tend to drag us into anarchy, and ultimately, into Communism? I believe in democracy, but not in democracy that supinely submits to every vexation or whatever attempt on its dignity or even its existence!'[69] The dynamic of provocation and reaction established in the university now threatened to extend to the Catholic Church and the entire town.

Confrontation became open conflict on the fourth day of the Anti-Lent. Around 1,000 persons gathered in the small space that separated the faculty of sociology from the cathedral of Trento. The fifty or so students conducting alternative readings were invited to retire, then put to flight. They sought refuge at the faculty. This time it was the students who called the police who formed a protective cordon. Rotten fruit, eggs and insults followed from the crowd: 'whores, hippies, get lost!'[70] The students responded by singing *La montanara*, the unofficial anthem of the Trentino. Incensed by the affront, some members of the crowd tried to break the police cordon and seize the students on the steps. More rotten fruit and eggs were launched. The sociologists retreated inside the university, barring the entrance. Several attempts to break down the doors failed. One member of the crowd set fire to the banner bearing the slogan of 'potere

---

[65] Ibid., 4. [66] Ricci, *I giovani*, 139.
[67] Adriana Zarri, 'Non piace ai giovani un cristianesimo troppo tranquillo', *Settegiorni in Italia e nel mondo* 44 (14 April 1968), 25.
[68] Marco Boato (ed.), *Contro la chiesa di classe: documenti della contestazione ecclesiale in Italia* (Padova: Marsilio Editori, 1969), 32.
[69] 'Il parere dei lettori', *L'Adige*, 28 March 1968, 6. [70] Vecchio, *Vietato obbedire*, 106.

studentesco'. The stand-off continued for hours, dissolving only towards midnight. The siege continued the following day. Rumours of a squad of fascists come to attack the institute circulated in the faculty. Police patrolled throughout the day. The crowd swelled again in the evening, attempting to break the police cordon. A barrage of stones and apples shattered the windows. The university remained surrounded well into the early hours of the morning.

While the challenge to the church had not been planned by the student movement, it transformed what had been primarily a conflict inside the university into a confrontation between the town and the institute it hosted. The broadening of the conflict proved to be the resolution to the stand-off within the university, as both students and faculty administrators sought to diffuse the situation. The student movement set a meeting with the 'coordinating committee' for what would be the third day of the siege. Beniamino Andreatta, Marcello Boldrini and Norberto Bobbio discussed the student demands with Marco Boato before the student assembly, while the crowd outside continued their vigil. More stones, apples and a bottle of petrol with a lighted fuse were thrown at the faculty. Inside, however, faculty and students came to an accord. The administration recognised the general assembly as the only legitimate representative of the students. The occupation became 'open' and courses resumed. In early April the coordinating committee accepted the 'charter of demands' almost in its entirety: a new director of the institute would be called, students would participate in equal numbers to faculty on a committee to decide future teaching and research programs, weekend seminars were scheduled for working students, discussion of exams would be held publicly, the library would be open until 11:00 p.m., rooms were put at the disposition of the students for whatever purpose they desired. In a press conference, Bobbio affirmed that 'on the whole the demands were acceptable'.[71] Asked by *L'Adige* about the graffiti on the walls, Boldrini replied 'if I had been in their position I would have done something worse'.[72]

'Student power' was victorious, the traditional representative organs vanquished, the structure of the faculty transformed, the politics of contestation triumphantly vindicated. The movement at Trento thus drew the same conclusion as that in West Berlin. They even adapted Peter Schneider's 'errors' speech to fit the local circumstances. 'We have committed errors', both speeches proclaimed. Schneider's declaration that 'We

[71] Ibid., 110.   [72] Ricci, *I giovani*, 145.

believed in the freedom of science, as others believe in the freedom of South Vietnam ...'[73] translated at Trento to 'We believed in the freedom of science, as others believe in the freedom of the workers of Michelin.'[74] Where Schneider identified Vietnam, Emergency laws and the university as the themes of protest, this became Vietnam, the exploitation of workers and academic culture at Trento. Schneider's speech elaborated the justification for the 'abolition of calm and order, it is about undemocratic behaviour, about no longer simply being realistic and objective' and affirmed that demands for calm and order, 'are exactly the bans with which the authorities ensure that the rage over crimes in Vietnam, about the Emergency Laws and the obsolete university constitution remain calm and without effect'.[75] So, too in Italy, the lesson learned was that peace and order needed to be abandoned:

> Finally, we understood that against exams in which we learn only fear, against an objectivity that signified nothing other than tiredness, against an authority that meant nothing but the protection of the bosses, against hypocritical rationality and the cautious dearth of feeling, against the tranquillity and order that peace concedes to the oppressors, against all this we argue in a more concrete way by ceasing to argue and beginning to enter the struggle together.[76]

The struggle within the university appeared to render a very simple lesson: rather than endless negotiations, compromises and political machinations, an occupation, an assembly or the interruption of an official speaker could shake 'the system' to its foundations. Politics begins in contestation.

If politics began in contestation, where did it end? The students at Trento had declared the need to stop arguing and fight, astonished and emboldened at the vacuum of authority that had suddenly emerged within the university when confronted with political rather than just intellectual opposition. Yet the analysis of Schneider, and the students who echoed him at Trento, undoubtedly overstated the extent to which the 'whole system' had been shaken to the core. If the university relied on student consent, many of the forms of protest that appeared to offer a way to shake the system relied on the overreaction of authorities. In the same way that student consent could no longer be guaranteed, neither could the tendency of authorities to overreact. The student victory at Trento exemplified the

---

[73] Schneider, *Ansprachen*, 7.
[74] CMR B.1 f.2 (Fondo Movimento Studentesco G. Palma), 'Abbiamo commesso degli errori'.
[75] Schneider, *Ansprachen*, 7.
[76] CMR B.1 f.2 (Fondo Movimento Studentesco G. Palma), 'Abbiamo commesso degli errori'.

problem: now that 'structural spaces' had been won within the university, could the protest movement regenerate itself given that so much of its dynamism had come from the refusal to grant it space within the university? If politics began with conflict, what happened once a major source of conflict was removed? Would the new conquests prove as fleeting and insubstantial as the traditional forms of politics? At the end of May, an 'official' Anti-Lent was held at the church of San Francesco Saverio where Sorbi and other students discussed the sermon with the priest. The boundaries of the possible had shifted. Another interruption at Trento could not produce the same results.

More than elsewhere, the movement at Trento successfully created a structural transformation of the university that conceded to the protest movement a large degree of autonomy. That success, however, owed much to the size of the institute, the ability of a small group of active protesters to paralyse it (with considerable support of the entire body of students) and the events of the Anti-Lent that forced faculty and students to collaborate in a crisis situation. Yet success bred its own problems: the question of how a student movement could perpetuate itself absent further attempts to repress it, the problem of embracing confrontation as an end in itself in order to shake the system and a powerful dynamic of politicisation that increasingly led students away from the university as a 'merely' academic site of struggle. In late April 1968, a little more than a year on from 'Vietnam week' when police had entered the faculty of sociology for the first time, another Vietnam sit-in occurred. In 1967, the demonstration's stated goal was to put pressure on the 'Italian government to finally disassociate immediately its own great political responsibility [for the war]'.[77] In 1968, despite insisting 'EVERYONE CAN EXPRESS THEIR OWN OPINION', the language of protest hinted that speaking must give way to a much broader struggle:

> To speak of Vietnam is not sufficient. It is necessary to understand but does not signify a struggle for the victory of the people. To be with Vietnam we must speak of OUR VIETNAM, of the Italian, Trentino, Vietnam, to know to struggle, not to settle our consciences. And the Vietnam at Trento is the situation in its poor quarters, the peasants in its valleys, of the tens of thousands of emigrants who daily leave their land, their family, to be able to survive.[78]

---

[77] CMR B.3 f.1, 'Documento politico del comitato permanente per la pace e la libertà nel Vietnam'.
[78] CMR B.3 f.4 (Fondo Movimento Studentesco G. Palma), 'Colleghi'.

Action soon followed. Not far from Trento, at the Marzotto textile factory of Valdagno in the Veneto, workers broke into the factory offices and destroyed the management's new time-charts. In a large demonstration, around 4,000 (including some students from Trento) clashed with police, damaged shops and tore down the statue of Count Gaetano Marzotto, founder of the textile business. The local Christian Democratic town council intervened to demand the release of the arrested. Mauro Rostagno exulted in the May Day celebrations at Trento: 'Until now we have been clubbed, hit, dispersed. We were bare-handed and up to now they hit us. But let us say clearly that it will not always be this way':

> I say to you that we do not have to hit those who are controlled by the police or carabinieri for seven, eight or more hours per day: we have to hit who commands, we have to create a violence that overturns the bourgeois state. ... Organisation is our strength. Political organisation and armed organisation: we must take arms, we must take arms so that there are no more arms.[79]

Guitar music, not violence, followed the speech, but within the next days events in Paris suggested the revolution had indeed arrived.

---

[79] 'Il primo maggio degli studenti', *Alto Adige*, 3 May 1968, 4.

CHAPTER 10

'An Asylum for Delinquents'
The Space of Revolt at Nanterre

Situated on a barren domain to the west of Paris previously used by the Ministry of Defence, the Faculty of Arts and Letters at Nanterre consisted of number of isolated buildings, in stark contrast to the usual urban implantation of Parisian universities. Not the Latin Quarter, but a *bidonville* of North African immigrants bordered the university.[1] A Moroccan worker, Bilani Lay Ben Lachen, died on the campus worksites in mid-March 1968, an event without echo in the student protest movement.[2] A satellite of the Sorbonne, Nanterre symbolised the expansion of French higher education. Yet it also cultivated an image of intellectual renewal, offering space to the new discipline of sociology, and overseen by a dean known for his liberal attitude. Nanterre owes its prominence in the history of the student movements of 1968 partly to its position as an experimental, modern university. This place within the national politics of higher education was compounded by a local situation that invited contestation, in particular the presence of the student residences which further served as an additional arena in which the revolt against authority incubated. While speech provided the backbone to the early revolt in West Berlin and the struggle over sociology forged the student movement at Trento, the politics of space set the stage for the revolt at Nanterre.

---

[1] Any account of the student movements at Nanterre before May 1968 must rely heavily on Duteuil's *Nanterre,* and the documents reproduced therein. On Duteuil's biography, see Robert Gildea, James Mar and Annette Warring (eds.), *Europe's 1968: Voices of Revolt* (Oxford: Oxford University Press, 2013), 27–29. For Duteuil's analysis of 1968, see Jean-Pierre Duteuil, *Mai 68: Un Mouvement politique* (La Bussière, 2008). For Duteuil interviewed by Cohn-Bendit, see Daniel Cohn-Bendit, *Nous l'avons tant aimé la revolution* (Paris: Bernard Barrault, 1986), 62–73. For the campus viewed from the bidonville, see Vincent Lemire, 'Nanterre, les bidonvilles et les étudiants', in Philippe Artières and Michelle Zancarini-Fournel (eds.), *68: Une histoire collective 1962–1981* (Paris: La Découverte, 2008), 137–143. See also Michael Seidman, *The Imaginary Revolution: Parisian Students and Workers in 1968* (New York: Berghahn, 2004) and Daniel Gordon, *Immigrants & Intellectuals: May '68 and the Rise of Anti-Racism in France* (Pontypool: Merlin Press, 2012).
[2] Lemire, 'Nanterre, les bidonvilles et les étudiants', 140; Gordon, *Immigrants & Intellectuals,* 39.

The student residences stimulated politics at Nanterre when other issues only inculcated apathy. By January 1967, the *groupuscules* admitted that neither university reform nor Vietnam – so important for the radical groups themselves – mobilised the student body.[3] The most successful incident – when anarchists wrested control of the philosophy-sociology-psychology office of the student union – came off only because of the general disinterest. A subsequent meeting to protest exams mobilised more than usual but still did not lead to conflict with the administration. Nonetheless, these early occurrences suggested that novel forms of protest could generate conflict. The anarchists followed their success protesting against exams by disrupting a 'happening' of Jean-Jacques Lebel (painter, artist and French exponent of the living theatre). As an actor moved about the amphitheatre addressing the audience, Daniel Cohn-Bendit burst out with 'Do you think he fucks? [*Tu crois qu'il baise?*]'[4] Others launched yoghurt and carrots at the stage. Despite the initial consternation, however, actors and protesters soon reconciled over beer. The discontent with exams and the theatrics attested to the degeneration of traditional political representation and the rise of provocation. Yet these incidents had thus far failed to generate a response from the university administration, thereby triggering the dynamic that at both West Berlin and Trento served to sustain the nascent protest movement. The residences provided the spark.

University Residences and the Politics of Space

The dean of Nanterre oversaw not only the faculty buildings but also the university residences. As in West Berlin, where the administration of building space rapidly became the axis of a conflict that opposed student self-government and the rector's traditional authority, so too at Nanterre, students began to challenge the dean's authority by imposing their own. The regulations of the university residences forbade visits in the rooms, any refurbishment of the bedrooms, disallowed any political or religious propaganda (authorising cultural meetings on request at 48 hours' notice),

---

[3] On the importance of Vietnam, see Salar Mohandesi, 'Bringing Vietnam home: The Vietnam War, internationalism and May '68', *French Historical Studies* 41.2 (2018), 219–251. See also Geneviève Dreyfus-Armand and Jacques Portes, 'Les interactions internationales de la guerre du Viêt-nam et Mai 68', in Geneviève Dreyfus-Armand et al. (eds.), *Les Années 68. Le temps de la contestation* (Bruxelles: Editions Complexe, 2000), 49–68.
[4] Jean-Pierre Duteuil, *Nanterre, 1965–66–67–68. Vers le movement du 22 mars* (Paris: Acratie, 1988), 94.

and banned males from the female buildings.[5] These regulations grated with the vast majority of the students. Residents flouted the rules, entering the girls' dormitories via open windows on the ground floor. On 16 March 1967, they formalised their disregard, unanimously resolving at an assembly that 'the interior regulations imposed by the administration being antiquated, they will be considered as of today to be NULL AND VOID'.[6] Henceforth, they proclaimed residents would have the 'free disposition of their room', 'total freedom of meeting, information and circulation', and affirmed mixed residences as the only possible solution. In the interim, 'the freedom to visit the female buildings WILL BECOME A STATE OF FACT'.[7] The declaration struck directly the authority of the dean, on an issue that drew widespread sympathy from the student body and required only a relatively small number of active protesters.

The residents demanded the same as at West Berlin and Trento: liberty and autonomy. As Pierre Grappin wrote to the rector of Paris a few days later, 'they have declared they no longer recognise any authority but their own'.[8] Without instructions to the contrary, the staff in charge of the buildings at first condoned infractions of the regulations. However, 'such a situation' wrote the dean, 'cannot be allowed to continue'.[9] Two solutions presented themselves to Grappin: the consideration of new regulations that responded to student objections and the placement of the residences directly under the control of the rector or the dean: 'if the whole of Nanterre is to exist, it is necessary that the institutions that it gathers together answer directly to the same university authority, in this instance the dean of the Faculty of Letters'.[10] Faced with a choice between negotiation and greater authority, the dean elected for the latter. Christian Fouchet, the Minister of Education, met with student delegations and intimated the possibility of new regulations with student consultation on condition the protests stopped – a proposal hardly likely to appease the protesters, who thought it should be the other way around. On the evening of 21 March a group of students gathered following the meeting of the Ciné-Club, and someone suggested 'Come on, let's go to the girls'.[11] So began the occupation of the girls' dormitory by some sixty students, with a slow decline in numbers as the night wore on. At dawn, just nine days after their first intervention at Trento and less than a month before

---

[5] For the regulations, see the reproduction in Ibid., 135.
[6] BDIC. F delta 813(1), A. R. C. U. N.   [7] Ibid.
[8] ADHS 1208W/180, 'Université de Paris. Faculté des Lettres et Sciences Humaines de Nanterre. Le Doyen. Nanterre, le 20 Mars, 1967'.
[9] Ibid.   [10] Ibid.   [11] Duteuil, *Nanterre*, 84.

they would attempt to clear the Freie Universität, the police arrived at Nanterre.

A stand-off ensued. Protesters blocked the elevators and controlled the narrow stairs. The police resorted to negotiation with the mediation of faculty members and the representatives of UNEF and ARCUN. By late morning the rector agreed to allow the students to leave if they could show a key to their room (to identify any outsiders), but with no other identity check and the promise of no sanction. Yet students now protested not only the regulations but the recourse to the police, 'even though the most complete calm reigned in the university city'.[12] To the residents, the police intervention signalled the intention to repress the nascent protest movement in the residences. Furthermore, they understood intervention over male access to the female dormitories as a means to isolate the demand for free circulation from the other principles of freedom of assembly and freedom of information, to 'make appear juvenile demands which aim in fact to democratise university life at every level'.[13] As elsewhere, police intervention served to designate the authority of the dean as reliant on the police rather than student consent. Repression confirmed the mental framework in which the regulation of dormitories formed one element of a broader authoritarianism in society.

Police action provided an important spur to political mobilisation, engendering protest not just in favour of the original demand but against the repressive response. The conflict over the residences escalated when twenty-nine students received letters informing them of sanctions for the action. Not only did this move contradict the promise of no official reprisals, but among the twenty-nine names figured some well-known militants who had in fact been absent that night. One student on the list wrote to the dean pointing out he did not even agree with the occupation and was in Paris on the date in question. Others protested the imposition of sanctions without any official inquiry or proof of participation.[14] These errors fomented rumours of 'blacklists' of the politically active students, thought to be based on information provided to the administration by plain-clothed policemen. The dean himself remembered the occupation as the moment when a government official pointed out Daniel Cohn-Bendit 'a student of red hair, the collar open wide, who seemed impatient to hold

---

[12] BDIC. F delta 813(1), 'Communiqué des residents de Nanterre'.
[13] Ibid. See Pierre Grappin, *L'Île aux peupliers: de la Résistance à Mai 68: Souvenirs du Doyen de Nanterre* (Nancy: Presses Universitaires de Nancy, 1993), 243.
[14] The various letters to the dean can be found in ADHS 1208W/180.

a rant' as someone 'sent to you to stir up the students and use them to ruin the faculty'.¹⁵ Dispute between the student body and administration thus came to be framed in terms of an existential crisis of the university (for administrators) and explicit political repression (for many students). The size of demonstrations increased. In April, a few hundred students protested the sanctions resulting from the occupation. To reaffirm the demands of the residents, they entered the faculty buildings and marched through the corridors.

The occupation of the residences confirmed the viability of the politics of provocation to students, not least because it led the administration to approach the problem as one of order. The *groupuscules* gradually drew closer together. The anarchists, the greatest proponents of direct action, felt vindicated. Although they had not instigated the conflict at the residences, the program they elaborated in November 1966 envisioned the possibility of occupying the girls' dormitory. The Trotskyist *Jeunesse Communiste Revolutionnaire*, which held the greatest influence in the student dormitories, judged that 'this movement was not in the least politically prepared',¹⁶ and concluded that 'a 'hard' movement against the administration and the minister must not be the kick-off for a campaign of demands but can only cap it'.¹⁷ For their part, the administration commissioned a review of the university residences that concluded 'the implantation at Nanterre of a mixed university city constituted an error.'¹⁸

Ominously for the prospects of peace at Nanterre, the report viewed the student body as incapable of self-control, let alone self-government:

> These boys and girls leaving adolescence, of whom a large number have only just escaped the regime of family monitoring or the boarding school, have not acquired the mastery which permits them to overcome the sexual psychosis favoured by the proximity of buildings thus located in an unfortunately disadvantaged suburb.¹⁹

The long-term solution to student sexual psychosis lay in limiting the residences to males only and providing other cultural activities. In the interim, measures of increased surveillance were stymied by the 'illiterate' night-watchmen and the physical construction of space: 'the placement of the concierge's lodge, which does not have a direct view of the stairs

---

¹⁵ Grappin, *L'Île aux peupliers*, 244.   ¹⁶ Duteuil, *Nanterre*, 30.   ¹⁷ Ibid.
¹⁸ ADHS 1208W/180, 'Rapport de Monsieur André Becane, Inspecteur général de l'administration sur certains incidents survenus à la cité universitaire de Nanterre, le 4 Juillet 1967'.
¹⁹ Ibid.

leading to the rooms, renders surveillance difficult'. The only possible course of action was the admission of residents to be 'more strictly controlled and subjected to more severe standards: many undesirables could thereby be discarded'.[20] The popular poster and slogan of May 1968 'we are all undesirables' responded to a specific remark about Cohn-Bendit as a German anarchist (understood by many as really meaning German Jew, rendered 'undesirables' after a debate in the General Assembly of the Atelier des Beaux-Arts judged that 'too violent').[21] But the phrase also pinpointed a wider ethos of repression in response to political struggle. The regulations that provoked the March occupation remained in place at the rentrée in late 1967. The occupation of the residences established a dynamic of provocation and reaction that slowly brought forth a broad student protest movement, crystallising the contrast between a movement that demanded democratisation and autonomy and an administration that responded through greater control and surveillance.

Spaces of Speech

The academic year of 1967–1968 brought further problems of governance for the dean of Nanterre, from both the Ministry of National Education and the students. In June 1967, the assembly of the faculty protested against the lack of personnel, exacerbated by the Fouchet reforms and the influx of new students.[22] Budgetary difficulties also hindered the control of space. In November, the dean wrote to the rector regarding the security of the university domain:

> The enclosure of our terrain is destroyed at multiple points and we do not dispose of any personnel of surveillance. Our budget difficulties prevent us from hiring, as last winter, contractual agents of a security company. Our paths of circulation and vast stretches of building therefore remain without any surveillance. If on this or that occasion, student demonstrations occur, we have not the least means to maintain order.[23]

The dean tried to pre-empt trouble by transferring Daniel Cohn-Bendit from Nanterre to the Sorbonne: 'many reports have been submitted to me of your subversive activities; not being obliged to keep you, we are

---

[20] Ibid.   [21] Christine Fauré, *Mai 68 jour et nuit* (Evreux: Gallimard, 1998), 98.
[22] ADHS 1208W/1, 'Faculté des lettres et sciences humaines de Nanterre. Assemblée de la faculté du 17 juin 1967. Procès-verbal de la séance'.
[23] ADHS 1208W/181, 'Le Doyen de la Faculté des Lettres et Sciences Humaines de Nanterre à Monsieur le Recteur-Adjoint de l'Académie de Paris. Paris'.

transferring you'.²⁴ But the protests of the sociology professors prevented his dispatch. The dean thus found himself constrained by a lack of financial resources on the one hand and the willingness of staff to intervene in favour of students on the other. Although it was yet to become obvious, Pierre Grappin presided over a vacuum of authority at Nanterre.

The position of dean increasingly lacked the consent of students, the unanimous support of staff and the means to enforce authority. Yet if any individual might have been expected to cope with student politics, it was Pierre Grappin, well-known as a man of the Left and a former general secretary of the Communist front organisation, the Movement for Peace. 'Today, less than ever', he wrote, 'we must not allow the difference of age ... to separate us from our students. We do not want them to accuse us of having retired to the illusory calm of our books, while outside the storm rumbles. We must go to them, speak often to them, even on political subjects...'²⁵ He bemoaned that students could endlessly discuss philosophy yet not know the basics of politics.²⁶ But this was the Grappin of the early 1960s. The brutal attack on Algerian demonstrators in Paris in October 1961 led to the 'grave decision' to break 'with the fundamental principle of neutrality and university teaching', when scholars denounced the repression in their lectures.²⁷ Grappin understood such action as the exception to the rule of neutrality, to be undertaken only when the right to speech, thought or protest was repressed. The power of denunciation drew on the conventional adherence to political neutrality. The movement of the late 1960s, however, rejected altogether the norm of neutrality as a disingenuous and suffocating convention that smothered political expression. His previous engagement notwithstanding, Grappin was unprepared for this wholesale rejection. Furthermore, like most of his peers, he was ill-equipped to deal with a politics of space and provocation. Perhaps most surprisingly, he proved unsympathetic to the rise of student politics on campus. While the events of 1961 'had to be denounced: it was no longer possible to remain silent', the same did not necessarily apply in 1967 and 1968.²⁸ The meaning of politics had changed.

The new politics of the late 1960s subjected the apparently neutral domain of university administration to a process of politicisation. Initially, the problems of overcrowding and curriculum reforms dominated late 1967, leading to the November strike that demanded equivalence between old and new degrees, student representation in university decision-making

---

[24] Duteuil, *Nanterre*, 125. [25] BDIC. F delta 1056(1)(9), 'Nos responsabilités d'universitaires'.
[26] Ibid. [27] Ibid. [28] Ibid.

bodies and smaller classes. Yet the strike served to legitimise further the culture of contestation that continued in its quotidian forms of clashes between administration and students over political speech and space. Interruptions of courses (used so successfully to gather support for the strike) no longer counted as isolated incidents. In early December a group of poets discovered that 'one doesn't put on a show at Nanterre without taking some risks'.[29] The following week, the dean forbade the projection of a film at the Ciné-Club, which he considered to have been 'diverted from its cultural meaning' into 'a public demonstration of political character'.[30] The film dealt with Vietnam. At Trento, such a film drew the police to campus. A ban sufficed at Nanterre. However, the authority of the dean became ever more entangled in the fine line between cultural expression and politics, while the administration of space increasingly operated as a regulation or repression of political activity – a mode that the majority of students found illegitimate.

In the face of growing political activism, ever stricter controls displaced the previously existing liberalism regarding use of university space. Initially, to obtain a room 'a written request with the guarantee of a professor sufficed. Then a student card number was needed. Then the card's deposit until authorisation of the room. Then the card was not returned until after the meeting. Now the card no longer suffices: a professor must commit to being in the room to guarantee the meeting.'[31] The implication that students were not responsible without professorial oversight stoked the widespread resentment. A movement that demanded representation in decision-making bodies of the university could hardly be satisfied with regulations that required greater supervision. Both the aggravating bureaucratic formalities required to obtain the use of a room and the withholding of rooms on the basis of 'political content' demonstrated the absence of student autonomy. The university refused to provide space for meetings on 'institutions and repressions' and the Fouchet reform of higher education 'on the basis of political content'.[32] The rejection of such requests – which, unlike some other forms of protest, did not disrupt teaching – marked a hardening of the self-representation of neutrality within the university. The limitations on such mildly political topics facilitated the acceptance of a much more provocative political content.

---

[29] Duteuil, *Nanterre*, 108.
[30] BDIC. F delta 1056(1)(6), Faculté des Lettres et Sciences Humaines de Paris Nanterre. Le Doyen.
[31] BDIC. F delta 1961(10) – VI, Nanterre Information.   [32] Ibid.

The most famous (or infamous) incident of speech occurred at the beginning of January 1968 as François Missoffe, the Minister of Youth and Sports, inaugurated the new swimming pool at Nanterre. Hearing of the event, a number of militants went to intervene, gathering a few eggs and tomatoes along the way. Upon arrival, Cohn-Bendit addressed the Minister, noting that the recently published *Livre blanc sur la jeunesse* (which noted the 'delay' of youth 'in engaging themselves in collective action in order to influence the evolution of society')[33] said nothing on the problem of sexuality. Missoffe replied that if he had such problems, he should throw himself into the swimming pool. 'Heil Hitler!' replied Cohn-Bendit, in an attempt to compare Missoffe's response to suppression of sexuality through sport in the Third Reich.[34] This trite exchange symbolised perfectly the new politics of speech: the disregard and desire to disrupt ceremony, the desacralisation of authority figures, and the generalised view of a diffuse repression present in every aspect of society from sexuality to sociology, an authoritarianism demonstratively overthrown in the act of provocation. The perception of repression could only be confirmed when the incident provoked measures once again to remove Cohn-Bendit – this time not just from the faculty, but (as a German citizen) from French territory altogether. In other attempts to reimpose his authority, the dean summoned a couple of pro-Situationists, the most persistent at interrupting lectures, while other students were threatened with expulsion from the university residences. Ever sensitive to any possible administrative sanction of political militants, the anarchists responded by taking politics inside the university buildings, thereby making manifest the latent conflict over space.

The January 1968 demonstration marked an escalation of protest, no longer simply aimed at freedom of speech or politics within the university but targeting the repressive power of the administration. Forms of authority – blacklists and the threat of sanctions – served to mobilise students more than the general proposition of liberty of speech on campus. The anarchists now identified undercover policeman who they presumed provided the dean with names of troublemakers. In late January, the anarchists arranged to photograph these police (students 'of an unlikely age in suit and tie walking in the hallway and casually stopping in front of each poster

---

[33] Ministère de la jeunesse et des sports, *Rapport d'enquête sur la jeunesse française: analyse des études et opinions exprimées 1966–1967*.

[34] As it was understood. See Dagmar Herzog, 'Sexual Morality in 1960s West Germany', *German History* 23 (2005), 370–383.

or inscription').³⁵ After accumulating a sufficient number of incriminating photos, they arranged them on placards. The Trotskyists of the JCR, informed of the operation, took no position as an organisation, but a number of their members promised their support. A group of around thirty gathered on 26 January for the march through the corridors. Events followed the script of provocation, confrontation, over-reaction and mobilisation. University staff told the students that political demonstrations were forbidden inside the university. Receiving no acknowledgement, they tried to seize the placards. The protesters resisted. Grappin then resorted to the police, calling them to disperse a demonstration protesting the presence of police within the university. The number of protesters had doubled by the time they arrived. Moreover, at precisely this moment, the lecture halls emptied and numerous students joined the protesters to oppose the entry of the police. Seizing the placards, tables and chairs to form makeshift barricades and projectiles, the students chased the police from the building. By provoking police intervention, the demonstration had succeeded better than its organisers could have hoped for.

The dean had not learnt the lesson from the occupation of the female dormitories the previous March. Unlike his counterparts at the Freie Universität and Trento, who invoked the police once, encountered passive resistance and widespread criticism, and never repeated the call, Pierre Grappin replayed the contest and converted passive into active resistance. The intervention of the police polarised the conflict. The CGT section of the staff at Nanterre sided with the students: 'pressure is exercised through the permanent presence of plain-clothes police, the expulsion of a foreign student, pressure against union leaders, notably a delegate of the CGT in the Faculty of Law'.³⁶ While the CGT distanced itself from 'a small group of exhibitionist students who discredit the action of the whole student body', they endorsed the 'immediate and energetic' response of students to police intervention.³⁷ UNEF also condemned the methods of the anarchists, 'a small inoffensive group who discredit themselves in the eyes of students and teachers' but proclaimed its solidarity with the 'many hundreds' who resisted the police.³⁸ The dean's intervention converted differences of opinion on the anarchists into universal condemnation of his own actions. The students in their majority converged around opposition to

---

³⁵ Duteuil, *Nanterre*, 120.
³⁶ BDIC. F delta 813(4), 'Section locale C.G.T. du personnel technique et des bibliothèques de la Faculté de Nanterre. Association Fédérative des Groupes des Etudiants de Nanterre U.N.E.F.'
³⁷ Ibid.
³⁸ BDIC. F delta 1056(1)(1), 'Association Fedérative des Groupes d'Etudes de Nanterre', UNEF.

police on campus and the right to speech on all topics: 'we demand as a minimum ... the freedom to speak aloud on terms that we choose ourselves'.[39]

While student opinion coalesced around the principle of free speech and freedom from police intervention, the administration and dean continued to understand 'the appearance of groups of violent action and provocation in the university domain of Nanterre' as 'a new problem of order and security'.[40] The assembly of the faculty that sat one day after the events failed even to recognise the purpose of the demonstration. In administrative eyes the protest appeared as a personal insult. According to the administration, the protesters 'brandished placards ... where the dean, whose past in the Resistance is not unknown, ... was labelled a "Nazi"'.[41] Police intervention became inevitable because 'the personnel of the faculty who attempted to stop the destruction of material having been mistreated and hurt, the dean had to call the police'.[42] The administration implied material destruction occurred not in response to the arrival of police but rather provoked the intervention of the personnel of the faculty, who most likely intervened due to the prohibition on political demonstrations (and who were, undoubtedly, resisted physically). Furthermore, as the anarchists who made them insisted, 'there was no 'Nazi dean' placard'. The point was important to the anarchists, for whom 'Nazism is a particular form of fascism ... By contrast, we say the dean is a cop.'[43] The cry of 'Nazi', almost certainly launched during the protest, occurred probably at the arrival of the police and presumably by the Situationists. In the following days the Situationists created a poster that condemned the dean in which swastikas served as commas. They prepared the text in common with the anarchists but the use of swastikas – not agreed upon – led to a rupture between the anarchists and the Situationists (who now called themselves the *enragés*, a name the press tended to use for all the revolting students). Such distinctions inevitably meant little to an administration that, fixated on the problem of order, failed to recognise the purpose of the

---

[39] BDIC. F delta 813(4), 'La glace est rompue' 'Groupe de soutien à rupture pour la constitution d'un front des artistes révolutionnaires'.

[40] ADHS 1208W/1, 'Faculté des lettres et sciences humaines de Nanterre. Assemblée de la faculté. Année universitaire 1967–1968. 3ème séance. Nanterre, le 27 Janvier 1968'.

[41] Ibid. Similarly, the assembly reduced the protests against at least four expulsions from the residences to the expulsion of one student 'pour trafic de stupéfiants'.

[42] Ibid.

[43] BDIC. F delta 1056(1)(8), Nanterre le 1er Février 1968. 'Monsieur le Directeur du Nouvel Observateur'.

demonstration, misunderstood how the confrontation escalated, and could not comprehend the solidarity it provoked.

The solidarity of students at the appearance of the police nonetheless led to some hesitation in contemplating sanctions. The dean considered prosecution for damages and the possibility of libel for defamation (precisely the action which would engender such controversy at the FU). Both options were set aside. Faculty agreed to read a common statement before their classes condemning the student protest. The only matter clarified at the end of January was the origin of the blacklists rumours. In June 1967, Henri Raymond, an assistant in the department of sociology who had submitted a list of students exempt from a final exam due to grades obtained in the partials, received a phone call from 'a member of the administration' who identified a name on the list as not meriting the favour of exemption. Raymond did not take up the suggestion, but did report the conversation to Henri Lefebvre, who headed the sociology department. This incident served to confirm the suspicion of blacklists, as the student in question figured on the list of the twenty-nine given suspended sanction over the occupation of the girls' dormitories in March 1967.[44] The existence of any other list was vehemently rejected.

Despite the clarification, the gulf between students and faculty could not be bridged. While many radicals understood the blacklists as very real, UNEF clearly interpreted the '*listes noires*' not as an actual list, but a metaphor for repression.[45] The 'denunciation of "listes noires" . . . is about shedding light on the way in which pressure is exercised on students considered as "agitators"', including the sanctioning 'of 29 students "chosen" from among the sixty or so who occupied the girls dormitory', the phone call of 1967, the expulsion of Cohn-Bendit and the presence of plain-clothes police.[46] Indeed, the denial of blacklists could not suffice to dissolve the tension as it accurately symbolised the way the administration understood the political problems of Nanterre as a small group of individuals. Where students saw repression, the dean beheld a problem of order. Where students viewed police intervention as a transgression of tradition, the dean understood the sanctity of the university served 'to safeguard freedom of expression, first of all that of professors' and not a 'place of

---

[44] ADHS 1208W/1, 'Assemblée de la faculté, le 27 Janvier 1968'.
[45] On blacklists, cf. Seidman, *The Imaginary Revolution*, 45; and in the West German context, Nick Thomas, *Protest Movements in 1960s West Germany: A Social History of Dissent and Democracy* (Oxford: Berg, 2003), 87–91.
[46] BDIC. F delta 1056(1)(1), 'Association Fedérative des Groupes d'Etudes de Nanterre', UNEF.

asylum for delinquents'.[47] The administration simply denied that there could exist a politics of the university sphere. As he later wrote, 'there is no power to seize or share in the university but simply the task of the best organisation of the transmission of knowledge. Professors and students have nothing but interests in common, there is no antagonism between them.'[48] This idealised image simply contradicted the experience of too many students.

If there was no power to seize within the university, nevertheless the lack of power haunted the dean in early 1968. Grappin felt himself confronted by the 'impossibility of making the house function without having the means to deal with disorder'.[49] As French students prepared a national day of protest over conditions in the university residences, Grappin wrote to the rector that he was 'firmly decided to abandon all responsibility concerning the university residences'.[50] Divesting the dean of the dormitories served two ends: removing from university authorities the function of maintaining order and limiting the opportunity for the residents to form a collective within the university, 'to return the students to the collective, to make them citizens like the others, to remove from them the temptation to constitute themselves as a state within a state'.[51] Grappin also requested the creation of new university institutes to absorb the influx of students, thereby pacifying Nanterre. While seeking to remove these sources of conflict, the dean simultaneously sought the ability to deal with others, requesting disciplinary powers currently held by the rector alone. The second occupation of the girls' dormitories passed off without great incident. Nantes, not Nanterre, was the scene of a violent confrontation between students and police. Awaiting a change in the regulations of the residences (which did not arrive), the administration tacitly tolerated their abrogation. New regulations introduced by the Minister of Education were honoured in the breach. Yet if the dean conceded ground in the residences, Nanterre now hosted a large body of students susceptible to the politics of provocation and protest against repression. The intervention of police had fused the spaces of local and national politics. If the next incident did not occur on the campus of Nanterre, that no longer mattered.

Vietnam once again provided the means whereby local, national and international politics aligned in the protesters' imaginary. Many activists

[47] BDIC. F delta 1056(1)(8), 'Sur les "franchises universitaires".
[48] Pierre Grappin, *Réflexions sur les Universités Françaises* (London: Athlone Press, 1971), 17.
[49] ADHS 1208W/1, 'Assemblée de la faculté, le 27 Janvier 1968'.
[50] BDIC. F delta 1056(1)(1), Letter from Pierre Grappin to Rector.
[51] BDIC. F delta 1056(1)(1), Pierre Grappin, 'Note sur la situation des residence universitaires'.

had travelled to the Vietnam Congress in February 1968 in West Berlin. They returned to France determined to 'break decidedly with the routine of nonchalant processions'.[52] On the evening of 20 March, the JCR-influenced Comité National Vietnam demonstrated in Paris. They marched to the offices of American Express, breaking windows and launching paint bombs and a Molotov Cocktail. Xavier Langlade, a student of Nanterre, was arrested nearby. Police arrested a further four demonstrators at their homes later that night. The news circulated slowly the next day at Nanterre (when a lecture on sexuality and repression took place on the anniversary of the occupation of the girls' dormitories). On Friday, when the protesters remained under arrest, demonstrations began in earnest. Initially, the protests followed a familiar routine. Demonstrators interrupted lectures to inform about the arrests and to demand a strike or discussions of Vietnam and police repression instead of the planned course content. In a move indicative of the breakdown of groupuscular isolation, the JCR wrote slogans on the university walls, a tactic they previously disdained. A meeting of militants considered various options – an occupation (suggested by the anarchists), a demonstration in Paris (the Trotskyists of the JCR) or a statement from UNEF. They deferred a decision until the meeting of the general assembly, called for 5:00 p.m. in an amphitheatre.

The 'Liaison Committee of Professors and Students', a residue of the November strike, sat at precisely the same time as the general assembly. Two forms of student politics competed side by side. In one meeting, four to five hundred students debated their response to police repression. In the other, thirteen professors and thirteen students discussed the *rentrée* of 1968 and recent incidents. The latter meeting confirmed the certainty of increasing enrolments and the absence of adequate means to deal with them. The administration reported that they had sent the Minister of Education 'a very firm note', but all discussion concerned how to manage the selection forced on the faculty. On the incidents at the Faculty, which included the boycott of an exam in sociology that week, both faculty and student representatives meditated on how to separate troublemakers from the majority. Philippe Meyer, who led the strike the previous November, acknowledged that 'the discontent is generalised', but was 'exploited by a handful of 'marginal students' who have managed to impose disorder and who have introduced forms of contestation that the majority of sociology

---

[52] '21 février, journée du Vietnam héroïque', *Avant-garde jeunesse* (Feb.–Mar. 1968), 14, as quoted in Mohandesi, 'Bringing Vietnam home', 236.

students reject'.[53] Alain Touraine likewise thought that 'the objective ... is to isolate a small group from the majority ... It would be advisable to take strong actions to identify possible troublemakers and take immediate sanctions.'[54] The committee thus approached the problem of student politics in the same framework as the dean. But student protest no longer concerned a few professional militants. For the moment, the numbers lay not with the thirteen students of the 'liaison committee of professors and students' but the five hundred in the amphitheatre. To those students, the official student representatives appeared not only fewer in number, but smaller in influence. Representation in university administration and joint committees offered little hope for change. Direct action mobilised more and promised an immediate impact.

Occupation of the Administrative Tower: The Birth of 22 March

The assembly of 500 met to consider their response to the arrests after the Vietnam demonstration. 'The militants who are here, they have come, I believe, because they are determined to act against police repression in France',[55] proclaimed Daniel Cohn-Bendit to applause. He proposed the occupation of the sociology department, but his fellow anarchist Jean-Pierre Duteuil disagreed: 'We must occupy the tower ... the administrative building of the Faculty of Nanterre.'[56] The second suggestion won immediate approval. Sociology housed the greatest number of militants. The administrative building reflected the increasing diversity of students. The assembled students thus embarked upon a university occupation to protest police actions against a demonstration by students undertaken outside the university. In the wake of police actions on campus, few cared to distinguish between the university administration and the actions of police against students elsewhere. The occupation once again proved the triumph of the anarchists' tactics. The alternatives considered earlier by the militants – demonstrations in Paris, or an official statement – offered no real challenge to the control of university space.

---

[53] BNF 'Les tracts de mai 68'. 1219. Université de Paris. Faculté des lettres et sciences humaines de Paris-Nanterre. Commission de liaison professeurs-étudiants. Réunion du 22 Mars 1968. Nanterre le 29 Mars 1968.
[54] Ibid.
[55] From a transcript of a tape recording by the Nanterre history student Patrice Louis as quoted in Jacques Baynac, *Mai retrouvé. Contribution à l'histoire du mouvement révolutionnaire du 3 mai au 16 juin 1968* (Paris: Éditions Robert Laffont, 1978), 37.
[56] Ibid., 38.

'An Asylum for Delinquents'   245

The occupation began haltingly when only 60 of the 500 from the general assembly reconvened at 8:00 p.m. Little by little the group swelled to around 100 and entered the ground floor of the administrative building, There, a debate ensued over whether to continue the occupation as planned. The suggestion to occupy sociology resurfaced but was rapidly rejected. Cohn-Bendit, sensing the hesitation, sought a compromise: to stay in the administrative tower, but not ascend to the conference room on the eighth floor. Such an action, he insisted, retained symbolic force.[57] The majority disagreed, and their leader followed them: 'I will rally behind the majority. ... But the problem is to know that people have the opportunity to express themselves.'[58] Once again, Cohn-Bendit's friend Jean-Pierre Duteuil captured the situation better, agreeing on the need for debate, but insisting it could not happen standing-up on the ground floor with half the protesters outside. Furthermore, 'It's not simply a symbolic action ... It's also ... a modification of the relations of power. ... this morning four militants were arrested, to gather here 150 persons ... to accustom the administration on the one hand and the police on the other, to an immediate reaction, is important.'[59] Pushing aside the few university officials, Duteuil made it to the stairs. Others entered the elevators. The rest followed.

Upstairs, differences between anarchists, Trotskyists, *enragés* (Situationists), and non-aligned students threatened to destroy the occupation almost before it had begun.[60] Furthermore, after a brief account of the Vietnam demonstration and arrests, the news of Nanterre student Xavier Langlade's release arrived. But the occupation now embodied goals beyond the protest against police repression. The *enragés* wanted to drink the whiskey reserved for the dean's special guests, steal a few symbolic objects and destroy student dossiers. Some anarchists wanted to search the desks and cabinets for the infamous blacklists. The self-consciously serious Trotskyists and the unaligned students disdained such actions. Before anything else, the assembly had to decide what to do with the two 'Stalinists' of the UEC (Union des Étudiants Communistes), whose forcible ejection from the occupation was briefly considered before acknowledgement that such an act would itself be 'Stalinist'. The *enragés*, receiving no support for their plan to destroy student dossiers, left the meeting,

---

[57] Ibid., 40.   [58] Ibid.   [59] Ibid., 41.
[60] For the full description of the events, see Duteuil, *Nanterre*, 158–164. Also among the occupiers was the Senegalese student Omar Blondin Diop (for further information on Diop, see Françoise Blum, 'Années 68 postcoloniales? "Mai" de France et d'Afrique', *French Historical Studies* 41.2 (April 2018), 193–218, 204).

calling the rest of the students 'dumb jerks'. Cohn-Bendit, the great compromiser, resolved the call to search for the blacklists when he pulled a set of keys from his pocket and declared if one fit the desks and cabinets, so be it; if not, too bad. A (fruitless) search for the blacklists thus proceeded without the destruction of furniture, too shocking for the rest of the assembly. The remainder of the evening evolved into an open discussion about Vietnam, repression and the university. News of the release of the remaining arrested students arrived. The original plan to remain all night appeared unnecessary, and the police were rumoured to be ready to clear the building. To end the occupation, the assembly delegated a committee to draw up an appeal for a day of assemblies to continue the debates begun that evening.

The 'manifesto of 142' was approved unanimously, except for the two Communists who voted against and three Lambertist Trotskyists of the CLER who abstained. The manifesto denounced police repression of political activity – 'the government has taken a new step. It is not at demonstrations that one takes militants, it's AT HOME', placed within a broader context ('a capitalist offensive sick from modernisation and rationalisation') which included workers' struggles and the university: 'the introduction of pseudo-sociological techniques in firms to dampen class conflict'.[61] The movement proclaimed the obsolescence of old forms of protest, declaring in capital letters that 'WE MUST BREAK WITH THE TECHNIQUES OF CONTESTATION THAT CANNOT DO ANYTHING'. The efficacious tactic proposed turned out to be 'to discuss these problems at university and to be able to develop our action there'. Such a program of course unerringly pinpointed the weakest link in the university: the control of speech and space. The manifesto ended with a call for an occupation on 29 March for small group discussion to debate capitalism, workers' struggles, the 'critical university', anti-imperialism and workers' problems in the Eastern Bloc.[62] The manifesto approved, the *Internationale* was sung. The administrative tower emptied before the police arrived. The occupation had not won the release of any protesters from prison (nor could it have), but it consolidated the anarchists, the Trotskyists and a significant number of non-aligned students into a new movement. The *groupuscules* of the early to mid-1960s all emerged via exclusions from larger parties. The movement of 142 brought together two distinct ideological groups, but also large numbers of fellow travellers beyond the small world of professional political militants. Within days,

[61] Duteuil, *Nanterre*, 165. [62] Ibid.

the growing number of adherents required a change of name: the 'Movement of 22 March' was born.

Administrative Shutdown

The Movement of 22 March emerged in the vacuum of authority created by a dynamic of provocation and repression generated by the administration's refusal to countenance politics in university space. The failure to embrace limited forms of student self-government led to much bolder expressions of autonomy. The administration confronted a fundamental problem in the broad student sympathy for the protesters, and a total absence of support for police repression. The new movement did not lack for critics. The Maoists of the UJCml, their simplicity matched only by their self-certainty, declared 'the character of this movement is 100% reactionary'.[63] Workers, not students, were the victims of the university, and the role of 'intellectual youth' was to place itself 'under the authority of the workers', and reject all 'reformist illusions of creating a "critical university", a socialist island in a capitalist society'.[64] The Communists of the UEC also dismissed the new movement as leading 'a sterile agitation which will resolve NONE of the true problems of students'.[65] UNEF, the least ideological organisation, recognised most quickly that 22 March represented the 'total outflanking of the traditional organisations'.[66] The bureau resigned. Others reacted to the earthquake of the occupation and the growing support for the new movement by adopting the administration's perspective that perhaps the leaders could be detached and dealt with. Student representatives of the language departments explained to the press that the leaders were 'obviously unbalanced', and demanded 'necessary measures be taken to establish … a normal atmosphere of work necessary to the Faculty'.[67] These reactions demonstrate the impact of the occupation on the other militants and the student body, each of them in their own way forced to acknowledge their own powerlessness and obsolescence. The university administration confronted the same problem.

---

[63] BDIC. F delta 813(4), 'Non aux manifestations réactionnaires! Non aux manoeuvres de l'adminstration!'
[64] Ibid.   [65] BDIC. F delta 813(4), Untitled.
[66] BDIC. GF delta 85, 'Association federative des groups d'études de Nanterre. Union Nationale des Etudiants de France. Rapport moral. présenté au Conseil d'Administration de l'A. F. G. E. N.-U. N. E. F. le 23 mars 1968 par Jean François Godchau, président, au nom du bureau fédéral démissionaire'.
[67] BDIC. F delta 1056(1)(8), 'Communiqué des délégués des départements de: Lettres modernes, Anglais, Espagnol, Italien, Allemand'.

An Assembly of the Faculty convened on 26 March to debate the response. On the evening of 22 March itself, the dean refrained from calling the police, a 'solution which would have given an inopportune publicity to the event and solidarised other students with the group'.[68] Yet if the lesson of past police interventions appeared clear, no new alternatives presented themselves. While the assembly unanimously condemned the demonstrations, it divided between the proposal for 'dialogue' and the call for greater police intervention, 'the passivity of the teachers and the faculty assembly having gone on too long'. A third solution envisaged 'a campaign of information designed to galvanise the mass of serious students'.[69] Of course, further police repression threatened merely to inflame the situation and had not proved successful previously. A campaign of information presumed the problem lay merely in a failure of communication rather than a fundamental difference of opinion on the role of politics in the university. The success of 'dialogue' was uncertain as well as untried and faced firm opposition from a significant number of academic staff.

While students coalesced around the Movement of 22 March, divisions between administration and faculty became more evident, personal and spiteful. In an acid evaluation of 1969, the historian François Crouzet faulted his colleagues for sympathy with 'extremists' (who he lumped together erroneously as *enragés*). Crouzet dismissed attempts to understand the student perspective as rooted in careerism or even baser motives. Alain Touraine was probably 'tempted to return to the extreme revolutionary romanticism of his early days', while Guy Michaud 'saw in the upheaval an opportunity to overthrow Grappin and succeed him'. Left-wing faculty were 'motivated by a thirst for popularity, bitterness, and ambition' while Paul Ricoeur (the foremost proponent of 'dialogue') was 'kindly and generous but, at least to some, unrealistic'.[70] No doubt this evaluation reflected the deep disappointments still to come, but the gap between the advocates of dialogue and of 'energetic action against the *enragés*' already looked irreconcilable. Most measures proposed by the assembly had drawbacks. 'Self-defence' was judged 'difficult to organise ... [and] risked leading to serious incidents'. The creation of the university's own police force confronted the perennial problem of money. University disciplinary procedures would take time. Charges for damage to public buildings

---

[68] ADHS 1208W/1, 'Faculté des lettres et sciences humaines de Nanterre. Assemblée de la faculté. Année universitaire 1967–1968. 4ème Séance. Nanterre, le 26 mars, 1968'.
[69] Ibid.
[70] François Crouzet, 'A university besieged: Nanterre, 1967–69', *Political Science Quarterly* 84.2 (1969), 343–344.

('minimal' according to the first report, although this estimate rapidly increased) were also considered before the assembly finally opted for the suspension of teaching (voted with forty-six in favour, fourteen against and five abstentions).[71] The Faculty of Arts and Human Sciences closed at Nanterre for two days, 'as a warning'.[72] Incapable of consensus, the assembly opted for a symbolic act. But the closure symbolised its own paralysis far more than the threat of future action.

The doors of the faculty shut, there could be no occupation of the amphitheatres as announced on 22 March. Yet the 'warning' proved ineffectual. Cancelling classes avoided a direct confrontation between politics and teaching. But it created thereby an unhindered space for political debate. With police stationed on the edge of campus, 500–600 students divided into groups and held debates on the lawn, putting into practice the demand for political debate on campus. The protesters proclaimed their defence of 'the principle of freedom of expression', and the 'right to political freedom'. They condemned Pierre Grappin for stating that university privileges 'apply only to the freedom of the expression of professors in their lectures'.[73] Nonetheless, some students proved just as liable to limitations of free expression. A journalist who questioned whether freedom of speech extended to the movement's opponents received the reply 'we do not support any freedom of expression for those who support the US aggression in Vietnam'.[74] Bolstered by the ever larger numbers, the movement decided that the occupation of faculty buildings would occur instead on 2 April in the presence of a delegate from the *Sozialistische Deutsche Studentenbund*. Yet another tactic to confront student politics had proven counter-productive.

The Faculty Assembly met again on Saturday 30 March. The meeting merely testified again to the disorientation of the institution in the face of the student challenge. After issuing yet another protest against ministerial education policy, the assembly confirmed that, after no incident the day before, classes would recommence Monday. Grappin responded to a declaration from the assistant faculty in the French department against any intervention of the police and in favour of freedom of speech by noting that 'the university freedoms are only a tradition', which 'aim to guarantee

---

[71] ADHS 1208W/1, 'Assemblée de la faculté. le 26 mars, 1968'.
[72] BDIC. F delta Res 106, 'Déclaration du doyen de la faculté des lettres et sciences humaines de Nanterre. Nanterre, le 28 mars 1968'.
[73] Duteuil, *Nanterre*, 181.   [74] Ibid., 174.

the freedom of professors in the exercise of their teaching'.[75] François Crouzet likewise insisted that alongside the rights of students, 'there is the need to take account of the right of teachers to carry out their lessons and teaching'. Such declarations ignored the fundamental problem indicated by other professors: that many students 'without approving the methods of the agitators, feel towards them a certain sympathy'.[76] The dean, although still determined to view the problem as one of power rather than policy, nonetheless recognised the absurdity of police intervention against students to ensure teaching: 'we have no means of our own to evade incidents, we cannot take any action and that's why we are obliged to call the police. It's ridiculous, because the means deployed are disproportional to the incidents, but again, we have not our own means'.[77] That analysis left little likelihood of amelioration in the situation. Above all, it failed to recognise that the problem was not just one of means but their legitimacy. Many students saw police intervention as illegitimate not only because it was disproportionate, but out of broad sympathy with the principles the movement espoused. Only a few recognised just how far the situation had progressed. 'We must not believe that things will return to order Monday', warned Alain Touraine, 'a certain form of contestation has been born ... we will be obliged to live with it'. The only solution was for the institution to 'make itself the protester' and embark on 'a deep reform of the university'.[78] But time was short. The assembly noted certain students would be summoned to the University Council for disciplinary measures at the beginning of May.

Touraine was right. The 'warning' failed. There was no return to order at Nanterre. The day after the university reopened, an unprecedented 1,500 students assembled in the amphitheatre to answer the call of the 22 March Movement. Paul Ricoeur wrote to Grappin noting a 'defeat': 'the brief closure of the faculty by the administration has proven ineffective and even harmful'.[79] The only possible response in the event of further troubles would be an unlimited suspension of teaching. Ricoeur insisted the dean not call the police. The Minister of National Education should answer for the buildings, while any suspension of teaching must be decided by the whole teaching body and not fall to the dean alone. While Ricoeur hoped to divest the university of a police function that distracted from and

---

[75] ADHS 1208W/1, 'Faculté des lettres et sciences humaines de Nanterre. Assemblée de la faculté. Année universitaire 1967–1968. 5ème séance. Nanterre, le 30 mars 1968'.
[76] Ibid.   [77] Ibid.   [78] Ibid.
[79] BDIC. F delta 1056(6)(2), Letter of Paul Ricoeur to Pierre Grappin. 'Cher ami, …'.

delegitimised teaching, a number of professors declared they would not guarantee their services unless order was restored. Grappin sided with the latter, and sought increased disciplinary and police powers for the dean and Faculty Council: 'a corps of internal police is an urgent necessity for the security of the Faculty and the domain, for the maintenance of order'.[80] The Faculty Council backed the dean, voting to create its own police force (twenty-five in favour, four against and six abstentions). Nineteen (seven against and nine abstaining) voted to declare the domain of the university other than the buildings 'public land' and thus open to the police.[81] These measures understood the rise of protest as a problem of order. They addressed the administration's sense of impotence but offered little by way of responding to student concerns or the ostensible grounds of discontent. As the number of protesters swelled to over a thousand, they least of all offered any practical hope of transforming the situation.

The polarisation that existed within the Council of the Faculty expressed itself even more strongly in a growing divide between the full professors (who alone sat on the Council) and the assistants. The assembly of assistants and maître-assistants declared itself opposed to a permanent police interior to the faculty, against any further closure of the university and stated that 'the student effervescence shows, even beneath its violence, problems which are serious and which apply to both students and teachers'.[82] Opposing any attempt to 'suffocate problems by neutralising or repressing the student movement',[83] they called for a serious reform. In yet another blow for the authority of dean and full professors, they demanded that the Faculty Council (of the full professors) sit after Faculty Assembly (where all teaching staff were represented), rather than prior (a practice which meant most decisions occurred in the Council and were merely confirmed at the assembly). The administration appeared increasingly isolated, abandoned by a large number of the students, its own teaching staff, and divided in the Council.

Multiple incidents punctuated the month of April. During the Easter holidays, a search of the university residences attempted to discover squatters ('above all the fact of boys ... of African or Middle Eastern origin' and therefore begun 'in the fourth wing where a large number of

---

[80] BDIC. F delta 1056(1)(1), Pierre Grappin, 'Note sur la police intérieure à la faculté de Nanterre'.
[81] ADHS 1208W/2, 'Faculté des lettres et sciences humaines de Nanterre. Nanterre, le 22 Avril 1968. Conseil de la faculté. Année universitaire 1967-1968. 10ème séance.'
[82] BNF 1156, 'Motion de l'assemblée des assistants et maître-assistants de Nanterre'.   [83] Ibid

coloured students are lodged').⁸⁴ Few offenders were discovered.⁸⁵ Those who were 'did not give the impression of being one of these '*enragés*' who organise and maintain the agitation in the university domain and particularly at the Faculty of Letters'.⁸⁶ Demonstrations over Vietnam continued. The Maoists, after performing self-criticism for labelling the 22 March Movement reactionary, returned to Nanterre. They prevented the Communist Pierre Juquin from speaking by reciting passages from the little red book while marching towards the lectern, forcing Juquin to flee. The action did not particularly please the 22 March Movement, which had planned to contest Juquin by letting him speak before grilling him about the Gulag and Stalinism. Their politics of speech was best expressed in another debate that threatened to end the same way. The left-wing French mathematician Laurent Schwartz (who favoured selection at entry to the university), unable to speak, could only shout 'it's not by paralysing the university that you will bring down de Gaulle'. Cohen-Bendit forged the consensus: 'Schwartz is certainly a scoundrel, but we must let him speak, and no-one will be deprived afterwards, in response to what he says, to make him know that he's a bastard'.⁸⁷ For itself, the movement no longer requested amphitheatres for political debate, but rather notified the dean when it would take them.

'Repression' dictated the pace of events. Cohn-Bendit was arrested on 29 April and accused of threatening to kill a right-wing student at Nanterre and for the publication of instructions how to make a Molotov cocktail in the first *Bulletin du 22 Mars*. More members of the movement were arrested for distributing tracts outside the lycée of Nanterre. A gathering of 1,500 students at the faculty demanded their release, which was obtained before the movement needed to carry through on its threat to assemble at the police station where they were being held. After more incidents inside the lecture theatre, Grappin decided to once again close the faculty. Regular lessons would not occur until the next academic year, by which time Grappin had resigned from his post: 'I no longer know well where is the Left and where the Right', he confessed.⁸⁸ Not Grappin, however, but the rector of the university of Paris committed the error that

---

⁸⁴ ADHS 1208W/180, 'Recherches effectuées pour déceler des occupants clandestins à la Résidence Universitaire de Nanterre'.
⁸⁵ Ibid. The report suggested 'Le "téléphone arabe" a facilité, n'en doutons pas, la disparition des autres'.
⁸⁶ Ibid.   ⁸⁷ Duteuil, *Nanterre*, 196.
⁸⁸ BDIC. F delta 1056(1)(1), '*Le Nouvel Observateur*. Interview du Doyen Pierre Grappin, jeudi 19 Septembre 1968'.

turned the impasse at Nanterre into conflagration in Paris. On Friday, 3 May, with 400–500 assembled in the Sorbonne to protest the disciplinary procedures against eight Nanterre students set for the following Monday, the rector called the police to clear the courtyard. As had happened in every previous instance of police intervention, the solidarity of the majority of the student body was immediate. The conflict expanded to the streets of Paris. The Movement of 22 March had, in its turn, been surpassed by events.

The rapid escalation of the revolt in May in Paris obscures that Nanterre had already fallen into a permanent state of revolt in April. Even when the optic is narrowed to the university, the revolt cannot be said to have come from nowhere, while France was 'bored'. Nanterre exemplified a similar crisis of authority to that at West Berlin and Trento. The authority of the dean had dissipated, beginning in the residences and evident across the university campus in the realm of teaching as much as spaces of paternal oversight. Repression – the generic term applied to all acts of authority now rendered illegitimate – propelled the revolt forward. Indeed, repression united the protest movement, swelled its ranks, and left unanswered complex questions of what new form of authority should emerge. Protesters asserted their own authority and the right to self-government, but this only avoided the problem of differences of opinion within the student body. Far fewer divergences existed over opposition to repression. So too, the expansion of the movement in May posed the question of self-government and created a space in which the basis of education, society and daily life could be discussed. There might be no universal agreement on the answers, but for the moment the act of calling into question the bases of society proved irresistible. Thus on the night of the barricades in Paris between 9 and 10 May, shortly before clashes between police and students, Daniel Cohn-Bendit declared 'We are sorry to hinder traffic. We really want to debate together in the courtyard of the Sorbonne. But the police bar us from access. So I declare this place a great amphitheatre and invite you all to sit down on the pavement. Who wants to speak?'[89] For those who took the invitation, the explosion of speech marked a profound reappraisal of every aspect of life.

---

[89] Daniel Bensaïd and Henri Weber, *Mai 68: une répétition générale* (Paris: Maspero, 1968), 128–129.

CHAPTER 11

'A Golden Ghetto'
The Critical University

The three student movements of Nanterre, Trento and West Berlin each reached an apogee of influence in a moment of intense politicisation. In Paris, with the campus of Nanterre paralysed, clashes with police in the Latin Quarter brought forth the general strike and month-long events of May 1968. At Trento, the 'Anti-Lent' of April 1968 swept aside objections to the movement's demands. The protest in West Berlin crescendoed in the wake of Benno Ohnesorg's shooting in June 1967. Clashes with police or the population defined these moments. The institutional disarray inside the university fused with social conflict outside higher education. The connection was not entirely new; protesters had persistently viewed the university through the lens of Vietnam or broader social authoritarianism. But while students previously understood their struggles as part of a latent or distant social conflict, now that confrontation had manifested itself. The intensification of protest prompted a shift from the politics of higher education to politics writ large. At the height of student protest within the university came the greatest temptation to abandon it.

The success of student protest thus created its own problems. Having paralysed the university, what to do with it? Having captured large numbers of new supporters, how to maintain their mobilisation? Movements that thrived on provocation and repression now faced the difficult task of defining in detail the institutions they sought. The project of the 'Critical University' fulfilled this function. West Berlin took the lead with its *Kritische Universität*, but the *Università Critica* at Trento went even further in transforming the established institution. So, too, at Nanterre discussions of a *Université Critique* dominated student debate on higher education in mid-1968. Complicating these projects, however, was the resurgent opposition between the struggle 'inside' and 'outside' the university. The wave of politicisation served primarily to strengthen those who dismissed any struggle within higher education as elitist, reformist and illusory. From their beginning the 'critical universities' had to defend themselves against the charge of creating a 'golden ghetto' in a 'society of shit'.

Kritische Universität

The *Kritische Universität* in West Berlin emerged from a sharp increase in the number of student demonstrators combined with the pessimistic evaluation of past protest. In the week after Benno Ohnesorg's shooting, SDS membership doubled from 1,200 to 2,500, while SHB membership grew from 1,500 to 2,000. The SDS thus became the larger organisation even while the SHB gravitated ever closer to its positions.[1] The unexpected transformation of small groups of activists into much larger organisations posed the problem of what to do with the new recruits. A variety of assemblies and action committees emerged to collect, analyse and distribute information on the shooting and on West Berlin. However, the euphoric subjective experience of those who 'overcame for the first time their isolation and found fellow students with whom they could spontaneously work together in solidarity'[2] confronted a downbeat assessment of the effects of a protest that 'came up against a complete lack of understanding of the Berlin populace'.[3] The successful scale of mobilisation stood in stark contrast to the failure of its efforts.

Both success and disappointment led towards a more substantial project of reform. The escalation of student mobilisation provoked plans 'to continue beyond this week the subjective emancipation from the current teaching activities as a cooperative public movement in and outside the university'.[4] Perhaps the new, emergent movement could do what years of previous activism had so far failed to achieved: 'Nothing happened the entire year at the universities – of reform there was only ever talk', judged one leaflet calling for the establishment of a *Kritische Universität*.[5] Sigrun Fronius' assessment was equally downbeat: 'Until now we have not been successful in politicising students via educational reform', but the

---

[1] One document reports the effect of 2 June 1967 as follows: the liberal LSD rose from 900 members to 1100, the SHB from 1500 to 2000 and the SDS from 1200 to 2500, while the right-wing RCDS remained at 2200. APO 12.12 FU KU Sammlung Fronius 1967. Christian Fenner, 'Kritische Universität: Selbstverständnis und Kritik', *X informationen. Berichte, Kommentare, Analysen* 70.67 (13.11.1967), 1–14, 1.

[2] Klaus Schroeder (ed.), *Hochschule im Umbruch: Teil V: Gewalt und Gegengewalt (1967–1969)* (Berlin: Pressestelle der FU Berlin, 1983), 201.

[3] APO 12.12 FU KU Sammlung Fronius 1967. '*X informationen*'.

[4] Schroeder (ed.), *Hochschule V*, 201.

[5] APO-Archiv APO 12.12 FU KU Sammlung Fronius 1967. 'KU. Kritische Universität'.

politicisation effected outside might be harnessed for the long-term goal of university reform.[6] As other students argued, such a judgment underestimated the impact of the struggles over university issues of speech and forced deregistration. Nonetheless, the meagre results of such campaigns predisposed the expanded movement to a marked qualitative shift in its goals. To maintain the mobilisation of June 1967 and overcome the stasis of past efforts, the SDS now promoted the scheme of a *Kritische Universität*.

The 'Critical University' drew on a decade of SDS engagement with the problems of higher education. The project can be traced back to the 1961 *Denkschrift* on university reform by Wolfgang Nitsch, Uta Gerhardt, Claus Offe and Ulrich Preuß, which became a book in 1965. The KU thus reflected a strand of SDS activism at first sidelined by the rise of tactics of provocation.[7] The 'Argument Club' that operated around the review *Das Argument* provided a more practical model: 'the Club consisted not only of reading groups, but reviews were written, the writing of reviews studied, research carried out and leaflets on atomic weapons put together'.[8] Thus although the *Kritische Universität* marked a qualitative leap in organisational plans, it required no great conceptual advance. The July 1967 'Provisional Schedule' stressed continuity, invoking the constitution of the FU student body, 'to demand political education and activity ... that serves the embodiment of democratic and constitutional relations through the use of scientific knowledge'.[9] Despite its proposal being a response to the effervescence of June 1967, the *Kritische Universität* embodied the principles of student agitation since the beginning of the conflict: 'critical reflection and scientific analysis for a democratic political practice'.[10]

The 'Critical University' was not the only model on offer. Talk also swirled around the idea of the *Gegenuniversität* or 'Counter-University'. At times, the terms were used interchangeably. Both projects, Critical- and Counter- Universities, existed prior to 1967, but they had very different provenances. They conformed to the growing divide between politics internal and external to the university. The *Kritische Universität* was

---

[6] Schroeder (ed.), *Hochschule V*, 204.
[7] Wolfgang Nitsch et al., *Hochschule in der Demokratie: Kritische Beiträge zur Erbschaft und Reform der deutschen Universität* (New York: Arno Press, 1977).
[8] Frigga Haug, 'Frauenpolitik galt als kleinbürgerlich,' in Kätzel, *Die 68erinnen: Porträt einer rebellischen Frauengeneration* (Berlin: Rowohlt, 2002), 183–184.
[9] Schroeder (ed.), *Hochschule V*, 219.   [10] Ibid., 52.

conceived 'primarily as an instrument of struggle directed at the current university',[11] and emerged out of detailed analyses of higher education. The *Gegenuniversität*, by contrast, was 'a distinctly Rudi-project' where the students would 'move out to Kreuzberg or Wedding, and plunge into the proletarian milieu'.[12] Dutschke described lessons for workers, students and apprentices in addition to 'medical, particularly sexual information ... particularly for young female and male workers along with legal aid for citizens or help organising rent-strikes'.[13] He felt financial feasibility posed the main obstacle. Yet Dutschke's model also lacked the cumulative weight of long-term elaborations of reform in SDS. Thus, as Wolfgang Lefèvre put it, the *Gegenuniversität* 'was only an idea'. With the *Kritische Universität* 'something would be done'.[14]

The Critical University thus followed the logic of student protest whereby the failure of reform led to the project of imposing a new reality. The KU marked a new phase of the struggle in which students sought to 'to realise themselves ... a part of [their] demands'.[15] The wave of recruits made such plans plausible. As early as 13 June 1967, barely two weeks after Ohnesorg's death, Wolfgang Nitsch produced a 'rationale for a student-organised "Critical University" at the FU'.[16] The *Kritische Universität*, wrote Nitsch, must continue the emancipatory activities of early June and defend against the expected 'backlash of academic and state authorities'.[17] The KU thus began from the acknowledgement that such tasks were 'with a few exceptions impossible within the official learning activities'.[18] At the height of student mobilisation, Nitsch envisioned a coming backlash, the failure of almost all efforts at reform, and the ebbing of political enthusiasm. However, even if, 'as is to be feared, other than partial successes in a few subjects, a significant student impact on the reform of studies and universities cannot be achieved', the *Kritische Universität* would prevent the 'splintering of student activities in numerous uncoordinated and small working circles or merely private student groups'.[19] The best that could be conceived was a framework within which the mobilisation of June 1967 would not totally be lost.

The pessimism was not confined to Nitsch. When members of SDS met to discuss his proposal, Sigrun Fronius admitted that past struggles had ended in 'defeat': 'The efforts at a more critical university in the

---

[11] APO Archiv Lönnendonker. Interview Wolfgang Lefèvre 30.12.1969, 29.   [12] Ibid., 29.
[13] See '"Wir Fordern die Enteignung Axel Springers": Spiegel-Gespräch mit dem Berliner FU-Studenten Rudi Dutschke (SDS)', *Der Spiegel* 29 (1967), 32.
[14] APO Archiv Lönnendonker. Interview Wolfgang Lefèvre 30.12.1969, 32.   [15] Ibid.
[16] Schroeder (ed.), *Hochschule V*, 201.   [17] Ibid.   [18] Ibid.   [19] Ibid., 202.

institutional framework have already failed. Nothing substantial has changed in the examination regulations. For lack of results we've withdrawn from the study reform commission.'[20] All that was left, she argued, was 'to make experiments with well-disposed professors'.[21] Equally lacking any illusions, Wolfgang Lefèvre insisted that 'we must assume that the established university has more power long term'.[22] This downbeat, pessimistic cast of mind reflected the length of time many of the more politically active students had sought reform of higher education. The SDS continued self-consciously to be a minority. The *Kritische Universität* aimed to move beyond the institutional defeat by harnessing the mobilisation of June 1967.

The SDS members were all too well aware that police violence outside the university, not the promise of educational reform, had served to escalate protest. The *Kritische Universität* perched precariously on the fault-line between the politics of society and the politics of intellectual engagement, seeking to draw on the impetus of the former to transform the latter. Within the institutions of higher education, the *Kritische Universität* would intensify 'the critique and exposure of irrational and repressive aspects of official teaching activities', promote the 'critical consciousness' of the students, and either foster the transformation of official teaching or supplement it where it was found lacking.[23] Not just the content would be new, but the practice of 'new, anti-authoritarian forms and methods of study'.[24] Perhaps with one eye on the straightforwardly political *Gegenuniversität*, the new institution also claimed to forge the nexus between 'enlightenment and political action'. The critical university would provide the 'scientific and theoretical preparation and analysis'[25] for 'enlightenment' of the population – about the student movement, the Federal Republic, the Third World – and for 'resistance against further or future emergency measures, betrayal of the constitution and police terror'.[26] There could be no isolation in the university sphere.

The founders of the *Kritische Universität* conceived it as a framework to serve both political and intellectual objectives. These two sites of confrontation – over educational reform with university administration on one side and over social politics with police and broader population – also functioned as the two incubators of the revolt. This division was not merely conceptual or historical but reflected the different wings of SDS – one more oriented towards the university and critically reasoned proposals for reform, the other tending towards provocation and

[20] Ibid., 204. [21] Ibid. [22] Ibid. [23] Ibid. [24] Ibid. [25] Ibid. [26] Ibid.

concerned above all with Vietnam, the Third World and the political struggle outside higher education. These alternatives implied very different choices in devotion of time and type of activity. Furthermore, the weight placed on politics created not only the two poles of SDS but structured the opposition between the 'political' SDS and the 'non-political' students. Plans for the *Kritische Universität* (that came largely from the education-oriented wing of SDS) aimed to accentuate the 'cross-over points ... instead of the emphasis on abstract academic controversies on one side and concrete political praxis on the other side'.[27] The success of the *Kritische Universität* depended on how successfully the politically-oriented wing of SDS subscribed to this vision. A member of Students for a Democratic Society from the United States ominously warned of the division between those who 'consider the university reform as educational reform and those who see it as a political movement'.[28]

Even more boldly, the Critical University sought to assert the political validity of professional outcomes of higher education. As Wolfgang Nitsch argued, 'It makes a difference, whether a critical or conformist sociologist works first on a new field.'[29] Whereas elsewhere professional concerns came to be disparaged as purely careerist, the provisional program of the *Kritische Universität* affirmed that 'students have a legitimate interest in security and success in their future professional development'.[30] Indeed, the KU aimed to overcome the 'division between political free-time and other-directed unpolitical work' by preparing 'students for a political praxis in their future professional positions'.[31] The program demonstrated a consciousness that one of the major obstacles to reform was the mutual prejudices of 'political' and 'non-political' students: 'It makes no sense, if the hitherto politically active students reject the rest as apathetic masses, if students with intellectual and aesthetic interests dismiss from the first the specialists and job-oriented students, or conversely if the unpolitical students brand the critically engaged as a left-radical minority'.[32] The *Kritische Universität* would cater to both the professionally and politically interested. But if the proposed counter-institution emerged as one answer to the problem of politics and professional development, aiming to reconcile the critical-intellectual and political drives of the protest movement, the university administration remained determined once more to exclude politics from the university sphere.

[27] Ibid., 205. [28] Ibid. [29] Ibid. [30] Ibid., 220. [31] Ibid., 221. [32] Ibid.

The Critical and the Free University

Administrative and faculty opposition to the *Kritische Universität* emerged from the moment of its proposal. In mid-July, the dean of the Law Faculty wrote to the rector that the law professors were 'extremely worried' and insisted no rooms at the FU be made available to the students.[33] H. J. Lieber, the outgoing rector, replied requesting a more detailed evaluation, but noted himself that the *Kritische Universität* 'is a part of the general plan to politicise the university and the teaching of science'.[34] In fact, just as important to the Critical University was to subject political activity to the rigours of scientific research, an aim lost on Lieber. As in previous conflicts with the students, the rector foresaw the constitutional and legal obstacles. To the West Berlin Senator for Science and Art, Lieber explained that the AStA as an executive organ of the student body could 'carry out activities within its area of responsibility' but 'cannot create its own university within the university'.[35] The conflicts of previous semesters had nonetheless made some impression on the rector, who admitted it was 'questionable whether it makes sense to distinguish again between scientific and other activities'.[36] Yet at the same moment that he doubted one distinction, the rector doubled down on another. Consideration of the 'social-political relations of science' and 'attempts to politicise science and the university', he wrote, must be 'radically distinguished'.[37] No such fundamental distinction was possible or likely to convince the students. Few could confuse crude 'indoctrination' with 'scientific research', but there was no easy way to distinguish debate on the politics of scientific research and scientific research on political topics from 'politicised' research.

Instead, authors most often used 'politicised activity' to designate research the politics of which they disagreed with. The *Kritische Universität* certainly abandoned the pretence to an apolitical science. As Wolfgang Lefèvre declared, the university must now 'in its content as a scientific working institution, make its contribution to the prevention of a second

---

[33] APO Berlin FU Allgemein. Kritische Universität Rektoratsakten 2 2098 2 'Freie Universität Berlin. Juristische Fakultät. Der Dekan. Berlin, den 14. Juli 1967. Eilt sehr! An den Rektor der Freien Univerität Berlin Herrn Prof. Dr. phil. Lieber'.
[34] APO Berlin FU Allgemein. Kritische Universität Rektoratsakten 2 2098 2 '18.7.1967 2249. An den Dekan der Juristischen Fakultät Herrn Professor Dr. Sieg'.
[35] APO Berlin FU Allgemein. Kritische Universität Rektoratsakten 2 2098 2 '5.8.1967 2250. An den Senator für Wissenschaft und Kunst Herrn Professor Dr. Werner Stein'.
[36] Ibid. [37] Ibid.

German fascism, therefore directly align its scientific work as politically defined'.[38] The crucial point here, however, was that while the end goal was explicitly political – the prevention of fascism – the methods remained those of a 'scientific working institution'. Rector and Senator, meanwhile, fumbled the distinction between methods and ends. Thus the Senator for Science and Art diagnosed the *Kritische Universität* as likely to replace 'objective scientific teaching activities ... by ideologically-determined politicising activities'.[39] In particular, a 'certain tendency towards the politicisation of the university' could be discerned from the reprinting of a statement by *Konvent* on Vietnam in which the student parliament condemned the silence of the university on the 'crimes in Vietnam' as a reflection of an ethos of conformist apoliticism.[40] Here 'politicisation' was equated with the critique of apoliticism. Explicitly political scientific practice undoubtedly contained its own dangers, but the approach of the *Kritische Universität* – to subject politics to the demands of science and demand critical consciousness of the politics of research – was a much more coherent intellectual response to the dilemma than that offered by the rector or senator.

Yet while politics lay at the heart of the contrasting ideas of the university from students, Senator, faculty and administration, the struggle played out in administrative and legal terms. The rector queried whether the students had a right to establish a 'university'. The Senator worried about 'the question of protecting the designation of "university"',[41] although he thought that, by and large, there was no basis pre-emptively to prohibit the *Kritische Universität*. To the rector, he stated that the boundary lay:

- where politicisation and transformation of the FU will be targeted.
- where the freedom of teaching and learning is endangered.
- where the independence of university teachers is put into question.
- where scientifically designated activities are no longer run impartially.
- where the university function is hindered ...

---

[38] APO Archiv Lönnendonker. Interview Wolfgang Lefèvre 30.12.1969, 28–29.
[39] APO Berlin FU Allgemein. Kritische Universität Rektoratsakten 2 2098 2 'Der Senator für Wissenschaft und Kunst. 1 Berlin 19, den 18. August 1967. Zur 'Kritischen Universität'.
[40] AStA der Freien Universität Berlin, *Kritische Universität. Freie Studienorganisation der Studenten in den Hoch- und Fachschulen von Westberlin. Programm und Verzeichnis der Studienveranstaltungen im Wintersemester 1967/68* (Berlin: Oberbaum Presse, 1967), 15–16.
[41] APO Berlin FU Allgemein. Kritische Universität Rektoratsakten 2 2098 2 'Zur "Kritischen Universität"'.

- where political actions against institutions, businesses and political and state authorities, in the form of tribunals and hearings among other things, are planned and carried out.
- where the task of student self-government is misused for unscientific and one-sided political actions and activities.[42]

However, in his public communication to the AStA, Senator Stein omitted the first and substituted the last two with 'where the activities of organs of the student body by form and content become carriers or facilitators of political actions on questions external to the university'.[43] Whereas adjectives such as 'unscientific' or 'politicised' played an important role in his first evaluation, they no longer occurred in his public statement, subsumed into the reading of the FU constitution, which denied the student body the right to deal with 'extra-university questions'. In response, the AStA simply denied the *Kritische Universität* aimed to disrupt the university, rejected the restriction of the student body to questions of higher education and pointed out that there were at the FU 'not a few teaching activities that serve the justification of preconceived political opinions'.[44]

The next steps of the FU Senate only confirmed the appearance that political bias already existed in the university. In late July, Lieber commissioned an evaluation of the *Kritische Universität*, which the students 'represent as a completely harmless undertaking even in the face of the evident intentions in the brochure'.[45] Fritz Borinski, a member of the education department at the FU and Georg Nicolaus Knauer, a classicist, co-authored the report. Unsurprisingly, given its remit, they condemned the *Kritische Universität*. More revealing was its method. Rather than simply analyse the provisional schema, the report first sought to demonstrate the Critical University's lineage in a flyer of a 'provisional committee' from late 1966. 'To what extent', Borinski and Knauer demanded, 'has the spirit of the provisional committee of 26.11.1966, which at that time appeared as an extreme wing of the SDS, penetrated the higher education action committee of the AStA and the founding circle of the "Critical University"'[46] The prime task of the report became not so much the value or otherwise of the *Kritische Universität* but rather the demonstration of the *Kritische Universität*'s origins in the 'extreme wing of SDS'. The report concluded that the *Kritische Universität* must be understood politically: 'it

---

[42] Ibid.   [43] Schroeder (ed.), *Hochschule V*, 229.   [44] Ibid.
[45] APO Berlin FU Allgemein. Kritische Universität Rektoratsakten 2 2098 2 '21.7.1967 2250. Herrn Professor Dr. Borinski'.
[46] Schroeder (ed.), *Hochschule V*, 230–231.

is only a phase in the efforts of left-extremist groups of current and former students of the FU'.[47] In apocalyptic tones, Borinski and Knauer concluded that 'if cause, authority and goal are exclusively political action, the seizure of power, the question stops being scientific. It approaches the consciously biased conduct of totalitarian ideologies and is the end of freedom of teaching and learning'.[48] For a significant section of the faculty of the FU, the *Kritische Universität* heralded an unparalleled assault on their understanding of the university.

The Critical University had undoubtedly struck at the authority of the existing institution, but as previously, the response was even more damaging. The Senate of the Freie Universität, on the basis of the Borinski-Knauer report and the views of the Senator for Science and Art, resolved not to support activities offered under the name of the *Kritische Universität*.[49] They published Borinski and Knauer's report, much to the annoyance of the students who pointed out that the rector had previously rejected publication of a joint student-professor commission.[50] The president of AStA, Hartmut Häußermann, resigned in protest from his position and described the Senate's decision at a press conference as a 'ban'. Some Senate members complained directly to the rector that their vote had not been intended as such.[51] The rector plaintively insisted the refusal to support the *Kritische Universität* was indeed provisional.[52] Yet the report of Borinski and Knauer only undermined further the authority of the rector and Senate. Helmut Gollwitzer publicly criticised the report for being rushed, for not having bothered to talk to the authors and for being simplistic: 'because the brochure *also* proposes the scientific preparation of political action, the committee sees "exclusively political action" as the meaning of the KU'.[53] The philosopher Peter Szondi scathingly criticised the Borinski-Knauer committee which 'cites from the documents what supports its thesis and ignores what contradicts it ... uses sources uncritically ... makes false claims ... [and] makes use of a demagogic

---

[47] Ibid., 232.   [48] Ibid., 234.   [49] Ibid., 230.
[50] AStA, *Kritische Universität. Wintersemester 1967/68*, 3–4.
[51] APO Berlin FU Allgemein. Kritische Universität Rektoratsakten 2 2098 2 'Institut für Volkswirtschaftslehre. 19.9.1967. An Se. Magnifizenz den Rektor der Freien Universität Berlin Herrn Professor Dr. Hans-Joachim Lieber'.
[52] APO 12.12 FU KU Sammlung Fronius 1967 H. J. Lieber to D. Helmut Gollwitzer.
[53] APO Berlin FU Allgemein Jul-Okt 1967. Helmut Gollwitzer, 'Bemerkungen zu dem Gutachten von Proff. Borinski und Knauer über die Broschüre "Kritische Universität"'.

terminology and method of citation'.[54] Indeed, the report incarnated what it sought to critique: superficial and sloppy intellectual production prompted by the authors' politics.

The authority of the Senate publicly crumbled on the issue of the *Kritische Universität*. When Rudolf Lennert wrote to the incoming rector to point out that 'the concepts "Science" and "scientific" have for some decades undergone a considerable, in part, tempestuous change ... and no-one should impose a claim of monopoly for his concept',[55] he received a censure for his 'disloyal' behaviour in copying his letter to a few colleagues.[56] At the sociology institute of the *Freie Universität*, professors and assistants requested that 'no general ban on rooms be pronounced for the Critical University' and any decision be preceded by a 'comprehensive internal university discussion'.[57] Around fifty professors (including some who had voted the original, provisional, Senate 'ban') issued another statement requesting any administrative measures against the KU be deferred and the opportunity taken 'to openly grapple with it'.[58] The new rector, dentistry professor Ewald Harndt, presided over a university publicly divided not merely between Freie Universität and Kritische Universität, but within the professorial body itself, and soon, between particular departments and the administration. For all the discussion about the attack on teaching and learning, it was the authority of the Senate and the rector that emerged most damaged from the confrontation.

Critique and Crisis

The founding assembly of the *Kritische Universität* occurred on 1 November 1967 in the Auditorium Maximum of the Freie Universität. This time the protests came from right-wing students who disrupted the meeting. In language similar to that used by faculty to describe left-wing demonstrations, Sigrun Fronius complained how these opponents 'did not want to enter into an in-depth discussion about the form and goals of the Critical

---

[54] Schroeder (ed.), *Hochschule V*, 243–244. The document is also available in Peter Szondi, *Über eine 'Freie (d.h. freie) Universität': Stellungnahmen eines Philologen* (Frankfurt am Main: Suhrkamp Verlag, 1973), 71–82.
[55] APO LV Berlin 1967 SDS 'Herrn Prf. Dr. Dr. Ewald Harndt. 6. Oktober 1967'.
[56] See APO Berlin FU Allgemein. Kritische Universität. Rektoratsakten 2 2098 2 'Prof Rudolf Lennert 14.10.1967 An den Rektor der Freien Universität Herrn Prof. Dr. Dr. Ewald Harndt'.
[57] APO Berlin FU Allgemein. Kritische Universität. Rektoratsakten 2 2098 2 'Institut für Soziologie der Freien Universität Berlin. 18.10.1967. An den Herrn Rektor der Freien Universität Magnifizenz Prof. Dr. E. Harndt'.
[58] Schroeder (ed.), *Hochschule V*, 247.

University, but rather sought to disqualify it completely as one-sided, doctrinaire and partisan. They supported their arguments by throwing leaflets, balloons, and numerous interruptions'.[59] The parallels only went so far. Fronius thought the debate 'exciting' and the organisers of the *Kritische Universität* were hardly likely to call the police to deal with the disruption. Nor did they need to. The spectacle of the *Kritische Universität* demanding a reasoned, in-depth debate about the politics of research and teaching in contrast to its opponents' politics of disruption demonstrated the extent to which the Critical University had seized the high ground of academic authority from the administration.

The winter semester program provided the most complete rebuttal of the Borinski-Knauer report. The *Kritische Universität* was 'an attempt at emancipation from sclerotic forms and content of academic teaching'.[60] It traced its origins not to the December 1966 flyer Borinski and Knauer identified, but to the resolution passed at the sit-in of June 1966 that 'decisions that affect students only be taken democratically with the participation of students'.[61] The division of politics from *Wissenschaft* was dismissed: 'It is not about political or unpolitical science. Much more it is about permanent scientific reflection, unseparated from practice, on the political goals of science'.[62] The emphasis on democracy continued in the structure of the university. The *Kritische Universität* 'planned for new democratic forms taken from practice: defences, tribunals, hearings, documentations'.[63] The traditional lecture was overthrown. Seminars abandoned the practice of a single seminar leader: 'Experts will occupy no further position of authority'.[64] For the ongoing traditional university, the KU planned 'critical study guides, reading plans and lecture scripts as a substitute for time-wasting, irrational, required courses whose attendance is to be avoided'.[65] The Critical University thus sought to inculcate a critical culture through the abandonment of lectures and seminar leaders and any other practices thought to promote student passivity, while furnishing an apparatus for the constant critique of the official university.

Political practice was nonetheless central to the KU. The winter semester program contained announcements for thirty-three working groups.[66] Twelve dealt with either the role of the intellectual, school and the university or pedagogy (Higher Education Law, Reform and Revolt;

---

[59] Ibid., 248.   [60] AStA, *Kritische Universität. Wintersemester 1967/68*, 2.
[61] Pressestelle der FU Berlin (ed.), *Hochschule IV*, 333.
[62] AStA, *Kritische Universität. Wintersemester 1967/68*, 34.   [63] Ibid., 42.   [64] Ibid., 43.
[65] Ibid., 45.   [66] Ibid., 2.

Technical Intelligentsia and Society; Lecture Reviews and Exam Criticism). Several broached topics underrepresented in the official curriculum (The Cuban Model and the Future of Latin America; Sexuality and Authority; Economic Crisis and Social Politics in West Berlin). A number of others aimed to promote a critical self-reflexive investigation of particular disciplines or professions (Doctors with Humanity; Architecture and Society; Law and Democracy in Germany). Another few analysed the politics of protest or sought to provide its intellectual foundation (Working Circle Springer Tribunal; Methods of Non-Violent Direct Action). True to its origins in the intersection of politics and research, even the most apparently apolitical topics were meant to lead towards a practical application, to 'find direct relations to social practice'.[67] The Seminar on Sexuality and Authority might create 'a well thought-out campaign for the diffusion of contraception, for the possibility of abortion, which will quickly impact on the social limits of erotic freedom once it leaves the realm of the university'.[68] The 'form of struggle' in German studies might be 'analysis of the fascistic jargon of the Springer newspapers, that can be used as expert opinion in a tribunal against these businesses'.[69] Reflecting its position within the protest movement, rejecting both the dismissal of scientific research and the call to form a more revolutionary political movement outside the university, the *Kritische Universität* sought to assert that scientific research could be politically useful without suggesting that it could replace political activism. Any idea of a 'scholar-leader' was dismissed. Revolution remained the privilege of the working class. The 'first spontaneous defensive combat of the workers will call the entire system into question', at which moment the Critical University would 'evolve into the practical revolutionary Counter-University'.[70]

While the plans for the *Kritische Universität* focused mainly on the thorny issue of its political and intellectual justification, the problems turned out to be much more mundane. The 1968 summer semester program reported very mixed results. Of the thirty groups begun in 1967, fifteen planned to continue their work through 1968. A further fifteen new *Arbeitskreise* were announced: The Tasks of Sociology in Technocratic Society, Armament and Disarmament in Late Capitalism, the Workers' Movement and the Party, Anti-Authoritarian Child-Rearing, Kafka, Alienation in the work of Georg Büchner and Agitation for a Democratic Church, among others. While occasionally the groups reported an unmitigated success – 'the constantly practiced critique at

[67] Ibid., 41.   [68] Ibid.   [69] Ibid.   [70] Ibid.

and in teaching activities has resulted in an enduring loss of authority for lecturers through their ignorance and lack of ideas'[71] – for the most part the *Kritische Universität* appeared beset by problems. Attendance fluctuated wildly. One working group noted a decline of half by mid-November.[72] The seminar on 'Considerations of Praxis in Teaching Activities' noted that 'the initially curious failed to come'.[73] The group on Keynesian theory observed an 'extremely strong fluctuation'.[74] As with the instability of numbers, innovations in pedagogy and practice often faded in the face of reality. One student from France had warned in early July that 'critical counter-activities merely become additional burdens'.[75] In this, the *Kritische Universität* proved no exception.

Time constraints proved merely the first problem. Much more fraught for the *Kritische Universität*, the various attempts to create critical pedagogical practices encountered unexpected obstacles. One group backtracked on the dismissal of the lecture, admitting that the 'varied levels of knowledge and interest necessitated holding short lectures'.[76] The seminar on psychosomatic medicine similarly confronted a 'lack of a theoretical basic knowledge'. Those 'already acquainted with the material' dominated the discussion while 'the majority of the participants stayed silent, abandoning themselves to passive perception'. In a damning verdict for the entire project, the organisers concluded that 'several founding presuppositions of the KU, namely to demand the development of individuals, to deconstruct their attitude as consumer and thereby boost their capacity for critique could no longer be guaranteed with this form of work'.[77] The format chosen worked best mainly for the self-selected elite already familiar with the material.

The experience of the *Kritische Universität* revealed that the problem lay less in the structure of education than within the students themselves. The familiar problem of student passivity reproduced itself: 'The victims of the seminars are also silent here, their expectations are disappointed, they became the frustrated, and not the initiators of the colloquiums. We do not stand outside the system which we are calling into question . . .'[78] The silent and the absentees suffered the ideological sneers of the most motivated. Attempting to establish an alternative pedagogy, the Keynesian group discovered that 'the functioning did not distinguish itself significantly from

---

[71] AStA der Freien Universität Berlin, *Kritische Universität. Sommer 68 – Berichte und Programm* (Berlin, 1968), 43.
[72] Ibid., 30.   [73] Ibid., 42.   [74] Ibid., 45.   [75] Schroeder (ed.), *Hochschule V*, 204.
[76] AStA, *Kritische Universität. Sommer 68*, 32.   [77] Ibid., 93.   [78] Ibid., 42.

a traditional seminar. Even the pressure to perform or rather the gladiatorial struggles reproduced themselves anew, just this time not mediated via the struggle for good grades'.[79] In the most scathing judgement, the colloquium 'Enlightenment and Revolution – Romanticism and Restoration' admitted the failure of all its goals: 'the colloquium fulfilled the feared fig-leaf function of a circle of leftists, who contented themselves on their own progressive consciousness. ... The curious at the beginning stayed away (the most often heard reason being "we didn't understand anything")'.[80] The new seminars thus benefited most those already critical of the current institution and already conversant with the theoretical or intellectual problem under consideration. If the goal was to educate the masses of students mobilised by June 1967, it failed. Those without a sufficient knowledge base or an ease with ideological and intellectual jargon opted out. The *Kritische Universität* functioned best as the organisation of a politicised, critical elite. However, the results were not uniformly negative. Many undoubtedly found the experience of small critical seminars liberating. The decline in professorial authority continued. To have identified the problem as within themselves rather than simply the structure of the university was in itself an achievement.

What of the political aims of the *Kritische Universität*? The assessment of the 'University of Students, Workers and School Students' as the program cover described it, was equally dispirited. While common action with school students was relatively easy, 'much harder was the collaboration of students and workers'.[81] An April 1968 report indicated that 20 per cent of participants in the *Kritische Universität* were school students, but only 2 per cent were workers.[82] The students identified three reasons for the failure: the 'spoken barriers' behind which 'were hidden the superficially disguised divisions of class society', the hatred for students generated by the popular press and the problem that 'wage-earners were hardly in the position to bring understanding' to the issue that mobilised students above all else – 'the ever more violent American-led war on Vietnam'.[83] Student protesters encountered the refrain of 'Always Vietnam – on the White Circle [the removal of a limit on rent charged for a property] you don't say anything. For that we would participate'.[84] The experience of the *Kritische Universität* led directly to the conclusion that its political activities were misplaced.

---

[79] Ibid., 47. [80] Ibid. [81] Ibid., 3. [82] See Schroeder (ed.), *Hochschule V*, 90.
[83] AStA, *Kritische Universität. Sommer 68*, 3–4. [84] Ibid., 4.

As with the broader university cohort, the activists found workers much more difficult to reach than expected. The assumptions behind their political activity crumbled. The group working on the Springer press found its expectations defeated such that 'the impossibility of developing even the simplest form of agitation on the basis of the distributed materials and analysis became the major problem of the working circle'.[85] The students felt compelled to abandon their view of *Bild* 'as a factory for the production of anti-democratic consciousness'.[86] The concepts with which the *Arbeitskreis* operated – manipulation (by *Bild* of its readers) and agitation (by the students through critique) had to be abandoned.[87] Instead of being passively manipulated by Springer, concluded the group, 'the oppression of the BILD reader occurs with his consent'.[88] As with the primarily university-oriented activities, the *Kritische Universität* encountered the limits of critique.

The seminars had also demonstrated that the consent of 'passive' students did not simply dissipate via the provision of practical, 'critical' alternatives. Yet this was the conclusion drawn by some of the political seminars:

> The problem of the BILD-reader is not his stupidity, but his powerlessness. He knows who runs the business, that the profit rates are too high, who is on top and who is below ... His consciousness of his own powerlessness must be broken through practical alternatives.[89]

Thus, the expressly political groups also found the *Kritische Universität* lacking. Instead of misplaced efforts at enlightenment, the 'preparation of practical alternatives and instigating the workers' self-understanding of his own interests'[90] took priority. After a year of experience, Wolfgang Nitsch's goal to provide the 'scientific and theoretical preparation and evaluation'[91] of political action was upended. As one group wrote in Summer 1968, 'work begins now no longer with the collection of 'objective' scientific materials – the starting point is now the in many places openly disregarded needs of workers, school students, mothers, pensioners, students, the unemployed'.[92] The *Kritische Universität* thus played out the division of university and politics present from its very beginning. Events outside the university continued the drive of politicisation. In April 1968, the attempted assassination of Rudi Dutschke created another impetus to radicalisation. In May 1968, the French general strike lent further power

---

[85] Ibid., 8.   [86] Ibid.   [87] Ibid., 9.   [88] Ibid., 10.   [89] Ibid.   [90] Ibid.
[91] Schroeder (ed.), *Hochschule V*, 201.   [92] Ibid., 6.

to those who sought a more straightforwardly political objective. In late May 1968 Daniel Cohn-Bendit arrived in West Berlin and addressed a general assembly of the *Kritische Universität* and 'contradicted the thesis of Marcuse, that it was no longer possible in late capitalist society to mobilise the entire working class'.[93]

While one part of the student movement increasingly moved away from the university under the politicising impulse, the other half was thrown back upon it, although not without itself employing an ever more confrontational style of politics. Having derided reform through the university itself, the initiative now came precisely from an alliance of students with the assistants and professors of the Otto-Suhr Institute. In June 1968, the Institute voted to reorganise itself on the basis of *Drittelparität* between professors, students and the *Mittelbau* (assistants and other teaching personnel). 'The primacy of full professors [*Ordinarienprinzip*] is abolished!" proclaimed the general assembly of the OSI.[94] The division at the FU clearly no longer lay between the rector and administration on the one side and the students on the other, but between the rector and Senate (which rejected the new constitution) and specific institutes of the university. More importantly, the Senator for Science and Art sided with the institute, passing a law to allow the experimentation to proceed. Within a year, the *Freie Universität* boasted no longer a rector but a president. The election fell to a 30-year old Assistant in the Sociology Department, Rolf Kreibich. Although the reform in no way ended the conflict within the university, the *Kritische* was reabsorbed into the *Freie Universität*.

Université Critique

The experience of the 'critical university' at Nanterre proved more fleeting than that at West Berlin, wilting under the intense politicisation of May.[95] On the night of 22 March at Nanterre, the students occupying the administrative building declared the following Friday to be 'a huge debate' on four themes – capitalism in 1968, the anti-imperialist struggle, the eastern bloc and the critical university.[96] The last of these drew the largest

---

[93] Ibid., 96.   [94] Schroeder (ed.), *Hochschule V*, 98.
[95] On the institutional and pedagogical innovations of May, see Dominique Damamme, 'Laboratoires de la réforme pédagogique' in Dominique Damamme et al (eds.), *Mai-Juin 68* (Paris: Éditions de l'Atelier, 2008). For a useful reminder of the reformist currents of May, see also Chris Reynolds, *Memories of May '68: France's Convenient Consensus* (Cardiff: University of Wales Press, 2011).
[96] Jean-Pierre Duteuil, *Nanterre, 1965–66–67–68. Vers le movement du 22 mars* (Paris: Acratie, 1988), 165.

'A Golden Ghetto'   271

crowd. The eastern bloc forum only attracted the political militants, eager to debate their differences. Their report could only note their division over whether the Communist states of eastern Europe were authentically socialist. On the anti-imperialist struggle the movement bemoaned the lack of militancy over Vietnam at Nanterre. The solution – an anti-imperialist day 'where comrades representing organisations that struggle against imperialism will be given the floor with films, exhibitions, debates, etc.' – hardly represented a radical novelty.[97] Of the four themes, the 'critical university' promised the most immediate, practical political objectives for students. Yet here too, divisions surfaced early.

As in West Berlin, differences emerged over the political justification for a university struggle. A commission on 'student struggles – workers struggles' reported how 'some refuse the specificity of the university contestation and others insist on the originality of this contestation as a matter of fact (awaiting theoretical justification)'.[98] There was nothing new in this debate, which subordinated higher education to the broader social struggle. The university could not become a 'socialist island' as the 'isolated students and professors will remain impotent, and their institution is an integral part of a global system which forms it'.[99] This appeal to totality was as much a political tool to vanquish opponents as an intellectually-grounded analysis, but it was widely accepted. In France, proponents of a '*université critique*' were thus on the defensive almost from the beginning. They could only point to the reality of the university contestation as having created de facto a new situation, despite a lack of theoretical justification.

Just as Wolfgang Nitsch and others justified the *Kritische Universität* as a contribution to the political struggle outside the university, so too ideas for the *université critique* came under pressure for being insufficiently political. In its first bulletin, the 22 March Movement sought a theoretical basis for its program: 'FROM THE CRITICISM OF POLITICS TO A POLITICS OF CRITICISM. FROM THE CRITICISM OF THE UNIVERSITY TO THE CRITICAL UNIVERSITY'.[100] On the one hand, the movement proposed that the antagonism between bosses and workers now functioned around the 'opposition between those who do and do not know, entailing the power of the first over the second'.[101] A related thesis posited the proletarianisation of the intellectuals: 'the production of intellectual goods ... is made by the exploitation of

---

[97] Ibid., 235.   [98] Ibid., 229.   [99] Ibid.   [100] Ibid., 269.   [101] Ibid., 229.

scientists, which entails for these last the status of proletarians'.[102] Typically, both arguments presented themselves as an updated or expanded version of Marxism. Neither rationalisation sufficed for the Maoists of the UJC(ml), who bluntly asserted that 'the university has the ultimate goal of exploiting the workers and nothing else'.[103] The Maoists mobilised the mythology of the working class to dismiss any university struggle as naïve: 'the sole "critique" possible of this university can only come from the workers. The true role of progressive students is therefore to put themselves in the service of the workers ...'.[104] The Lambertist Trotskyists likewise lambasted the theory of the *université critique* as 'wrong, fundamentally reactionary'.[105] From this perspective, as other students correctly noted, there could not possibly exist a Critical University.[106]

Proposals for experiments in higher education thus began in a difficult environment in which the working class constituted the cornerstone of radical politics, all reforms would be judged by their impact on the workers and where political rivalries operated via the deployment of theoretical differences that proclaimed themselves the key to unlocking the revolutionary potential of the proletariat. Yet the protest movement of early 1968 emerged largely by operating outside this framework of an ideologically laden language that disdained the politics of higher education. The demand to recognise the 'fact' of the successful agitation within the university despite its poor theoretical underpinning admitted as much. Thus, at a meeting in late April 1968, Cohn-Bendit attempted to put aside the problem of actions outside the campus. The Critical University, he argued, must be a question of what 'actions of contestation ... can be led inside the Faculty... that is to say that it isn't brought up again now that we must make connection with the workers and all that, that's agreed, there are other commissions ...'[107] The goal was to 'fundamentally contest certain precise points in this university, but we are not agreed to stop it from functioning'.[108] Others needed to be reminded even more bluntly that 'you've already been told that we aren't [North Vietnamese military commander Vo Nguyen] Giap here. You are only a guerrilla when there is the possibility for it'.[109] The idea of the *université critique* existed in a space defined defensively by what it was not: by the provisional exclusion of

---

[102] Ibid., 230.   [103] Ibid.   [104] Ibid.
[105] Alain Schnapp and Pierre Vidal-Naquet, *Journal de la Commune Étudiante: textes et documentes. Novembre 1967–juin 1968*, edition augmentée (Paris: Éditions du Seuil, 1969), 332.
[106] Duteuil, *Nanterre*, 231.
[107] BDIC. F delta 1961(10) – VI, 'Meeting: Université Critique. 23/4 Nanterre 1968'.   [108] Ibid.
[109] Ibid.

actions outside the university, by the agreement the university was not to be prevented from functioning and by the exasperated insistence that this was no guerrilla war.

When discussion turned to what the 'Critical University' was rather than what it was not, proposals emerged similar to those in West Berlin. Like their West German counterparts, the French students proposed group study or working groups as a practice that the current system made impossible.[110] Collective study was, however, 'a good start, but ... absolutely insufficient'.[111] A critical university also meant both contestation within the classroom, critique of the ends of the university, and the use of research within the university outside academia. The movement stressed the imperative to analyse critically graduates' future professions: 'the goal of the Critical University would be to do a little sketch on each profession where this Faculty leads ... what is essential, in my opinion, is not so much as to criticise the course as to criticise the profession ... both, agreed...'[112] The proposed analysis and critique rested often on no more than a summary of a book, a sign of how much appeared to be at stake in merely challenging the monopoly of knowledge and reading lists held by the professor. In this, the *Université Critique* sought to formalise the most successful actions undertaken in the prior year.

Yet the Movement of 22 March also demonstrated an awareness of its newfound power: 'At Nanterre, the movement is strong enough that the first task to do is to take the timetable of courses, and make a selection ... we believe we have the ability to say yes or no, this or that must be taught.'[113] The functioning (or 'capitalist needs') of the university could not be changed, absent a wider revolution, but 'in our combat inside the Faculty we will have points of impact, we have possibilities of destruction, even at a minimal level, of certain courses. That is a first thing.'[114] While one target remained the official university, other proposals sought to move from the campus to society. As a practical initiative, one person in the discussion on the critical university proposed 'a tract in collaboration with the people unemployed at Nanterre' and the demand that someone in the sociology department 'deal with the situation of unemployment in France and in particular at Nanterre ... That is to say that our political action reconnects directly with the function of the scientific ... university.'[115] Once again in imitation of West Berlin, the *université critique* sought to

---

[110] Duteuil, *Nanterre*, 231.
[111] BDIC. F delta 1961(10) – VI, 'Meeting: Université Critique. 23/4 Nanterre 1968'. [112] Ibid.
[113] Ibid. [114] Ibid. [115] Ibid.

make scientific research function as the basis of politics. Yet the events of May 1968 swept aside the plans of April. Outright political confrontation replaced long-term goals.

Amid the revolutionary fervour of mid-1968, even greater schemes appeared imaginable than at Nanterre in April. As Dominique Damamme has argued, it is important to recognise 'the realist character of the innumerable university assemblies, committees, commissions or conventions as well as the theoretical character or 'limit-idea' of certain texts.'[116] The events of May had expended the horizon of expectations. One platform invoked 'the Critical University – ... self-governed – open to all – critical'.[117] This program presumed not a movement that could exert pressure on specific parts of the university, but one that could control the whole institution. Emphasising the breadth of its ambition, the manifesto insisted this critical university was neither 'A PARALLEL UNIVERSITY' nor 'A CRITICAL CORE IN THE TRADITIONAL UNIVERSITY'.[118] Yet while May initially expanded the realm of the possible, it also brought forth two important new actors – the government and the working class. The former invoked 'participation' and an 'autonomy', which would satisfy some in the university. The latter, through the general strike, decisively shifted the political focus away from the university. The Maoists, who had never stopped insisting that the only progressive role for young intellectuals was to 'place themselves under the authority of the workers' finally found many to agree with them.

The most radical militants framed the choice between the university and the workers as stark alternatives. Going to the workers meant one 'rejects reformist illusions of creating a "critical university, socialist island in a capitalist society"'.[119] The best those who defended a 'critical university' could do was to insist 'the "Critical University"... is not a socialist island in a bourgeois society, but a "red base" from which the student movement will set out on the conquest of the vanguard of the working class'.[120] Some members of the 22 March Movement attempted to fight a rear-guard action against the revolutionary euphoria: 'Before saying "The worker is essentially revolutionary", the movement of the factory occupations must be analysed. ... The students want to lead the worker into the revolutionary struggle, but one cannot force on the worker a revolutionary tendency

---

[116] See Damamme, 'Laboratoires de la réforme pédagogique', 251.
[117] BDIC. F delta 1961(10) – V, Plate-forme Z.   [118] Ibid.
[119] BDIC. F delta 813(4), 'Non aux manifestations réactionnaires! Non aux manoeuvres de l'administration!'
[120] Daniel Bensaïd and Henri Weber, *Mai 68: une répétition générale* (Paris: Maspero, 1968), 131.

that he possesses "essentially".[121] However, such calls for study and caution were difficult to sustain mid-1968.

The explosion of May exposed a multitude of contradictions in the French student movement. The concept of 'system' helped to identify the university as a site of politics but undermined any political program to be enacted there – the pretension that any single part of the system could somehow be radically restructured easily dismissed as illusory reformism. Similarly, most if not all of the radical groups at Nanterre understood the working class as the sole possible revolutionary force, yet any sustained political program within the university required this affirmation to be either set aside and temporarily ignored or rationalised in justifications of varying credibility. Above all, the student movements, emerging in a crisis of political parties and institutions, exhibited a phobia of institutionalising themselves. Their capacity for critique existed in inverse proportion to their ability to create enduring structures. There was no equivalent at Nanterre to the *Kritische Universität* in West Berlin. In the 1968–1969 academic year, the university administration and students once again faced off with neither able to break the stalemate. The first initiative at structural change came with the advent of Paul Ricoeur to the position of dean of Nanterre in April 1969. As in West Berlin, as the politicisation of the student movement increased, the initiative returned to reformers within the university. Even so, Ricoeur experienced no more success than his predecessors.

The closest parallel to the *Kritische Universität* in France was instead the *Centre universitaire expérimental de Vincennes*. Unlike the institutions of West Berlin and Trento, however, the initiative came from the government, seeking to draw protesters away from the other institutions.[122] As de

---

[121] BDIC. F delta 813(8), 'Section d'Allemand. 17 mai 1968 –25 mai 1968. Critique de l'université: Université critique'.
[122] Christelle Dormoy-Rajramanan, 'From Dream to Reality: The Birth of 'Vincennes', in Julian Jackson, Anna-Louise Milne and James S. Williams (eds.), *May 68: Rethinking France's Last Revolution* (Basingstoke: Palgrave Macmillan, 2011), 245–262, 252. See also Laurène Le Cozanet and Christelle Dormoy-Rajramanan, 'Une origine, deux destins? Les centres universitaires de Dauphine et Vincennes de 1968 aux années 1970', in Loïc Vadelorge, Florence Bourillon, Stéphanie Méchine and Éléonore Marantz-Jaen (eds.), *De l'Université de Paris aux universités d'Île-de-France* (Rennes: Presses Universitaires de Rennes, 2016), 271–283. For a more nostalgic view, see Paul Cohen, 'Happy Birthday Vincennes! The University of Paris-8 Turns Forty', *History Workshop Journal* 69 (2010), 206–224; Charles Soulié (ed.), *Un mythe à détruire? Origines et destin du Centre universitaire experimental de Vincennes* (Paris: Presses universitaires de Vincennes, 2012); Guy Berger, Maurice Courtois and Colette Perrigault (eds.), *Folies et raisons d'une université: Paris 8: de Vincennes à Saint-Denis* (Paris: Éditions Pétra, 2015). See also Michel Debeauvais, *L'université ouverte: les dossiers de Vincennes* (Grenoble: Presses Universitaire de Grenoble, 1976).

Gaulle put it, 'Vincennes is for *emmerdeurs*.'[123] The Centre was open to students without the baccalauréat, held longer teaching hours and aimed to abandon the lecture for seminars. But the Communist students, rather than the gauchistes or Maoists, dominated at the centre (later university) of Vincennes, which once again reproduced the divisions between those 'who favoured an avant-garde university and those who wanted an "open" university' as well as a '"technocratic" centre in tune with the job market'.[124] The experimental nature of Vincennes should not be underestimated, but it was not driven by the protest movement.

Università Critica

The French *Université Critique* never left the realm of imagination, while the West German *Kritische Universität's* system of parallel structures foundered in mid-1968. At just that moment began the experiment of the *Università Critica* at Trento. Unlike the West German model, however, this would not be a set of parallel structures, but rather a joint enterprise led by students and staff of the Faculty of Sociology. The students at Trento knew of the *Kritische Universität*. Two representatives visited West Berlin in July 1967 and witnessed the reception given to Marcuse and the first adumbrations of the critical university.[125] Mauro Rostagno and a group of militants spent the summer organised in three groups, studying imperialism, the revolution of 1917 and the student movement, including documents from West Berlin. The students decided to attempt a critical university, inspired by the West German model, but divergent in two respects. Firstly, instead of an autonomous parallel structure as in West Berlin, 'at Trento it was proposed to make the KU basically coincide with the "official university" by intertwining the one inside the other institutionally and organisationally'.[126] Secondly, by virtue of being directed at the entire institution, the *Università Critica* aimed to 'involve the entire student "mass" in political and theoretical work'.[127]

Circumstances explained the differences. The long occupation that began on 31 January 1968 ended in April with the triumph of the students

---

[123] Raymond Krakovitch, *Edgar Faure. La virtuose de la politique* (Paris, 2006), 269, as quoted in Cohen, 'Happy Birthday Vincennes!', 211.
[124] Dormoy-Rajramanan, 'From Dream to Reality', 259.
[125] See Concetto Vecchio, *Vietato obbedire* (Milan: Rizzoli, 2005), 70.
[126] M. Boato, *Il movimento studentesco trentino: origine storica esperienze di lotta, prospettive politiche*, Tesi di laurea, 23 as cited by Aldo Ricci, *I giovani non sono piante* (Milan: SugarCo, 1978), 183.
[127] Ibid.

and the resignation of Mario Volpato as director of the Institute. This left the Institute of Sociology ripe for a radical overhaul. In contrast to the bleak student outlook in West Berlin, marked foremost by the consciousness of defeat and the futility of 'dialogue', the occupation in Trento concluded with an amicable conversation. In April the 'organising committee' responsible for the Institute had accepted that students would participate in equal numbers on a committee that decided on teaching and research. Indeed, as a single faculty rather than an entire university, experiments were much more feasible at Trento than elsewhere. Furthermore, the lack of significant urban infrastructure somewhat held in check the temptation of students to abandon the university for full-time political struggle. Finally, Trento boasted in its new rector – Francesco Alberoni – an individual willing to take on the challenge of a 'Critical University'.

Alberoni arrived on the recommendation of Norberto Bobbio, who saw him as 'the only one who could tame the revolt'.[128] Alberoni had found his way to sociology through psychology, studied the Berkeley Free Speech movement first hand and had recently left the chair of sociology at La Cattolica in Milan. As he put it to the Bishop of Trento, he had 'left not only La Cattolica, but also the Catholic religion and my wife; in the eyes of the Church here at Trento, I am publicly cohabiting'.[129] He arrived at Trento in early July to face a general assembly of students. Rather than address them from the lectern, Alberoni sat on the floor: 'I am here to listen to you.'[130] He moved his office to the ground floor of the faculty building to be near the students and adopted the student mode of expression: *documenti di lavoro* or working documents, duplicated and distributed like flyers. To the press he announced 'the Critical University is that which debates its own presuppositions, that is, itself; critical is the opposite of dogmatic, the opposite of alienated, the opposite of passive, the opposite of hypocritical'.[131] The embrace of the movement merely recognised the fact that any other line would be contested and overthrown by the students, but no one had had the temerity or humour to try so much before.

Alberoni sought to create an intellectual space not defined by political confrontation. He renounced any possibility of policing the university. Neither force nor traditional or bureaucratic authority held any sway: 'Everything that can be done, unless things change, must be done via

---

[128] Vecchio, *Vietato obbedire*, 119. [129] Ricci, *I giovani*, 154.
[130] Vecchio, *Vietato obbedire*, 121. [131] Ricci, *I giovani*, 186.

charismatic leadership', he wrote.[132] While rejecting the politics of administrative power, Alberoni sought to recast the space of dialogue as one which aimed 'not to obtain anyone's integration into the system or for manipulative purposes, but to create new types of relations that can bring about new sorts of critical consciousness'.[133] More broadly, Alberoni forcefully sought to prevent politics from overwhelming every other aspect of the Institute: not to put politics 'in parentheses' but to avoid 'the sectarian illusion that man, society and creativity are consumed by the political label'.[134] This was a bold claim in mid-1968, but the power of Alberoni's personality and the renewal of teaching staff that accompanied his arrival threatened for the first time seriously to rival the authority of the student movement.

The *Università Critica* functioned similarly to that of West Berlin, abandoning the professorial lecture, privileging seminars (some run by advanced students), identifying topics neglected by the traditional university and emphasising practical research. Thus, the seminar on 'Division of Labour and Bureaucracy' envisaged 'interviews of students who work in the local bureaucracy – studies of the bureaucracy in small centres around Trento or elsewhere'. 'The Sociological Problem of Anomie' was to be observed in 'houses of workers, ex-peasants, those let go from psychiatric hospitals ... veterans'. Other seminars included the 'Family as a Social Institution', 'Weber and Rationalisation in Western Society', 'Economic Rationality', 'Class and Class Struggle', 'Religion and Society' and 'The Methodological Problem of Marx, Durkheim and Weber'.[135] In the greatest contrast to West Berlin, student-run seminars counted towards the degree. Exams were sometimes collective. Alberoni thought that 'the result at the level of seminars is to be judged positively', even if 'today the suggestions to return to the lecture with discussion are not few in number'.[136] The results thus mirrored that in West Berlin: a mixed experience that raised new problems and calls for more traditional pedagogy, without ever becoming a demand for the *status quo ante*.

The research endeavours of advanced students also yielded varying results. The arrival of Alberoni heralded the functioning of the 'research laboratory' which outlined a research program for 1968/1969 on four topics: total institutions (prisons, psychiatric hospitals etc.); the education

---

[132] CMR B.1 f.5 (Fondo Movimento Studentesco G. Palma), 'Documento di lavoro n. 2'.
[133] Ibid.   [134] Ibid.
[135] CMR B.1 f.5 (Fondo Movimento Studentesco G. Palma), 'Didattica per la sociologia. 1. Documento di lavoro n.1'.
[136] CMR B.1 f.5 (Fondo Movimento Studentesco G. Palma), 'Documento di lavoro n.5'.

system; socio-economic and political structures (big industry, the peasants of Trento, local press) and religious sociology.[137] These collective research projects avoided some of the criticism of more general seminars. The research program produced a number of student theses, all of which had to be justified and reported to the general assembly. Aldo Ricci, who worked on prisons, described how 'to clarify our position and to reaffirm the – even relative – utility of the Critical University, Paolo and I convoked a general assembly'. The form of authority most respected in the general assembly at this point was the approval of workers. As Ricci remembered, 'since we didn't have in hand one or more members of the working class to validate what we had to say, we arrived in the assembly with ex-prisoners ... of whom a few were students and others members of the local mob'.[138] The experiment of the *Università Critica* opened up new avenues of research but succumbed simultaneously to the political dynamics of the protest movement.

The political drive of the movement increasingly undermined the university experiment. When Alberoni arrived at Trento, Mauro Rostagno declared 'the phase of struggle for university problems is over, now the contestation becomes global, whether at national or international level'.[139] Yet this statement reflected bravura more than anything else. Slightly earlier, Rostagno articulated a much more downbeat political assessment, admitting that 'there has been no success in dragging behind us (other than in an insignificant dimension) ... either the working class or the workers on the land, and not even the parties or unions ...'.[140] The French May created some euphoria, but the summer of 1968 was still marked by 'the nausea of activism' which 'led to the almost biological necessity to "eat books" together. Then commenced the theoretical summer seminars.'[141] As in West Berlin, the *Università Critica* occurred in a breathing space marked by both a wave of politicisation and a pessimistic assessment of past struggles. The experimental university appealed as a practical, concrete struggle that promoted the long-term goal of a march through the institutions, 'conserving the institutional structure while overturning its function. No longer a factory of Pavlovian graduates to insert servilely in the system, but a factory of militants, theoretically armed, practically subversive, capable today of beginning the long march, tomorrow to

---

[137] The full description is in V. Capecchi et al., 'Dall'avarizia alla politica', *Bozze 1978* 1.3 (1978), 60–61.
[138] Ricci, *I giovani*, 219.   [139] Vecchio, *Vietato obbedire*, 122.
[140] Rostagno, 'Anatomia della rivolta', *Problemi del socialismo* 28–29 (1968), 285.
[141] Renato Curcio e Mauro Rostagno, *Fuori dai denti* (Milan: Gammalibri, 1980), 35.

continue it in the specific institutions in which they will be immersed.'[142] Much like the *Kritische Universität*, the *Università Critica* proposed a politics of the professions rather than a profession of politics.

This intellectual rationale held fast while the protest movement remained poised between the success of student mobilisation and the perception of political defeat. Yet the compromise was fragile. The protest movement at Trento embarked on the *Università Critica* at Trento, as Alberoni put it, 'founded on a pact (covenant) between students and teachers ... that presupposed reciprocal autonomy and non-acceptance of the principle of co-government'.[143] Strident student assertions that they did not seek 'a "golden ghetto in a society of shit"' accompanied participation. As Rostagno emphasised 'there is not, there cannot be a "different", a "better" university'.[144] Engagement with the Critical University could only occur under the cover of declarations of its impossibility.

Collaboration was somewhat foreign to the protest movement, which had been forged in head-to-head conflict. The proposal of the long march through the institutions envisaged a much greater time-span than customary in student battles. Indeed, the success of the student movement in bringing about the *Università Critica* could also mean its dissolution, with little left to fight for within the university. While the first three occupations of the faculty of sociology occurred, at least in part, with objectives to be achieved within the university, the fourth occupation, from 2 to 5 December 1968, was an act of solidarity after two deaths when police fired on striking workers at Avola in Sicily. At the fifth, in January 1969, students divided openly into those in favour of continuing the struggle 'outside' or 'inside' the university. For the first time, Alberoni came into conflict with the student movement. With no intention of calling the police, he pled the case for the *Università Critica* 'that is of the experimentation, the delimitation of a governed and not "wildcat" political-expressive space, anti-authoritarian and anti-intimidatory engagement of everyone'.[145] While Alberoni argued for the uniqueness of the university, and its distinctiveness within Italian higher education, the attempt to delimit political confrontation clashed with the nature of the protest movement.

The students judged the *Università Critica* on political grounds by which standard it could only fail. Marco Boato lamented an institution

---

[142] Ibid., 44.
[143] CMR B.1 f.5 (Fondo Movimento Studentesco G. Palma), 'Documento di lavoro n.6 (Al Plenum del 22 marzo)'.
[144] Rostagno, 'Anatomia della rivolta', 280.
[145] CMR B.1 f.5 (Fondo Movimento Studentesco G. Palma), 'Documento di lavoro n. 3'.

with the greatest interest for the most varied 'theoretical' problems of Marxist, neo-Hegelian, Luxemburgian, Freudian, Reichian, Lukacsian imprint etc. etc. but with by now the most insufficient political presence in the class contradictions and social struggles of Trentino and with a social practice reduced to pure 'experimentation'. In the faculty there is a lot of talk (and writing) about Marxism, socialism, revolution, anti-authoritarianism, emancipation, etc. but the 'glorious' days of the Trentino May of 1968 (with 5000 workers and students in the piazza and the struggle at Michelin in the vanguard) are now only a memory or little more.[146]

While the leaders of the movement temporarily acceded to Alberoni's request and ended the occupation, the experiment slowly suffocated. Alberoni himself expected 'the defeated maximalist fringe ... [to] counter-attack, accusing of revisionism (or even of fascism) every type of university activity identifying [it] wholesale ... as manipulation'.[147] A protest movement in search of revolution had little time for enlightened experiments.

The protest movement had held in tension two distinct drives – university reform and political protest. While that tension proved productive in the first years of revolt, these goals now diverged. One side of the protest movement thus undermined the other. The West German Peter Schneider arrived in Trento from West Berlin in late 1968: in 'two weeks I got to know a thousand persons, in two weeks I became a charismatic leader in a language I barely knew!' he remembered.[148] In alliance with the 'outsiders' (*esternisti*) against the 'insiders' (*internisti*), he sought 'to break out of the "ghetto" of the university and look for the striking workers'. At the textile factory of Marzotto he found what he was looking for in the strike leader Carlo Alberganti:

> It was the first time in my life that I came in contact with a living example of the mythical 'revolutionary subject' ... In my euphoria he seemed to me the hero of the future world revolution modelled by Dutschke and Che Guevara. I took back his criticism of the Trentino student movement to the general assembly and for the first time encountered reserved reactions.[149]

Whatever the initial reservations, the leaders of the movement were trapped by their language, by the difficulty of maintaining a political

---

[146] Marco Boato, 'Sottosviluppo e repressione: la via trentina al centro-sinistra,' *Giovane Critica* 25 (1971), 69.
[147] B.1 f.5 (Fondo Movimento Studentesco G. Palma), 'Documento di lavoro n.6'.
[148] CMR B.14 f.1 (Fondo Calì), A Trento Venti'Anni Dopo. Peter Schneider. (assemblea).
[149] Peter Schneider, *Rebellion und Wahn: Mein '68: Eine autobiographische Erzählung* (Köln: Kippenheuer & Witsch, 2008), 321.

movement within the *Università Critica* and because many had all but finished their degrees and were ready to move on. The most important figure of the movement, Mauro Rostagno, 'abandoned the city out of fear of being considered a traitor to the working class', admitting later that 'I could not resist the attack on me made from the Left . . . They attacked me saying the university was aristocratic, anti-worker, a golden ghetto, etc. They made me ashamed to the point that shortly after I left.'[150] As in West Berlin and Paris, politics vanquished the project of university reform.

The protest movements found themselves trapped in part by their revolutionary rhetoric and the pressure of events, much to their later regret. Rostagno abandoned the *Università Critica*, acknowledging a decade later that 'we committed an error, we should have continued the experiment, preserved the university . . . in spite of all'.[151] Marco Boato, who dismissed the *Università Critica* as 'a colossal collective illusion'[152] at the time, would twenty years later 'challenge anyone, on the level of historical comparative research to demonstrate that elsewhere there existed a model as advanced as the critical university of Trento at that time, even if it lasted only a short while'.[153] In retrospect, the experimental university appeared a much more significant innovation than it did at the time. The pressure of politics and of revolutionary time swept aside long-term intellectual endeavours for immediate political engagement.

The *Università Critica* finally collapsed in April 1969 when, after the closure of a tobacco factory at Battipaglia in Naples, the police fired on demonstrators, killing 2 and wounding around 200. The events sounded 'the alarm bell that said to the students: people are dying outside and here we are inside studying while outside the class struggle continues'.[154] In a foretaste of what was to come in the 1970s, two bombs exploded at Trento, suspicion falling on a worker close to the student movement. Police sought to search the headquarters of the student movement. Alberoni convinced Rostagno to allow it, in a compromise that only hastened the decline of the *Università Critica*. The student movements of Trento, Turin and Pisa formed *Lotta continua*, Italian workers entered a year of strikes, and the political climate deteriorated in the shadow of bombs. Alberoni admitted the end: 'the process of fusion is finished: possibly not

---

[150] Ricci, *I giovani*, 220. [151] Ibid.
[152] Marco Boato, *Il '68 è morto: viva il '68! Prima del '68: origini del movimento studentesco e della nuova sinistra; dopo il '68: abbiamo 'sbagliato tutto'. . .?* (Verona: Bertani Editore, 1979), 337.
[153] CMR B.14 f.1 (Fondo Calì), A Trento Venti'Anni Dopo. Intervento di Boato.
[154] Ricci, *I giovani*, 221.

in Italy, but it is finished at Trento'. Somewhat bitterly, he noted that the student movement at Trento was itself 'intimidatory':

> it remained in the old logic of shit, it hasn't managed to shake it off. It's seen the shit on others: recognised their repressive, persecutory, oppressive mode of thought but in the struggle has not known how to come outside of itself ... different bodies were experienced as a menace to its identity: politics formalised in Marxist-Leninist terms. The hegemonic group did not speak to all men, neo-humanism is finished.[155]

The Università Critica came to an end and Alberoni too departed Trento.

All three student movements – West Berlin, Nanterre, Trento – split between wings directed at the university and at the workers (or society more broadly), a division which corresponded to that between those oriented more towards theory and research and those inclined towards politics and action. The 'critical university', as conceived in Berlin and Trento, aimed to overcome the opposition of theory and practice – linking research to pragmatic contexts or establishing the intellectual bases for political action. Instead, the institution succumbed to the division. The reasons were partly external: the reappearance of strikes and the working class in May in France or throughout 1969 in Italy fostered the divisions between 'inside' and 'outside' the university. However, another reason was internal: a peculiar combination of success and failure of the protest movements. At Nanterre and West Berlin, few concessions had been wrung from reluctant university administrations. The major achievement of the students was rather the creation of the movement itself, and the ability to paralyse classrooms or academic ceremonies.

The program of the *Kritische Universität* clearly predicted total failure should the students fail to connect with social groups outside the university: 'If the students stay quarantined on campus, they will find no allies in the relevant social strata of the population, and so the Senate will be able to assert itself and choke the student movement.'[156] At Trento, the inverse was the case. Having triumphed in mid-1968, and with a new rector willing to participate in a novel institutional experiment, the conflicts around which the movement had come into being faded. The movement itself would either follow and gradually dissolve into the new *Università Critica* or needed to find a new political arena. Furthermore, the practices that fostered the growth of the student movements undermined its institutionalisation. The tendency to avoid compromise and negotiation in

[155] CMR B.1 f.5 (Fondo Movimento Studentesco G. Palma), 'Documento di lavoro n.6'.
[156] AStA, *Kritische Universität. Wintersemester 1967/68*, 40.

order to denounce, provoke or disrupt, and the rejection of political parties or bureaucratic order was not a stable basis for a long-term organisation. A movement, precisely, was neither institution, nor organisation, and could only transform itself into one of the latter by losing some of the features most important to its participants. One of the characteristics of 1968, as Francesco Alberoni had noted, was the tendency of politics to consume the students entirely, leaving less and less room for a politics of or within the university. Politicisation tended to promote simplification. Alberoni found himself defending the need to research: 'Knowledge ... cannot be reduced to the discovery that the data is manipulated. Agreed, the data is manipulated, but what is the exact data? Will we do without it? ... The difficulty is getting it, the critical university means gathering exact information.'[157] The Critical University, so defined, however, needed no student movement nor student participation in university government. Its strength was critique and contestation, not research and theorisation. As a political movement, the student rebellion contested the authority of professors and administrators, the limits of speech, the social exclusions of higher education and the claims to objectivity and value-neutral science, but as a political movement, it was ill-adapted to run a university.

[157] CMR B.1 f.5, 'Documento di lavoro n.3'.

Conclusion

'We lost', admitted Mauro Rostagno at the twentieth anniversary of 1968, 'Thank goodness we lost.'[1] Another speaker agreed: 'it doesn't interest me if we were defeated at a political level. Who gives a damn? Rather I agree with those who say it is better that way. Who knows what success would have been? Ultimately the most beautiful revolutions have always been defeated.'[2] Among themselves, the protagonists of 1968 found the consolations of failure. At other times, to other audiences, they defended their experience, especially in the face of derisory accounts. The ironic retrospective self-assessment was only to be expected. Outside the revolutionary atmosphere of the late 1960s, other priorities prevailed. As has been seen in the preceding chapters, experiments dismissed as illusory or maligned as reformist in 1968 quickly recaptured their historic importance in the aftermath of the events. Conversely, political revolution, which appeared so imminent in '68, could only elicit more cautious consideration in subsequent decades. For the historian, the important task is neither to romanticise the retrospectively 'important' aspects of the late 1960s nor dwell on what dated quickly even to the protagonists, but rather to explain how these two sides belonged together. The protests of 1968 proved far more capable of exposing the hypocrisies and inequalities of authority, both within the university and more generally, than they were in establishing alternatives. The failure of some of those alternatives can only elicit a 'thank goodness'. Others are undoubtedly a source of regret. If nothing else, the protesters forcefully demanded a rethinking of political and cultural power, and exposed, via their own errors, the paradoxes of the search for more democratic forms of authority.

Thus 1968 appears, both in retrospect and at the time, as unfinished business. The revisioning of West European democracy in the 1960s raised

---

[1] Interview with Marta Losito, 7 December 2004.
[2] CMR B.14 f.1 (Fondo Cali), A Trento Venti'Anni Dopo. Assemblea, 19.

complicated and intractable problems. What role did higher education play in a democratic society? How might that 'democratic' education be conceived? How feasible were forms of direct democracy in complex societies, and what forms of authority were legitimately democratic? What were the limits of self-determination? Did cultural 'democratisation' mean political democratisation? What did cultural self-determination or personal fulfilment mean in the context of rampant consumerism? These questions took on particular urgency in the late 1960s when new answers to them appeared both urgent and imminent. The revolts of 1968 in no way provided final resolutions to these problems, but served thereafter as a defining moment of their most utopian conceptualisation and their practical failure.

The preceding chapters explored these dynamics of democratisation in a series of fields connected to the university. To be sure, the revolts of 1968 both had origins and expanded well beyond the realm of higher education. The protest movements in each of these three case studies never focused solely on educational politics. After crucial incidences of violent interaction with the state (the shooting of Ohnesorg, the 'night of the barricades') or with society (the Anti-Lent) they no longer found their main antagonist even primarily in university administrations. These moments of violent conflict proved especially productive, aligning the relations of cultural authority within the university to that of state and social authority, creating the impression of a single anti-authoritarian or revolutionary struggle. That illusion did not last. A multiplicity of anti-authoritarian revolts co-existed and at times rivalled each other for priority.[3] The revolt that had festered in higher education no longer existed in the same social context after the crisis of 1968, marked by these moments of deeply charged symbolic (and actual) violence. Yet limiting the perspective to higher education allows a focused analysis of the dilemmas of anti-authoritarian revolt. The university was just one sphere in which an anti-authoritarian revolt developed. Given its reliance (for the most part) on consent and cultural authority rather than state power, it proved one of the most fertile fields for rebellion, yet one in which the paradoxes of anti-authoritarianism rapidly revealed themselves.

---

[3] For a decade-long 'radical challenge to structures of authority in the factories' in France see Xavier Vigna, 'Beyond Tradition: The strikes of May-June 1968', in Jackson et al. (eds.), *May 68*, 47–57, 48. See also *L'insubordination ouvrière dans les années 68: essai d'histoire politique des usines* (Rennes: Presses universitaires de Rennes, 2007).

The university, conceived as an instrument of modernisation and social mobility, wracked with problems of expansion, epitomised the dilemma of democratisation. Dreams of degrees for all transmuted (in the absence of greatly increased funding) into a nightmare world of overcrowding and attrition. Protesters rejected both selection at entry to university and the wastage of non-completion as two forms of elitism. But absent a social and political revolution (of which no one could foresee the outcome) these were the two alternatives. The protest movements often successfully prevented new restrictions on access at entry, but they were less well equipped to address the problem of attrition. That defeat made the dismissal of the university and the turn to politics even more tempting. The failure, of course, was much more that of governments than protest movements. It would be perverse to expect social movements to successfully accomplish what governments consistently failed to achieve. Attrition remained a pervasive feature of higher education. Higher education emerged from 1968 chastened, much less easily viewed as the motor of revolutionary social change.

The protest movements had much more success shaping the curriculum, styles of teaching and assessment, all fields in which their numbers could be more easily brought to bear. Such was the case of sociology. The social movements of the mid-late 1960s fundamentally shifted the discipline away from the technocratic vision of administrative experts. Although the figure of the expert never disappeared, sociology was the last place to look for them. Instead, numerous radical democratic sociologists and protesters took the values of the protest movements and marched into the professions, with the experience of social protest behind them. Within the university, while experiments such as the *Kritische Universität* and the *Università Critica* collapsed in the short term, the ideas they embodied were adopted in varying degrees within the official institutions.

The pressures of democratisation and consumerisation created shockwaves within the realm of high culture. As with the university, the meaning of these changes proved contentious. Did democratisation mean greater access to high culture? Or did a democratic society imply the overthrow of elite definitions of culture? Social movements certainly played their part in deconstructing the cultural canon and exposing its social prejudices. They powerfully asserted the politics of all culture. Protestors rode the desacralisation of high culture, but found it hard to impose a new definition amid the ruins. Few were comfortable, longer-term, with the anti-intellectualism that could arise in the wake of high culture's fall. The collapse of high culture's privileged status inaugurated a more democratic cultural regime, in which no single definition of culture reigned. This inability to assert an uncontested cultural authority was felt most keenly by defenders of the old guard. However, hierarchies still marked the disenchanted world of mass culture, which offered fewer defences against anti-intellectualism, and the intensity of political conflict threatened to subordinate culture to politics entirely.

The protesters of the late 1960s also sought to reinvent the political process more generally. Parties, perceived as authoritarian and hierarchical, initially fell out of favour, and students widely asserted the demand for autonomy, devolution of power and control over institutions and organisations in which they participated. Calls for representation were the most easily met, especially within the university; once granted, however, most often felt symbolic rather than effective. Nonetheless, representation within university structures proved an enduring result of student protests in the 1960s. Attempts to run or co-run university institutions had notable successes, but often foundered in the face of institutional or government intransigence. The activist minority also found it difficult both to retain support for those experiments beyond their own politically active base, and to convince that base that the university and not broader social conflict demanded their time and attention. Furthermore, the demand for devolution and autonomy increasingly appeared a liability in terms of political efficacy, leading to the return of hierarchical political parties that fostered an even greater self-identification with the party's ideological goal than those of the early 1960s.

1968 was undoubtedly an anti-authoritarian revolt, but one which primarily targeted traditional and bureaucratic forms of authority. Their collapse (drawing on the mass university and the affluence of post-war society) was frequently experienced as one of genuine liberation. The revolt permanently undermined the status of major authority figures, particularly professors, some of whom keenly felt the decline in their status. Into the vacuum crept other forms of authority. Male charismatic authority featured notably in student assemblies, a problem the protesters identified but to which they found few resolutions. The turn to new political parties amid the intense politicisation of the revolts marked a re-embrace of hierarchy and authority. Bureaucratic authority, rejected during the revolts as a mask for capricious and personal power, re-established itself to the extent that it could appear depersonalised. The changing balance of forms of authority is evident in the similarities across the three states examined here. Everywhere, police intervention within the university proved unifying, exposing university authority as reliant on force and thereby delegitimising it. The logical (if not the actual) response to the protest movements was to refrain from the use of police. The protest movements themselves relied far too often on provocation, absent which they found it much harder to generate momentum. The political practices of the protest movements traced an arc from regulative ideals of reasoned political debate and the public use of criticism to a less-intellectually reasoned but more politically productive cycle of provocation, overreaction and mobilisation. Although provocation often successfully opened a space for politics within the institution, the democratic public sphere was not always a locus of rational debate, but rather one where domination and simplification thrived.

There is much, therefore, to be thankful about in the failure of student radicalism, but such a view cannot be cause for condescension or complacency. The attempt to democratise education, relations of authority, culture and society remains one possible horizon for contemporary society. The legacy of the movements of 1968 is a powerful assertion of that goal, but also a recognition of the difficulties inherent in working towards it. That struggle continues.

Select Bibliography

ARCHIVES

Archiv APO und soziale Bewegungen [APO]
Archives départementales Hauts-de-Seine [ADHS]
Bibliothèque de documentation internationale contemporaine [BDIC]
Bibliothèque nationale de France [BNF]
Centro di documentazione Mauro Rostagno [CMR]
Centre d'histoire sociale du XXe siècle [CHS]
Museo storico del Trentino [MST]

SECONDARY WORKS

Agostini, Aldo, Passerini, Luisa and Tranfaglia, Nicola (eds.), *La cultura e i luoghi del '68* (Milan: FrancoAngeli, 1991).

Ambrosoli, Luigi, *La Scuola in Italia dal dopoguerra ad oggi* (Bologna: Il Mulino, 1982).

Aron, Raymond, *La révolution introuvable: réflexions sur la révolution de mai* (Paris: Fayard, 1968).

Artières, Philippe and Zancarini Fournel, Michelle (eds.), *68: Une histoire collective 1962–1981* (Paris: La Découverte, 2008).

Barbagli, Marzio, *Educating for Unemployment: Politics, Labor Markets and the School System. Italy 1859–1973*, trans. Robert H. Ross (New York: Columbia University Press, 1982).

Bolte, Karl Martin and Neidhardt, Friedhelm (eds.), *Soziologie als Beruf. Erinnerungen westdeutscher Hochschulprofessoren der Nachkriegsgeneration* (Baden-Baden: NOMOS Verlagsgesellschaft, 1998).

Bourdieu, Pierre, *Homo Academicus* (Stanford: Stanford University Press, 1988).

Bourdieu, Pierre and Jean-Claude Passeron, *The Inheritors: French Students and Their Relation to Culture* (Chicago: University of Chicago Press, 1979).

Brown, Timothy Scott, '1968. Transnational and Global Perspectives', *Docupedia-Zeitgeschichte*, 11.06.2012: DOI: http://dx.doi.org/10.14765/zzf.dok.2.272.v1

West Germany and the Global Sixties (Cambridge: Cambridge University Press, 2013).

Bude, Heinz and Kohli, Martin (eds.), *Radikalisierte Aufklärung: Studentenbewegung und Soziologie in Berlin 1965 bis 1970* (Weinheim: Juventa Verlag, 1989).
Caute, David, *The Year of the Barricades: A Journey through 1968* (New York: Harper & Row, 1988).
Chaplin, Tamara and Pieper Mooney, Jadwiga E., *The Global Sixties: Convention, Contest and Counterculture* (Abingdon: Routledge, 2018).
Chen, Jian et al. (eds.), *The Routledge Handbook of the Global Sixties: Between Protest and Nation-Building* (Abingdon and New York: Routledge, 2018).
Cohn-Bendit, Daniel and Cohn-Bendit, Gabriel, *Le gauchisme: remède à la maladie sénile du communisme* (Paris: Seuil, 1968).
Cook, Alexander C. (ed.), *Mao's Little Red Book: A Global History* (Cambridge: Cambridge University Press, 2014).
Cornils, Ingo and Waters, Sarah (eds.), *Memories of 1968: International Perspectives* (Oxford: Peter Lang, 2010).
Damamme, Dominique, Gobille, Boris, Matonti, Frédérique and Pudal, Bernard (eds.), *Mai-Juin 68* (Paris: Editions de l'Atelier, 2008).
Davis, Belinda et al. (eds.) *Changing the World, Changing Oneself: Political Protest and Collective Identities in West Germany and the U.S. in the 1960s and 1970s* (New York: Berghahn, 2010).
De Certeau, Michel, *The Capture of Speech and Other Political Writings*, trans. Tom Conley (Minneapolis: University of Minnesota Press, 1997).
Dreyfus-Armand, Geneviève, Frank, Robert, Lévy, Marie-Françoise and Fournel-Zancarini, Michelle (eds.), *Les années 68. Le temps de la contestation* (Brussels: Editions Complexe, 2000).
Dreyfus-Armand, Geneviève and Gervereau, Laurent, *Mai 68. Les mouvements étudiants en France et dans le monde* (Nanterre: Bibliothèque de la Documentation Internationale Contemporaine, 1988).
Duteuil, Jean-Pierre, *Nanterre, 1965–66–67–68. Vers le mouvement du 22 mars* (Paris: Acratie, 1988).
Dworok, Gerrit and Weissmann, Christoph (eds.), *1968 und die 68er: Ereignisse, Wirkungen und Kontroversen in der Bundesrepublik* (Vienna: Böhlau Verlag, 2013).
Eley, Geoff, *Forging Democracy: The History of the Left in Europe* (Oxford: Oxford University Press, 2002).
Fichter, Tilman and Lönnendonker, Siegward, *Kleine Geschichte des SDS: Der Sozialistische Deutsche Studentenbund von 1946 bis zur Selbstauflösung* (Berlin: Rotbuch Verlag, 1977).
Fink, Carole, Gassert, Philipp and Junker, Detlef (eds.), *1968: The World Transformed* (New York: Cambridge University Press, 1998).
Fischer, Didier, *L'Histoire des étudiants en France de 1945 à nos jours* (Paris: Flammarion, 2000).
Frei, Norbert, *1968: Jugendrevolte und Globaler Protest* (Munich: Deutscher Taschenbuch Verlag, 2008).

Frese, Matthias, Pauls, Julia and Treppe, Karl (eds.), *Demokratisierung und gesellschaftlicher Aufbruch: Die sechziger Jahre als Wendezeit der Bundesrepublik* (Paderborn: Ferdinand Schöningh, 2003).
Gilcher-Holtey, Ingrid, *Die Phantasie an die Macht: Mai 68 in Frankreich* (Frankfurt am Main: Suhrkamp, 1995).
Gildea, Robert, Mark, James and Warring, Annette (eds.), *Europe's 1968: Voices of Revolt* (Oxford: Oxford University Press, 2013).
Gobille, Boris, 'L'événement mai 68: Pour une sociohistoire du temps court', *Annales. Histoire, Sciences Sociales* 63.2 (2008), 321–348.
Gordon, Daniel A., *Immigrants & Intellectuals: May '68 and the Rise of Anti-Racism in France* (Pontypool: Merlin Press, 2012).
Grappin, Pierre, *L'Île aux peupliers: de la Résistance à Mai 68: Souvenirs du Doyen de Nanterre* (Nancy: Presses Universitaires de Nancy, 1993).
Gruel, Louis, *La rébellion de 68: Une relecture sociologique* (Rennes: Presses Universitaires de Rennes, 2004).
Habermas, Jürgen, *Toward a Rational Society: Student Protest, Science and Politics*, trans. Jeremy J. Shapiro (Cambridge: Polity Press, 1987).
Herbert, Ulrich, 'Liberalisierung als Lernprozeß. Die Bundesrepublik in der deutschen Geschichte – eine Skizze', in Ulrich Herbert (ed.), *Wandlungsprozesse in Westdeutschland. Belastung, Integration, Liberalisierung 1945–1980* (Göttingen: Wallstein Verlag, 2002), pp. 7–49.
Hilwig, Stuart J., *Italy and 1968: Youthful Unrest and Democratic Culture* (London: Palgrave Macmillan, 2009).
Horn, Gerd-Rainer, '1968: A Social Movement *Sui Generis*', in Stefan Berger and Holger Nehring (eds.), *The History of Social Movements in Global Perspective: A Survey* (London: Palgrave Macmillan, 2017), pp. 515–542.
  The Spirit of '68: Rebellion in Western Europe and North America 1956–1976 (Oxford: Oxford University Press, 2007).
  The Spirit of Vatican II: Western European Progressive Catholicism in the Long Sixties (Oxford: Oxford University Press, 2015).
Horn, Gerd-Rainer and Kenney, Padraic, *Transnational Moments of Change: Europe 1945, 1968, 1989* (Oxford: Rowman and Littlefield, 2004).
Jackson, Julian, 'The Mystery of May 1968', *French Historical Studies* 33.4 (2010), 625–653.
Jackson, Julian, Milne, Anna-Louise and Williams, James S. (eds.), *May 68: Rethinking France's Last Revolution* (Basingstoke: Palgrave Macmillan, 2011).
Jobs, Richard Ivan, 'Youth Movements: Travel, Protest, and Europe in 1968', *American Historical Review* 114.2 (2009), 376–404.
Johannot, Yvonne, *Quand le livre devient poche: une sémiologie du livre au format de poche* (Grenoble: Presses Universitaires de Grenoble, 1978).
Kätzel, Ute, *Die 68erinnen: Porträt einer rebellischen Frauengeneration* (Berlin: Rowohlt, 2002).
Klimke, Martin, *The Other Alliance: Student Protest in West Germany and the United States in the Global Sixties* (Princeton: Princeton University Press, 2010).

Klimke, Martin and Scharloth, Joachim (eds.), *1968 in Europe: A History of Protest and Activism, 1956–1977* (New York: Palgrave Macmillan, 2008).

Koenen, Gerd, *Das rote Jahrzehnt: Unsere kleine deutsche Kulturrevolution 1967–1977* (Cologne: Fischer Taschenbuch Verlag, 2001).

Kraushaar, Wolfgang, *1968 als Mythos, Chiffre und Zäsur* (Hamburg: Hamburger Edition, 2000).

Krippendorff, Ekkehart, *Lebensfäden: Zehn autobiografische Versuche* (Heidelberg: Verlag Graswurzelrevolution, 2012).

Labro, Philippe et al. (eds.), *Ce n'est qu'un début* (Paris: Éditions et publications Premières, 1968).

Lefebvre, Henri, *L'irruption de Nanterre au sommet* (Paris: Éditions Syllepse, 1998).

Lönnendonker, Siegward (ed.), *Linksintellektueller Aufbruch zwischen 'Kulturrevolution' und 'kultureller Zerstörung'. Der Sozialistische Deutsche Studentenbund (SDS) in der Nachkriegsgeschichte (1946–1969). Dokumentation eines Symposiums* (Wiesbaden: Westdeutscher Verlag, 1998).

Lumley, Robert, *States of Emergency: Cultures of Revolt in Italy from 1968 to 1978* (London: Verso, 1990).

Marwick, Arthur, *The Sixties: Cultural Revolution in Britain, France, Italy, and the United States, c.1958–c.1974* (Oxford: Oxford University Press, 1998).

Mohandesi, Salar, 'Bringing Vietnam Home: The Vietnam War, Internationalism and May '68', *French Historical Studies* 41.2 (2018), 219–251.

Monchablon, Alain, *Histoire de l'UNEF de 1956 à 1968* (Paris: Presses Universitaires de France, 1983).

Morin, Edgar, Lefort, Claude and Castoriadis, Cornelius, *Mai 68: La brèche, suivi de vingt ans après* (Paris: Editions Complexe, 1988).

Müller, Jan-Werner, *Contesting Democracy: Political Ideas in Twentieth-Century Europe* (New Haven: Yale University Press, 2011).

Ortoleva, Peppino *I movimenti del '68 in Europa e in America*, 2nd ed. (Rome: Editori Riuniti, 1998).

Passerini, Luisa, *Autoritratto di gruppo* (Florence: Giunti, 1988), p. 75.

Petrucci, Armando, 'Reading to Read: A Future for Reading', in Roger Chartier and Guglielmo Cavallo (eds.), *A History of Reading in the West*, trans. Lydia G. Cochrane (Amherst: University of Massachusetts Press, 1999), pp. 345–367.

Pressestelle der FU Berlin (ed.), *Hochschule im Umbruch: Teil III: Auf dem Weg in den Dissens (1957–1964)* (Berlin: Pressestelle der FU Berlin, 1974).

(ed.), *Hochschule im Umbruch: Teil IV: Die Krise (1964–1967)* (Berlin: Pressestelle der FU Berlin, 1975).

Prost, Antoine, 'La démocratisation de l'enseignement: histoire d'une notion', in Claude-Isabelle Brelot and Jean-Luc Mayaud (eds.), *Voyages en histoire: mélanges offerts à Paul Gerbod* (Paris: les Belles Lettres, 1995), pp. 119–129.

Reynolds, Chris, *Memories of May '68: France's Convenient Consensus* (Cardiff: University of Wales Press, 2011).
Ricci, Aldo, *I giovani non sono piante* (Milan: SugarCo, 1978).
Rohstock, Anne, *Von der "Ordinarienuniversität zur "Revolutionszentrale"? Hochschulreform und Hochschulrevolte In Bayern und Hessen 1957–1976* (Munich: R. Oldenbourg Verlag, 2010).
Ross, Kristen, *May '68 and its Afterlives* (Chicago: University of Chicago Press, 2002).
Rossanda, Rossana, *L'anno degli studenti* (Bari: De Donato, 1968).
Rüegg, Walter (ed.), *The History of the University in Europe. Volume IV: Universities Since 1945* (Cambridge: Cambridge University Press, 2011).
Schildt, Axel and Siegfried, Detlef (eds.), *Between Marx and Coca-Cola: Youth Cultures in Changing European Societies, 1960–1980* (New York: Berghahn, 2006).
Schildt, Axel, Siegfried, Detlef and Lammers, Karl Christian (eds.), *Dynamische Zeiten: Die 60er Jahre in den beiden deutschen Gesellschaften* (Hamburg: Hans Christians Verlag, 2000).
Schnapp, Alain and Vidal-Naquet, Pierre, *Journal de la Commune Étudiante: textes et documents. Novembre 1967–juin 1968*, édition augmentée (Paris: Éditions du Seuil, 1969).
Schneider, Peter, *Rebellion und Wahn. Mein '68: Eine autobiographische Erzählung* (Cologne: Kippenheuer & Witsch, 2008).
Schroeder, Klaus (ed.), *Hochschule im Umbruch: Teil V: Gewalt und Gegengewalt (1967–1969)* (Berlin: Pressestelle der FU Berlin, 1983).
Seidman, Michael, *The Imaginary Revolution: Parisian Students and Workers in 1968* (New York: Berghahn, 2004).
Slobodian, Quinn, *Foreign Front: Third World Politics in Sixties West Germany* (Durham: Duke University Press: 2012).
Tent, James F., *The Free University of Berlin: A Political History* (Bloomington: Indiana University Press, 1988).
Thomas, Nick, *Protest Movements in 1960s West Germany: A Social History of Dissent and Democracy* (Oxford: Berg, 2003).
Università: l'ipotesi rivoluzionaria. Documenti delle lotte studentesche Trento, Torino, Napoli, Pisa, Milano, Roma (Vicenza: Marsilio Editori, 1968).
Varon, Jeremy, Foley, Michael S. and McMillian, John, 'Time is an ocean: The past and future of the Sixties', *The Sixties: A Journal of History, Politics and Culture* 1.1 (June 2008), 1–7.
Vecchio, Concetto, *Vietato obbedire* (Milan: Rizzoli, 2005).
Von der Goltz, Anna, 'Other '68ers in West Berlin: Christian Democratic students and the Cold War city', *Central European History* 50 (2017), 87–112.
Von Hodenberg, Christina, 'Mass media and the generation of conflict: West Germany's long Sixties and the formation of a critical public sphere', *Contemporary European History* 15.3 (2006), 367–395.

Von Saldern, Adelheid, 'Markt für Marx: Literaturbetrieb und Lesebewegungen in den Sechziger- und Siebzigerjahren', *Archiv für Sozialgeschichte* 44 (2004), 149–180.
Wehrs, Nikolai, *Protest der Professoren: Der "Bund Freiheit der Wissenschaft" in den 1970er Jahren* (Göttingen: Wallstein Verlag, 2014).
Zancarini-Fournel, Michelle, *Le Moment 68: une histoire contestée* (Paris: Seuil, 2008).

Index

1968
  68 years, 9
  consequences, 8, 17, 19
  contingency of, 14
  global Sixties, 12–15
  long 1960s, 10
  as myth, 7
  and progress, 16
  as psychodrama, 7, 9, 158
  as revolution, 18

Adenauer, Konrad, 116
Alberganti, Carlo, 281
Alberoni, Francesco, 89, 162, 277–278, 280, 282–284
Albertz, Heinrich, 203
Algerian War
  at FU, 133, 135
  demonstration of October 1961, 236
  in French politics, 114, 121–122, 170
  in West Germany, 118
Althusser, Louis, 166
anarchists, 136, 138–139, 234, 238, 243–246
Andreatta, Beniamino, 48, 63, 223, 226
Anselm, Sigrun, 167
Anzieu, Didier, 169
Argument Club, 256
Aron, Raymond, 7, 25, 38, 41, 43, 51, 53, 67, 158
authority
  after anti-authoritarian revolt, 288
  challenge to deference, 161
  charismatic, 131, 169, 277
  crisis of, 108, 253
autonomy
  absence of in university, 146
  in choice of study, 62
  demand for, 148, 214
  as goal of education, 142
  of SDS from SPD, 118
  within university, 134, 192

Berkeley, 137, 172, 179–180, 183, 198, 210, 215, 277
Bettermann, Karl August, 42, 185, 189–190, 198
Boato, Marco, 57, 143, 149–150, 165, 168, 208, 226, 280, 282
Bobbio, Norberto, 113, 223, 226, 277
Boldrini, Marcello, 223, 226
books
  as authoritarian, 96
  deconstruction of, 93
  dismemberment of, 97
  dismissal of, 98
  as elitist, 99
  fetishisation of, 96
  little red, 98
  pirate editions, 90
  theft of, 97
Borinski, Fritz, 262
Bourdieu, Pierre, 41, 53, 172
Brandt, Willy, 194

Catholicism
  and creation of Sociology at Trento, 56
  and French youth groups, 123
  and political parties, 128
  anti-Lent, 223–226, 228
  at Nanterre, 140
  at Trento, 143, 223, 277
  Intesa Universitaria Cattolica. *See* Intesa Universitaria Cattolica
  Jeunesse Étudiante Chrétienne. *See* JEC
  Jeunesse Universitaire Chrétienne. *See* JUC
  reformist, 49
  Vatican II, 224
CGT (Confédération Générale du Travail), 122, 239
Christian Democrats, 112, 127, 211
Cohn-Bendit, Daniel, 46, 70, 149–152, 154, 165, 172–173, 231, 233, 235, 238, 241, 244–246, 252–253, 270, 272

Cold War, 33
  at the FU, 135
  context in West Berlin, 180
consumerism
  in books, 78
  caricature of consumer, 84
  commodification of knowledge, 78
  decline of metaphor, 102
  as fostering criticism, 95
  as irrational, 82
  in libraries, 91
  reader as consumer, 81
  as seduction, 79, 81
  student as, 267
Cros, Louis, 35, 44
Crouzet, François, 5, 248, 250
Crozier, Michel, 50, 163
culture
  access to, 91
  anti-intellectualism, 99, 168
  critical attitude towards, 86, 93
  decline of, 68
  desacralisation of, 72
  division of two cultures, 52
  mass, 71
  modernisation of, 48
Curcio, Renato, 100, 148

Dahrendorf, Ralf, 31
Damerow, Peter, 191
Damisch, Hubert, 80, 84
de Gaulle, Charles, 65, 114–115, 141, 276
democracy
  and authority, 177
  deficit of, 141, 190
  direct
    at the Free University, 133
    demand for at Nanterre, 138, 142
    in student assemblies, 57, 144, 148
  dissatisfaction with, 119
  at FU, 132
  parliamentary, 111, 115
  participatory, 21
  plebiscitary
    at FU, 197
    in France, 115
    referenda in FRG, 116
  as public use of criticism, 187
  representative
    crisis of, 130
    demand for by faculty, 141
    elections in 1968, 154
    failure of at Nanterre, 137
    as powerlessness, 141
    as regressive, 146
  as result of 1968, 288
  within university, 63, 146, 223
  as self-government, 184
democratisation, 18
  cultural, 20, 73, 84–85
  of debate, 160
  disillusionment in, 129
  as effacement of hierarchy, 161
  failure of postwar, 110, 120
  as growth of tolerance, 159
  of high culture, 67, 100
  linguistic, 164
  meaning, 2
  as meritocracy, 43
  as self-government, 148
  of social life, 134
  of university, 44, 62, 127, 143, 157, 182
desacralisation
  of professors, 204, 214
  of speech, 161
Diepgen, Eberhard, 132, 184
Duteuil, Jean-Pierre, 244–245
Dutschke, Rudi, 118–119, 149–152, 171, 173,
  193, 201, 204, 224, 257, 269, 281
Dutschke-Klotz, Gretschen, 164

enragés. See Situationist International
Enzensberger, Hans Magnus, 78, 80, 85, 95, 102
Erhard, Ludwig, 111, 193
Escarpit, Robert, 72, 74, 78, 84, 91

fascism, 20
  heritage of, 57, 113, 209
  as term of abuse, 221, 281
  rumours of fascists, 226
Feltrinelli, Giangiacomo, 98
Ferrarotti, Franco, 62
FNEF (Fédération nationale des étudiants de
  France), 122
Fouchet, Christian, 232
Fourastié, Jean, 52
Fraenkel, Ernst, 94, 203
Francès, Robert, 94
Free University of Berlin
  Berlin Model, 131–136, 177, 184, 186–187,
    191, 197, 199
  deregistration of students, 41
  Diplom in sociology, 64
  escalation of protest, 192–204
  fraternities at, 132, 182, 189
  Krippendorff Affair, 187
  Kritische Universität, 255–270
    curriculum, 265
    and Gegenuniversität, 256
    problems of, 266

Free University of Berlin (cont.)
  Kuby Affair, 178–187
  origins, 4
Freud, Sigmund, 69, 89, 281
Fronius, Sigrun, 184, 255, 257, 264

gender
  of literature, 86
  male charismatic authority, 168
  of speech, 167
  in student assemblies, 148
  of university expansion, 39
Gerhardt, Uta, 256
Gollwitzer, Helmut, 204, 263
Gottardi, Alessandro Maria, 224
Grappin, Pierre, 5–6, 25–26, 43, 51, 232, 236, 239–242, 248–252
Guevara, Che, 281

Habermas, Jürgen, 18, 119–120, 170
Harndt, Ewald, 264
Häußermann, Hartmut, 94, 263
Heinitz, Ernst, 183, 201
high culture, 82, 86
  abolition of barriers to, 75
  boundary with mass culture, 84, 101
  challenge of paperbacks to, 73
  challenge to guardians, 92
  debasement of, 77
  definition of, 69
  desacralisation of, 86
  Kultur versus *Zivilisation*, 78
  as origin of revolt, 72
  redefinition of, 95
higher education. *See* university

ideology
  end of, 9, 112
Intesa Universitaria Cattolica, 61, 127
Istituto Universitario di Scienze Sociali. *See* Trento, Faculty of Sociology

Jaspers, Karl, 188–189, 191
JCR (Jeunesse communiste révolutionnaire). *See* Trotskyists
JEC (Jeunesse Étudiante Chrétienne), 122–124
JUC (Jeunesse Universitaire Chrétienne), 123
Juquin, Pierre, 252

Kessler, Bruno, 47–49, 52, 144, 223
Knauer, Georg Nicolaus, 262–265
Kommune I, 200, 202
Kotowski, George, 183
Kreibich, Rolf, 270
Krippendorff, Ekkehart, 161, 187–192

Kröger, Hanna, 167
Kuby, Erich, 178–186

Langlade, Xavier, 243, 245
Lebel, Jean-Jacques, 231
Lefebvre, Henri, 241
Lefèvre, Wolfgang, 133, 179, 184–187, 191–192, 257, 260
Lennert, Rudolf, 264
Lieber, Hans-Joachim, 64, 150, 182, 191, 193–199, 203–204, 260, 262
Losito, Marta, 167
Lotta Continua, 98, 282
Lüers, Herbert, 179, 182–185, 188–191, 196, 201
Lukács, Georg, 70, 79, 90

Maoism, 98, 136, 166, 220, 247, 252, 272, 274, 276
March 22 Movement. *See* Movement of 22 March
Marcuse, Herbert, 69–72, 89–90, 270, 276
Martinoli, Gino, 36, 52, 60, 62
Marxism, 69–70, 111, 118, 123, 136, 191, 266, 272, 275, 281, 283
Marzotto, 281
Maspero, François, 74, 79, 83, 97, 170
Memmi, Albert, 77, 85
Meyer, Philippe, 243
Michaud, Guy, 248
Milani, don Lorenzo, 69, 225
Missoffe, François, 238
Mitterrand, François, 115
Montale, Eugenio, 82
Montanelli, Indro, 214
Moravia, Alberto, 84
Moro, Aldo, 49, 113
Movement of 22 March, 153–154, 247, 252, 271, 273–274
  and crisis of representation, 142
  formation of, 247
MSI (*Movimento Sociale Italiano*), 112, 209

Nanterre, University of
  bidonville next to, 230
  closure of, 249
  November 1967 strike, 139
  occupation of administrative tower, 244
  occupation of residences, 232
  origins, 5–6
  politics before 1968, 136–142
  protests about exams, 139
  response to overcrowding, 43
  sociology at, 51
  student politics at, 125

Index

unemployed at, 273
université critique, 270–276
Nazism
  as insult, 240
  commemoration of end of, 191
  heritage of, 117, 120, 132–133, 188, 190, 202, 261
Nevermann, Knut, 120, 150, 197, 203
Nitsch, Wolfgang, 256–257, 259, 269
NPD (Nationaldemokratische Partei Deutschlands), 109–111

Occident, 126
Offe, Claus, 256
Ohnesorg, Benno, 204, 254–255
Otto-Suhr Institute, 183, 186, 188, 270

Passerini, Luisa, 167
PCF (Parti communiste française), 114–115
PCI (Partito Comunista Italiano), 112, 127, 211
Piccoli, Flaminio, 222
Picht, Georg, 29–32, 110
Pizzorno, Alessandro, 163
Poignant, Raymond, 33
police
  called by students, 225
  charges against students, 209
  in FRG, 110
  intervention, 288
    demand for, 225
    in France, 124
    at FU, 202–203
    in Italy, 210
    at Nanterre, 233, 239, 242, 250
    at Sorbonne, 253
    at Trento, 212
  proposal for university police at Nanterre, 248, 251
  restraint from calling, 216, 248
  undercover in university, 238
  violence, 112, 202, 280, 282
Political Science, 57
politics
  and the university, 133, 156–157, 196, 211, 242, 260, 264–266, 269, 278
  groupuscules, 125
  occupations, 138, 147, 156
    1964 in France, 124
    at Trento, 60
    in Italy, 210
  of administration, 155, 181, 184, 195–196, 203, 209, 212
  of residences at Nanterre, 231
  of assemblies, 220
    authoritarian, 220
    criticism of leaders, 152
    as form of domination, 167
    leaders in, 151
  of civil disobedience, 187, 203
  of compromise, 57, 117
    dissatisfaction with, 112
    opposed by SDS, 117
  of confrontation, 227
  of criticism, 156, 188
  of direct action
    at Nanterre, 138
  of disorder, 171, 227
  of groupuscules, 136
  of long march, 279–280
  of order, 59, 112, 190, 234
    blacklists, 203, 233, 238, 241, 246
  of provocation, 119, 171, 194
    reliance on, 289
  of realism, 59, 121, 138
  of reform, 113, 127
  of violence, 229
    revolutionary, 111, 153
    strikes, 183, 186, 211–212
Preuß, Ulrich, 256
PSI (Partito Socialista Italiano), 113, 127
PSIUP (Partito Socialista Italiano di Unità Proletaria), 113, 127

Rabehl, Bernd, 118, 151, 193
Raymond, Henri, 241
RCDS (Ring Christlich Demokratischer Studenten), 179, 201–202
reading
  as a social act, 103
  as poaching, 102
  order of, 81–82
  library, 91
  practices, 83
Reich, Wilhelm, 90, 281
Ricci, Aldo, 279
Ricoeur, Paul, 43, 248, 250, 275
Rostagno, Mauro, 5, 100, 144, 149–152, 169, 211, 221, 229, 276, 279–280, 282, 285
Rüger, Sigrid, 198

Sartre, Jean-Paul, 71
Sbalchiero, Igino, 224
Schelsky, Helmut, 54
Schneider, Peter, 171, 226–227, 281
Schwartz, Laurent, 173, 252
Sclavi, Marianella, 71, 168

SDS (Sozialistische Deutsche Studentenbund), 116–121, 126, 128, 132, 150, 152–153, 183, 192, 195, 201–202, 204, 249, 256, 258–259, 262
  exclusion from SPD, 117
  growth of membership, 255
  konkret faction, 117
  recognition by FU, 136, 202
SHB (Sozialdemokratische Hochschulbund), 117, 183, 255
  convergence with SDS, 120
Situationist International, 70–72, 80, 100, 119, 136, 138, 150, 238, 240
  enragés at Nanterre, 245
Snow, C.P., 52
Socialisme ou Barbarie, 150
sociology, 20
  and Vietnam, 212
  as emancipation, 55
  careers, 54, 57, 63, 65
  degree
    in France, 52
    in Italy, 55
    in West Germany, 54
  empirical versus theoretical, 53, 61, 64
  modernity of, 57, 60
  politics of, 66
  struggle over curriculum, 60
Sontheimer, Kurt, 110, 183, 188, 191, 195
Sorbi, Paolo, 128, 224–225, 228
SPD (Sozialdemokratische Partei Deutschlands), 111, 117, 132
speech
  academic, 168
  in assemblies, 157, 169
  as barrier to working class, 268
  censorship of, 159, 171, 179, 189, 193, 212
  as disobedience, 157
  experience of, 158
  freedom of, 160, 173, 181, 188
  gendered, 167
  graffiti, 72
  hierarchies of, 164
  informalisation, 162
  laughter, 163, 169, 214
  mastery of by student leaders, 101
  opacity, 70, 164
  politicisation of, 166
  as provocation, 163, 169, 172, 238
  and rational debate, 172
  regulation of, 196
  as self-discovery, 159
  seizure of, 68, 72, 158, 200
  vulgarity, 162
  within Church, 224

Spellman, Francis, 224
Spiegel Affair, 110, 170
Springer Press, 183, 190, 194, 203, 266, 269
students
  apathy of, 107, 120, 133, 139, 171, 185
  as apolitical, 107
  collaboration in own domination, 157, 219
  decline of politics of, 125
  general assembly
    at FU, 183
  leaders, 149, 164
  non-political, 259
  passivity of, 93–94, 218
    in assemblies, 149
    attempts to counter, 265
    breaking of, 172
    countering, 215
    in Kritische Universität, 267
    as target of protest, 157
  powerlessness, 214
  as readers, 76
  right-wing, 132
  reinvention through protest, 220
  representation, 131, 133
    marginality of, 181
  reprisals against, 145, 208, 233
  as revolutionary, 222
  sexual psychosis of, 234
  student power, 215, 222
Subversive Aktion, 118, 150
Suhrkamp, 88, 98
Szondi, Peter, 263

Tambroni, Fernando, 112
Taubes, Jacob, 202
teaching
  anti-authoritarian methods, 217, 258, 265, 273
  as authoritarian, 218, 265
  exams
    boycott of, 243
    criticism of, 139
  lectures
    as authoritarian, 92, 95, 157
    challenge to, 92
    desacralisation of, 94
    return to, 267, 278
    reviews of, 94
    reviews of at FU, 203
technocracy, 31, 50, 54, 66, 266
Touraine, Alain, 53, 150, 244, 248, 250
Trento, Faculty of Sociology
  Anti-Lent, 223–226
  fifth occupation, 280
  first occupation of, 58

fourth occupation, 280
origins, 4–5, 47
second occupation, 60
statute of, 146
struggle over *laurea*, 55
student organisations at, 142
student power, 148
third occupation, 147, 215–226
Università Critica, 276–284
  definition of, 277
Vietnam Week protests, 210
Trotskyists, 124, 136–138, 245–247
  JCR (Jeunesse communiste révolutionnaire), 125–126, 137, 234, 239, 243

UEC (Union des étudiants communistes), 123, 245, 247
UGI (Unione goliardica italiana), 127
UJC(ml) (Union des jeunesses communistes marxistes-léninistes). *See* Maoism
UNEF (Union nationale des étudiants de France), 121–127, 136–140, 153, 233, 241, 243, 247
  decline of, 125
  obsolescence of, 140
university
  access to, 41
  and social selection, 45
  attrition in, 40
  Bildungskatastrophe, 28–31, 50
  democratisation of, 33, 37
  expansion of, 36
  objectivity within, 261
  overcrowding in, 25, 42
  politicisation of, 260
  reform of, 27, 198
    demand for, 251
    Fouchet, 43, 138–139, 235, 237
    as illusory, 274
    Italy, 127
    rejected, 222
    undermined by politics, 282
UNURI (Unione nazionale universitaria rappresentativa), 126–127, 143, 153

Vietnam War, 2, 13, 171, 216, 249, 272
  at FU, 191, 193–195, 201, 261
  at Nanterre, 137, 237, 242, 246
  at Trento, 155, 210–214, 224, 226–229
  in French politics, 114
  unable to mobilise students, 231, 271
Vincennes, Centre universitaire expérimental de, 275
Volpato, Mario, 55, 61–62, 146, 212–215, 277
von der Gablentz, Otto, 190

Zanzara Affair, 170
Ziebura, Gilbert, 188

Printed in Great Britain
by Amazon